SHAKESPEARE'S EARLY TRAGEDIES

A Collection of Critical Essays

Edited by
Mark Rose

Prentice Hall, Englewood Cliffs, New Jersey 07632

Library of Congress Cataloging-in-Publication Data

Shakespeare's early tragedies : a collection of critical essays /
   edited by Mark Rose.
       p.   cm. — (New century views)
   Includes bibliographical references (p.   ).
   ISBN 0–13–035544–5
       1. Shakespeare, William, 1564–1616—Tragedies.   2. Tragedy.
   I. Rose, Mark.   II. Series.
   PR2983.S4485   1994
   822.3′3—dc20

                                                    94–11740
                                                       CIP

Acquisitions editor: Alison Reeves
Editorial assistant: Lee Mamunas
Editoral/production supervision and
   interior design: Joan Powers
Copy editor: Garland Scott Pass
Cover design: Karen Salzbach
Production coordinator: Tricia Kenny

© 1995 by Prentice-Hall, Inc.
A Paramount Communications Company
Englewood Cliffs, New Jersey 07632

Printed in the United States of America
10   9   8   7   6   5   4   3   2   1

ISBN 0-13-035544-5

Prentice-Hall International (UK) Limited, *London*
Prentice-Hall of Australia Pty. Limited, *Sydney*
Prentice-Hall Canada Inc., *Toronto*
Prentice-Hall Hispanoamericana, S.A., *Mexico*
Prentice-Hall of India Private Limited, *New Delhi*
Prentice-Hall of Japan, Inc., *Tokyo*
Simon & Schuster Asia Pte. Ltd., *Singapore*
Editora Prentice-Hall do Brazil, Ltda., *Rio de Janeiro*

CONTENTS

Introduction

Mark Rose

This collection of critical essays on *Titus Andronicus, Romeo and Juliet,* and *Julius Caesar,* is one of three volumes on Shakespeare's tragedies in the New Century Views series. Others collect studies of Shakespeare's middle tragedies, *Hamlet, Othello,* and *King Lear,* and of the late tragedies, *Macbeth, Antony and Cleopatra,* and *Coriolanus.* The sequence as a whole thus provides a nearly comprehensive representation of contemporary critical discussion of Shakespearean tragedy. Of those plays usually treated as tragedies in modern editions of Shakespeare only *Timon of Athens* is not included.

All nine plays represented in this series are identified as tragedies in the First Folio, the posthumous collection of Shakespeare's comedies, histories, and tragedies assembled by his theatrical colleagues in 1623. But it is worth noting that the Folio also calls *Cymbeline* a tragedy, a play that today is considered a romance, and identifies *Richard III* and *Richard II* as histories, when they might well be called tragedies on the basis of their subjects. Why should *Richard III* and *Richard II* be histories, and *Macbeth* and *King Lear,* both of which employ chronicle history materials and dramatize the reigns of kings, be tragedies? In fact, when *King Lear* was first printed in 1608, the title page identified it as a chronicle history. What is apparent is that there is inevitably a degree of arbitrariness about how Shakespeare's plays are assigned to categories, and the student ought not to suppose that any list of Shakespeare's tragedies, including the Folio's, has final authority.

It is worth noting, too, that the Folio shows no consistent attempt to present the plays in order of composition. Thus the comedies open with *The Tempest,* one of Shakespeare's last plays, and the tragedies with *Coriolanus,* which is also late. The one section of the Folio that shows a clear interest in chronology is that devoted to the histories, which are arranged in order of monarchical reign, starting with *King John* and ending with *Henry VIII.* This reveals much about seventeenth-century priorities and the central position of the monarch as the ordering and explanatory principle in this period. Modern editions generally follow the Folio in arranging the plays according to genre, adding a fourth category, romances, to the Folio's comedies, histories, and tragedies; nevertheless, within these categories modern editions present the plays, including the histories, in order of composition. This practice is perhaps no less revealing about our assumptions and priorities than the Folio arrangement is about those of the seventeenth century, for the modern

arrangement, unlike the Folio's, places the plays within a frame of authorial development. It implies that for us the crucial ordering and explanatory principles with
respect to these plays are genre and author, and that these texts are the product of
a kind of dialectic between convention and originality, between the received forms
and Shakespeare's personal development as an artist.

It must be stressed that this conception of authorship—the notion of the author
as an original genius who creates works that bear the stamp of his or her personality—is specifically modern, the product of social and cultural changes that came to
a head in the eighteenth century when the notion of original genius was born. As a
member of an Elizabethan and Jacobean theatrical company, Shakespeare partici-
pated in a process of cultural production that was essentially cooperative and col-
laborative. It is unlikely that Shakespeare felt any obligation to be original or that
he would recognize himself in our conception of him as a creative genius. Thus his
stories typically come from historical sources or popular narratives, and sometimes
his plays appear to be reworkings of older scripts. *Titus Andronicus*, for instance,
is probably a dramatization of a story that was circulating in chapbook form in the
late sixteenth century. Likewise, *Romeo and Juliet* is a dramatization of a well-
known love story that had recently been retold in Arthur Brooke's poem, *The
Tragical History of Romeus and Juliet*. Moreover, *Julius Caesar*, which is based on
material that Shakespeare read in Sir Thomas North's translation of Plutarch's
Lives, dramatizes what was probably for the Elizabethans the single most famous
story from classical antiquity. From these examples, and nearly all his other plays
as well, it would be appropriate to characterize Shakespeare as a reteller of tales,
an adapter of materials for the stage.

Nor, in all likelihood, would Shakespeare quite recognize his plays as "works" in
the sense of distinct aesthetic objects characterized by integrity and individuality.
This, too, is a modern conception born together with the idea of the author as a
creative individual. In the sixteenth and seventeenth centuries, it was usual to
think of a text less as a kind of object than as an action, a way, for example, of moving an audience to laughter or tears, or perhaps, in Hamlet's phrase, of showing
"virtue her feature, scorn her own image, and the very age and body of the time his
form and pressure" (3.2). Shakespeare's plays were made for performance, and
the scripts were evidently subject to continuing adaptation by the company. There
would, for instance, be cut-down versions to be used when the company was tour-
ing, and very likely there would be new scenes added from time to time to keep a
play fresh. Several of the witches' scenes in *Macbeth*, for instance, are thought to
be late additions of this sort, perhaps composed by Thomas Middleton. Moreover,
the two texts of *King Lear* that have come down to us, the Quarto of 1608 and the
Folio of 1623, each of which contains scenes that the other does not, are now
believed by many to represent two fundamentally incompatible versions of the
play from different moments in its early stage history.

The process of transforming Shakespeare's plays into "works" and of fashioning
Shakespeare himself into an "author" in the modern sense began in the First Folio
with its title page dominated by the now famous Droeshout engraving of

Shakespeare. But, as Margreta de Grazia has recently shown in *Shakespeare Verbatim* (Clarendon Press, 1991), the production of Shakespeare as an individuated author was the work of the great Shakespeare scholar, Edmond Malone, whose monumental edition of *The Plays and Poems of William Shakespeare* was published in 1790. It was Malone who first included the sonnets in his edition, who constructed a biography based on facts, and who worked out a full chronology for the plays. Modern Shakespearean scholarship in large part descends from him, and the assumptions that underlie his edition are directly related to the assumptions that underlie a collection such as the present one. When was a play written? What are its distinctive characteristics and concerns as an individual work and as a representative of a particular dramatic kind? What specifically Shakespearean qualities does it reveal? What relation does it have to other works in the Shakespearean canon? These are among the questions that a volume of essays on early Shakespearean tragedies will by its very conception encourage the reader to entertain as significant, and a few general words about the early tragedies along these lines are in order.

Titus Andronicus, *Romeo and Juliet*, and *Julius Caesar* are all plays from the 1590s, the first half of Shakespeare's roughly twenty-year period of productivity as a playwright. Perhaps what is most striking about these early tragedies, most critics would agree, is how different they are from each other, which may be why they have only rarely been considered together as a distinct body of work. Possibly as a group they might best be considered imitative experiments in strikingly different styles of tragedy. The earliest, *Titus Andronicus*, which was probably first performed in the early 1590s, is a version of Senecan revenge tragedy in the mode popularized by Thomas Kyd's *The Spanish Tragedy*. The next, *Romeo and Juliet*, which most likely dates from about 1595, is a tragedy of love in a Petrarchan vein and is plainly very different. For one thing, the protagonists are not proud rulers or other figures of political consequence but young aristocrats driven by love. For another, in this play, unlike *Titus Andronicus*, there are no villains. It would be hard to predict from *Titus Andronicus* that Shakespeare would go on to write *Romeo and Juliet*; it would be equally hard to predict from *Romeo and Juliet* that he would go on to write *Julius Caesar* about four years later. In this third play, Shakespeare returns to the ancient world, but he treats his subject in a style that is conspicuously chaste and restrained compared to *Titus Andronicus*. Here he is perhaps attempting to write a play that will bring famous classical figures to life in high Roman style.

Romeo and Juliet and *Julius Caesar* have been consistently successful both on the stage and with readers. *Titus Andronicus*, however, which was evidently very popular in the 1590s, has not been much in favor since. Traditionally critical discussion of *Titus Andronicus* has turned on questions of quality and attribution. Is the play good enough to be considered Shakespeare's? Few today would doubt Shakespeare's authorship, which is strongly indicated by inclusion in the First Folio and by contemporary references. Moreover, *Titus Andronicus* has verbal and thematic links with Shakespeare's early narrative poem *The Rape of Lucrece*, and insofar as it portrays a headstrong patriarch who brings disaster on himself and those near him, it may be said to anticipate *King Lear*. Lately the critical fortunes of *Titus Andronicus* have risen dramatically. Peter Brook's important production at Stratford-upon-Avon in 1955 with Laurence Olivier as Titus and Vivien Leigh as Lavinia demonstrated how effective the play can be in the theater, and there have been many subsequent performances in recent years. Furthermore, the present interest in depictions of violence, rape, and the body have made *Titus Andronicus* the focus of much recent critical attention.

As I have indicated, *Romeo and Juliet* represents a radical departure from *Titus Andronicus* in style, theme, and treatment. Indeed, it is hard to see that apart from participating in the broad category of tragedy, the two plays have much in common at all. Not surprisingly, perhaps, *Romeo and Juliet* is less often discussed in relation to *Titus Andronicus* than in relation to two other plays of the mid-1590s, *Richard II* and *A Midsummer Night's Dream*, which echo its lyrical verse style. Nor has it escaped notice that the tragedy of Pyramus and Thisbe that Peter Quince and his troupe perform in honor of Theseus and Hippolyta in *A Midsummer Night's Dream* parallels *Romeo and Juliet* in theme. As a tragedy of love *Romeo and Juliet* is also frequently discussed in relation to *Othello* and *Antony and Cleopatra*. But the difference in tragic power between *Romeo and Juliet* and these later plays has led to debate over whether the early drama is a true tragedy or merely a pathetic tale of unfortunate circumstances. Recent discussion, however, has been less concerned with comparative evaluation of the play than with analyzing such matters as the play's portrayal of gender roles, its dialectical concern with the private world of the lovers in conflict with the public world of Verona, and its extraordinary deployment of the rhetorical materials of the sonnet tradition.

Julius Caesar has long been read as an anticipation of the later tragedies in terms of portrayal of character. Thus the portrait of Brutus, who is presented as a reflective man weighing alternatives in solitude, is frequently seen as a sketch for Hamlet. *Julius Caesar* is also often associated with *Antony and Cleopatra*, which continues the story of the fall of the Republic, and these two tragedies, along with *Titus Andronicus* and *Coriolanus*, are sometimes considered together as Shakespeare's Roman plays. Critics have debated whether the play is really about Caesar, who dies long before the end, or about Brutus, and they have discussed the notably restrained style of the verse, which contrasts with both the elaborate brocade of *Titus Andronicus* and the lush lyricism of *Romeo and Juliet*. There has been much discussion, too, of the play's politics—what, exactly, is Shakespeare's attitude toward the assassination of Caesar?—and its sense of historical process. Recent criticism has also stressed *Julius Caesar*'s ritualized violence, its concern with the power of rhetoric, and its treatment of what might be called the epistemological theme—that is, the theme of the difficulty of interpreting people, events, and purposes correctly.

Here, of course, I can only hint at what the shape of critical discussion concerning these three early tragedies has been. Nor does this collection attempt to provide a historical survey of criticism, but merely to suggest a range of current critical concerns and to do so with essays that are in themselves excellent. I have included some pieces that are established as classics such as Eugene Waith's essay on *Titus Andronicus*, which can perhaps be said to have initiated the recent critical interest in that play, or Kenneth Burke's "Antony in Behalf of the Play," which imagines Mark Antony stepping forward to address the audience directly in order to explain the rhetorical organization of *Julius Caesar*. I have also included some pieces that are recent and likely to be controversial such as Gail Kern Paster's discussion of blood in *Julius Caesar*. A number of the essays, including Rosalie L. Colie's important discussion of *Romeo and Juliet*, are concerned with the ways in which the plays transform earlier materials; several, including C.L. Barber and Richard P. Wheeler's attempt to assess structural problems in *Titus Andronicus*, deal with tragedy as a genre; and several are concerned with how these plays work on stage. There are essays here that might be taken as representing various current schools of criticism, including studies that could be termed psychoanalytic, deconstructive, feminist, or new historicist in orientation. But these essays have been chosen more for their excellent discussions of the particular issues raised by these three early plays than for their display of a range of methodologies.

In every stage of my preparation of this volume from the compiling of initial bibliographical surveys to the final selection of essays I have been helped by my research assistant Steve Cohen. Without his energetic and insightful assistance I certainly could not have completed this task while serving in a full-time administrative position. Indeed, Steve has been as much a colleague as an assistant, and the table of contents as it stands is the product of the many stimulating conversations about these essays that we have had.

Shakespeare's Earliest Tragedies: *Titus Andronicus* and *Romeo and Juliet*

G. K. Hunter

It is commonly accepted that Shakespeare's earliest essays in tragic form are *Titus Andronicus* and *Romeo and Juliet*[1]—accepted, that is, among those who allow that Shakespeare was responsible for *Titus Andronicus*. But few critics, even among the accepters, seem willing to go beyond the merely chronological point to take up the critical consequence: that we might expect to be able to analyse here an early but characteristic Shakespearian mode of tragedy.[2] The two plays are so obviously unlike one another that it is hard even to think of adding them together to make up any description of a unified mode. Whatever the reason, it is a clear critical fact that these plays are not normally considered together, or even apart, in a description of Shakespearian Tragedy. Shakespeare, it is implied, had to throw away this dispersed prentice work, set it against experience rather than achievement, when he began to compose the sequence of truly 'Shakespearian' tragedies beginning with *Julius Caesar* and growing out of the political interests of the English history plays.

These pre-judgements bear more heavily against *Titus Andronicus* than *Romeo and Juliet*, for *Romeo* has, whatever its generic implication, the refuge of being a 'well-loved' play, where *Titus* can only be called 'much disliked'. I begin, however, by assuming an equality of interest and importance, taking it that in both plays Shakespeare was writing as well as he knew how. The subsequent reputations of the plays may be thought to tell us more securely about audience preferences in the period between Shakespeare and the present than about the author's intention. My concern in this paper is not with differences of valuation

From *Shakespeare Survey* 27 (1974), 1–9. Reprinted by permission of the author.

[1]The exact chronology of these early plays is too uncertain to bear any weight of consequential argument. It is worth noticing that modern scholarship (following E. K. Chambers) has tended to keep the two tragedies within two or three years of one another; so there is nothing on this side to impede the idea of a close relationship. . . .

[2]The obvious exception to this blanket statement is Nicholas Brooke (*Shakespeare's Early Tragedies*, London, 1968). Professor Brooke's brief is, however, much larger than mine; he includes *Julius Caesar* and *Hamlet* (also *Richard III* and *Richard II*) within his survey. Brooke's sense of 'the mode of tragedy' is also rather different from that pursued here, so that the question of 'early tragedy' can, I believe, be rehandled without culpable repetition.

but with the formal similarities and relationships that can be established between the two tragedies.

In making this point I am not, of course, forgetting that *Titus* is the most horrific of Shakespeare's tragedies. To some minds this implies that it is exceptional and that its evidence about Shakespeare's tragic mode is out of court. The idea that true tragedy is essentially about the mental suffering of noble natures, and therefore unbloody, is, however, probably a delusion, based on the social assumptions of a post-Enlightenment society which has shown itself incapable of writing tragedy. The Victorian sub-genre, 'the tragedy of blood', invented to deal with plays like *Titus Andronicus,* offers us, in fact, only a pointless tautology: the *Oedipus Rex, The Bacchae, King Lear, The Duchess of Malfi,* are all blood-spattered and horrific; but who would be so bold as to confine such plays to a sub-genre?

That Shakespeare when he wrote *Titus* was under the influence of classical exemplars must also be allowed; but this does not mean that his mind can be cleared of responsibility for it. Shakespeare was no doubt like other artists, and achieved his own voice by working through aesthetic enthusiasms and derivative exercises, and in this *Titus* is no different from other early plays. Like *Lucrece* and its comic counterpart, *Venus and Adonis, Titus Andronicus* is deeply indebted to Ovid's sense of human mutability, the frailty of man's happiness and of his capacity for reason. In a similar way *The Comedy of Errors* is indebted to Plautus, *The Taming of the Shrew* to Italianate comedy, *Romeo and Juliet* to the atmosphere and conventions of the Italian novella. The real difference between *Titus Andronicus* and *Romeo and Juliet* seems to emerge not from the derivativeness of the one and the originality of the other, but from the different implications of the genres used. If *Titus* is exceptional among Shakespeare's tragedies in its devotion to a hysterically bleak view of human potential, *Romeo* is exceptional also, in its general sunniness, its closeness to comedy. It is, of course, particularly close to the kind of comedy that Shakespeare was writing in these years, 'Italian', courtly, exploring the romantic sensibilities of well-bred youth. It goes without saying that we are the better able to understand *Romeo and Juliet* because we know these cognate comedies.

The distinction I have so far made between the two plays suggests that Shakespeare's first move in tragedy was to seek to delimit the space within which he could operate, marking out the extreme polarities of his tragic range. He was never again to pursue the image of man's bestiality with the single-mindedness he showed in *Titus.* And likewise he was never, after *Romeo,* to write another tragedy which was so clearly a diversion by malign fate of materials that would normally form the basis of comedy. From time to time hereafter he will, of course, come close to one pole or the other, but always in a manner which invokes the presence of its opposite. *King Lear,* for example, can be regarded as in some ways a reworking of themes from *Titus Andronicus.* We have the same grieved and deprived father, hounded from dignity into madness by a malignant group whose authority comes from his gift, and rescued in the end by a foreign invasion led by his loyal child. We have the same pervading image of man as a beast of prey, the same contrast between extremes of female rapacity and female innocence, the same overlapping of lust and political ambition. But the role of the family in society is very different in the two plays. In both, the good and evil quickly sort themselves out as opposing forces. In *Titus* the social gap between the two groups is what is emphasised: on the one hand we have the barbarian outsiders, on the other the Andronici, the pious Roman family. In *Lear*, however, the opposition of good and bad emerges from the matrix of a single family. Among the sufferings of Titus the fact that Saturninus betrayed the favour he received does not bulk large; but for Lear the ingratitude of the daughters is the central agony. Thus the social rituals through which the conflict is expressed in *Titus* (feasting, family reading, the birth of a child, etc.) must give way in *Lear* to more unstructured domestic confrontations, and in these the side of Shakespeare's tragic vision represented by *Romeo* re-emerges. Something of Old Capulet's irascible absurdity survives into the very different world of Lear and his daughters.

Not only in *Lear* but throughout Shakespeare's mature tragedies the ritual of *Titus* is complemented by the domesticity of *Romeo*, the hieratic flanked by the familiar. Shakespeare achieves his later tragic centrality not only by diluting the unreality of *Titus* but also by making more remote and overpowering the cosinesses of Verona. Among the later tragedies *Antony and Cleopatra* is probably the one that most closely resembles *Romeo and Juliet*: in both plays the poetic power is centrally involved in projecting the love emotions of a socially significant couple, whose relationship defies the prevailing political and ethical assumptions of their society. Both are plays whose minor characters (Nurse, Mercutio, Enobarbus, Charmian, Alexis) are much given to comic routines. The lovers are finally united by quasi-sacrificial deaths; their deaths open the way to a unification of their society; and they are memorialised by joint tombs of exemplary splendour. But *Antony and Cleopatra*, in spite of its high comedy, does not in any sense give us a comic world wrenched by fate to a tragic conclusion. The characters are not like us; they are colossuses, and their laughter shakes the world. Here there is no private sphere into which lovers can escape from the pressures of other men's expectations. The love gestures of Antony and Cleopatra, all made in the world's eye, have to have the ritual quality of great public occasions. Their quarrels mirror the clash of alternative moral systems, Roman severity and barbarian self-indulgence. And in these respects the play may be seen to be closer to *Titus Andronicus*, or at least to the pole of tragedy it represents, than to *Romeo and Juliet*.

I have been arguing for a relationship between *Titus Andronicus* and *Romeo and Juliet* and between these two and the rest of Shakespeare's tragedies in terms of the polar characteristics of tragedy they exhibit. But *Titus Andronicus* and *Romeo and Juliet* are not related only as opposites. As one might expect with a playwright finding his way into his craft, similar structural skeletons serve for both plays, though the flesh hung on top of them is very different. We may note how the two plays open:

> *Flourish. Enter the Tribunes and Senators aloft; and then enter below Saturninus and his followers at one door, and Bassianus and his followers at the other, with drums and trumpets.*

The scene that follows fleshes out the diagram thus established: first Saturninus (the elder) speaks, claiming his right to the crown, derived from primogeniture; then Bassianus (the younger) repeats the speech claiming the crown as his right, derived from election. Then

> *Enter Marcus Andronicus aloft, with the crown.*

Marcus tells us that the *populus Romanus* has chosen Titus Andronicus as its representative to take to himself the issue being contested. The contenders then leave the stage to allow Titus to enter in his *triumphus*.

The opening diagram of the forces in *Romeo and Juliet* is extraordinarily similar:

> *Enter [at one door] Sampson and Gregory, of the house of Capulet . . . Enter [at the other door] two other Servingmen, Abraham and Balthazar [of the house of Montague] . . . Enter [at one door] Benvolio [a nobleman of the house of Capulet] . . . Enter Tybalt [a nobleman of the house of Montague] . . . [they fight] . . . Enter an Officer and three or four citizens . . . Enter [at one door] Old Capulet . . . and his wife . . . Enter [at the other door] Old Montague and his wife . . . Enter [? above] Prince Escalus with his Train.*

In both plays the opening movement establishes discord against rule. The formalised stage-pictures set one competitor for power against another, the greater social range of the representatives of faction in *Romeo and Juliet* measuring the variety of social experience that play will draw on, the more concentrated concern with political power in *Titus Andronicus* marking that play's range of significant action. In both cases power is denied to the competitors. A central justice in the possession of power is demonstrated, and the establishment of this central authority over the brawling factions leads to their departure from the stage at the end of this dramatic phrase or movement.

In both tragedies, however, the remedy for discord which this opening diagram displays is a matter for display rather than acceptance. The failures to accept are, of course, very different. In *Romeo and Juliet* the Prince remains throughout the action an objective and unsubverted guarantor of order. The discord that persists is, in political terms, a hole-and-corner affair, dealt with by easy penalties. In *Titus Andronicus,* however, the supreme authorities of the opening, Marcus and Titus Andronicus, the representatives of the citizens and of the army, quickly lose their central position *aloft*. Titus is soon self-subverted and then hounded into grotesque subservience and madness. Astraea leaves the country; justice and order cease to have a political dimension. The movement by which moral order vanishes from Rome is, of course, without parallel in *Romeo and Juliet*. But the process by which Titus, in his wrong-headed and high-principled choice of Saturninus, his abject surrender of all rights to the new Emperor, falls from arbiter to suppliant does not end by breaking the parallel with *Romeo*. It ends, in fact, by re-forming the opening diagram of strife into a more stable and more exactly parallel shape.

The central conflict of *Titus Andronicus* stabilises itself as the story of two family groupings, whose conflict destroys (or threatens to destroy) the civilisation represented by the city. The opening chorus of *Romeo and Juliet* can easily be adapted to fit the other play:

> Two households, both alike in dignity,
> In Rome's fair city, where we lay our scene,
> From early grudge break to new mutiny,
> Where civil blood makes civil hands unclean.

It must be confessed, of course, that the 'two households' of *Titus* are less obvious than those of *Romeo*. By the middle of act 2, however, it is clear that the action is going to hinge on the conflict between the Andronicus family and that alternative 'household' of Saturninus/Tamora/Aaron with Tamora's assorted children, Chiron and Demetrius (later joined by the black baby). That this latter grouping can only be called a 'family' by a radically deformed definition does not reduce the significance of the parallel; indeed it strengthens it. The family ties of the Andronici suggest the strength of the family unit as the basis of all social order, and particularly that of Rome, demonstrating loyalty, mutual support and above all *pietas*, drawing on the dutifulness of the past to secure the dutifulness of the future. The household of husband, lover and assorted children that clusters round Tamora suggests the opposite: a dreadful burgeoning of uncontrolled nature into a rank and unweeded plot, where parental love cannot compensate for the various disorders and mismatings that result. Within a short time we are shown the wife over-ruling the husband, the mismating of Emperor and enemy, of Empress and slave, of white and black, the mother encouraging the sons to rape and murder, the brothers ready to kill one another until reduced to 'order' by the black lover (acting as surrogate father). Finally we have the black baby itself 'as loathsome as a toad', the complete image of instinctual wickedness.

In the two plays the conflicts of the households are handled, of course, in very different terms. In *Romeo and Juliet* the conflict between Montagues and Capulets has little political reality. It exists to maintain a certain pressure on what the play presents as more real—the personal emotions of the two lovers. In *Romeo and Juliet* evil exists only in so far as the traditional conflict exists. It is not presented as a facet of the normal human will (even in the case of Tybalt); stability and concord are always possible, as a result of spontaneous human action, and we are always aware that peace is only a hand's breadth away. The narrow distance between tragedy and comedy is of course one of the principal effects of the play. But in *Titus* the political conflict remains central and cannot possibly be evaded. It arises from the fact of being human, from the need to resist destruction, the imposition of chaos, the reduction of civilisation to appetite, and man to beast, all of which here grows out of a personal will to evil, deeply implanted in human nature, and requiring for its neutralisation every energy and every resource available in the play. Here no aspect of life can be thought of as merely personal and private, and so exempted from the struggle. The loves of Aaron and Tamora, the rape of Lavinia, are political as well as moral offences. There is no Duke to intervene; the conflict is not simply a relic of past bitternesses, but a monstrous burgeoning of manic energies; death or flight are the only alternatives to absorption into the system.

And in the end, flight is not possible either. The world of the play demands a return to the scene of the struggle. This is equally true of both tragedies: the two plays are (uniquely among Shakespeare's tragedies) tales whose significance is expressed in terms of single cities, though *Rome* has, of course, a very different civic resonance from *Verona*. Verona suggests to us when we hear that it is in 'fair Verona, where we lay our scene' the anticipation of Italian passions, Italian family honour, the hot blood stirring in the sun, balconies, friars, domestic luxury and homely social display, a cosy familiarity of masters and servants, a world poised between the bourgeois and the aristocratic; though we must try to beware of finding in the play an 'Italianism' which entered English literature through *Romeo and Juliet*. Rome on the other hand suggests *ab initio* a military civilisation, severity, self-conscious masculinity, stoical self-denial, the inexorable rule of law—the collection of ethical icons that long dominated the European sense of culture: Horatius defending the bridge, Mutius Scevola burning off his right hand, Regulus returning to Carthage, Lucretia preferring death to dishonour, Manlius Torquatus killing his son for disobedience, etc., etc.

It appears in consequence that the two cities are well chosen by Shakespeare as points of focus, for a love story on the one hand, and on the other hand for a story of civilisation and its enemies, concerned with fortitude and brutality. In both plays the city walls measure the limit of the ordered world.

> There is no world without Verona walls

says Romeo with what might seem merely adolescent exaggeration; but the exaggeration is in fact quite close to truth. Meaning does not exist for the play outside Verona; the only non-Veronese of whom we hear is the Apothecary, who is death's emissary:

> Famine is in thy cheeks,
> Need and oppression starveth in thy eyes,
> Contempt and beggary hangs upon thy back,
> The world is not thy friend, nor the world's law . . .
> (5.1.69–72)

The balance of love and hate, of personal life and public reputation, the context within which meaning exists—this can be found only in Verona.

In *Titus*, very similarly, the play's meaning can only be brought to focus inside the walls of its city. Of course the focus is very different, the city being so different. We are here concerned with self-sacrifice and self-indulgence, rule and disobedience, with suffering and cruelty, with the destructive will to chaos, set against personal commitment to justice as the only meaningful basis for society. Only in Rome, it is implied, can the victory of cosmos or chaos be fully significant; Rome is seen as the hub of things, where final decisions are made and known to be final. This is why at the end of the play:

> As for that ravenous tiger, Tamora,
> No funeral rite, nor man in mourning weed,
> No mournful bell shall ring her burial;
> But throw her forth to beasts and birds to prey.
>   (5.3.195–8)

Rome is here finally returned to the status appropriate to it, a status it has seemed to lose in the course of the action, when the city came to seem no different from the barbarism outside. When, as Titus tells us,

> Rome is but a wilderness of tigers,

when Lucius has to flee to the Goths to raise an army 'to be revenged on Rome and Saturnine', Rome clearly has forgotten how to be Rome. It takes a political convulsion and a blood-bath to re-establish the city as different from the wilderness of tigers. In the meantime Titus is required to carry the role of Rome's speaking conscience, when Rome cannot speak for herself. Where is Astraea gone? Why do the gods not answer, or not listen? Such questions keep continuously before our minds a sense of meaning in the city which is elsewhere out of sight. Meaning cannot be given to the world again, it is implied, till the mind of Rome and the mind of Titus are at one, when Moors and Goths know their place outside the walls and Roman *severitas* rules all within.

The only locale established in *Titus Andronicus* outside the walls of Rome is the forest of act 2 where the major crimes are committed. It is to be noticed that those who are at home and effective here are Aaron and Tamora, Chiron and Demetrius. For Tamora everything in the forest 'doth make a gleeful boast':

> The snakes lie rolled in the cheerful sun;
> The green leaves quiver with the cooling wind
> And makes a chequer'd shadow on the ground;
> Under their sweet shade, Aaron, let us sit . . .
>   (2.3.13–16)

For Lavinia, however, the forest scene is, like Aaron, dark and evil:

> let her joy her raven-coloured love;
> This valley fits the purpose passing well.
>   (2.3.83–4)

Aaron is skilful in the use of forest pits and stratagems; his energy sprouts at the thought of them. The young Andronici, however, grow uncertain and dim of sight:

> Quintus. My sight is very dull, whate'er it bodes.
> Martius. And mine, I promise you; were it not for shame,
>   Well could I leave our sport to sleep awhile.
>   . . . . . .
> Quintus. I am surprised with an uncouth fear;
>   A chilling sweat o'er-runs my trembling joints;
>   My heart suspects more than mine eye can see.
>   (2.3.195–7, 211–13)

Within the dim light of the forest meanings change at the whim of the observer; this is no place for the hard clear minds of the Andronici. It is, however, a natural context for Tamora's Gothic deceptions and shifts of role. At one point the forest is for her, as noted above, a place of love and repose. It is also Tamora, however, who expresses most eloquently the idea of the forest as a place of horror—without even the excuse that it is 'another part of the forest':

> A barren detested vale you see it is:
> The trees, though summer, yet forlorn and lean,
> Overcome with moss and baleful mistletoe;
> Here never shines the sun; here nothing breeds,
> Unless the nightly owl or fatal raven.
>   (2.3.93–7)

This description, like the previous one designed to encourage Aaron to acts of love, is, of course, not organised as a scientific account of a place actually there, but presents a rhetorical backdrop, appropriate in this case to murder, rape and mutilation. When Titus asks for 'proof' that his sons performed the murder he brings a Roman attachment to the rules of evidence to a Gothic dream of total personal fulfilment, where the world becomes what the dreamer desires it to be. At the end of act 2 when the night-world of the forest is giving way again to the daylight clarities of Rome, Marcus Andronicus sees the nightmare figure of his niece; he remarks:

> If I do dream, would all my wealth would wake me!
> If I do wake, some planet strike me down,
> That I may slumber an eternal sleep!
>   (2.4.13–15)

Henceforth in the play, however, such nightmare shadows have to be allowed as part of the daylight population of Rome. The ghosts are only laid, the shadows of the forest dispelled, when nightmare and truth have faced one another in Tamora's last disguise—as Revenge, the mother of Rapine and Murder ('A pair of cursed hell-hounds and their dam' as Titus puts it)—so that mutilators

and mutilated can perish together in a shared universe of absurdity and Rome
be restored to rule and the daylight processes of justice.[3]

At the centre of the city, as its soul you may say, stands the family of the
Andronici, and at the centre of the Andronici's sense of themselves stands one
essential object, which the stage-picture should surely highlight—the tomb. The
structural use of the family vault or tomb provides another point of correspon-
dence between *Titus* and *Romeo*. We are shown the tomb of the Andronici very
early in the play: when Titus first enters in his Roman Triumph, bearing the
Gothic family into Rome among his prisoners, the first action he undertakes is the
burial of the dead in the family vault:

> Romans, of five and twenty valiant sons . . .
> Behold the poor remains, alive and dead!
> These that survive let Rome reward with love;
> These that I bring unto their latest home,
> With burial amongst their ancestors . . .
> Make way to lay them by their brethren.
> There greet in silence, as the dead are wont,
> And sleep in peace, slain in your country's wars.
> O sacred receptacle of my joys,
> Sweet cell of virtue and nobility,
> How many sons hast thou of mine in store
> That thou wilt never render to me more!
>   (1.1.79–95)

And it is the tomb that stimulates the first statement of the conflict that will dominate the play. Lucius demands, in what is clearly part of a controlled ritual:

> Give us the proudest prisoner of the Goths,
> That we may hew his limbs, and on a pile
> Ad manes fratrum sacrifice his flesh
> Before this earthy prison of their bones,
> That so the shadows be not unappeas'd,
> Nor we disturb'd with prodigies on earth.
>   (1.1.96–101)

Shakespeare seems here to be dramatising a clear conception of the religious basis
of the Roman way of life; there is no suggestion that he is criticising the system.
The dead citizen-warriors claim the right to be returned to their family place
within the city. There they will rest in peace, provided the appropriate honour is
paid to them; and the appropriate honour is that the living should hear their claim
for the propitiatory sacrifice of 'the proudest prisoner of the Goths', and be
absolutely obliged to fulfil this claim.

Against this Roman ritual Shakespeare sets the personal plea of Tamora:

---

[3]In these terms *Titus* looks like a tragic version of the city–forest–city pattern found in *A
Midsummer-Night's Dream*—a play which also has close affinities with *Romeo and Juliet*.

> Victorious Titus, rue the tears I shed,
> A mother's tears in passion for her son.
> (1.1.105–6)

Modern readers naturally feel more sympathy for the personal position taken up by Tamora and argued by her with eloquence and passion. But the play hardly supports the view that these Roman rituals are in themselves barbarous, or that Tamora is in some sense 'justified' in taking up revenge against the Andronici. The stern suppression of self in the interest of family, community or state is certainly presented in an extreme form, but it is the extreme form of a value-system consistently preferred in the play before subjective passion or individual emotionalism. The military dead are represented as an essential part of the living family and of the national destiny; they cannot be fobbed off with something less than their right. As in other military civilisations, the valiancy of the living is preserved by the promise that they, too, in their turn will have the right to enter the family tomb, to join the honoured bones of their ancestors and be rewarded with reverence and with sacrificial victims. This is why the tomb becomes the primary focus again at the end of the play. The new conqueror and paterfamilias, Lucius Andronicus, throws out the tiger Tamora for birds to peck at; Aaron is treated very similarly— half buried in the earth and left to the mercies of a Nature that 'swallows her own increase'. Both are replaced in the extra-mural world of unhallowed appetite. But

> My father and Lavinia shall forthwith
> Be closed in our household's monument.
> (5.3.193–4)

Interment in the tomb validates the efforts of the life preceding, and ensures the continuity of past, present and future under the same standards of civilisation.

The parallel importance of the tomb in *Romeo and Juliet* suggests that the Andronicus 'household's monument' reflects more than Shakespeare's study of Roman antiquities. It implies that Shakespeare found the tomb property a convenient expression of his sense of the tragic importance of family and social continuities. The Capulet family monument is not, of course, a military symbol. But the choice of it as the most appropriate final setting for the tragedy brings out the structure of significances this play shares with *Titus Andronicus*. It is entirely appropriate that the 'public' wedding-bed of Romeo and Juliet (as against their previous private bedding) should be placed in the Capulet tomb, for it is there that Romeo may be most effectively seen to have joined his wife's clan, there where their corporate identity is most unequivocally established:

> Where all the kindred of the Capulets lie,
> (4.1.112)

> Where for this many hundred years the bones
> Of all my buried ancestors are pack'd.
> (5.3.40–1)

The rash and personal passion of Romeo and Juliet can hardly claim a truly tragic significance if it cannot be caught up in the corporate and continuing life of Verona. Here, as in *Titus Andronicus*, the presence of the tomb assures us that the extreme acts of tragic individuals contribute to the past and future as well as to the brilliant present of personal assertion, here where they join the confluence of acts that make up social continuity.

In both plays a woman as well as a man is placed in the tomb at the end of the action. One might have expected the Andronicus tomb to exclude women; but Lavinia is clearly said to be Titus's companion in death. I do not think, however, that this implies any weakening of the military significance of the family monument. Lavinia, too, has like a soldier triumphed over her enemy. The battle has, of course, been a strange and even a grotesque one. The code of military ethics does not provide much guidance for dealing with a wilderness of tigers; and the cunning ploys of the mad Titus are only marginally 'Roman'. But it is worth noticing that the appeal to Roman precedent and tradition returns at the moment of Lavinia's death:

> Was it well done of rash Virginius
> To slay his daughter with his own right hand.
>   (5.3.36–7)

asks Titus, and, being told by the Emperor, 'It was, Andronicus', he stabs and kills her. This is often seen as yet another senseless butchery; but in the light of the precedent explicitly established one may prefer to see it as the restoration of truly Roman or meaningful death. To have killed Lavinia earlier would have been an act of despair, for the standards by which such an act might be justified seemed to have vanished. To have enclosed her in the tomb then would have devalued the generations of soldiers already inhearsed. Now, with the mutilators mutilated, and with Tamora and Saturninus securely within the grasp of punishment, the practical possibility of justice reappears, the tomb can reopen and receive the honourable dead. Their presence there can now give meaning to the continuing efforts of the living. The persistent *Romanitas* of the family is spelt out in Marcus's submission of the 'poor remainder of Andronici' to the will of the Roman people:

> Now have you heard the truth: what say you,
>   Romans?
> Have we done aught amiss, show us wherein,
> And, from the place where you behold us pleading,
> The poor remainder of Andronici
> Will hand in hand all headlong hurl ourselves,
> And on the ragged stones beat forth our souls,
> And make a mutual closure of our house.
>   (5.3.128–34)

On the contrary, of course, the people exalt the family and the family, in its turn, must exalt the dead. It is in this context that Lavinia, like another Lucrece, comes to represent something like a Roman tutelary deity, raped, mutilated, rendered incapable of crying out against these invasive barbarisms, but, by virtue of family *pietas* and unflinching self-sacrifice, enabled to take up her niche in the household monument and to represent to later ages a mode of tragic experience appropriate to a meaningfully 'Roman' world.

Part 2
TITUS ANDRONICUS

The Metamorphosis of Violence
in *Titus Andronicus*

Eugene Waith

It is surprising to find Shakespearian critics in agreement, yet almost to a man they have concurred in their verdict on the merits of *Titus Andronicus*. The word which most nearly sums up their feelings is "disgust". Ravenscroft called the play "a heap of rubbish"; Coleridge said that it was "obviously intended to excite vulgar audiences by its scenes of blood and horror—to our ears shocking and disgusting"; Dover Wilson recently called it a "broken-down cart, laden with bleeding corpses from an Elizabethan scaffold".[1] Only a few critics have had so much as a word of praise for this early Shakespearian tragedy.[2]

The features of *Titus Andronicus* which have had such enduring power to repel the critics are easy to identify. The succession of extraordinarily violent episodes has given rise to the opinion that the play is crude—fit only for "vulgar audiences". The florid style of many of the speeches has seemed appallingly overwrought. Now it is a curious fact that this second feature should logically lead to a quite different opinion about the play Miss M. C. Bradbrook has well characterized the tone as "cool and cultured".[3] If the style is crude in a way, it is not the crudity of the bear-baiting pit or the Elizabethan scaffold. The trouble seems to be an excess of refinement, or an overloading with classical allusion—surely caviare for the bear-baiting crowd.

Taken separately, these two features of *Titus Andronicus* have seemed bad enough; taken together, they have served to damn the play utterly, for even if we grant the author of a thriller his right to bring the heroine on the stage, "her hands cut off, and her tongue cut out and ravisht" (2.4, stage direction), must we endure a description of the "crimson river of warm blood, like to a bubbling fountain" on her "roséd lips" (2.4.22–4)? The combination of crude violence with

From *Shakespeare Survey* 10 (1957), 39–49. Copyright © Cambridge University Press 1957. Reprinted with the permission of Cambridge University Press.

[1]Edward Ravenscroft, *Titus Andronicus, or The Rape of Lavinia* (1687), sig. A2; *Coleridge's Shakespearean Criticism*, ed. T. M. Raysor (Cambridge, Mass., 1930), II, 31; *Titus Andronicus*, ed. J. Dover Wilson (Cambridge, 1948), p. xii.

[2]I do not deal in this article with the problem of authorship, which has been thoroughly treated most recently by J. C. Maxwell in the new Arden Edition (London, 1953), pp. xxiv–xxxiv; I agree with him that the play is substantially Shakespeare's. I am deeply indebted to all the critical apparatus of this edition.

[3]M. C. Bradbrook, *Themes and Conventions of Elizabethan Tragedy* (Cambridge, 1935), p. 99.

this sort of fanciful description is so incongruous that Dover Wilson has suggested that Shakespeare was burlesquing the style of his contemporaries.[4] Though this view has not so far prevailed, the incongruity has troubled every critic. It has seemed impossible to see a meaningful relationship between action and style.

A further objection to the play is the flatness of the characters. Critics have complained that only Titus and Aaron have any life in them, while the formal, rhetorical style tends to make of all the rest purely emblematic figures. Once again, style is to blame: caught in some fantastic pose in the midst of their most violent actions, the characters are petrified by a blast of eloquence—plunged, as it were, in the deep-freeze of rhetoric.

There is, however, a relationship between the violence of *Titus Andronicus* and the style in which it is written. My object in this paper is to examine that relationship with the intention, not of rehabilitating the play, but of placing it in a stylistic development of some consequence for the English drama. The direct source of *Titus Andronicus* appears to have been a prose account which survives in an eighteenth-century chapbook. This account purports to be translated from the Italian, which may have been a tale of the order of those in the *Gesta Romanorum*. The exact nature of this source must remain a matter for speculation. We can be sure, however, that behind it lie the stories of the rape of Lucretia, of Appius and Virginia, probably of Thyestes, and most certainly of the rape of Philomela. Shakespeare of course knew these stories as well as the Titus-story which they influenced. How much he may have been affected by Seneca is debatable. Though *Titus Andronicus* used to be called a Senecan play, critics such as Howard Baker and E. M. W. Tillyard[5] have shown the many respects in which it is not Senecan, and it seems fair to conclude that however important the Senecan model may have been, Ovid exerted a more direct influence. References in the play leave no doubt that his telling of the Philomela story in his *Metamorphoses* was fresh in Shakespeare's mind. This well-known fact provides a point of departure. We may ask how Ovid renders the violence of Tereus' attack and of the dire revenge of Philomela and her sister Procne, and what meaning he sees in these dreadful events.

If we turn to the latter part of Book VI and begin reading this story, we shall be struck immediately by the emphasis on pathos: King Pandion's tearful farewell to his daughter Philomela, and his injunction to Tereus to "guard her with a father's love";[6] the rape itself in a "hut deep hidden in the ancient woods", where Philomela, far from all help, calls vainly for her father and sister; the

---

[4]*Titus Andronicus*, ed. Wilson, pp. li–lvi. I have taken all quotations from the play from this edition since the readings which Wilson takes from QI are preferred by most modern editors to those of F printed in the standard Globe edition.

[5]Howard Baker, *Induction to Tragedy* (University, Louisiana, 1939), pp. 119–39; E. M. W. Tillyard, *Shakespeare's History Plays* (New York, 1946), pp. 135–41.

[6]Ovid, *Metamorphoses, with an English translation* by Frank J. Miller, Loeb Classical Library (London, 1936), VI, 499, 521. Unless otherwise indicated, all the English translations from Ovid are Miller's or are closely modelled on his.

efforts of Itys, the little son of Procne by Tereus, to throw his arms around his mother's neck as she murders him. Along with the feelings of the victims we find other emotions: the raging lust of Tereus at the sight of Philomela, Procne's fierce devotion to revenge, Philomela's unspeakable joy as she hurls the head of Itys in his father's face. At such feelings we can only be horrified. But if the mixture of pity and horror is reminiscent of the Aristotelian account of tragedy, the ending of the story hardly fulfils our expectations of tragedy. Every schoolchild who has been brought up on the explanatory notes to *The Waste Land* knows what follows: Tereus draws his sword after the cannibalistic feast, and pursues the revenging sisters, who turn into a nightingale and a swallow as he turns into a hoopoe. Of the sisters, Ovid's final words are "One flies to the woods, the other rises to the roof. And even now their breasts have not lost the marks of their murderous deed, their feathers are stained with blood" (6.668–70). Of Tereus, "Upon his head a stiff crest appears, and a huge beak stands forth instead of his long sword. He is the hoopoe with the look of one armed for war" (6.672–4). This is not "How are the mighty fallen!" nor "How horrible!" nor yet "How pathetic!" It is more as if Ovid were saying, "Strange, isn't it?"

We cannot expect to penetrate Ovid's meaning by looking at only one out of his vast collection of myths. When we read one or more entire books of the *Metamorphoses* certain predominant attitudes toward the material begin to emerge. The theme of metamorphosis, which gives the work its title, is a vital part of the meaning. It appears in several variant forms. Most obviously there are the physical transformations, such as those I have just mentioned, or of Ceyx and Alcyone, also changed into birds, of Daphne or Myrrha into trees, of Niobe into stone, of Hecuba into a dog. These characters also undergo a kind of psychic transformation. In certain cases the change is of a moral order: Tereus, possessed by lust, becomes a cruel monster; so do Procne, Philomela, and Hecuba when they devote themselves to revenge; Niobe is changed from a proud boaster to a suppliant, paralysed by grief. It is tempting, of course, to equate these two sorts of metamorphosis by saying that the physical change symbolizes the moral change and the punishment fits the crime. This is a temptation that the commentators of the Middle Ages and the Renaissance did not resist. To take one example from the hundreds of possible ones, when George Pettie comes to the end of his retelling of the story of Tereus, he says of the three principal characters, "and as Ovid reporteth [they] were turned into birds, meaning they were not worthy human shape or the use of reason, which were such cruel monsters altogether devoid of ruth and reason".[7] If one succumbs to this sort of interpretation, it is easy enough to see a moral emblem in the transformation of Hecuba into a dog after she has gouged out Polymestor's eyes, or in the change of proud Niobe into a weeping stone. But one is apt to have misgivings about some of the other cases, even though the hardened allegorizers apparently had none. If Tereus, Procne and Philomela were turned into birds, so were Ceyx and

---

[7] *A Petite Pallace of Pettie His Pleasure*, ed. I. Gollancz (1908), 1, 70.

Alcyone, those models of marital devotion. Were they also unworthy of human shape? Ovid tells us only that the pity of the gods was responsible for the transformation. Then too we notice that while Daphne is turned into a tree to save her from Apollo's embraces, Myrrha is turned into a tree after her incestuous union with her father to keep her from contaminating either the world of the living or the world of the dead. The teaching of this last story is, to say the least, rather oblique, and in none of the instances we have just been considering is there any clear-cut moral transformation.

Psychic metamorphosis of another sort is clearly common to all the stories I have cited. In the execution of their vengeance Procne and Philomela are transported by emotions which rise steadily to the point of obliterating their normal characters; when Tereus discovers what vengeance has been taken on him, he too is transported by overmastering emotions. At this moment of crisis the feelings of the three characters are alike in intensity, though as different as exultant vengeance mixed with fear is from grief mixed with rage. In each case the emotion is unbearable; the character is literally beside himself. And this is the moment in which all three are metamorphosed. In Ovid's telling of the story of Niobe we watch the mounting intensity of the mother's grief to the point where it can no longer find expression in words and her tongue is frozen to the roof of her mouth. This is the moment of her transformation. The mingled love and grief of widowed Alcyone are similarly unbearable, like the virginal terror of Daphne, and the fear, the guilt, and above all the utter weariness of Myrrha, fleeing alone, month after month. These examples suggest that Ovid was more interested in the transforming power of intense states of emotion than in pointing a moral. Hecuba's story makes this especially clear. Her suffering is extraordinary as is the vengeance to which it drives her. Ovid's comment on her transformation into a dog is this: "Her sad fortune touched the Trojans and her Grecian foes and all the gods as well; yes, all, for even Juno, sister and wife of Jove, declared that Hecuba had not deserved such an end" (13.573–5). In this case the actual transformation is anticipated in the description of the moment in which vengeance is planned. When the body of Polydorus is discovered, the Trojan women shriek, but Hecuba, like Niobe, is dumb with grief and stands immovable as a rock, looking at the corpse of her son. When her anger rises, however, Ovid tells us that she is "wholly absorbed" by the idea of vengeance and goes off to Polymestor like a lioness whose suckling cub has been stolen from her. Two sorts of transformation are suggested here of which only the latter, the raging animal, materializes. But in both are portrayed the transforming power of great emotion.

I have dwelt upon this point at length both because the tendency to allegorize is by no means absent from some modern criticism and because the emphasis on emotional states is important in itself. Seneca the Rhetorician observed in his *Controversiae* (2.2.12) that Ovid, who had a considerable reputation as an orator, was not so interested in arguments as in the depiction of character and behaviour. In the *Metamorphoses* this interest appears chiefly in the representa-

22   *Eugene Waith*

tion of the various passions and their extraordinary effects on various natures, human or divine. Yet, despite such variety, one of the lasting impressions from reading this work is of the unity of all creation, informed by one vital force. The idea, as Miss Bradbrook has pointed out, is closely related to that of Lucretian Nature.[8] In the moments of greatest emotional stress Ovid's characters seem to lose not only individuality but even humanity as if sheer intensity of feeling made them indistinguishable from other forms of life. Often a physical transformation completes the suggestion. Thus, in the depiction of these legendary figures individuality is built up only to be obliterated by an impersonal force working from within. Character and personality miraculously give way to naked, abstract emotion.

It is obvious that incidents of great violence lend themselves well to the portrayal of character under emotional stress. Outrage is the prime mover in the story of Philomela, forcing the protagonists to that final crisis in which they lose themselves utterly. And in some of the other gruesome stories, such as the battle of the Lapiths and the centaurs, where physical transformation is rather a minor part of the action, the violent carnage is in itself a powerful means of portraying the senseless fury which has transformed both men and centaurs.

Ovid's style reinforces in several ways the effects I have been describing. Both horror and pathos are pointed up by brilliant touches, often given in a very few words. When Tereus boards the ship with Philomela in his power he exclaims to himself, "We have won!" (6.513). This single utterance conveys the elation of a man who thinks of his lustful scheme as an exciting game. The brief description of the "hut deep hidden in the ancient woods" is most evocative, and the gesture of Itys, seeking to embrace his mother, condenses the pathos of an entire incident.

At the same time, the elegant urbanity of these narrations implies a considerable detachment. With great suavity Ovid leads us from one story to another, scarcely seeming to alter the tone of his voice, as if the story of Philomela did not really affect him very differently from that of Pelops, which it follows. His use of narrators further increases the psychic distance. The story of Venus and Adonis, for instance, is one of a group of stories told by Orpheus, and it is interrupted by the story of Atalanta, which Venus tells Adonis. Perspective opens within perspective.

The seemingly illogical combination of emotional excitement and psychic distance contributes to the effect of impersonalization. The metamorphosis of the character is of absorbing interest; the individual who is transformed is only interesting as an example of metamorphosis. Ovid's descriptions of violence illustrate such an attitude. The battle of the Lapiths and the centaurs contains some sensationally gory exploits by the infuriated opponents. Ovid does not spare detail, but his descriptions are sometimes surprisingly matter of fact. A flaming brand plunged into an open wound is like the hot iron which the blacksmith plunges in

[8]M. C. Bradbrook, *Shakespeare and Elizabethan Poetry* (1951), pp. 51–3.

water (12.276–7); a mangled body is compared to a common and pleasant household sight (12.434–8). In the story of Philomela, the tongue, when it has been cut out, is compared to the severed tail of a snake, still twitching (6.557–60). In every case the visual image is exact and thus the horror more vivid, yet at the same time our minds are turned away from the individual as a whole to a minute contemplation of what has happened to one part of his body. Looking thus through the microscope, as it were, we momentarily forget the sufferer in the overwhelming reality of the wound, and beyond the wound we glimpse its analogies in an everyday world. The comparisons are often extended, usually unexpected, sometimes even fanciful, always neatly phrased. What may seem at first an incongruous elegance is perfectly suited to the process of transforming a character into an emotional state. Violence, as Ovid describes it, is an emblem of the transformation. In a sense, it is itself transformed in the process into an object of interested but somewhat detached contemplation.

It would be risky to assume that this descriptive technique or the reduction of character to abstract passions had for Augustan Romans or for Renaissance Englishmen the inhibiting effect upon emotional response which I think they have for us today. It is less risky to suggest that even if these devices were considered very moving, the effect they produced was less that of sharing a great emotional experience with another human being than of wonder at the extraordinary manifestations of familiar emotions raised to a most unfamiliar pitch. Ovid sometimes points up this effect by a comment. Of Alcyone leaping into the sea, "It was a wonder that she could do it" (11.731); of Procne and Philomela fleeing from the enraged Tereus, "You would have thought they were on wings; they *were* on wings!" (6.667–8). We are left with these moments of wonder, caught in a series of vivid pictures, elegantly framed by the style of a master-narrator.

Before turning to *Titus Andronicus* to see how certain Ovidian effects are reproduced in the play, a few words must be given to a matter previously alluded to—the attitude of Renaissance readers towards the *Metamorphoses*. Douglas Bush points to the multiple attitude composed of the medieval moralizing tradition, the beginnings of a new paganism which admired Ovid's depictions of nature and love, and perhaps most important of all, the great respect for Ovid as a model of style.[9] In generation after generation students were encouraged to imitate him.

The new pagan attitude towards Ovid left, so far as I know, no coherent interpretation of the *Metamorphoses*. One can only surmise that from this point of view the stories might have seemed to illustrate the miraculous vitality of nature. As for the grammarians and textual critics, the Italian Regio will serve as an example of their attitude towards violence. His frigid observation on the description of Philomela after her rape is that Ovid "beautifully expressed virgin fear" by comparing her to a lamb and a dove. Clearly, it is elegance of style which interests Regio.[10]

[9]Douglas Bush, *Mythology and the Renaissance Tradition in English Poetry* (Minneapolis, 1932), pp. 68–81.
[10]Ovid, *Metamorphoses*, ed. R. Regio (Venice, Bonetus Locatellus, 1493), sig. G7.

There remains the moralizing tradition. By and large, the Renaissance commentators did not pursue the medieval *Ovide Moralisé* to its *o altitudo!* of allegorical interpretation. Golding, the famous Elizabethan translator of Ovid, lays
greatest stress on a general point of moral philosophy: not all "that bear the
name of men" are truly men; many are like beasts or even worse than beasts.[11]
The notion is essentially what emerges from Pettie's interpretation of the story
of Tereus, Procne, and Philomela. In addition to this kind of lesson there
appeared to the Renaissance commentators to be certain broad underlying
themes in Ovid's work. His account of the Creation interested them especially.
They found it in accordance with the Biblical story, and some of them, as T. W.
Baldwin has shown,[12] also saw in it the transformation of chaos into order by the
power of love as portrayed in Hesiod and Plato. Such Biblical and philosophical
associations seemed to provide an important theme of order versus chaos in the
Metamorphoses. Golding gives a political formulation of the theme in a passage
which also brings in the theme of transformation: if the States, which are God's
representatives on earth, "Decline from virtue unto vice and live disorderly, / To
eagles, tigers, bulls, and bears" they change both themselves and their people.[13]
To allegorical interpreters like Golding the most violent episodes were obviously acceptable as rewards of wickedness or emblems of disorder.

The theme of *Titus Andronicus* is too commonplace to attribute to any one
source. It is, I take it, the opposition of moral and political disorder to the unify-
ing force of friendship and wise government, a theme in which Shakespeare was
interested all his life. Tillyard noted several years ago the relation of this tragedy
to the history plays,[14] and it extends to the Roman plays, to *King Lear, Macbeth*
and much else that Shakespeare wrote. Marcus states the theme at the end of
the play:

> You sad-faced men, people and sons of Rome,
> By uproar severed, as a flight of fowl
> Scattered by winds and high tempestuous gusts,
> O, let me teach you how to knit again
> This scattered corn into one mutual sheaf,
> These broken limbs again into one body.
> (5.3.67–72)

The rape and mutilation of Lavinia is the central symbol of disorder, both moral
and political, resembling in this respect the rape of Lucrece as Shakespeare portrays it. The connexion between the two sorts of disorder is made explicit in the
play's two references to Tarquin, once as ravisher (4.1.64–5) and once as the evil,
exiled king (3.1.299). The association is still present in Shakespeare's mind many

[11]Epistle, ll. 55–62; *Shakespeare's Ovid* . . . , ed. W. H. D. Rouse (1904), p. 2 (I have modernized
the spelling).
[12]T. W. Baldwin, *On the Literary Genetics of Shakespeare's Poems and Sonnets* (Urbana, Ill., 1950),
pp. 49–72.
[13]Preface to the Reader, ll. 89–92; *Shakespeare's Ovid*, p. 16.
[14]*Op. cit.* p. 139.

years later, when he and Macbeth speak of "wither'd murder" moving "with Tarquin's ravishing strides". (2.1.55)

The integrating force, which through most of the play is too weak to impose itself upon chaos, appears in the guise of friendship, brotherly love, justice, and gratitude. Marcus addresses Titus at the beginning of the play as the "friend in justice" to the people of Rome (1.1.180), and at the end calls Lucius "Rome's dear friend" (5.3.80). Brotherly love is demonstrated in the bizarre episodes of Quintus losing himself in the effort to help his brother Martius out of the pit, and of Marcus offering his hand for that of Titus. The absence of brotherly love appears in the first scene in the quarrel of Saturninus and Bassianus, and injustice and gratitude are the subjects of complaint throughout the play.

The theme of *Titus Andronicus* is at least consonant with what many interpreters supposed Ovid to be saying. Friendship is one of the ordering forces; Golding uses this word in translating Ovid's account of how the strife between the elements was ended. He says that God, separating "each from other did them bind / In endless friendship to agree" (1.24–5). Titus laments the departure of justice by quoting "Terras Astraea reliquit" from Ovid's description of the iron age, just before the time of the giants and the flood. Disorder is represented by the acts of wanton violence and one of the most powerful metaphors in the play, "Rome is but a wilderness of tigers" (3.1.54), seems to echo Golding's lines about disorder in the state.

We may ask then whether any of the characterization is in an Ovidian mode. "Tiger" is one of several animal and bird epithets applied to the passionate Tamora, whose story would fit easily into the scheme of the *Metamorphoses*. When we first see her, she is a captive "distressèd queen", pleading for mercy to her son. We must sympathize, though we are given very little time to do so, with her protest against Titus's inflexibility: "O cruel, irreligious piety!" (1.1.130). Demetrius then compares her to Hecuba, who was given the opportunity to revenge the loss of her son on Polymestor. The allusion reminds one of the guile and the ferocity of Hecuba in carrying out her vengeance and of her final transformation into a dog. The end of Tamora's career is quite consistent with this introduction. Her disguise as Revenge, though part of her plot to deceive Titus, obviously labels for us the passion which dominates her character. She dies a victim of an outrage prompted by the outrage in which she had assisted, and the last words of the play leave no doubt of her complete assimilation into the animal kingdom:

> As for that ravenous tiger, Tamora,
> No funeral rite, nor man in mourning weed,
> No mournful bell shall ring her burial;
> But throw her forth to beasts and birds of prey.
> Her life was beastly and devoid of pity,
> And being dead, let birds on her take pity.

Golding or Pettie could not make the moral more clear.

The character of Tamora is so intimately related to the character of Titus, for which it is a foil, that the two must be discussed together. Once more we have a story which would easily be put with the *Metamorphoses*. We see Titus at the beginning a man of absolute integrity but cursed, somewhat like Coriolanus, with an unbending and blind fixity of character. If his piety, ignoring all pleas for mercy, warrants Tamora's adjective, "cruel", his slaying of Mutius and his refusal to have him entombed deserve the charges of injustice, impiety, and barbarity brought by his brother and sons. His choice of a principle rather than a man, when he throws the election to Saturninus, is palpable folly. Thus his closely related virtues and faults are well established in the first act. In the succeeding acts the cruelties of his enemies are heaped upon him in a steady succession. After he has cut off his hand, the unbearable horror of his situation causes him to exclaim,

> Is not my sorrow deep, having no bottom?
> Then be my passions bottomless, . . .
> If there were reason for these miseries,
> Then into limits could I bind my woes.
>   (3.1.217–218, 220–1)

If this speech suggests some of the attitudes I have pointed to in Ovid, so do the comments of Marcus after the messenger has brought Titus the heads of his sons:

> These miseries are more than may be borne! . . .
> Ah! now no more will I control thy griefs: . . .
> Now is a time to storm, why art thou still?
>   (3.1.244, 260, 264)

From this point the character of Titus is markedly altered by grief. Although Marcus says that Titus is "so just that he will not revenge" (4.1.129), it gradually becomes clear that revenge is his obsession. At first he takes refuge in fantasy, but when he finally has Chiron and Demetrius in his power his words reveal clearly his true state of mind and do so in a series of Ovidian allusions. After a grisly account of his plans for the banquet, he says:

> This is the feast that I have bid her to,
> And this the banquet she shall surfeit on;
> For worse than Philomel you used my daughter,
> And worse than Progne I will be revenged. . . .
> Come, come, be every one officious
> To make this banquet, which I wish may prove
> More stern and bloody than the Centaurs' feast.
>   (5.2.193–6, 202–4)

Here surely is a psychic metamorphosis which provides one of the truly powerful moments in the depiction of the hero. His cruelty is monstrous yet, thanks to the indications of the first act, not incredible.

Because of this consistent development Titus is a more successful character than Tamora, who is not always depicted as the woman obsessed by revenge. In the second act we find her more lustful than revengeful, while Aaron, described in terms of the same birds and beasts to which Tamora is compared, becomes in a sense the projection of her revenge. But unfortunately for the unity of design, Aaron, though a brilliant dramatic creation, belongs to the un-Ovidian tradition of Barabas and Eleazar. His villainy invites a less complicated response than does the obsessive behavior of Tamora and Titus.

Although the references to Procne and to the battle of the Lapiths and the centaurs show the horrifying effect of the fixation on revenge, Titus, unlike Tamora, is not finally shown as bestial or degenerate. His slaying of Lavinia, also somewhat prepared for by the first act, has overtones of nobility, though Saturninus' comment "unnatural and unkind", is uncomfortably close to the truth. The final comments on his character are all praise and pity, sharply contrasted with the abuse heaped on Aaron and Tamora. Marcus gives the core of the defence:

> Now judge what cause had Titus to revenge
> These wrongs, unspeakable, past patience,
> Or more than any living man could bear.
> (5.3.125–7)

So at the end it is Titus rather than Tamora who produces an effect like that of Ovid's Hecuba, for whom even the gods felt pity when revenge had dreadfully transformed her. Or we might describe the difference by saying that the depiction of Tamora is in the mode of the moralized Ovid, while the depiction of Titus more closely resembles Roman Ovid.

The underlying theme of *Titus Andronicus*, to which I have referred, is not so important an organizing principle as Shakespeare's themes are in his later tragedies. I think that, like Ovid, he was more interested here in portraying the extraordinary pitch of emotion to which a person may be raised by the most violent outrage. The passions of Titus transcend the limits of character to become in their own right, so to speak, phenomena of nature: his grief, like the Nile, "disdaineth bounds" (3.1.71). The grotesqueries of his mad scenes contribute to this effect, and the end is pure frenzy. If the violence of the play serves the theme as an emblem of disorder, it also serves as both agent and emblem of a metamorphosis of character which takes place before our eyes. Character in the usual sense of the word disintegrates completely. What we see is a personified emotion.

We come finally to Lavinia, the third character who may profitably be seen against this Ovidian background. She has been one of the chief stumbling-blocks to the appreciation of the play: to many critics she has seemed smug in her contemptuous speeches to Tamora (2.3.66 ff.), and intolerably pathetic or ludicrous thereafter. Dover Wilson gave the most unkindest cut of all when he likened her to "a little puppy-dog", trotting after Titus with his severed hand in her teeth.[15] Yet as an inhabitant of the Ovidian world she is neither absurd nor difficult to under-

---

[15]*Titus Andronicus*, ed. Wilson, p. xi.

stand. Her proud self-confidence with Tamora clearly points up the shocking suddenness of her change to a weeping suppliant—an initial metamorphosis somewhat comparable to Niobe's.

Lavinia's second metamorphosis is accomplished in a description which has
proved to be the most unpalatable passage in the play. It is also the most Ovidian.
This is the passage in which Marcus compares Lavinia to a tree whose branches
have been cut, her blood to a river, a bubbling fountain, her lips to roses, her
cheeks to the sun, her lost hands, once more, to the leaves of a tree (2.4.16–57). In
a somewhat different category is the comment on her loss of blood "As from a conduit with three issuing spouts", a comparison reminiscent of Ovid's description of
the death of Pyramus: ". . . the spouting blood leaped high; just as when a pipe
has broken at a weak spot in the lead . . ." (4.121–3). Like Ovid's comparisons,
these of Shakespeare's are unexpected, fanciful, and yet exact. Miss Bradbrook has
pointed to Shakespeare's use of opposites in description in *Venus and Adonis* and
here in *Titus Andronicus*. The imagery of the description of Lavinia is meant, she
believes, to "work by contrast. . . . The writer is saying by means of the images,
'Look here upon this picture, and on this'."[16] It is the "contrast of remembering
happiness in misery" to which she refers, and agreeing that the observation is just,
I should like to add some other ways in which contrast works here. These pleasant
and familiar images of trees, fountains, and conduits bring the horror that has
been committed within the range of comprehension. They oblige us to see clearly
a suffering body, yet as they do so they temporarily remove its individuality, even
its humanity, by abstracting and generalizing. Though not in themselves horrible,
they point up the horror; though familiar, they point up the strangeness. The suffering becomes an object of contemplation.

This technique of description is not inappropriate to this sort of situation. The
trouble is that it is a narrative rather than a dramatic device. Though many writers
have used it in plays, its function is to present to the mind's eye something which
is not on the stage for the physical eye to see. When Duncan is described, "His
silver skin lac'd with his golden blood" (*Macbeth*, 2.4.118), there is also an incongruity between mortal wounds and decorative language, but Duncan himself is
not there to compete with the description. The imagination of the spectator is
free to contemplate a spectacle simultaneously horrible and kingly. The narrative
intrusion is brief and clearly separated from dramatic action. For the Ovidian
description of Lavinia to work as it might work in the *Metamorphoses* an even
greater freedom is required. A physical impersonation of the mutilated Lavinia
should not block our vision.

Though this objection sounds like Lamb's criticism of *King Lear*, I believe it is
more valid because of the different way in which metamorphosis is related to the
meaning of *Titus Andronicus*. In *King Lear* the transformation brought about by
extraordinary suffering is not a loss of humanity but a step toward greater understanding. Dramatic action reinforces at every point what the poetry suggests. In
Ovid's *Metamorphoses* the unendurable emotional state robs the character of his

---

[16]Bradbrook, *Shakespeare and Elizabethan Poetry*, pp. 64, 108.

humanity and the story ends, so to speak, with a point of exclamation. It is easy to see that the melodramatic tale of Titus, Tamora, and Lavinia, partly inspired by Ovid, is susceptible of the full Ovidian treatment. It ends logically with what Joyce might have called an "epiphany" of the state of mind at which each of the principal characters has arrived. This would be shown by a physical metamorphosis or by a passage of description or by both together. In *Titus Andronicus* we have the many speeches insisting upon what is extraordinary in the situation of the hero—what makes it beyond human endurance—but the final transformation which would complete the suggestion cannot take place. We have the description which almost transforms Lavinia, but in the presence of live actors the poetry cannot perform the necessary magic. The action frustrates, rather than re-enforces, the operation of the poetry.

A simple formulation of the source of critical dissatisfaction with the play might seem to follow logically here: the style is inappropriate. Shakespeare, like some Elizabethan builders, has reached out for a bite of classical design and has come up with some decoration which does not fit his basic structure. But this pronouncement rests on an oversimplification, for the Ovidian borrowing in *Titus Andronicus* has more significance than the mere application of decorative detail.

In taking over certain Ovidian forms Shakespeare takes over part of an Ovidian conception which cannot be fully realized by the techniques of drama. This is the conception of the protagonist as a man so worked upon that by sheer intensity of passion he ultimately transcends the normal limits of humanity. I believe that there is a reason why such a treatment of character might appeal to an Elizabethan writer of tragedy, and hence why he might attempt what seems to us a patently impossible task.

In describing the proper effect of tragedy many Renaissance critics emphasized what they called "admiration". In the sixteenth century the word was sometimes used with approximately its modern meaning, but usually retained its basic meaning of "wonder" or "astonishment". The point of exclamation was commonly referred to as a "note of admiration". In a familiar passage of his *Defense of Poesie* Sidney speaks of tragedy "stirring the affects of admiration and commiseration",[17] where "admiration" oddly replaces Aristotle's terror. Minturno makes admiration the final aim of all poetry but particularly of tragedy. "That especially belongs to the tragic poet which fills the hearer with astonishment by horrifying him or moving him to compassion. . . . Whoever suffers a marvellous thing, if it is horrifying or causes compassion, will not be outside the scope of tragedy, whether he be good or whether he be evil".[18] There is no doubt that such ideas about tragedy were in the air at the end of the sixteenth century and hence that playwrights, whether or not they read the theorists, might look for material

---

[17]*Literary Criticism Plato to Dryden*, ed. Allan H. Gilbert (New York, 1940), p. 432; see also pp. 459–61.

[18]Gilbert, pp. 292–3. On "admiration" see also Marvin T. Herrick, 'Some Neglected Sources of *Admiratio*'. *Modern Language Notes*, 62 (1947), 222–6; and J. V. Cunningham, *Woe or Wonder* (Denver, 1951).

and language suitable to arouse admiration. Seneca was obviously a rich mine, but often it was the Latin writers of verse narrative who furnished models; astonishing passages were freely borrowed or imitated from Virgil, Lucan, Statius. Marlowe and Chapman each developed what might be called a rhetoric of admiration; one thinks of Tamburlaine's "high astounding terms" and of the "glaring colours" which "amazed" the young Dryden.[19] By the time of Buckingham's *Rehearsal*, "to elevate and surprise" are the chief objectives of the satirized playwright. This genre of tragedy is most uncongenial to our times. We are inclined to deny that it is tragedy at all and to dismiss it as mere posturing and rant. Even in its own day it never lacked the mockery of critics.

Titus Andronicus is Shakespeare's contribution to a special tragic mode. Its final spectacle is both horrible and pathetic, but above all extraordinary. Ovid more than Seneca or the epic poets was the model for both characterization and style, with the result that Shakespeare's rhetoric of admiration, as seen in such lines as Marcus' description of Lavinia, is more elegantly florid than that of his contemporaries. The hero, in this respect like Tamburlaine or Bussy D'Ambois, is almost beyond praise or blame, an object of admiration.

[19]Dedication of *The Spanish Friar*.

The Aesthetics of Mutilation
in *Titus Andronicus*

Albert H. Tricomi

When T. S. Eliot so flamboyantly denounced *Titus Andronicus* as 'one of the stupidest and most uninspired plays ever written', he naturally invited rebuttal.[1] But while an apology for *Titus* can certainly be erected, the fact is that the imputed stupidities of the tragedy attract far more interest than any of its mediocre achievements. Indeed, if we would only persist in the study of those very 'stupidities' that many critics would rather forget, we would discover that the ways in which the figurative language imitates the literal events of plot makes *The Tragedy of Titus Andronicus* a significant dramatic experiment. In the play's spectacularly self-conscious images that keep pointing at the inventive horrors in the plotting, in its wittily-obsessive allusions to dismembered hands and heads, and in the prophetic literalness of its metaphors, *Titus* reveals its peculiar literary importance.

The peculiar language of *Titus Andronicus* is particularly apparent in the literalness of its central metaphors. In a play preeminently concerned with the mutilation of the human body, *Titus* makes nearly sixty references, figurative as well as literal, to the word 'hands' and eighteen more to the word 'head', or to one of its derivative forms.[2] Far from being divorced from the action as many critics claim,[3]

From *Shakespeare Survey* 27 (1974), 11–19. Copyright © Cambridge University Press 1974. Reprinted with the permission of Cambridge University Press.

[1]*Selected Essays: 1917–1932* (London, 1932), p. 82. Effective rebuttal has occurred with relative infrequency. See Hereward T. Price, 'The Authorship of *Titus Andronicus*', *The Journal of English and Germanic Philology*, XLII (1943), 55–81; E. M. W. Tillyard, *Shakespeare's History Plays* (New York, 1962), pp. 158–65; Alan Sommers, ' "Wilderness of Tigers": Structure and Symbolism in *Titus Andronicus*', *Essays in Criticism*, x (1960), 275–89; and A. C. Hamilton, *The Early Shakespeare* (San Marino, 1967), pp. 63–89. For a superb theory concerning the language of *Titus Andronicus*, see Eugene Waith, 'The Metamorphosis of Violence in *Titus Andronicus*', *Shakespeare Survey 10* (Cambridge, 1957), pp. 39–49.

[2]Laura Jepsen, 'A Footnote on "Hands" in Shakespeare's *Titus Andronicus*', *Florida State Univ. Studies*, XIX (1955), 7–10; *Oxford Shakespeare Concordance: Titus Andronicus* (Oxford, 1972), pp. 95–6, 99.

[3]The works of Muriel Bradbrook, *Themes and Conventions of Elizabethan Tragedy* (Cambridge, Eng., 1935), pp. 98–9, and *Shakespeare and Elizabethan Poetry* (New York, 1952), pp. 104–10; J. Dover Wilson (ed.), *Titus Andronicus* (Cambridge, Eng., 1948), pp. ix–xii; and Wolfgang Clemen, *The Development of Shakespeare's Imagery* (New York, 1951), pp. 22–7, have provided deservedly influential insights into the discontinuity between image and occasion in *Titus Andronicus*, but the sense in which the figurative language embodies the events in *Titus* has never been analyzed. An explanation of the decorous tone of the poetry in *Titus* can, however, be found in Waith's essay, 'Metamorphosis of Violence'.

the figurative language points continually toward the lurid events that govern the tragedy. The figurative language, in fact, imitates the gruesome circumstances of the plot, thus revealing that Shakespeare subordinates everything in *Titus*, including metaphor, to that single task of conveying forcefully the Senecan and Ovidian horrors that he has committed himself to portraying.

Such a relationship between language and event is really quite strange. Ordinarily metaphor is endowed with the capacity of extending almost infinitely the imaginative compass of a play. Through its embedded metaphors especially, a play usually translates its immediate events in images that reach far beyond the poor limitations of the stage. In *Titus Andronicus*, however, metaphor, for the most part, draws its images directly from the narrower events of plot. It becomes literalized. This is a very daring and even dangerous enterprise to undertake. Deliberately relinquishing its natural prerogatives, metaphor strives instead to unite language and action in an endeavour to render the events of the tragedy more real and painful. When Marcus offers Titus the throne, for example, he employs a peculiar metaphor, saying, 'And help to set a head on headless Rome' (1.1.186). Since Titus is being offered the throne of Imperial Rome, Marcus's statement seems to be a happy one. As such, the metaphor appears to be just that, an embellished phrase, a polished, if affected, mode of speech. But, as it happens, this mere metaphor, with all its ominous overtones, is later raised to factual reality when Saturninus, ironically made that 'head' of Rome through Titus's support, beheads two of Titus's sons. In a more specific sense as well, the figures employed direct our perceptions toward isolated parts of the human body. When in the first act Lavinia asks her father to bless her, she uses the rather precise phrase, 'with thy victorious hand' (1.1.163), and Bassianus does likewise when he explains how Titus, 'With his own hand' slew his youngest son (1.1.418). In both instances the figurative phrasing points ahead to the mutilations of future events, to the shearing off of Lavinia's hands, and then, to Titus's willing sacrifice of his own hand when bargaining for the lives of two of his sons.

But while the keen critic may discover a rather brutal principle of retribution in Titus's loss of a hand for having killed—with his own hand—one of his sons, I am more concerned here with the oddly alluring relationship between language and event. Constantly pointing toward and underlining the events that we witness upon the stage, metaphor in this tragedy strains to keep the excruciating images of mutilation ever before our imaginations even when the visual spectacle is no longer before us. The words 'hand' and 'head' appear copiously as figures of speech whose effect is to saturate every aspect of the play with remembered or foreshadowed horror. Following the scene of Lavinia's mutilation, Marcus presents his niece to Titus whose first words to her,

> Speak, Lavinia, what accursed hand
> Hath made thee handless in thy father's sight?
> (3.1.66–7)

recreate the horrible event in the imagination. Of course, the literate response is so artificial as to invite derision, and, no doubt, the whole idea of asking the dumb to speak is a questionable way of inviting pathos. But the pun on hands, which is equally self-conscious and full of artifice, is not without its redeeming features. Titus's paronomasia rests on two notably dissimilar kinds of usage. When he refers to 'the accursed hand', he employs a simple form of synecdoche, but when he speaks of Lavinia's handlessness, he alludes to nothing but the visual reality before him. Furthermore, the paronomasia draws our attention to the image of the rapist using his hand in the act of shearing off Lavinia's own, effectively underlining, Hamlet-like, the 'unkindness' and unnaturalness of the act. So while we may argue that Titus's self-conscious word-play largely replaces genuine personal response, we must acknowledge that the bitter contrast between the mere metaphor and the experienced reality of Lavinia's handlessness is powerfully conceived.

This remark of Titus's illustrates one of the play's basic concerns—exploring the gulf between metaphoric descriptions of events and the irrefutable realities they purport to communicate. Shakespeare's interest in these matters, so abstract in its way, appears grounded, however, in the dramatist's involvement in the relative merits of words as contrasted with dramatic events. So concerned is the play with the deceptive powers of poetic description that it offers several instructive lessons contrasting the vacuous rhetoric of rape and the palpable reality of Lavinia's ravishment, hands lopped off, mouth bleeding. As the play opens, Saturninus, who has just announced his betrothal to Lavinia, finds that Bassianus has already married her and berates him in an exaggerated rhetorical outburst, saying, 'Thou and thy faction shall regret this rape' (1.1.404). Bassianus, sensitive to the proper signification of words, rejoins hotly,

> Rape call you it, my lord, to seize my own,
> My true-betrothed love . . . ?
>
> (1.1.405–6)

In this way the play continually investigates the chasm between the spoken word and the actual fact, an investigation, incidentally, whose meaning is fully experienced only when Lavinia appears before us raped and bleeding in fact. Similarly, this ironic denigration of metaphor occurs again when Lucius, hearing the villainous Aaron explain how,

> They cut thy sister's tongue and ravish'd her,
> And cut her hands and trimm'd her as thou sawest.
>
> (5.1.93)

seizes on the disgustingly prettified figure and retorts, 'O detestable villain! call'st thou that trimming?' (5.1.93). Far from being used inadvertently then, the language self-consciously focuses upon itself so as to demonstrate the manner in which figurative speech can diminish and even transform the actual horror of events. But since the purpose of the tragedy is not to dilute but to highlight the nightmare that befalls the Andronici, the play deliberately 'exposes' the euphemisms of metaphor by measuring their falseness against the irrefutable realities of dramatized events. On these occasions, the play turns its back on metaphor, rejecting it as a device that tends to dissipate the unremitting terrors of the tragedy. Only in the literalization of its metaphors, it appears, does the tragedy seem to be at ease with itself.

II

Such a self-consciously didactic use of metaphor is really quite distinctive in Elizabethan drama, to say nothing of Elizabethan tragedy, but far more strange is the deliberate constriction of the figurative language as it binds itself to the gory plot. So firmly does the figurative language yoke itself to the action of *Titus* that mere rhetorical flourishes tend, prophetically, to realize themselves in actual events. In the scene where Titus first bears witness to his daughter's mutilation, for example, he expresses his grief, not unexpectedly, in hyperbolic outburst,

> My grief was at the height before thou cam'st,
> . . . .
> Give me a sword, I'll chop off my hands too,
> For they have fought for Rome, and all in vain
> (3.1.70–3)

To be sure, the unusual nature of the event goes far to justify the strained pitch of the rhetoric, but the speech fully realizes its tragic possibilities only in subsequent events. For while Titus begins by speaking an exaggerated language of sorrow, Shakespeare forces his hero to live up to the terrible potential of his hyperbolic outburst. Shylock-like, the dramatist takes Titus's speech out of the realm of mere rant and exacts of him the pound of flesh he promises. That is to say, the exaggeration of Titus's rhetorical figure is, through an act of the dramatist's imagination, realized in terms of a hyperbole of plot, which acts as if it were a figure of speech brought to monstrous birth. Thus, in a vain effort to save his two imprisoned sons, Titus renders up his hand to the ravenous Emperor of Rome. The words he speaks at the time explain precisely the bizarre relationship between language and events that typifies the method of the play. 'Come hither, Aaron . . .' he says, 'Lend me thy hand, and I will give thee mine' (3.1.186–7).

Since *The Tragedy of Titus Andronicus* is predicated on the notion that the most excruciating horrors pertain to the experienced reality of events, the metaphoric impact of the tragedy can only be realized by forcing the metaphors to take on dramatic life. Accordingly, hands become powerful dramatic symbols, not simply because they are mentioned sixty times in the text, but because they become *images in action* whose significance we experience visually and not merely verbally, in abstraction. Stated metaphorically, the most profound impulse in *Titus* is to make the word become flesh. That the literary symbolism of hands indeed becomes flesh is obvious, not only in Titus's hand-lopping scene, but also in the scene in which Titus's son Quintus offers to assist his brother Martius after the latter has fallen into a pit that the cunning Aaron has prepared. Trapped inside, Martius implores Quintus's aid, crying, 'O brother, help me with thy fainting hand' (2.3.233), and Quintus in turn replies, 'Reach me thy hand, that I may help thee out' (2.3.237). After his first effort fails, Quintus again underscores the dramatic significance of hands, saying,

> Thy hand once more; I will not loose again,
> Till thou art here aloft, or I below.
> Thou canst not come to me—I come to thee.
> [*Falls in.*]
>
> (2.3.243–5)

Here the hands of Titus's kin, vainly stretched to help one another, epitomize a central tragic movement in the play. Symbols of Rome's defense, civic pride, and filial love, the hands of the Andronici are, in the aftermath of the Gothic war, rendered useless, not metaphorically, but literally.

Moreover, even while Quintus's allusion to hands attunes us to future events, his specific remark about 'loos[ing]' hands becomes, by virtue of the hand mutilations that are to follow, a visual, theatrical device for dramatizing the helplessness of the Andronici. Like Titus's witticism on Aaron's lending him a hand and like his imaginative question to Lavinia, 'What hand hath made thee handless . . . ,' Quintus's remark reveals again Shakespeare's unstinting exploration of the gap between a metaphoric use of language and a referential use of language anchored in the afflictions of actual events. Indeed, considering the contrast that exists between Quintus's fear of 'losing' his brother's outstretched hand and the actual lopping off of Lavinia's hands, which immediately follows this first event, we must admit that Shakespeare confers upon the ghoulish notion of losing hands, not one, but several literal meanings!

III

This unrelieved and, in truth, witty exploration of the relationship between language and event marks a notably disinterested, even detached, involvement in the values of language with respect to dramatic events. This cool distance between the playwright and his materials helps to explain one of the distinguishing features of *Titus Andronicus*—the odd way that this tragedy leaps with an inextinguishable wittiness toward the multiple perceptions that ordinarily belong to the world of intellectual comedy. From incidents like the one in which Titus asks his mute daughter to speak or like the one in which he wonders whether the Andronici should

bite our tongues, and in dumb shows
Pass the remainder of our hateful days
(3.1.131–2)

it becomes obvious that these gruesomely ironic perceptions are rooted in an irrepressible wittiness. This witty impulse expresses itself further in a hideously satanic atmosphere that permeates the unbelievable events of the tragedy, and the personification of this atmosphere is Aaron, whose satanic drollery is not unworthy of his spiritual brother, Richard Crookback. When the fiendish black-amoor instructs Tamora's oafish sons to ravish Lavinia in the woods, he employs an evocatively poetic language that lasciviously focuses upon the image of physical violation:

The woods are ruthless, dreadful, deaf, and dull.
There speak, and strike, brave boys, and take
    your turns;
There serve your lust, shadowed from heaven's
    eye,
And revel in Lavinia's treasury.
(2.1.128–31)

The source of Aaron's wittiness, we find, emerges from the deliberate exposure of the literal meanings that underlie our figurative use of language. The poetic decorum of the clause, 'And revel in Lavinia's treasury' is savage in that it simultaneously creates, in prurient delight, a literally-imagined picture of Lavinia's ravished chastity at the moment of violation. Enveloped as it is in a dark language of hushed expectancy, the picture creates an ugly beauty. Like Iago and Richard III, Aaron relishes poetic language because he can force it to serve the baser appetites, which is to say that Aaron appropriates the beauties of language for foul purposes, rapes it as it were, so that it may serve the literalness of his own coarse imaginings.

This deliberate transformation of the beauties of lyrical poetry into a house of horrible imaginings is, however, not just Aaron's, but Shakespeare's, for in *Titus Andronicus* brutality, which is always conceived with the utmost literalness of imagination, continually parades in the parodic disguise of metaphoric loveliness. In the scene where Titus rouses the court and bids them to join him in the sport of hunting a proud panther, Demetrius declines the invitation, saying to his brother,

Chiron, we hunt not, we, with horse nor hound,
But hope to pluck a dainty doe to ground
(2.2.25–6)

Expecting to use his time to rape Lavinia in the forest, Demetrius riddles shallowly on the instrument with which he and his brother will 'hunt' Lavinia. But the couplet is more than indecent; it is brutal and obscene. The venereal suggestiveness of the hunt itself, combined with the image of the 'pluck[ed]' doe being brought to the ground, focuses with salacious relish on the anticipated act of violation. Here again, the poetry, which seems at first to offer only a metaphoric suggestion of Lavinia's rape, is in reality shackled—through the salacious wit—to the literal ugliness of the rape itself.

Whatever we may think about the success of this use of figurative language, there is no escaping the fact that *Titus Andronicus* is, in the broadest sense of the term, a very witty play. It is, in fact, as witty in the circumstances of its plotting as it is in its exploitation of metaphor and in its evocation of atmosphere. The two outstanding cases in point occur in the hand-lopping scene in the third act and in the special technique Lavinia uses to reveal her assailants in act IV. The former instance comes about when Aaron convinces Titus to cut off his right hand as ransom for his two sons imprisoned by the Emperor. Throughout the scene Aaron displays an odd kind of detached artistry, a lunatic humor. After Aaron chops off Titus's hand, he commends the old warrior, saying,

> for thy hand
> Look by and by to have thy sons with thee
> [*Aside.*] Their heads, I mean.
> (3.1.201–3)

A crude joke indeed. In a play filled with the devices of metonymy and synecdoche, especially on the subject of the human body, Aaron employs the same device with respect to the action. Metaphorically speaking, Aaron does engineer the return of Titus's sons in that he returns the part for the whole. Like a literary artist Aaron has created an act of synecdoche. For the two sons he has returned a metaphor!

This irrepressible wit of plotting is, however, only partly explicable as an expression of Aaron's personality, which in some important measure derives from the ingenious vice figures of the medieval moralities. The wit of plot is, finally, much larger than Aaron's; it is Shakespeare's, and it is worth noting that the scene most universally scored for its ludicrous flight of lyric poetry, the one in 2, 4, where Marcus first spies the ravished Lavinia wandering in the woods, keeps pointing to its own achievements in rendering Ovid's pathetic tale of Tereus's rape of Philomel even more pathetic:

> *Marcus.* Fair Philomel, why, she but lost her tongue,
>   And in a tedious sampler sew'd her mind;
>   But, lovely niece, that mean is cut from thee.
>   A craftier Tereus, cousin, hast thou met,
>   And he hath cut those pretty fingers off
>   That could have better sew'd than Philomel.
>   (2.4.38–43)

The explicit allusions to Ovid's tale invite comparison. That 'craftier Tereus' Marcus speaks of is really Will Shakespeare laying claim to having out-witted the Roman poet in the telling of a tale. In *Titus* the young playwright even invites the audience to ponder how Lavinia, his heroine, unable to 'sew her mind' as Ovid's Philomel did, will be able to reveal her ravisher's identity. Lavinia's rapists, unschooled as they are, make quite a bit of the problem they have raised:

> Chiron. [to Lavinia].   Write down thy mind, bewray thy meaning so,
>   And if thy stumps will let thee play the scribe.
> Demetrius.   See how with signs and tokens she can scrowl.
>
>   (2.4.3–5)

But if the shearing off of Lavinia's hands raises a kind of suspense because we are uncertain how she will be able to expose her assailants, the solution to this puzzle is that much more unexpected and original than Ovid's. In having Lavinia scrawl out the names of her ravishers by holding a pole between her stumps and grasping the pole's end inside her mouth, Shakespeare effects a most witty poetic justice. Lavinia's lips do speak; her handless hands, indeed, do write.[4]

IV

In this witty competition with Ovid and Seneca, Shakespeare is just what Greene said he was, 'an upstart Crow' striving to overreach his masters in their own vein.[5] In *Titus* the especial competition with Ovid fully insinuates itself into Shakespeare's poetic statement and is one of the basic reasons why the tragedy sometimes runs aground on the shoals of Ovidian lyricism. As Eugene Waith points out, the play apparently fails to transpose a narrative tale of horror into a convincing dramatic story.[6] The characters, he observes, respond to events with poetic declamations that lack psychological appropriateness or verisimilitude. Yet, the problem is not one of dramatic ineptitude, pure and simple. The scenes derived from Ovid's story are confidently aware of their transposed existence in the added dimension of drama.[7] When Titus first beholds his ravished daughter, he laments,

[4]Although Shakespeare courts comparison with Ovid, he makes no effort to disclose his own native sources. The story of Lavinia's scribbling the names of her assailants by the use of her two stumps occurs in a prose narrative, which in all probability Shakespeare knew. The convincing evidence is set forth by Ralph M. Sargent, 'The Source of *Titus Andronicus*', *Studies in Philology*, XLVI (1949), 167–84. The prose narrative itself is reprinted by Sylvan Barnet (ed.), *The Tragedy of Titus Andronicus* (New York, 1963), pp. 135–48. See also, Geoffrey Bullough (ed.), *Narrative and Dramatic Sources of Shakespeare* (New York, 1966), VI, 7–13. The witty justice that emerges from Lavinia's using her stumps *and her mouth* to reveal her rapists is, however, Shakespeare's own invention.
[5]G. B. Harrison (ed.), *Robert Greene, M.A.: Groats-Worth of Witte* (1592; New York, 1966), p. 45. Although the context in which the phrase appears shows that Greene was thinking of Shakespeare as actor as well as playwright, the colorful phrase aptly captures the ambitiousness that is evident in the writing of *Titus Andronicus*.
[6]'Metamorphosis of Violence', pp. 47–8.
[7]Hamilton, *The Early Shakespeare*, pp. 68–9.

> Had I but seen thy picture in this plight
> It would have madded me; what shall I do
> Now I behold thy lively body so?
> (3.1.103–5)

So too, when Marcus first spies the mutilated Lavinia wandering in the woods, his monologue effectively underlines the dramatic mode of Shakespeare's story:

> *Marcus.*   Cousin, a word; . . .
>
> . . . .
> Speak, gentle niece . . .
> . . . Why dost not speak to me?
>
> . . . .
> Shall I speak for thee? Shall I say 'tis so?
> (2.4.12–33)

That the anticipated dialogue is denied Marcus only emphasizes how effectively Shakespeare has exploited the visual resources of drama. Moreover, inasmuch as dialogue is necessarily impossible in this episode, Shakespeare casts the greater focus upon the visual spectacle of the mutilated Lavinia. Through Marcus who acts as commentator on the event, Shakespeare forces us to see, detail by descriptive detail, the spectacle that we are already beholding:

> Speak, gentle niece, what stern ungentle hands
> Hath lopp'd and hew'd and made thy body bare
> Of her two branches . . . ?
>
> . . . .
> Alas, a crimson river of warm blood,
> Like to a bubbling fountain stirr'd with wind,
> Doth rise and fall between thy rosed lips,
> Coming and going with thy honey breath.
> But, sure, some Tereus hath deflow'red thee,
> And, lest thou should'st detect him, cut thy tongue.
> Ah, now thou turn'st away thy face for shame!
> And, notwithstanding all this loss of blood . . .
> (2.4.16–29)

Clearly enough, the visual image is intended to be so powerfully immediate that the characters themselves believe the image of Lavinia must be imaginary. Among Marcus's first words in the above speech are, 'If I do dream, would all my wealth would wake me' (2.4.13). Later, Titus complains, 'When will this fearful slumber have an end?' (3.1.252). The fact that the characters often react to the play's events as if they had been transported into another realm altogether demonstrates Shakespeare's endeavor to reach the utmost verge of realizable horror. By utilizing Ovid's already affecting narrative in a theatrical context that exploits Lavinia's presence upon the stage, Shakespeare reaches to outdo the Roman poet for pathos, and Seneca as well for horror.

But despite the resourcefulness of this theater of horrors, there are unavoidable limits in *Titus Andronicus* to dramatic spectacle. For all the severed heads, for all the poignance of Lavinia's mutilated beauty, the one horror the dramatist could not depict upon the stage was the fact of Lavinia's violated chastity, which loss was to Titus the worst violation of all,

> that more dear
> Than hands or tongue, her spotless chastity
> (5.2.176–7)

In overcoming this necessary limitation, however, Shakespeare chooses to identify Lavinia's violation with the violation of Rome and of all civilized value. It is upon this enlarged conception of violation—Lavinia's and Rome's—that Shakespeare does confer visual life by introducing the enduring and theatrical symbol of the middle acts, the pit. As Tamora's premonitory speech indicates—

> And when they show'd me this abhorred pit,
> They told me, here, at dead time of the night,
> A thousand fiends, a thousand hissing snakes,
> Ten thousand swelling toads, as many urchins,
> Would make such fearful and confused cries,
> As any mortal body hearing it
> Should straight fall mad, or else die suddenly
> (2.3.98–104)

—the pit symbolizes an inferno of evil and is directly associated, as Professor Hamilton has shown, with the classical underworld.[8] The demonic portentousness of the pit is further highlighted by Lavinia's own ironic protestations, made before her captors. Fearing rape, she begs of Tamora,

> one thing more
> That womanhood denies my tongue to tell:
> O, keep me from their worse than killing lust,
> And tumble me into some loathsome pit.
> (2.3.173–6)

Speaking a language of chaste circumlocution, Lavinia asks to die rather than to be sexually defiled, but her inadvertent pun upon the word 'tumble', meaning, as Eric Partridge records, 'To copulate with (girl or woman), to cause to *fall backward*,'[9] ironically prophesies the circumstances of her later violation. Just ten lines later Lavinia is dragged off the stage to her rape, and the pit, just alluded to, becomes the central image upon the stage.

In the passage immediately following, Bassianus's bloody corpse is heaved into the pit and Lavinia's brothers, Martius and Quintus, deceived by the cunning

---

[8]*Ibid.*, pp. 69–72.
[9]*Shakespeare's Bawdy* (1947; rpt., London, 1961), p. 210.

Aaron, become entrapped within it. Already depicted vividly by Tamora as an abyss in which a world of evil spawns, the pit is now described as a womb, malignant and devouring.[10] Pictured by Quintus and Martius as 'this unhallow'd and blood-stained hole' (2.3.210), then as a

> fell, devouring receptacle,
> As hateful as Cocytus' misty mouth
>   (2.3.235–6)

and, finally, as

> the swallowing womb
> Of this deep pit
>   (2.3.239–40)

the pit reveals the dark recesses of evil and also carries at least a suggestive reminder of the rape of Lavinia that is simultaneously transpiring off-stage. Moreover, with Bassianus's blood upon it, his body within, and the two entrapped Andronici accused of his murder trapped inside, the pit—that is, the trap door at the front of the Elizabethan stage—becomes not only a symbol of the demonic power, but a theatrical embodiment of it. Grotesque then as the image appears, the pit creates, by virtue of its visibility and concreteness as a device of theater, a powerful and synthesizing poetic image of the horrible fecundity of evil.

This éclat in exploiting the resources of the stage is just what we should expect from a wit-enchanted and ambitious poet who has lately discovered the wider world of theater. Just as the young Shakespeare endeavors to out-plot Plautus in *The Comedy of Errors* by doubling the number of identical twins, and just as he tries to out-marvel Marlowe by creating in *Richard III* a villain more joyous in the performance of evil than Barabas, so in *Titus Andronicus* Shakespeare seeks to outdo both Seneca and Ovid by utilizing his living stage in the telling of a tale more horrifying and pathetic than that of either of his models.[11] Small wonder that the characters in this earliest of Shakespeare's tragedies appear to participate actively in the dramatist's own ambitious search for ever more fabulous events:

---

[10]This association is characteristically Shakespearian. Most strikingly, it appears again in *King Lear* (Kenneth Muir (ed.), London, 1959), where Lear imagines the female sexual organs as the pit of hell:

> Down from the waist they are Centaurs,
> Though women all above:
> But to the girdle do the Gods inherit,
> Beneath is all the fiend's: there's hell,
>   there's darkness,
> There is the sulphurous pit—burning, scalding,
> Stench, consumption; fie, fie, fie! pah, pah!
>   (4.6.123–8)

[11]For a close analysis of the influence of these models, see Bullough (ed.), *Narrative and Dramatic Sources*, VI, 23–33.

> *Titus.*   shall we cut away our hands like thine?
> Or shall we bite our tongues, and in dumb shows
> Pass the remainder of our hateful days?
> What shall we do? let us that have our tongues
> Plot some device of further misery,
> To make us wonder'd at in time to come.
>
>   (3.1.130–5)

Whatever our final aesthetic judgment concerning the merits of *Titus Andronicus,* we must understand that we are dealing, not with a paucity of imagination, but with an excess of dramatic witness, with a talent untamed. However flawed the tragedy may be in other respects, we must grant that the playwright has exploited the language of the stage with inventive brilliance and has taxed the resources of drama in making death and mutilation vivid to us.

If we wish, we can, of course, treat this tragedy with orthodox sobriety in order to demonstrate its thematic integrity, but the real vitality and interest of *Titus Andronicus* lies, it seems to me, in just those parts that are in some ways speculative, or even impossible dramatically. By shackling the metaphoric imagination to the literal reality of the play's events, the tragedy strives for an unrelieved concentration of horrific effect. Through its prophetic allusions to physical dismemberment, its incurably literalized figures of speech, and its ambitious use of the stage as a dramatic metaphor, *Titus Andronicus* strives to exhaust the language as well as the events of tragedy. We do not all have to like the tragedy, but we ought to recognize that *Titus* is a uniquely important experiment in drama, for in it Shakespeare is exploring the resources inherent in a referential use of metaphor and is trying to integrate the power of the poetic language with the immeasurable potential of dramatic action itself.

The Device of Wonder:
Titus Andronicus and Revenge Tragedies

Lawrence N. Danson

The proliferation of generic categories for Elizabethan drama is a problem as ancient as Polonius' naming of the parts: "tragedy, comedy, history, pastoral, pastoral-comical, tragical-historical, tragical-comical-historical-pastoral, scene individable, or poem unlimited." One firmly entrenched category is that of the tragedy of revenge, which (according to Fredson Bowers) "has been classified as a definite, small subdivision of the Elizabethan tragedy of blood"; plays belonging to that category "treat, according to a moderately rigid dramatic formula, blood-revenge for murder as the central tragic fact."[1] But the rigidity of the formula is, in fact, questionable. Indeed a striking characteristic of the most notable of the so-called revenge tragedies is that "the central tragic fact," the act of revenge itself, when it finally comes, seems something of an after-thought, is, at any rate, quite muddied in its motivations. Hamlet, for instance, never really does discover his means of revenge, or consciously overcome whatever scruples or fastidiousness has kept him so long from it; rather, he stumbles into it when the Claudius-Laertes plot misfires. Kyd includes in Hieronimo's revenge at least one character (the Duke of Castile) who seems extraneous to his revenger's concerns; while Titus Andronicus (most bafflingly, if revenge is what the play is about) kills his daughter Lavinia. By the time of Webster, in a play like *The White Devil*, the question of who is revenging himself on whom for what is almost impenetrably unclear. So badly, indeed, do these plays fulfill the expected formula that we must begin to suspect either that the greatest dramatists were very imperfect at their craft, or that the critical category describes plays that they had little intention of writing.

Something, I suggest, other than revenge ought to be sought as the "central tragic fact" of those plays for which it is really worth speaking of a "central tragic fact." For a play like Chettle's *Hoffman*, "revenge" will do as well as anything else; but it makes, I think, imperfect sense to class *Hoffman* with *Hamlet*. For the greater so-called revenge tragedies something is wanted which will show their

From *Texas Studies in Literature and Language*, Vol. 16:1 (Spring 1974), pp. 27–43. Copyright © 1974 by the University of Texas Press. Reprinted by permission of the author and the University of Texas Press.

[1]*Elizabethan Revenge Tragedy 1587–1642* (Princeton: Princeton Univ. Press, 1940), p. 62.

affinities with other great tragedies of the period rather than isolating them in a separate, mechanically derived category. But that is an enormous task, and what I intend to do here is something much more modest: to look for that tragic fact (by which I mean something of the deepest concern to the protagonist as well as, esthetically, to his creator) in a single early play, Titus Andronicus; and only incidentally (by way of excursions, when they are warranted, into other plays, especially The Spanish Tragedy) to push that fact towards greater generality.

And we can begin by remembering that, however despised Titus Andronicus may have become, it was throughout Shakespeare's career a very successful play. Ben Jonson, with his own career to protect in 1614, had reason to be contemptuous of old workhorses like Titus and The Spanish Tragedy: "Hee that will sweare, Ieronimo, or Andronicus are the best playes, yet, shall passe unexcepted at, heere, as a man whose Iudgement shewes it is constant, and hath stood still, these five and twentie, or thirtie, yeeres."[2] But if we today share Jonson's superior smile we should do so uneasily, for we have learned not to be complacent about that audience whose taste for blood and bombast made possible, not only Hieronimo and Titus, but Hamlet and Lear as well. The popularity of the old plays well into the Jacobean period is a fact of significance for the history of drama: by Jonson's time, the parts of Titus and Hieronimo had become closely associated with the player's amazing power to force a responsive passion in his listeners.

This simple historical consideration leads immediately to something approaching a paradox. For while Titus Adronicus is a play that could elicit an audience's sympathetic response, it presents to us the image of a world in which a man's words go unheeded and his gestures unacknowledged, a world unresponsive to his cries, demands, prayers. The world of tragedy is (to borrow a phrase from Northrop Frye) "the world that desire totally rejects: the world of the nightmare";[3] and in Titus the nightmare is that widely familiar one of the unutterable scream, the unattainable release from horror through outcry or gesture. Now there is a relationship to be observed between these two facts, that (on the one hand) the play found a responsiveness in its audience and that (on the other) the material with which the play deals is the characters' inability, within the world of the play, to find an adequate hearing. It is a relationship which, because it bears upon a basic aspect of tragic theory—that things painful to behold in life can yet give us pleasure when transmuted into art—may point the way towards our "central tragic fact." But to find that relationship we must turn to the play and trace its pattern of withered gestures and virtual silence.

The first instance I cite is one which, like much in the play, teeters on the brink of the ludicrous—for Titus (like King Lear) is a play that deals so insistently with man in extremis that the comic grotesque is always available to relieve us from the burden of its inordinate vision. At the beginning of Act 4, young Lucius enters

[2]Induction to Bartholomew Fair, in C. H. Herford and Percy and Evelyn Simpson, Ben Jonson (Oxford: Clarendon Press, 1925–52), VI, 16.
[3]Anatomy of Criticism (Princeton: Princeton Univ. Press, 1957), p. 147.

fleeing from his aunt Lavina; deprived of her tongue and hands, Lavinia, by her incomprehensible gestures, can only terrify the child as she tries to calm him. Now Titus and Marcus enter and interpose for Lavinia:

> *Tit.* Fear her not, Lucius: somewhat doth she mean.
> *Marc.* See, Lucius, see how much she makes of thee;
> Somewhither would she have thee go with her.
> Ah, boy, Cornelia never with more care
> Read to her sons than she hath read to thee
> Sweet poetry and Tully's Orator.[4]

Lucius is carrying his copy of Ovid; in it Lavinia directs their attention to "the tragic tale of Philomel," and then painfully writes in the sand the names of her ravishers.

Now amidst all this pathos, the egregious touch is the reference to "Sweet poetry and Tully's Orator." For Tully's Orator is, in all probability, *Ad M. Brutum Orator,* the epistle in which Cicero depicts his ideal orator. And the reference underscores how nearly Lavinia has been reduced to the barely human, the almost-monstrous: her grotesque inability to communicate sets her at the opposite pole from Cicero's orator, the man who is able to bring to bear all the distinctively human characteristics in the accomplishing of his high art. The reference might almost seem a cruel joke—but it is not meant to be one, for to the Elizabethans this matter of speaking well, of oratory, was a matter of the highest seriousness: "*Oratio* next to *Ratio,* Speech next to Reason, [is] the greatest gyft bestowed vpon mortalitie."[5] The idea ran deep: in the earliest English-language textbook of logic, Thomas Wilson's *Rule of Reason* (1551), the example given of "an undoubted true proposition" is "*Homo est animal ratione praeditum, loquendi facultatem habens.* A man is a liuing creature endewed with reason, having aptnesse by nature to speake."[6] We shall have to return to the question of oratory and rhetoric later; here it is only necessary to realize what it means to be deprived of the humanizing gift of speech, and to follow out the image that Lavinia presents and that comes to dominate the play: the image of man tongueless, limbless, sunk in a world inimical to his fundamental need to be understood, but still trying by every means to speak—to make known his pain and (by the act of making it known) his very humanity to the gods and his fellow men.

It would be tedious to record all the instances of beseeching and petitioning in *Titus*; there are too many of them. It is, however, worth noting that the first disap-

[4]J. C. Maxwell, ed., The Arden Edition (London: Methuen, and Cambridge, Mass.: Harvard Univ. Press, 1961). All other references to *Titus Andronicus* are to this edition.

[5]Sir Philip Sidney, "An Apologie for Poetry," in Gregory Smith, *Elizabethan Critical Essays* (Oxford: Oxford Univ. Press, 1904), I, 182. Sidney's commonplace must be allowed to stand here for the wealth of texts which might be cited. Among modern scholars who have studied the relationship between the rhetorical tradition and Elizabethan drama, my greatest debt is to Madeleine Doran, *Endeavors of Art* (Madison: Univ. of Wisconsin Press, 1954).

[6]Quoted by W. S. Howell, *Logic and Rhetoric in England 1500–1700* (Princeton: Princeton Univ. Press, 1956), p. 18.

pointed petitioner is the (temporarily) conquered Queen of Goths, Tamora, and that it is Titus to whom she prays for her son's life:

> Stay, Roman brethren! Gracious conqueror,
> Victorious Titus, rue the tears I shed,
> A mother's tears in passion for her son:
> And if thy sons were ever dear to thee,
> O, think my son to be as dear to me.
>
> . . . .
> Thrice-noble Titus, spare my first-born son.
>   (1.1.104–08, 120)

But what Tamora calls a "cruel, irreligious piety" demands the sacrifice of her son; and the only response to her entreaty is the announcement (in what may be Shakespeare's worst half-line), "Alarbus' limbs are lopp'd" (1.143). Within the same act, Titus' sons and brother kneel and beseech him to allow Mutius burial (which, grudgingly, he does); and Titus, his sons, his brother, and Tamora plead for favor from Saturninus.

One may be tempted to say that all the succeeding instances of Titus' own inability to gain an adequate response to his entreaties arise from that first instance of his deafness to Tamora—as (to take a comparable instance) one might be tempted to say that Lear's sufferings all result from his willful deafness to Cordelia's expressive silence. But that would be too narrow a view of either play. Like Lear's, Titus' punishment so far exceeds the crime that the prevailing deafness to the human voice in its cries for mercy or justice is made to seem endemic to the play's world, beyond any one man's causing. In Act 2, Lavinia's mutilation takes place against the ironically gay noise of dogs and horns (2.2.1–6); but for Aaron the Moor, "The woods are ruthless, dreadful, deaf, and dull" (2.1.128), and there Chiron and Demetrius are to "strike her home by force, if not by words" (l. 118). As Tamora had pleaded, now Lavinia pleads:

> *Lav.* O Tamora, thou bearest a woman's face—
> *Tam.* I will not hear her speak; away with her!
>   (2.3.136–37)

And even as Chiron and Demetrius (offstage) slake their lust (and incidentally Tamora's revenge) on Lavinia, it becomes Titus' turn to plead. Aaron has arranged matters so that Titus' sons seem guilty of Bassianus' murder; and, like Lavinia's plea, Titus' plea on their behalf is cut off in mid-cry:

> *Tit.* High emperor, upon my feeble knee
>   I beg this boon, with tears not lightly shed,
>   That this fell fault of my accursed sons,
>   Accursed, if the fault be prov'd in them,—
> *Sat.* If it be prov'd! you see it is apparent.
>   (2.3.288–92)

The need to find a satisfactory response to these interrupted pleas becomes (as the incidents of frustration mount) an overwhelming concern. Lavinia, *"her hands cut off, and her tongue cut out, and ravish'd,"* is, as we have seen, the monument that most forcefully figures this need. But we must notice, too, the response of the other Andronici to Lavinia. Marcus, for instance, is the first to encounter his mutilated niece, and he gives us one of the clearest statements of the motif:

> Shall I speak for thee? shall I say 'tis so?
> O, that I knew thy heart, and knew the beast,
> That I might rail at him to ease my mind.
> Sorrow concealed, like an oven stopp'd,
> Doth burn the heart to cinders where it is.
> (2.4.33–37)

Lavinia's case, Marcus says (in one of the numerous echoes of the Ovidian tale), is worse than Philomela's:

> Fair Philomel, why, she but lost her tongue,
> And in a tedious sampler sew'd her mind:
> But, lovely niece, that mean is cut from thee;
> A craftier Tereus, cousin, hast thou met. . . .
> (2.4.38–41)

The means of expression lost to Lavinia, the burden of expression now falls on others: "Do not draw back, for we will mourn with thee: / O, could our mourning ease thy misery!" (2.4.56–57).

And on Titus himself the burden of expression falls most heavily. At the opening of Act 3, we find Titus pleading with the judges and senators for his sons' lives. When his words fail, he falls upon the ground to write in dust "My heart's deep languor and my soul's sad tears" (3.1.13). Although the tribunes will not heed Titus, "yet plead I must," and

> Therefore I tell my sorrows to the stones,
> Who, though they cannot answer my distress,
> Yet in some sort they are better than the tribunes,
> For that they will not intercept my tale.
> (3.1.37–40)

Now Lavinia is brought before Titus. The imperious need for relief through expression, which has already led to his writing in dust and pleading with stones, leads now to the contemplation of a further series of fantastic actions:

> Shall thy good uncle, and thy brother Lucius,
> And thou, and I, sit round about some fountain,
> Looking all downwards to behold our cheeks
> How they are stain'd, like meadows not yet dry,
> With miry slime left on them by a flood?
> And in the fountain shall we gaze so long
> Till the fresh taste be taken from that clearness,
> And made a brine-pit with our bitter tears?

Or shall we cut away our hands like thine?
Or shall we bite our tongues, and in dumb shows
Pass the remainder of our hateful days?
What shall we do? let us that have our tongues
Plot some device of further misery,
To make us wonder'd at in time to come.

(3.1.122–35)

"Plot some device of further misery, / To make us wonder'd at in time to come": Titus' final lines are worth some attention, for in them is found the motivation for the grotesque actions that are to follow, as well as an important clue towards that "central tragic fact" we are seeking. To "plot some device" can mean simply "to plan, contrive, or devise" (*OED*, "Plot," v^1.3) "an arrangement, plan, scheme, project, contrivance; an ingenious or clever expedient; often one of an underhand or evil character: a plot, stratagem, trick" (*OED*, "Device," 6). But both "plot" and "device" have other connotations, of a specifically artistic and dramatic nature, which indicate that Titus' lines have significance for the playwright's as well as the revenger's craft. The word "plot" is, of course, especially common in this double sense throughout the drama of the period, and requires no special comment here. "Device," as Titus uses it, carries a related double sense which, although less common than "plot," can yield even richer insights into the relationship between the esthetic requirements of the playwright and the existential concerns of his characters. According to the *OED* (whose definitions I quote at length because they form a progression, of immediate relevance to us, from a type of nonverbal expression to purely verbal expression to verbal and gestural combined), "device" can mean: "8. Something artistically devised or framed; a fancifully conceived design or figure. 9. *spec.* An emblematic figure or design, *esp.* one borne or adopted by a particular person, family, etc., as a heraldic bearing, a cognizance, etc.: usually accompanied by a motto. 10. A fanciful, ingenious, or witty writing or expression, a 'conceit.' 11. Something devised or fancifully invented for dramatic representation; 'a mask played by private persons,' or the like." In *Titus Andronicus,* as well as *The Spanish Tragedy, Tamburlaine*—indeed in most of the tragic drama from the late eighties and the nineties—we find these various forms of expression (the related senses of "device") in more or less uneasy mixture. Marlowe's "mighty line" is no more striking, for instance, than his use of essentially nonverbal tableaux (Tamburlaine's shifting colors, from white to red to black, is an example), which are the stage equivalent of heraldic bearings. Hieronimo's "play . . . in sundry languages," with which *The Spanish Tragedy* culminates, is a "device" in the final sense cited from the *OED*. But before reaching it there have been other, less variously expressive, sorts of "devices." Hieronimo has staged an entertainment made up of a series of heraldic bearings, which he interprets for the benefit of his stage audience (1.4). And throughout the play Kyd more subtly introduces "devices" that figure forth the play's central concerns. What is for our purposes most interesting to observe is how many of Kyd's "devices" comprise more or less static conceits for the difficulty Hieronimo and others find in achieving justice through the use of words—as if the variety of dramatic techniques were mirroring the characters' own wrestling with the problems of expression; to cite only a few examples: an old man who has lost his son pleads for redress to a Knight Marshall who has lost *his* son; Pedringano goes blithely to his death while a messenger points to an empty box that is supposed to contain a written pardon; Bel-imperia, who knows the truth of Horatio's murder, drops a message written in blood to Hieronimo—who suspects a trick (or "device," in the related sense) and fails to heed its contents.

   Titus Andronicus similarly contains a series of devices that adumbrate the imperious need for relief through expression. The mutilated Lavinia is, as we have seen, the central such device, a conceit for the nearness of man to monster when deprived of the humanizing gift of expression, and (more narrowly) an emblematic figure for the plight of the voiceless Andronici in a now-alien Rome. The responses Titus proposes—weeping all day into a fountain, passing their days in dumb-shows—are related devices, here with the added implication of dramatic spectacle. A bare recital of the actions that do follow will sound ludicrous, unless we recognize them for the devices they are, intentionally conceited, emblematic—and each related to the same basic problem of expression needed but denied: Titus sacrifices a hand to save his sons' lives; thus mutilated he and Lavinia pray to heaven—and receive his sons' severed heads in reply. Lavinia writes the names of her ravishers in the sand, and Titus proposes transferring the words to brass. Titus sends weapons wrapped in a riddling message to Chiron and Demetrius. At Titus' bidding the Andronici shoot petitioning arrows at the gods; and because *Terras astraea reliquit,* Titus proposes searching for the goddess at sea or underground. Finally there is Titus' revenge itself, in all its elaboration (for here the sense of dramatic performance, "a masque played by private persons," is strong) and apparent excessiveness (involving his own and Lavinia's deaths); but of this example, where tableau, words, and gesture combine in a culminating action, we must reserve discussion until we can explore the latter part of Titus' injunction: "Let us that have our tongues / Plot some device of further misery, / *To make us wonder'd at in time to come.*"

   Here it is necessary to acknowledge an anomaly that will already have been apparent. *Titus Andronicus* is, I have said, a play about silence, and about the inability to achieve adequate expression for overwhelming emotional needs; but the thing we may notice before all else in it, before even its physical horrors, is its extreme, obtrusive rhetorical elaboration. Again the situation is similar to that in *The Spanish Tragedy*: surely there is something absurd about the loquacity of Titus and Hieronimo, endlessly talking and with endless elaboration about their inability to make their cries for justice heard. Indeed it is an absurdity that was not lost on the play's near-contemporaries, as the many parodic echoes (especially of Kyd's play) attest. Hieronimo's famous speech, "O eyes, no eyes, but fountains fraught with tears; / O life, no life but lively form of death" (3.2.1–2) is remarkable for various reasons, not least of which is its excellence as a rhetorical showpiece. In fact it is so remarkable, so insistently calling attention to its own artifice, that it inevitably provoked the backhanded compliment of parody. In Marston's *Antonio and Mellida*, for instance, Piero's hysterical commands, "Fly, call, run, row, ride, cry, shout, hurry, haste; / Haste, hurry, shout, cry, ride, row, run, call, fly" (at which point he lapses into Italian: 3.2.262), makes farce of the rhetorical ideal of *copia* (the use, to put it crudely, of the most words to say the least) which is realized in the completion of the first movement of Hieronimo's lament: "Eyes, life, world, heavens, hell, night, and day, / See, search, shew, send, some man, some mean, that may—" (3.2.22–23).[7]

But it did not really need a Marston to prick the bubble of Hieronimo's rhetoric: a glance at the situation shows that Kyd has built in his own criticism. For just as Hieronimo is so copiously and asyndectically pleading for the means of discovering his son's murderer, "*A letter falleth*"; it is Bel-imperia's, and it contains most succinctly all that Hieronimo needs to know—but, as we have seen, it goes unregarded, to become another in the play's series of thwarted communications. Hieronimo is so caught up in his own elaborate rhetoric that he can no longer effectively connect with the words of others, a dilemma that culminates in his "play . . . in sundry languages" where (to quote Jonas Barish's excellent account),

> The effect, perhaps, would have been to suggest the extremes to which language can evolve, the lengths to which verbal ingenuity can be carried and how unintelligible words can become when they lose their moorings in the reality they are meant to express. The jabbering in four languages turns the whole phenomenon of speech under a strange phosphorescent glare, revealing it as a kind of disembodied incantation, a surrealistic dance of abstractions, divorced from roots in lived existence.[8]

The confusion that Hieronimo's playlet breeds is the perfect epitome of Kyd's larger theatrical world, in which the greatest gift of man's reason, the faculty of speech, has only contributed to man's undoing.

Kyd, as Professor Barish suggests, is aware not only of "the pleasures" but also of "the perils of rhetoric"; and so, I believe, is Shakespeare. And this self-consciousness in regard to their chosen medium is most significant, for it points towards the very close but very uneasy relationship between drama and rhetoric in this period. To the Elizabethans, indeed, orator and actor were essentially the same. In one of his additions to *The Overburian Characters*, for instance, Webster asserts that "Whatsoever is commendable in the grave Orator, is most exquisitly perfect in ['An Excellent Actor']."[9] Curiously, it seems to have been as much the use of action as of language which established this identity; the Overburian sketch justifies the comparison of actor and orator by noting that "by a full and significant

[7]*The Spanish Tragedy*, ed. Philip Edwards (London: Methuen, 1959). *Antonio and Mellida The First Part*, ed. G. K. Hunter (Lincoln: Univ. of Nebraska Press, 1965).
[8]"*The Spanish Tragedy*, or The Pleasures and Perils of Rhetoric," *Stratford-upon-Avon Studies*, 9 (1966), 81.
[9]*The Overburian Characters, to Which is added A Wife*, ed. W. J. Paylor (Oxford: Blackwell, 1936), p. 76. The character of "An Excellent Actor" was added in the sixth impression, 1615; its attribution to Webster is generally accepted, and the piece is included in F. L. Lucas' edition of Webster.

action of body, he [the actor] charmes our attention." This apparent anomaly, that action should be the quality which links orator and actor, is taken up by Francis Bacon in his "Of Boldness":

> It is a trivial grammar-school text, but yet worthy a wise man's consideration. Question was asked of Demosthenes, *what was the chief part of an orator?* he answered, *action:* what next? *action:* what next again? *action.* He said it that knew it best, and had by nature no advantage in that he commended. A strange thing, that that part of an orator which is but superficial, and rather the virtue of a player, should be placed so high, above those other notable parts of invention, elocution, and the rest; nay almost alone, as if it were all in all.[10]

The commonness of the relationship is worth noticing here, but so too is Bacon's contemptuous tone. For by "action" (that "virtue of a player") Bacon means only the particular gesture of hand and body which must accompany speech; it is a merely technical skill, the suiting of the action to the word and the word to the action which Hamlet recommends to his Players; and it is a sufficiently limited notion of action to justify Bacon's contempt.

Most importantly for us, this relationship between oratory and acting, based on a rather mechanical notion of "action," indicates a real danger for the dramatist. In some of the "devices" we have noticed in *Titus* and *The Spanish Tragedy* the danger is apparent, for such passages tend to be more or less static—speaking pictures unnaturally situated within the frame of the surrounding action. If drama was in debt to "Tully's Orator" and the other textbooks of rhetoric that were at the heart of Elizabethan education, it was also possible that drama would perish beneath the burden of the loan. Much of Elizabethan drama did in fact succumb; *Gorboduc,* for instance, although Philip Sidney (since he was not a playwright) could afford to luxuriate in its "stately speeches and well sounding Phrases," is dead to us because it remained rhetoric and never found any really organic way to suit its words to its actions. Inevitably, therefore, it became the superior playwright's task to broaden the notion of "action" beyond the particular gesture until it encompassed the whole play, to find the "action"—now in a sense closer to Aristotle's (in the *Poetics)* than to Bacon's—that would convert the raw materials of drama (including language) into the form of drama. In *Titus Andronicus* we see that conversion taking place before us; here the struggle is in the open, the struggle to turn the language of words into the language of action, to convert (even by way of rhetoric) rhetoric itself into dramatic, and specifically tragic, form.

We see Shakespeare's recognition and handling of the problem in the paradoxical ineffectuality of the play's rhetoric—paradoxical, because however stirring it may be to the audience it is useless to the character in achieving, in his fictive world, the results he intends. Titus has cried out to the very heavens (having exhausted the world of men, of dust and stones) and, through elaborate imagery,

---

[10]*The Works of Francis Bacon* ("Popular Edition"), ed. Spedding, Ellis, and Heath (Boston: Houghton, Mifflin, 1857), II, 116.

sought to involve the most elemental forces of nature in his lament. His words are of no avail, yet he must speak:

If there were reason for these miseries,
Then into limits could I bind my woes:
When heaven doth weep, doth not the earth o'erflow?
If the winds rage, doth not the sea wax mad,
Threat'ning the welkin with his big-swol'n face?
And wilt thou have a reason for this coil?
I am the sea. Hark how her [Lavinia's] sighs doth blow;
She is the weeping welkin, I the earth:
Then must my sea be moved with her sighs;
Then must my earth with her continual tears
Become a deluge, overflow'd and drown'd;
For why my bowels cannot hide her woes,
But like a drunkard must I vomit them.
Then give me leave, for losers will have leave
To ease their stomachs with their bitter tongues.
Enter a Messenger with two heads and a hand.
(3.1.219–33)

Here again is recognition that "Sorrow concealed, like an oven stopp'd, / Doth burn the heart to cinders where it is." But though "action" may be the chief part of oratory, for Titus it is the vast gap between even the most rhetorically elaborate speech and effective action which is most painfully noticeable. The action that breaks off Titus' lament is one of the play's most horrifying devices for that gap. Titus' lamenting is compulsive: men in such extremes must speak out; but it is also, apparently, useless.

And it can be worse. For as the need to find relief through expression becomes more pressing, and as the rhetoric in response becomes more extreme and obtrusive, we find that from the heights of linguistic invention we are plunged into the nadir of madness and mad-speech. Thus Titus, having sought to ease his stomach with his bitter tongue and receiving his sons' heads and his own hand in response, is for a moment ominously still; Marcus prompts him: "Now is a time to storm"—but Titus' only reply is the laughter of the mad (3.1.264). There may, however, be another way of looking at this descent into madness: the plunge may be, like Gloucester's from the cliffs near Dover, no plunge at all; it may be a mere step, an inevitable progression from linguistic elaboration to the dissolution of language itself. What is it, after all, that disturbs us about the rhetorical showpieces? Is it not that in them language has become too prominent, breaking the expected bonds between words and world until we feel that the former has gained mastery over the latter? Mad-speech is similarly a language that has lost its connections with objective reality, words without referents in the shared world of the sane. The art of rhetoric, which can be the index of man's reason, can also, when it grows to a surfeit, become the token of madness.

So crucial is the matter of madness to most of the great Elizabethan tragedies, and so important for this discussion is the relationship between mad-speech and rhetoric, that a brief look at Shakespeare's greatest portrait of madness is justified here. And we may notice that, as Titus sought "some device of further misery / To make us wonder'd at in time to come," so King Lear, driven to desperation by the insouciance of Goneril and Regan, utters the strangled vow:

> No, you unnatural hags,
> I will have such revenges on you both
> That all the world shall—I will do such things,
> What they are yet I know not, but they shall be
> The terrors of the earth.
>
> (2.4.280–84)[11]

Weeping is not the language Lear needs:

> You think I'll weep;
> No, I'll not weep:
> I have full cause of weeping, but yet this heart
> Shall break into a hundred thousand flaws
> Or ere I'll weep.
>
> (2.4.284–88)

But, as he has feared from the start, only one mode is left, that last desperate means (to which Titus and Hieronimo also are brought) to fulfill the human imperative to speak: "O Fool! I shall go mad" (1.288).

When we discover Lear on the heath (3.2) he has become almost incapable of hearing any voice but his own and that of the thunder. Only fitfully is he aware of those around him; but those few moments of awareness are most significant, for breaking through the obsessive language of invective are the first tentative sounds of a new language that might serve to bind man to man:

> My wits begin to turn.
> Come on, my boy. How dost, my boy? Art cold?
> I am cold myself. Where is this straw, my fellow?
> The art of our necessities is strange,
> And can make vile things precious. Come, your hovel.
> Poor Fool and knave, I have one part in my heart
> That's sorry yet for thee.
>
> (3.2.67–73)

But this language and the communion it allows is premature. The process of dissolution is only beginning, and Lear's wits must turn utterly before they can turn again.

The hectic riddling of the fool and the cacophony of Poor Tom are stages on the way to the linguistic disintegration reached in Lear's great mad-speeches. A capa-

[11]Kenneth Muir, ed., The Arden Edition (London: Methuen, 1952).

ble editor, like Professor Muir, can provide the missing clues that will reveal what he calls the "undertone of meaning" in those speeches; but while the meaning is important, so too is the mode of speech itself, a mode defined in the New Cambridge edition as "ideas following each other with little more than verbal connection":

> No, they cannot touch me for coining; I am the king himself. . . . Nature's above art in that respect. There's your press-money. That fellow handles his bow like a crow-keeper: draw me a clothier's yard. Look, look! a mouse. Peace, peace! this piece of toasted cheese will do't. There's my gauntlet; I'll prove it on a giant. Bring up the brown bills. O! well flown, bird; i' th' clout, i' th' clout: hewgh! Give the word.
>
> (4.6.83–93)

Associations of sound more than of meaning provide the structure of Lear's discourse. The meaning of Lear's interior drama is determined by the whim of his words.

And the drama remains private: only Lear can know the infinitely complicated rules that generate his mad language. "I will preach to thee. Mark," says Lear; and his sermon begins well enough: "When we are born, we cry that we are come / To this great stage of fools" (1. 184). But immediately the discourse is shunted off onto a detour created by a secondary association of sound or meaning: "This' a good block!" And suddenly Lear's sermon gives way to "a delicate stratagem to shoe / A troop of horse with felt," and the wish to steal "upon these son-in-laws, / Then, kill, kill, kill, kill, kill, kill!" The sermon returns upon itself to the world of Lear's private obsessions, excluding any conceivable congregation of listeners.

Lear's mad-speech isolates the speaker, thus subverting one essential function of language. In *Titus Andronicus* there are also moments when a speaker's words reveal him locked in the privacy of his obsessions—and those moments are precisely those of the fullest, most magniloquent rhetorical elaboration. Such a moment we have encountered in Titus' extended comparison of himself as earth and Lavinia as "weeping welkin" (3.1.219). A more subtle and perhaps more significant example comes in 3.2; it begins with Titus' promise to the silenced Lavinia that she will still, somehow, be heard:[12]

> Speechless complainer, I will learn thy thought;
> In thy dumb action will I be as perfect
> As begging hermits in their holy prayers:
> Thou shalt not sigh, nor hold thy stumps to heaven,
> Nor wink, nor nod, nor kneel, nor make a sign,
> But I of these will wrest an alphabet,
> And by still practice learn to know thy meaning.
>
> (3.2.39–45)

It is a noble speech in its determination that human ingenuity can overcome the

[12]The authenticity of this scene has been questioned, especially on the grounds that it necessitates the re-entry of characters who have exited at the end of the immediately preceding scene. The scene may be a later addition, but I see no reason to attribute it to any hand other than Shakespeare's.

barbarity that has silenced Lavinia; and here Titus' rhetorical copiousness is ironically appropriate and moving. But almost immediately the optimism is shattered: Marcus strikes at a fly which has settled on his dish, and Titus launches into a series of fantastic speeches—speeches that seem still to have been reverberating in Shakespeare's mind when he came to write *King Lear:*

> *Tit.* Out on thee, murderer! thou kill'st my heart;
> Mine eyes are cloy'd with view of tyranny:
> A deed of death done on the innocent
> Becomes not Titus' brother. Get thee gone;
> I see thou art not for my company.
> *Marc.* Alas, my lord, I have but kill'd a fly.
> *Tit.* "But"? How if that fly had a father and mother?
> How would he hang his slender gilded wings,
> And buzz lamenting doings in the air!
> Poor harmless fly.
> That, with his pretty buzzing melody,
> Came here to make us merry, and thou hast killed him.
> (3.2.54–65)

With Marcus' explanation that "it was a black ill-favour'd fly / Like to the empress' Moor," Titus swings violently about; now killing the fly becomes "a charitable deed," and Titus demands,

> Give me thy knife, I will insult on him;
> Flattering myself as if it were the Moor
> Come hither purposely to poison me.
> There's for thyself, and that's for Tamora.
> (3.2.71–74)

Titus' prosopopoeia on the harmless fly, with his "lamenting doings" and "pretty buzzing melody," is an extraordinary thing—purposefully sentimental, beautifully realized as poetry. And considering Titus' mental state, one is even able to forgive the illogic by which a murdered fly laments his parents' bereavement. Fine: but what has become in all of this of Lavinia? And what of the effort to "wrest an alphabet" from her gestures? The possibility of communion is shattered as Titus wanders off in his acrid smoke of rhetoric. At the very moment that the need for human communication is most forcefully presented, we witness words destroying their natural function.

We arrive here at a nexus of concerns which can reveal that "central tragic fact" we are seeking. The playwright in the world of his craft and his characters in their created world are faced each with an analogous problem: how to break out of rhetoric, that high gift which has become a prison, and achieve the action which will suffice? For the playwright, as I have said, that action must be one broadly conceived, sufficient to transform the language of words into the language of drama, to create (to put it simply) a stageworthy tragedy. And how this can be achieved is indicated by Titus' desire to "Plot some device of further mis-

ery, / To make us wonder'd at in time to come." The theatrical implications of
the first part of Titus' line we have already glanced at; and we may notice that, as
the moment of Titus' revenge approaches, such *double entendre* becomes more
frequent: Tamora, creating a masquelike "device" of her own (she is disguised as
Revenge, Chiron and Demetrius as Murder and Rape), comes to where Titus
"ruminate[s] strange plots of dire revenge" (5.2.6); Titus plans to "o'erreach
them in their own devices" (5.2.143); and when he has killed Chiron and
Demetrius he announces as the next part of his plan that "I'll play the cook"
(5.2.204). Through such suggestions of a play-within-a-play, the world of reality
and the world of the stage begin to merge in a way that animates Ralegh's poetic
cliché, "Thus march we playing to our latest rest, / Only we die in earnest; that's
no jest." In *Titus Andronicus*, the earnest of death becomes inextricably bound
up with the jest of playing.

But in what way can the play's "plot of dire revenge," which includes the
deaths of Lavinia and Titus himself, satisfy the demand that it be a plot "To make
us wonder'd at in time to come"? Again we must attend to a special sense of Titus'
language. According to J. V. Cunningham, the word "wonder" (L. *admiratio*), in a
tradition descending from Aristotle, was closely associated with the particular
emotion supposed to derive from tragedy. "The effect of astonishment or wonder
is the natural correlative of unusual diction, as it is of the unusual event," he
writes; in particular, "The high style, the forceful, the grand—the style of
Demosthenes and Aeschylus—will evoke that wonder which is akin to fear, and
will be especially appropriate to tragedy."[13] But we have already seen that *Titus
Andronicus* carries with it, just as it is exploiting the language of wonder, the
recognition that even the most unusual diction and the highest style will not suffice: action, and that a very special action, must animate the otherwise imprison-
ing rhetoric. And the action that will not only fit but transform the words is death:
for the Elizabethan dramatist, death is what can provoke "wonder" in time to
come. J. V. Cunningham explains:

> The tragic fact is death. Even the most natural death has in it a radical violence, for it is
> a transition from this life to something by definition quite otherwise; and, however much
> it may be expected, it is in its moment of incidence sudden, for it comes as the thief in
> the night, you know not the day nor the hour. Hence the characteristics of suddenness
> and violence which are attached to death in tragedy may be viewed as artistic heighten-
> ings of the essential character of death: the unnaturalness of the tragic event is only
> pointed and emphasized by the unnatural precipitancy of its accomplishment.[14]

In this play, when words have done their uttermost and failed, Titus breaks
through the barriers of incommunicability with the gesture that, because it is the
gesture most provocative of wonder, is definitive of Elizabethan and Jacobean
tragedy. He takes the final step from rhetoric through madness to death.

If the assertion that death is our "central tragic fact" seems something of an

[13]*Woe or Wonder* (Denver: Univ. of Denver Press, and Toronto: Burns & MacEachern, 1951),
p. 73.
    [14]Ibid., p. 59.

anticlimax, the fault may be that we know so much more than the Elizabethans—and (as Mr. Eliot said), "they are that which we know." But why, if the simple (but also infinitely complex) fact of death is all that we arrive at, not accept the term "revenge" and leave it at that? The answer, I think, is suggested in a phrase used (in a different context) by a recent critic, who writes of "The choice of revenge as *the metaphor for action.*"[15] Revenge itself, that is to say, is subsumed in a larger purpose; and one aspect of that purpose is immediately pertinent to this discussion: the need for a culminating action that will bring "wonder" out of rhetoric in time to come. Revenge is only one of the various routes to the ritualization of death which permits the Elizabethan dramatist to conclude his tragedy with the expressiveness of a *consummatum est.* The sense of something attained, at once fearful and wondrous, is the playwright's solution to the problem that haunts so much of Renaissance literature, be it sonnet or tragedy; the problem, to use Spenser's word, of mutability. The resolution in death will assure the sort of enduring memorial Titus and his creator seek.

The demand for permanence explains a function of that saving remnant which is present at the tragedy's close, the Horatios and Edgars, who promise to remember the events and report them "aright / To the unsatisfied." In *Titus*, it has to be admitted, the remaining Andronici are annoyingly wordy, a fact that may be in part forgivable under the circumstances: they have been voiceless in Rome long enough. Still, this is a long way from the more honest ending of *King Lear*, with its bathetically simple, "Speak what we feel, not what we ought to say," and its recognition that not all the words in the world can balance the weight of the action we have witnessed. The great tragedies of this period—whether of blood, revenge, or tragedy pure—culminate, like their important precursor *Titus Andronicus*, in the acting out of death, and the rest is, necessarily, silence.

[15]Philip J. Finkelpearl, *John Marston of the Middle Temple* (Cambridge, Mass.: Harvard Univ. Press, 1969), p. 160. My italics.

Shakespeare and the Soil of Rape

Catharine R. Stimpson

Shakespeare's sympathy toward women helps to create an attitude toward rape that is more generous and less foolish than that of many of our contemporaries. He never sniggers and assumes that women, consciously or unconsciously, seek the rapist out and then enjoy the deed: brutal, enforced sex; the ghastly tmesis of the flesh. He never gives "proud lords" the right to "Make weak-made women tenants to their shame."[1] Nor does the act dominate his imagination, as it might that of a lesser writer as concerned with violence, war, and sexuality as Shakespeare is. In the complete works, the word "rape" occurs only seventeen times; "rapes" three; and various forms of "ravish" thirty-eight.[2] "Ravish" is perhaps like a poetic gloss that both hints at and denies rape's brutal force.

When rape occurs, it is terrible in itself. Like murder, it displays an aggressor in action. Shakespeare and his rapists use stridently masculine metaphors of war and of the hunt to capture that flagrant energy. Tarquin

. . . shakes aloft his Roman blade,
Which, like a falcon tow'ring in the skies,
Coucheth the fowl below with his wings' shade, . . .
(*Lucrece*, 505–7)

Like murder, rape also pictures a helpless victim, powerless vulnerability. Because rape's violence is sexual, an audience watching it can live out voyeuristic fantasies. Moreover, Shakespearean rape signifies vast conflicts: between unnatural disorder and natural order; raw, polluting lust and its purification through chastity or celibacy; the dishonorable and the honorable exercise of power; "hot-burning will" and "frozen conscience" (*Lucrece*, 247); and the sinful and righteous begetting of children. A chaste wife, a "clean" marriage bed, guarantee that property rights will pass to a man's blood heirs. For a man to rape a woman, then, is to take sides; to make a series of choices. Rape tempts and tests him, physically and morally.

From *The Woman's Part: Feminist Criticism of Shakespeare*, ed. Carolyn Ruth Swift Lenz, Gayle Greene, and Carol T. Neely (Urbana, IL: University of Illinois Press, 1983), 56–64. © 1980 by the Board of Trustees of the University of Illinois. Reprinted by permission.

[1]*The Rape of Lucrece*, lines 1259–60. All quotations are from *The Complete Works of Shakespeare*, ed. by George Lyman Kittredge (Boston: Ginn, 1936).

[2]Marvin Spevack, *A Complete and Systematic Concordance to the Works of Shakespeare*, V (Hildesheim: Georg Olms, 1970), 2713–14, 2718.

The structure of Shakespearean rape scenes itself embodies a conflict. The language in which rapes are imagined and then enacted is vivid, immediate, extended, garish, sometimes hallucinatory: "Night-wand'ring weasels shriek" (*Lucrece*, 307); Lucrece's breasts are "like ivory globes circled with blue" (407). The breast, at once erotic and maternal, swells to symbolize the body that will be overcome. However, the setting of the rape scenes in the plays is remote in time or place or both, usually near Italy, if not actually within it. The result is a dramatic sexuality that has the simultaneous detail and distance of a dream/nightmare. The dream/nightmare also contains frequent references to past rapes, to the Trojan War, to the legend of Philomel. Shakespeare compares Lucrece to "lamenting Philomele" (1079), a bitterly poignant allusion she herself will make. In *Titus Andronicus*, both Aaron and Marcus will join Philomel and Lavinia in a female community of suffering (2.3.43; 2.4.26). Aaron judges Lavinia as pure as Lucrece (2.2.108). Such reminders give the dream/nightmare the repetitive weight of myth and history, of experiences that have occurred before and will occur again.

When a man pursues, besieges, and batters a woman's body, he assaults a total world. The female flesh is a passive microcosm. Lucrece is a world, a "sweet city" (469). In *Coriolanus*, Cominius says to Menenius:

> You have holp to ravish your own daughters and
> To melt the city leads upon your pates,
> To see your wives dishonour'd to your noses—
>
> .   .   .   .
>
> Your temples burned in their cement, and
> Your franchises, whereon you stood, confin'd
> Into an auger's bore.
>
> (4.6.81–83, 85–87)

In *Titus Andronicus*, "Lavinia and Tamora may be seen as symbolic personifications of female Rome."[3] The question then becomes, "To whom does the world belong?" The order of Cominius's clauses, as well as his pronouns, provides an answer. The world belongs to men: fathers, husbands, lovers, brothers. Because in Shakespeare only well-born women are raped, their violation becomes one of property, status, and symbolic worth as well. The greater those values, the greater the sense of power their conquest confers upon the rapist.

Because men rape what other men possess, rape becomes in part a disastrous element of male rivalry. The woman's body is a prize in a zero-sum game that men play. Collatine's boasting about Lucrece, an act of excess that is a rhetorical analogue to Tarquin's sexual will, helps to provoke the ruler's desire to conquer the pride of his subordinate. In *Titus Andronicus*, the vicious competition of Demetrius and Chiron parallels the sibling hostilities between Saturninus and Bassianus. However, Demetrius and Chiron stop fighting over Lavinia

[3]David Wilbern, "Rape and Revenge in *Titus Andronicus*," *English Literary Renaissance*, 8 (1978), 164.

when it comes time to rape, mutilate, and humiliate her. The joys of controlling a woman together subsume the difficulties of deciding which one will control her independently. Their horrible, giggling plan—to use Bassianus's "dead trunk" as "pillow to our lust" (2.3.130)—deflects and satisfies their need to defeat other men, to deprive them of their rights and gratifications. When their mother gives birth to Aaron's child, their half-brother, Demetrius and Chiron also unite in their disgust, an emotion that yokes Oedipal jealousy, racist revulsion at miscegenation, and fear of the Roman political consequences of their mother's adultery.

Such rivalry can occur within a man as well as between men. Tarquin, in his long internal debates, struggles between the good self, who argues against rape, and the bad self, who demands sexual triumph. Tarquin is unable to use the common justifications for rape: political or familial revenge. He is equally unable to forget that Collatine is a principal man in his army, a kinsman, and a friend; these are male bonds that invert and undermine male rivalries. Tarquin mourns:

> Had Collatinus kill'd my son or sire,
> Or lain in ambush to betray my life,
> Or were he not my dear friend, this desire
> Might have excuse to work upon his wife,
> As in revenge or quittal of such strife;
> But as he is my kinsman, my dear friend,
> The shame and fault finds no excuse nor end.
> (232–38)

In psychoanalytical terms, Tarquin's ego is torn between the demands of a libido and a superego whose appeals Lucrece vainly tries to reinforce. After the rape, the superego takes its belated revenge. Guilt immediately deprives Tarquin of any sense of sexual pleasure. In *Measure for Measure,* Angelo will later act out Tarquin's struggle. He will put Isabella in the position of a potential rape victim, for the "choice" he offers her—submit to me sexually or commit your brother to death—is a version of the "choice" Tarquin presents to Lucrece—submit to me sexually or commit yourself to death.[4]

For women, rape means both submission, death, and more. Shakespeare never falters, never hedges, as he shows how defenseless women are before sexual violence and the large destructiveness it entails. Forced sexual submission enforces female death. For the loss of chastity, "a dearer thing than life" (*Lucrece,* 687) stains women irrevocably. Lavinia knows that being murdered is better than being subjected to a "worse than killing lust" (*Titus,* 2.3.175) that will deprive her of her reason for living. Women are unwillingly responsible for a "cureless crime" (*Lucrece,* 772). Lucrece, her act at once sacrificial, redemptive, and flamboyant

---

[4]In contrast, the deceiving of Angelo in the matter of the bed-trick, though underhanded, is not comparable to rape. Angelo is neither forced into something against his will nor conscious of pain and humiliation during the sexual act.

enough to make her husband's friends wish to revenge her, must kill herself. Because "the girl should not survive her shame" (5.3.41), Titus stabs Lavinia. Their deaths purge the lives and honor of the men whom they have ornamented: Lucrece's husband and father, whose mournings mingle over her corpse; Lavinia's father alone, her husband being dead.[5]

Few of Shakespeare's dramas about traumatic injustice are as clear, or as severe, as those about the raped woman who must be punished because she endured an aggression she never sought and against which she fought. Shakespeare deploys the voice of moderate men to comment on such unfair expiations. In *The Rape of Lucrece*, Brutus thinks Lucrece's suicide a final act of excess in a Rome Tarquin and his family have ruled. Discarding the mask of silliness he has expediently worn to now reveal an authentic self, he tells Collatine not to "steep thy heart / In such relenting dew of lamentations . . ." (1828–29). He urges Collatine to abandon private grief for political action and rid Rome of Tarquin. In a sense, Brutus uses Lucrece's anguish as a weapon in a struggle between men for power. In *Titus Andronicus*, Marcus asks for compassion for his niece and shows her how to publicize her plight. The reasonableness of a Brutus or Marcus contrasts to the despicable excesses of will of the rapist and the dangerous excesses of rhetoric of husbands who brag about their wives' chaste fidelity. Oddly, moderate women (like Paulina) who play prominent, articulate roles defending the victimized woman in Shakespeare's explorations of sexual jealousy, are missing from the examinations of rape.[6] Their absence starkly points to women's inability to control and to influence in benign ways the public structures that judge rape and the psychosexual needs that generate it.

Indeed, women assist in the rapes that attack other women. In *Lucrece*, night is allegorically female, a sable "mother of dread and fear" (117). In *Titus Andronicus*, Tamora wants to destroy Lavinia. Like Clytemnestra, she seeks revenge for the sacrifice of her children. She is also annoyed and threatened because Bassianus and Lavinia have discovered her sporting with Aaron in the woods. However, Tamora's encouragement of her sons to rape not simply Lavinia but any Roman woman has a lascivious quality that flows beyond these motives. Letting her boys "satisfy their lust" (2.3.180) expresses her enjoyment of her sons' potency, which veers toward and approaches a sublimated incest.

Tempting such taboos, Tamora deliberately turns away from Lavinia. She ignores the plaintive cry, "O Tamora! thou bearest a woman's face—" (2.3.136) and denies, as Lady Macbeth will do, her own femaleness. This is but one act in a series that will end when she eats her dead children; when she incorporates them back into her body it is an inversion of the release of a living child that

---

[5]Leo C. Curran, "Rape and Rape Victims in the Metamorphoses," *Arethusa*, II, Nos. 1/2 (1978), 223, also points out that rape is "perceived primarily as an offense against the property or honor of men." In brief, rape in a shame culture makes women guilty.

[6]Because husbands perceive rape as a form of infidelity, their psychic response to the raped wife has similarities to the attitude toward a possibly unfaithful wife: a disruptive suspicion, confusion, anger, and sense of loss, conveyed metaphorically through references to the sheets of the marriage bed that no longer seem white.

marks natural maternity. The forest setting of Lavinia's rape increases the play's sense of distorted, squalid sexuality. The soil is soiled in a perversion of nature comparable to the perversion of domesticity Tarquin creates in Collatine's and Lucrece's marriage bed. The pit that becomes Bassianus's grave, "unhallowed and blood-stained" (2.3.210), symbolizes the violated female genitalia and womb as well.

Self-reflexive Shakespeare, ever rewriting his materials, also offers a darkly comic study of imagined rape. In *Cymbeline,* Posthumus flaunts Imogen's virtue before Iachimo and dares him to assail it. Iachimo does not physically rape Imogen, but his theft of her good reputation, like his penetration of her bed-chamber, is a psychic equivalent. He admits this when he compares himself to Tarquin. Learning that Posthumus thinks her a strumpet and her sex a regiment of strumpets, Imogen begins to imitate Lucrece by stabbing herself in the heart. In addition, clod Cloten sees Posthumus as his rival. Cloten's fantasies parody a conflict between men in which victory means the right to assume the identity of the vanquished, to wear his clothes, to have his wife. Cloten also desires to revenge himself upon the woman who, defending herself against his advances, has offended him. With the encouragement of his mother, he imagines his sexuality as a vehicle of punishment. So he mutters:

. . . With that suit [Posthumus's] upon my back will I ravish her; first kill him, and in her eyes. There shall she see my valour, which will then be a torment to her contempt. He on the ground, my speech of insultment ended on his dead body, and when my lust hath dined (which, as I say, to vex her I will execute in the clothes that she so prais'd), to the court I'll knock her back, foot her home again. She hath despis'd me rejoicingly, and I'll be merry in my revenge.

(3.5.140–50)

However, crude Cloten cannot transform fantasy into act. Such inadequacies become a grossly comic figure. In *Cymbeline,* comedy blunts the force of Shakespeare's analysis of male enmity and the reunion of Posthumus and Imogen mitigates the force of his brief against the wagers, literal and figurative, that men place on women's virtue.

The fact of having been raped obliterates all of a woman's previous claims to virtue. One *sexual* experience hereafter will define her. Such a strict interpretation of rape may be an index to a shift in the position of women during Shakespeare's time. One historian has suggested: "What the Reformation era witnessed was the changing delineation of women's roles. As this period drew to a close, women's roles became defined increasingly by sex—to the detriment of all women—rather than by class."[7] Other historians have postulated that the more controlled female sexuality is in particular societies, the less power women have. Shakespeare warns his audience about breakdowns in the boundaries on

[7]Sherrin Marshall Wyntjes, "Women in the Reformation Era," *Becoming Visible: Women in European History,* ed. Renate Bridenthal and Claudia Koonz (Boston: Houghton Mifflin, 1977), p. 187. See, too, in the same volume, Joan Kelly-Gadol, "Did Women Have a Renaissance?" pp. 137–64, and Richard T. Vann, "Toward a New Lifestyle: Women in Preindustrial Capitalism," pp. 192–216.

male sexuality, showing rapists as vicious and out of control. However, he also reminds his audience about the boundaries that marriage places on female sexuality. His protest is not against such confinements, but against assaults upon them. If Shakespearean rape does indeed signify such a double retraction—of female identity to sexual identity, of female sexual expressiveness to marital fidelity—it might illustrate the intricate development, between 1580 and 1640, of what Lawrence Stone has named the Restricted Patriarchal Nuclear Family. Stone writes: ". . . both state and Church, for their own reasons, actively reinforced the pre-existent patriarchy within the family, and there are signs that the power of the husband and father over the wife and the children was positively strengthened, making him a legalized petty tyrant within the home."[8] Coppélia Kahn then correctly reads *The Rape of Lucrece* as the poetic version of an ideology that justifies this male power through imputing "a sort of natural inevitability to the relationship between men and women as the relationship between the strong and the weak. . . ."[9] In brief, the rape victim may be painfully emblematic of the plight of women during a period of constriction. Her sexual terror stands for the difficulty of her sex. Men, who have more power than women, abuse it. Women, who have less power than men, must absorb that abuse. In Shakespeare, women also have language and the dignity of stoicism as well as the choral commentary of decent men to provide a sympathetic response to their condition.

Psychologically, Shakespeare's rape sequences shrewdly unravel some of the reasons why men rape and the justifications they offer for such exploitation of their strength. Morally, the sequences compel sympathy for women, though they offer, as an inducement to the audience, some recoiling titillation. Shakespeare acutely shows—through Lucrece's speeches, through Lavinia's amputations—the agony a woman experiences after rape. Yet breeding that agony is the belief that the unwilling betrayal of a man's patriarchal position and pride matters more than the destruction of a woman's body and sense of being. Shakespeare deplores warped patterns of patriarchal authority but not the patterns themselves. I cannot prove that the Judith Shakespeare Virginia Woolf imagined in *A Room of One's Own* would have more skeptically asserted that patriarchy itself, not simply malicious and overweening representatives of it, helps to nurture rape. No fabulist, I cannot manufacture texts for history, a

[8]Lawrence Stone, *The Family, Sex and Marriage in England, 1500–1800* (New York: Harper & Row, 1977), p. 7. Others have likewise claimed that the junction of the sixteenth and seventeenth centuries was "an important crisis in the historic development of Englishwomen." I quote from Alice Clark, *Working Life of Women in the Seventeenth Century* (New York: Harcourt, Brace and Howe, 1920), p. 2. Stone, though he realizes that women were important economic assets, denies the view "that the economic contribution of the wife to the family budget necessarily gave her higher status and greater power, and that her progressive removal from the labour force as capitalism spread prosperity slowly downward was the cause of her social degradation" (p. 200). Clark supports such a theory.

[9]Coppélia Kahn, "The Rape in Shakespeare's *Lucrece*," *Shakespeare Studies*, 9 (1976), 68. After giving the first version of this paper, I read in manuscript Kahn's essay which explores several of the same issues with admirable depth, subtlety, and persuasiveness.

"Lucrece" by Judith Shakespeare. We must attend to what we have: Shakespearean victims to mourn, victimizers to despise, and a hierarchical order to frame them both.

"Scars Can Witness": Trials by Ordeal and Lavinia's Body in *Titus Andronicus*

Karen Cunningham

Criticized as immature and sensational dramaturgy for its bloodbaths, Shakespeare's *Titus Andronicus* recently has begun to be retrieved from the dustbin where Ravenscroft's indictment of it as "a heap of Rubbish" sent it centuries ago.[1] At its center stands the particularly troublesome figure of Lavinia, her mutilated body blazoning forth her own victimization and visually uniting scenes in which limbs are lopped, entrails burned, trunks decapitated, hands amputated, throats slit, and bones pulverized. In this context of horror, the violence to Lavinia may seem relatively indistinguishable from other bloodlettings that signal the disintegration of the Roman state and its aristocratic families. Yet it seems to me that a local English practice—the trial by ordeal—enables us to understand Shakespeare's heroine as much as does ancient Roman politics.

Exploiting staged violence to create justice, the early English trial by ordeal was the chief means of determining whether a crime had been committed, of discovering the criminal, of establishing the facts of a case, and, under pressure from local interested parties, of advancing specific individuals or classes.[2] The ordeal was a formalized practice that relied on social consent to produce an outcome called "justice," which it achieved *through* tests of the body, privileging the flesh in producing meaning. Yet ordeals were also fundamentally ambiguous and subject to manipulation: on the one hand, they were presented as impartial manifestations of divine justice; on the other hand, they were dependent upon the skills and motives of mortals for their interpretation and application. The interpretive uncertainties implied in the ordeal's doubleness parallel the interpretive uncertainties Shakespeare exploits in *Titus Andronicus*. Proceeding from

From *Women and Violence in Literature: An Essay Collection*, ed. Katherine Anne Ackley (New York: Garland Publishing, 1990), 139–162. Reprinted by permission of Garland Publishing, Inc. The original footnotes for this essay have been shortened.

[1]Ravenscroft's 1687 evaluation, along with J. Dover Wilson's 1948 criticism of the play as "some broken-down cart, laden with bleeding corpses from an Elizabethan scaffold, and driven by an executioner from Bedlam," is cited in J. C. Maxwell's introduction to the Arden edition, xxxiv. An overview of criticism is in Nicholas Brooke, *Shakespeare's Early Tragedies*, London: Methuen, 1968, 13–15.

[2]To avoid endless footnotes, I would like at the outset to acknowledge my debt to several authors of sixteenth-century legal history: Paul Hyams (1981); John Bellamy (1984); John Laurence (1932); and R. C. Van Caenegem (1973). Outlawed as a mode of proof by the Lateran Council of 1215, the ordeal survived in practice in local franchises administered by lords, and it survived in theory in folklore well into the eighteenth century (Hyams 123).

the significant violence of the ordeal, the play traces a shift in the modes of establishing justice from corporeal to rhetorical means. Before it achieves its rationalist conclusion, however, Shakespeare uses the theme of ordeals to raise a series of questions: what is signified by these tests of the body? And how is one to interpret—or to control the interpretation of—these visions of maimed flesh? Confronted with his speechless, bleeding daughter, Titus desperately demands, "what means this?" (4.1.30). Shakespeare's response is Lavinia's voluble flesh.

Although in a sixteenth-century public execution violence was deployed after a trial to validate a jury's judgment, to circulate images of royal power, and to punish convicts, in ordeals violence had priority as a chief means of discovering and evaluating character and events. Both these spectacles suggest that the early English common law "thought" in terms of the body, and that the body acquired at least some of its significance from its uses in legal practice.[3] Accused or convicted criminals generally could expect to be mutilated in some way, and extreme conventions of violence accompanied treason: criminals were displayed in carts, hung until "half dead," castrated, disemboweled, and decapitated. Their heads were then deposited on stakes upon London bridge, presumably as warnings to other malefactors (Thomas 1:39–40).

Rather than inventing this demonstration of inequitable power, however, the Tudors derived it from the trial by ordeal. In practice, almost any physical test could be declared legally binding: pronouncing a specific oath, triumphing in physical combat of all sorts, and surviving in boiling water were variations that implied the intimate connection between taxing a body and discovering truth:

> The trial by ordeal rests upon the belief that God will intervene by a sign or miracle to determine a question at issue between contending parties. . . . We find that the person who can carry a red-hot iron, who can plunge his hand or his arm into boiling water, [or] who will sink when thrown into the water, is deemed to have right on his side. . . . (Holdsworth 1:310–311).[4]

In the ordeal, judgment was represented as absolute and error-free: God was the judge, the ordeal His method. Aligned with divine will, the structure of ordeals implied impartiality, displacing judgment from earthly to heavenly courts. In this context, the local justice was a humble interpreter of the apparent who read the self-evident marks on the bodies of participants. Bodies were crucial sites not only

[3]Michel Foucault's observation that a history of sexuality is a history of a field of truth (*Sexuality* I, 56–57) provides a convenient context for considering the juridical theme; his comments imply the complex link between a legal discourse trying to represent itself as "truth" and the deployment of sexuality in that discourse. Law itself, Foucault states, "was not simply a weapon skillfully wielded by monarchs, [but] was the monarchic system's mode of manifestation and the form of its acceptability. In Western societies since the Middle Ages, the exercise of power has always been in terms of law" (*Sexuality* I, 87).

[4]The *OED* defines ordeal as "an ancient . . . mode of trial, in which an accused or suspected person was subjected to some physical test fraught with danger, . . . the result being regarded as the immediate judgement of the Deity."

for apportioning punishment, but more importantly, for producing meaning, for resolving conflicts, and for testing truth; they were objects of interpretation identified with manifestations of divine judgment, valued for their representational possibilities, and essential to heavenly and earthly revelations. Despite their announced claim to so unimpeachable a judge as God, then, ordeals were often subject to political manipulation, and in practice judges seem to have wielded interpretation as a form of power, creating their own versions of the body's story to repress dissent or to advance prominent members of the community (Hyams 97, 107). And ordeals could certainly miscarry, as is evidenced in the tale of a slave who, having carried a hot iron, was pronounced innocent of any wickedness despite the signs of guilt—the pus and infection—that the assembled observers saw clearly on his hands (Hyams 97). Silent about their own political implications, however, ordeals fit within the contemporary system of jurisprudence and publicly identified violence with the creation of truth that was verified, to use Othello's words, by "ocular proof."

II

Shakespeare embodies this ambiguous relation between scarred flesh and revealed truth in *Titus Andronicus*'s central problem, Lavinia, who begins as an archetypal virgin and submissive daughter. Initially a peripheral figure in this martial tale, she is progressively transformed through violence into the focal point of the play's insistent appeals to justice.[5] Certainly Lavinia's mutilation by the Goth warriors, Demetrius and Chiron, contains her within the play's dynamic of power relations by encoding her body with the visible signs of her impotence—the absence of her hands and tongue—and ultimately by making her flesh the herald of her own "shame," just as convicts' bodies proclaimed their criminality by the absence of ears or hands.[6] More than this, however, Lavinia's rape transfers the site of aggression from the Roman-Goth battlefield, evoked in the opening scene by the funeral cortege conveying Titus' sons to their tomb, to her body, where sexuality and criminality become intertwined, hidden possibilities. The inherent ambiguity of an ordeal as both a mode of inquiry into facts (which might render one innocent of any wrongdoing) and a mode of punishment for guilt (implicitly presumed by one's having been

---

[5]*Titus Andronicus* (with the more obvious instances of *Measure for Measure* and *The Merchant of Venice*) has among the highest number of direct references to justice and legalisms. Saturninus opens the play with his legal claim to the empery on the basis of primogeniture; Bassianus relocates justice in "free election" when he claims the throne; Saturninus and Bassianus both base their claims to Lavinia on legal issues—Saturninus on the right of the monarch, Bassianus on prior contractual betrothal; Tamora undertakes the destruction of the Andronici as "revenge," a matter of justice; Titus' sons Quintus and Martius are executed as legal punishment; Saturninus defends his decisions on the basis of law; and so on.

[6]A useful discussion of the ways bodies are encoded with their own positions in power relations is Foucault's *Discipline and Punish*, especially pp. 43–49.

accused) is analogous to the ambiguity of rape as a transgression against the female and also a sign of her pollution; as Coppelia Kahn has shown in her discussion of *Lucrece*, the victim of rape in Shakespeare adheres to the patriarchal values of chastity even as she acquires a stigma from *being* raped (46);[7] she is tainted (or criminalized in its sixteenth-century sense of "decided upon") by her own victimization. In Lavinia's victimization, Shakespeare's plot pivots from a tale of political strife into a mystery inscribed in and on her flesh, a "whodunit" in which the main goal of the Andronici is to discover the crime and to expose and punish the criminals.

A summary of the plot may help us establish Lavinia's role. The venerable Roman general Titus Andronicus returns to Rome from ten years of war with the Goths to find two brothers—Saturninus and Bassianus—competing to become emperor. Called upon to resolve the quarrel, Titus selects the elder, Saturninus, who rewards Andronicus by choosing his only daughter, Lavinia, as empress. Almost immediately Bassianus claims Lavinia as his wife on the basis of their prior betrothal, initiating another rivalry in which Titus' sons join Bassianus against their father and Saturninus. During the ensuing swordfight, Titus denounces all his sons and kills one of them, while Saturninus hastily discards Lavinia for the erotic Goth Queen, Tamora. By the end of the lengthy first scene, Titus has been alienated from Saturninus' favor, and Tamora has sworn to destroy the Andronicus family as revenge for their ritual sacrifice of her son Alarbus. These confrontations precipitate the variations on revenge that follow: Aaron the Moor is introduced as Tamora's lover, and the pair in various ways bring about Bassianus' murder, Lavinia's rape and dismemberment, and Quintus' and Martius' (Titus' sons) imprisonment and execution for murder; Aaron dupes Titus into severing one of his hands to save his sons, but they are decapitated nonetheless; seemingly driven mad at the injustices to his family, Titus swears revenge on Tamora and her sons, traps the sons, and with Lavinia's participation, slits their throats, bakes them in a pie, and serves them to their mother at the play's final banquet; Titus then stabs Lavinia to end her "shame," and stabs Tamora to fulfill his vengeance; Saturninus stabs Titus; Titus' son Lucius, having converted the Goths to allies, stabs Saturninus; and amid a pile of bleeding corpses, order is restored to Rome as the surviving citizens proclaim Lucius their new emperor.

What is evident in this recapitulation is less the disintegration of Rome than the exaggeration of rivalries that produce Lavinia—the emblem of a ritual mode of justice in which the bodies of competitors are both the sites and resolutions of conflict. In the opening scene, Shakespeare foreshadows Lavinia's subsequent violent exploitation by establishing her as a silent, submissive setting for the play's sexual politics. Saturninus' preemptive decision to marry her, Bassianus'

---

[7]Four works have proved particularly helpful in considering Lavinia's rape and the rivalries acted out across her body: Kahn (1976); Catharine R. Stimpson (1980); Nancy J. Vickers (1986); and Eve K. Sedgwick (1985).

counterclaim to his "betrothed," and Marcus' support for Bassianus are all presented in legal terminology: what to Saturninus and Titus is "treason" (1.1.283) to Bassianus and Marcus is "justice" (1.1.280); what to Saturninus is "rape" (1.1.404), by which he means Lavinia's abduction or theft, to Bassianus is merely the act of seizing his own (1.1.405).[8] Throughout the scene, Lavinia is identified variously and aggressively with replication of the family, political advancement, and Roman ornamentation, as each character bases his play for political power and progeny on the possession of her body.[9] Those rivalries culminate in a crucial description that proves prophetic of Lavinia's role: intending to insult parent and child and to justify his desire for Tamora by tainting Lavinia with promiscuity, Saturninus discards "that changing piece" (1.1.309). Saturninus' image signifies not only his scorn for the Andronici but, more importantly, Shakespeare's conception of Lavinia: like the subject of a Renaissance anamorphic painting, which can be seen from one point of view as a vital, dynamic figure, and from another point of view as a decaying corpse, Lavinia is indeed a "changing piece," a cipher and repository of meaning continually reinterpreted through the observations and voices of others.

The problem of voicing, of putting into words the multiple meanings of Lavinia's body, pervades *Titus Andronicus* after she returns to center stage to take her "silent walks" (2.4.). She re-enters accompanied by rather startling stage directions that call attention to her visible dismemberment and invisible rape: "enter Lavinia, her hands cut off, her tongue cut out, and ravished." And she re-enters accompanied by the brutal tongue-lashings of the rapists, in which Shakespeare demonstrates his skill with the phenomenal force of speech by bringing words dangerously close to instruments of torture that produce a real flinch:

[8]The *OED* defines "rape": "the act of taking anything by force; violent seizure of goods; robbery"; "the act of carrying away a person, especially a woman, by force"; and finally, "violation or ravishing of a woman."

[9]The sexual politics begins with the play's first scene, where Bassianus singles out Lavinia as his motive for ending the conflict with Saturninus over the throne: "And her to whom my thoughts are humbled all, Gracious Lavinia, Rome's rich ornament" (1.1.52–53). Instances of her appropriation in the competition among the males include: Saturninus' vow to recompense Titus by marrying her "to advance/[Titus'] name and honorable family" (1.1.238–239); Titus' acceptance of this patronage as his own, "in this match/I hold me highly honored of your grace" (1.1.242–243); and Bassianus' counterclaim, "this maid is mine" (1.1.276). The first act concludes with a precarious image of suspended rivalry: ignoring Bassianus, Saturninus takes *two* brides into a wedding feast, "Come, if the emperor's court can feast two brides,/You are my guest, Lavinia, you and your friends" (1.1.489–90). This early instance of doubling serves the pattern of exchange: two brothers—Saturninus and Bassianus, Titus and Marcus, Demetrius and Chiron; two brides—Tamora and Lavinia; two sons—Demetrius and Chiron; two executed sons, Quintus and Martius; and so on. Shakespeare returns to the pairings to undermine the "truce" in act five: Saturninus, jealous of Lucius' show of military power, querulously asks, "What, hath the firmament moe suns than one?" (5.3.17). Lavinia's submissiveness throughout these exchanges is perhaps more understandable when we recall that during the sixteenth century for a woman to complain was a punishable offense. See Belsey 181.

Dem: So, now go tell, an if thy tongue can speak,
           Who 'twas that cut thy tongue and ravish'd thee.
Chi: Write down thy mind, bewray thy meaning so,
           An if thy stumps will let thee play the scribe.
Dem: See how with signs and tokens she can scrowl.
                        (2.4.1–5)[10]

Glossed as a form of "scrawl," to gesticulate, with a play on "scroll," to write down, Lavinia's "scrowl" (1.5) ironically points toward her disclosure of the rapists, etymologically uniting allusions to bodies (gesticulating) and texts (writing) as modes of making meaning. Whatever she is at this moment—an emblem of patience or sorrow, or as Titus later labels her, a "map of woe" (3.2.12)—whatever conventional descriptions she elicits, she is most certainly, like the figure in an ordeal, an assertion of the significance of bodiness over other kinds of expression. Lavinia is the body fully problematized, the interpretive problem made flesh, in which lies the revelation of truth if her family could decipher it, and the definition of justice if revenge could provide it. Taken metadramatically, Lavinia's body represents Shakespeare's arena for trying out the possibilities of dramatic representation. Taken thematically, however, her body achieves a kind of metaphysical density like that Foucault describes as belonging to a publicly maimed figure: she is "the synthesis of the reality of the deeds and the truth of the investigation, of the documents of the case and the statements of the criminal, of the crime and the punishment" (*Discipline* 47).

Shakespeare has prepared for the interpretive challenge Lavinia poses as "the documents of the case" when her two brothers, Quintus and Martius, are framed for murdering Bassianus (2.3.). The scene's interest is divided between their ability to see at all and their ability to interpret what they see. Neither can see clearly (2.3.195 ff.), and Martius quickly falls into the camouflaged pit that holds Bassianus' corpse; unable to recognize him readily, Martius can identify Bassianus only through the token of "a precious ring" (2.3.227); and unable to lift his brother from the "detested, dark" pit (2.3.224), Quintus tumbles into it. Rather too easily duped by the manufactured evidence of Aaron's forged letter, the self-satisfying Saturninus orders that the two be imprisoned (2.3.284–85); but his sentence produces a series of ironic responses that raise the specter of false witnesses and call into question the central issue of proof in accusing and judging those suspected of a crime. Sounding like a malicious parody of Chaucer's narrator in "The Nun's Priest's Tale," who insists that "Mordre wol out" (l. 3057), Tamora gloats, "How easily murder is discovered!" (2.3.287). But Titus resists that easy discovery and petitions:

---

[10]Shakespeare derives the rape and severed tongue from his Ovidian and prose sources. However, in the source Philomela's hands are not amputated, and she is able to weave a tapestry that reveals her attackers. Closer to Shakespeare's own day, it was typical for figures charged with various crimes— theft or seditious writing, for example—to have a hand cut off. Perhaps relevant to Lavinia's mutilation is the punishment of John Stubbs, who, having written to queen Elizabeth opposing her marriage to Anjou, had his hand severed to prevent him from writing such documents in the future. The incident is described in Tennenhouse, 21–22.

Tit: High emperor, upon my feeble knee
        I beg this boon, with tears not lightly shed,
        That this fell fault of my accursed sons,
        Accursed, if the fault be prov'd in them—
Sat: If it be prov'd! you see it is apparent.
                                                (2.3.288–292)

Prefiguring Shylock, and accommodating sixteenth-century trial protocol in preventing the accused from speaking in their own behalf, Saturninus silences Quintus, Martius, and Titus: "Let them not speak a word; the guilt is plain" (2.3.301). But plain to whom? We have been provided with privileged knowledge of Quintus' and Martius' innocence, a knowledge that places us without our consent among the perpetrators. In the context of early common law, that knowledge contains its own suppression, for figures accused of crime could offer no witnesses in their defense; to speak for the accused was to speak against the interests of the king, a potentially treasonous act (Bellamy 48). Still, by assigning Titus the task of seeking additional "proof," Shakespeare exploits Saturninus' blindness to raise questions not only about Saturninus' character, but also about the crime (what precisely is it?), its perpetrators (who did it?), and the circumstances that would constitute sufficient signs of guilt, guilt that is represented here not as criminal behavior nor moral taint, but as the result of machinations by Aaron and Tamora, and "proved" by the presence of the two Andronici in the pit. The repetition of "proof" is the sign of Shakespeare's dramatic intention: as the *OED* defines it, "proof" means "evidence such as determines the judgment of a tribunal"; "the action or act of testing or making trial of anything, experiment, examination"; and "evidence sufficient to establish a fact or to produce belief in the certainty of something." In short, proof is both the evidence and the test of the evidence, and justice is the "belief in the certainty of something" produced by proof.

Basing the exchange between Saturninus and Titus on the multiple meanings of "proof," Shakespeare flaunts the ambiguities of circumstantial evidence and reveals how easily the apparently self-evident is misread or manipulated "to produce belief" that is unwarranted. Titus' reservation ("if it be prov'd") and Saturninus' scoffing reply ("you see it is apparent") call into question not merely the effectiveness but the possibility of justice in a world where what the eyes see is not sufficient explanation for what men have done: Quintus and Martius saw briars and weeds, not a camouflaged pit, and they saw a shining ring, not Bassianus' distinct if bloodied features; Saturninus sees two murderers trapped with their victim, not two brothers victimized by the artistic evil of Aaron and Tamora; only Titus, who might be accused of having his vision blurred by kinship, sees room for doubt and reason to withhold a verdict.[11] When subsequently he is called upon to defend his judgment and the execution of Quintus and Martius, Saturninus allies himself "with law" (4.4.8) that has already lost its underpinnings: evoking "egal justice" (4.4.4), he repetitiously insists that the "traitorous sons" "died by law" (4.4.53–54). To paraphrase Samuel Johnson, a rigid legalism is the last refuge of this scoundrel. What Shakespeare offers in this scene of crime and mis-discovery is an image of jurisprudence desperately needing to be set right: eyewitnesses err or lie, upholders of law figure justice as self-interest, and accusation substitutes for proof. It is no wonder that the Andronici mourn the absence of justice in the world, and that Titus proclaims Astraea's flight from the earth (4.3.4). When goddesses abandon the task of righting wrongs, justice falls to the manipulations of mortals.

The dramatization of justice gone wrong in Quintus' and Martius' arrests immediately precedes and precipitates the play's most sustained visual assault, the display of the mutilated Lavinia (2.4.), which challenges characters and spectators to play the jurists and negotiate between the visible and the inferential.[12] To get at the story inscribed on Lavinia's flesh, Shakespeare makes her a public issue; and although he represents the character's requisite modesty in her pleas to evade display ("tumble me into some loathsome pit,/Where never man's eye may behold my body" [2.3.176–77]), he continually exploits the theatricality of violence by subjecting Lavinia to different kinds of scrutiny that range from the mocking, aggressive observations of Demetrius and Chiron that I discussed earlier to the sympathetic but distorting gaze of her uncle Marcus.

The sight of Lavinia so disturbs that gaze that Marcus is thrown back into confusion and begins to rattle off lines as though he would talk his eyes out of what they see, attributing this version of Lavinia to a horrible dream (2.4.11–15). The result of her mutilation is his failure of speech, as he almost loses his own ability to make sense and lapses into a series of relentlessly troublesome metaphors that strain to evade monstrosity even as they reveal the violence rhetoric does to nature:

> Alas, a crimson river of warm blood,
> Like to a bubbling fountain stirr'd with the wind,
> Doth rise and fall between thy rosed lips,
> Coming and going with thy honey breath.
>
> (2.4.22–25)

Marcus' wrenched images mark the first of many speeches that attempt to trans-

---

[11]Titus repeats the common play on the visible body as an organizing principle when he tells the disguised Tamora/Revenge that he does indeed know her: ". . . I know thee well enough":

> Witness this wretched stump, witness these crimson lines;
> Witness these trenches made by grief and care;
> Witness the tiring day and heavy night;
> Witness all sorrow that I know thee well
> For our proud emperess, mighty Tamora.
> Is not thy coming for my other hand?
>
> (5.2.21–27)

[12]It may be useful here to recall that although we know, with Aaron, Tamora, and her sons, that Lavinia has been raped and Bassianus murdered by Demetrius and Chiron, no one else in the play—including the putative voice of "law," Saturninus—possesses that knowledge. For a discussion somewhat different from mine, one that takes Lavinia as the "aristocratic body" of Rome, see Tennenhouse. He argues that Shakespeare's version of the rape revises the images of penetration found in the classical sources into images of "dismemberment."

late the deformed Lavinia into naturalized images that, as A.C. Tricomi has shown, link her to the allusions to mutilated gardens and eroticized settings in conflict with the images of predators (90).

Yet in an assertion of phenomenal presence that will not yield to words, Lavinia's garrulous flesh also remains beyond the taming power of linguistic tropes, her body a reservoir of half-glimpsed truths and insufficient syllables, the dwelling place and the expression of cries for vengeance. Demonstrating a remarkable capacity to disturb or to absorb all the language that tries to explain it, Lavinia's body becomes a cipher for significant disclosures and the source of revelations that extend beyond her—revelations that explain her two brothers' decapitations, her father's madness, and her rapists' grisly executions. Like the scarred figure in a trial by ordeal, Lavinia is conceived as a deeply disturbing phenomenon that demands and simultaneously resists interpreting; transformed into a visual prompt, she is a cue for moralizing about the vicissitudes of political and domestic life. In Marcus' presentation of her, with its nostalgic past tense, "This was thy daughter" (3.1.63); in Titus' aggressive insistence that Lucius must "arise, and look upon her" (3.1.65); and ultimately in Titus' display of her when he indicts her attackers, "here stands the spring" (5.1.170)—over and over Lavinia is offered as a sight to excite and engage the spectators' powers of reading a mutilated icon, to make them infer events and their meanings from the sight before them.

What needs stressing is the obvious but often overlooked point precisely put by Bert O. States "that theater . . . is really a language whose words consist to an unusual degree of things that *are* what they seem to be" (20). In the theater, Lavinia's scars are her words, and they bring us to an impasse, paradoxically requiring and thwarting their transformation into verbal structures. Violently deprived of her own position as a speaker, and dependent on observers to solve the problem of her meaning, she becomes the generative source of unstoppable commentary, verbally dissected and reconstituted outside herself.[13] Yet Shakespeare is careful to point out that the reconstitution is ambiguous and untrustworthy: faced with her tears, Marcus cannot be certain whether she weeps because her brothers *did* kill Bassianus or because they did *not*, and thus were executed erroneously (3.1.114–115); struggling to understand her meaning when she raises one handless arm, then the other, Marcus infers that she means there was more than one rapist *or* that Marcus and Titus should leave the revenge to heaven (4.1.40); foolishly assuring her that the law has taken revenge on her criminal brothers, Titus initially misinterprets her tears as hatred for her siblings and mourning for her husband (3.1.117); and terrorized by her pursuit, young Lucius fears violence from his aunt (4.1.4). Despite all the attempts to

---

[13]In her suggestive work on female subjectivity and tragedy, Catherine Belsey argues that women deprived of speech are deprived of a position as subjects (149 and *passim*). In this context, Lavinia's speechlessness is certainly a sign of her impotence. Yet it seems to me also that the context of the trial by ordeal, which emphasized the body's language, acts as Lavinia's alternate mode of speech and constitution of subjectivity.

"say for" Lavinia (3.1.87), her body threatens to silence her family by transforming them into the image that anticipates the scene's macabre conclusion: "Or
shall we bite our tongues, and in dumb shows/Pass the remainder of our hateful
days?" (3.1.130–131).

In an ordeal, the local adjudicator was a sort of designated "truth-giver" who
acted out a quasi-divine role as a reader of God's text by interpreting signs on
the body—infected burns or unblistered skin, for example—and providing closure. Similar mystical empathy and authority is hinted at in Titus' remarks about
his access to Lavinia: he vows to "interpret all her martyr'd signs" (3.2.36); to
"learn [her] thought" (3.2.39); to "wrest an alaphabet" from her body (3.2.44).
But Titus' promises of interpretive certainty dissolve in the face of Lavinia's
actions: befuddled by her pursuit of young Lucius and his books, Marcus
queries, "What means my niece Lavinia by these signs?" (4.1.8); Titus can comment only generally, "somewhat doth she mean" (4.1.9), and return the question
to Marcus, "what means this?" (4.1.30), "what would she find?" (4.1.46). The
desperate meaning-mongering here echoes Marlowe's *Doctor Faustus*. Like
Lavinia's descent into dismemberment and disarticulation, the learned scholar's
descent into irrationality and sensate damnation results from an inability to
interpret phenomena; continually questing for definitive explications, Faustus
repeatedly demands, "what means this show?" Like Marlowe, Shakespeare in
Titus Andronicus dramatizes a search for an authoritative interpreter, clearing
the ground for the expert adjudicator by holding up a naive logic of justice: *if* one
could properly read the signs on Lavinia's body, this logic suggests, justice would
be the inevitable result.

The point is that no one can interpret those corporeal signs with certainty;
ultimately, Shakespeare turns to inscription in a series of textual allusions that do
not replace so much as supplement the messages written in violent lines. Most
notable is the climactic scene of disclosure (4.1.), in which Lavinia seizes Ovid's
"Metamorphoses" and hieratically elevates it with her handless arms, juxtapos-
ing her expressive flesh to violent stories of Lucrece and Philomela.[14] Bearing a
striking resemblance to an exorcism, which aims to force a demon under torture
to reveal itself, the scene proceeds ritualistically to force the secret inhabitants
from Lavinia's body.[15] Melding her hands to the text, Lavinia discloses her own
truth by exposing its pages, remaking Ovid (as she has remade her family) into a
commentator on her fate. Again as he has throughout, the playwright stages his
bravado on her body in a moment as potentially comic as tragic when Lavinia
transforms herself into a writing instrument, distorting herself to clasp a staff
with her mouth and feet in order to write "Stuprum—Chiron—Demetrius"
(4.1.78). In this unparalleled scene of self-translation, Lavinia brings forth the
crime and its solution, exposing "the traitors and the truth" (4.1.76), and verify-
ing both with her body.

---

[14]Compare Eugene Waith (1957), who interprets *Titus Andronicus* in light of an Ovidian "metamorphosis of violence," which presents the transformational power of passion.
[15]The formal aspects of exorcisms are detailed in Peter Brown, 109–111.

Shakespeare embeds this externalizing of "the documents of the case" in a series of acts of writing and erasing that intensify his emphasis on the exchanges between kinds of expression. Ranging from Marcus' making the ground into a *tabula rasa* metaphorically equivalent to Lavinia's virgin flesh; through Lavinia's erasing his name and overlaying it with the names of Chiron and Demetrius; and to Titus' wishing this indictment might be etched in brass rather than on shifting sands (4.1.104)—each stage in this dramatization of inscription and erasure represents a slight gain in interpretive clarity. Transferred from its mysterious and multivalent form as scarring on Lavinia to the more directly referential key three terms—rape, Chiron, Demetrius—the crime is part of a larger pattern of mutual explication among bodies and texts, a simple noun in a grammatical fragment whose referentiality produces relief by resolving ambiguity.

Yet the resolution offered by texts is not absolute, but has been eroded in advance by the characters' easy exploitation of the classical analogues Lavinia draws on, Lucrece and Philomela. Like Lavinia's body, these references are appropriated to the needs of those who mention them, functioning as codes for personal and political strategies: to quell the rivalry between Demetrius and Chiron over Lavinia, Aaron emphasizes Lucrece's chastity and makes her into the motive for "force" (2.1.118); to whip up his sense of revenge, Lucius turns the reference to Lucrece's rapist, Tarquin (3.1.296–298), a self-exhortation Marcus reiterates when he too links Lucrece's rape to revenge (4.1.89–93); to pursue the question of what has happened to Lavinia, Marcus alludes to a third mutilated female, Philomela (2.4.26, 38, 41–43), uncannily implying in his references a knowledge of rape that he does not yet possess; and to guess at Lavinia's rape and the name of her attacker (about which he errs), Titus recalls "the tragic tale of Philomel" (4.1.47–49) and relies too closely on his knowledge of Lucrece—"What Roman lord it was durst do the deed:/Or slunk not Saturnine, as Tarquin erst,/That left the camp to sin in Lucrece's bed?" (4.1.62–64). The point is that texts carry no special privilege as reliable guides to interpretation; they, too, can be made to say what the interpreter desires, even if the interpreter is obviously wrong.

Such Shakespearean undermining of Titus' interpretive authority precedes and colors his rationalization for killing Lavinia, which he expresses in terms of another literary analogue, or, in the play's diction, "precedent." The "pattern, precedent, and lively warrant" of the story of Virginius subjects the progress of revenge to a curious pause for a bit of literary explication when Titus asks if "rash Virginius" was right to kill his daughter because she had been "enforc'd, stain'd, deflow'r'd" (5.3.35–37). Saturninus' conventional patriarchal response in arguing that "the girl should not survive her shame,/And by her presence still renew [Virginius'] sorrows" (5.3.40–41) merely confirms what has been Titus' interpretation throughout, which he hastily uses to justify killing Lavinia, transforming stabbing into sacrifice: "Die, die, Lavinia, and thy shame with thee:/And with thy shame, thy father's sorrow die!" (5.3.46–47). Conceived of as a conduit for her father's emotions, as she has been conceived of throughout as the conduit for others' desires,

Lavinia is refigured by textual "precedent" into an explanation for her own slaughter, thematically assimilated at the last into an alien text. Both the knowledge and resolution of her violation are enabled by classical allusions that allow Titus to contextualize murder as "justice."

But this archaic solution to the problem of justice, like the failed allegory of Revenge enacted by Tamora, is rejected and replaced in the play's final scene by a rhetorical mode that is closely linked to trial by jury. In a highly declamatory style, in diction punctuated with references to law and judgment, and in a tone that evokes nothing so much as a courtroom performance, Lucius pleads the case for the Andronici, persuading the assembled citizens to embrace a new "truth-giver" capable of managing the evidence by wielding the power of interpretation. Physical evidence that might require assessment—including the corpses of Titus and Lavinia, the unrepentant Aaron, and the offspring of the Moor and Tamora—is annexed to the needs of adjudication as the survivor verbally disentangles the bodies and assigns guilt, publicizing and distributing knowledge of villainy. Repeating "be it known to you" to bolster the knowledge he here constitutes, Lucius names Chiron and Demetrius, "deciphered villains" (4.2.8), as the sources of Bassianus' murder, Lavinia's rape, Quintus' and Martius' decapitations, Titus' rejection, and Lucius' own banishment. Shakespeare had been complicating the notion of self-evidence by subjecting sights and texts to variable interpretations. Here he reverses himself, limiting interpretive possibilities by providing only Lucius' and Marcus' shared perspective and validating their arguments with the unanimous support of "the common voice" (5.3.140). In the creation of Lucius, who is wholly absent from the prose source, Shakespeare turns solicitations of judgment achieved through violence into solicitations of approbation and public position achieved through rationalization. Designed to assert the force of rhetoric over flesh in apportioning law, the final scene enunciates Shakespeare's complex transfers between bodies and speeches in the pursuit of justice and distills them in Lucius' plea to the citizens:

> Alas, you know I am no vaunter, I;
> My scars can witness, dumb although they are,
> That my report is just and full of truth.
> (5.3.113–115).

Titus Andronicus reflects a time in legal and dramatic history that asserted what now seems an alien proposition: in producing truth and justice, in producing "a belief in the certainty" of an interpretation, scars must witness; the body, especially as it sustains violent abuse, is an "honest" signifier. Set in the gap between the invisible, secret crime of Lavinia's rape and the emphatically visible, public form of the trial by ordeal, the play shows its own elements in transit: exposing the ambiguities that undermine ordeals as proofs of crime and methods of justice, it concludes by pointing toward a juridical successor, trial by jury.[16] Despite

---

[16]"The English jury . . . could plausibly be represented as a new type of ordeal . . ." (Hyams 106).

Shakespeare's exposure of the ambiguities at the core of crime, punishment, and proof; and despite the problems of secrecy and visibility dramatized in Lavinia's body, spectators are consoled at the end by what is "apparent," a consolation itself weakened in advance when Saturninus reassured himself by taking the guilt of Quintus and Martius as "apparent." Within this structure of problematizing the apparent, Lavinia mounts no challenge to the patriarchy that identifies her as the site of political rivalry nor to the legal structure that identifies her as a territory for expropriation. Yet despite her silence, Lavinia is meaningful, harkening back to a fading time when not to speak was not only to possess but indeed to *be* meaning.

Works Consulted

Bellamy, John G. *Criminal Law and Society in Late Medieval and Tudor England.* New York: St. Martin's, 1984.

Belsey, Catherine. *The Subject of Tragedy.* London and New York: Methuen, 1985.

Brooke, Nicholas. *Shakespeare's Early Tragedies.* London: Methuen, 1968.

Brown, Peter. *The Cult of the Saints.* Chicago: U of Chicago P, 1981.

Chaucer, Geoffrey. *The Works of Geoffrey Chaucer.* Ed. F. N. Robinson. Boston: Houghton Mifflin, 1957.

Foucault, Michel. *Discipline and Punish.* Trans. Alan Sheridan. New York: Random House, 1977.

———. *The History of Sexuality.* 3 vols. Trans. Robert Hurley. New York: Random House, 1978. vol. 1.

Holdsworth, W. S. *A History of English Law.* 3rd. ed. 7 vols. London: Methuen, 1922. vol. 1.

Hyams, Paul R. "Trial by Ordeal: The Key to Proof in the Early Common Law." In *On the Laws and Customs of England.* Ed. Morris S. Arnold et al. Chapel Hill: U of North Carolina P, 1981. 90–127.

Kahn, Coppelia. "The Rape in Shakespeare's *Lucrece*." *Shakespeare Studies* 9 (1976), 45–72.

Laurence, John. *A History of Capital Punishment.* Port Washington, NY: Kennikat, 1932.

Maxwell, J. C. Introduction to *Titus Andronicus.* By William Shakespeare. Arden edition. London: Methuen, 1968. xi–xl.

Sedgwick, Eve K. *Between Men: English Literature and Male Homosocial Desire.* New York: Columbia UP, 1985.

Shakespeare, William. *Titus Andronicus.* Arden Edition. Ed. J. C. Maxwell. London: Methuen, 1953.

States, Bert O. *Great Reckonings in Little Rooms.* Berkeley: U of California P, 1985.

Stimpson, Catharine R. "Shakespeare and the Soil of Rape." In *The Woman's Part: Feminist Criticism of Shakespeare.* Urbana, IL: U Illinois P, 1980. 56–64.

Tennenhouse, Leonard. *Power on Display.* New York and London: Methuen, 1986.

Thomas, Donald, ed. *State Trials: Treason and Libel.* 2 vols. London: Routledge & Kegan Paul, 1972. vol. 1.

Tricomi, Albert H. "The Mutilated Garden in *Titus Andronicus*." *Shakespeare Studies* 9 (1976), 89–105.

Van Caenegem, R. C. *The Birth of the English Common Law.* Cambridge: Cambridge UP, 1973.

Vickers, Nancy J. "This Heraldry in Lucrece's Face." In *The Female Body in Western Culture.* Ed. Susan Rubin Suleiman. Cambridge, MA: Harvard UP, 1986. 209–222.

Waith, Eugene. "The Metamorphosis of Violence in *Titus Andronicus.*" *Shakespeare Survey* 10 (1957), 39–49.

Wilson, J. Dover, ed. *Titus Andronicus.* New Shakespeare Edition. Cambridge: Cambridge UP, 1948.

Titus Andronicus:
Abortive Domestic Tragedy

C. L. Barber and Richard P. Wheeler

Designed in obvious imitation of Kyd's *Spanish Tragedy*, *Titus Andronicus* has an aged, worthy pillar of social piety, who suffers outrage to his children, is driven to desperate, extravagant grief and protest, "takes false shadows for true substances" (3.2.80) under the intolerable pressure of feeling, and finally, by turning dramatic fiction into physical action, achieves outrageous revenge. Much of the play is constructed with considerable dramatic skill and written with truly astounding verbal and imaginative energy. Shaping the whole is mythopoeic power which, far from being deficient, is too strong for the structure as developed. Because motives remarkably similar to those handled in *King Lear* are projected in symbolic action for which there is no adequate social matrix, there can be no control by ironic recognition, no clarification of what these motives mean as they are expressed in relation to a plausible community whose stability they disrupt. *Titus Andronicus* fails, by contrast with *The Spanish Tragedy* (let alone *King Lear*), because there is in effect no larger social world within which the outrage takes place, no ongoing business of state and private life within which the isolation and impotence of the injured hero can be presented, in the way that Hieronimo's desperate, helpless isolation is conveyed. The revenge motive as a struggle for vindication of what is at the core of society is only formally present in *Titus Andronicus*.

The limitation of *The Spanish Tragedy* lies in the fact that we have to take Hieronimo's emotions, his total absorption in Horatio, as given, and attend to the beautifully clear way this bond interacts with circumstances that develop in the ongoing social and political reality. We cannot know what the deeper roots of Hieronimo's attachment to Horatio are; Kyd's art does not go down or back to the level at which so nearly monomaniacal a dependence could be understood. In *Titus Andronicus* the circumstances are nearly absurd, while motives are explored far beyond the capacity of the plot to socialize them. From the outset, all that is artistically realized is family piety and pride concentrated in the aged hero's egotism. Shakespeare multiplies the outrages done to Titus by the destruction of two sons, not just one, by the useless sacrifice of Titus's hand, and by creating in the raped and mutilated Lavinia an always present, walking version of Hieronimo's

From *The Whole Journey: Shakespeare's Power of Development* (Berkeley: University of California Press, 1986), 125–157. Copyright © 1986 The Regents of the University of California. Reprinted by permission.

murdered son, Horatio. The result is a father-daughter situation where total sympathy is demanded for an incestuous relationship expressed as suffering and violence. Those who commit the outrages are figures in whom sexual potency is fused with violence: Rape and Murder in the persons of Tamora's sons; Tamora herself, the overpowering Queen of the Goths; and her exotic lover, the Moor Aaron, to whom she bears a black child, and who is the arch-contriver of the villainies. The revenge is to turn nurturance into its opposite, to make "that strumpet, your unhallowed dam, / Like to the earth swallow her own increase" (5.2.190–91).

Shakespeare finds dramatic equivalents for social realities much earlier in his comedies and histories. We have seen that in *The Comedy of Errors* an important part of the success of the farce is the author's skill in creating as a setting for the play's confusions an ongoing, credible mercantile world. He brings the whole family constellation into play by framing the farcical action with the romantic separation and final reunion of his twins' parents. In *A Midsummer Night's Dream*, a comedy with a surprising number of similarities in materials and style to *Titus Andronicus*, we can see him finding effectual, native embodiment in folk custom for erotic symbolic action. The early tragedy is abortive in dramatizing eros engulfed in family ties; the comic action of *Dream*, shaped by native, outgoing communal festivity, provides a way of leading eros out of family bonds into nature and its larger rhythms. The series of festive comedies follows; *Romeo and Juliet* starts out as a festive comedy, to turn into a tragedy of young love destroyed by family ties.

In his English history plays, Shakespeare enters on a long discipline in presenting complex social and national action where family ties and motives are seen as crucial. Here the central concern, however, is the nation as a whole, beyond any one destiny. Even in the two histories that center on tragic careers, *Richard III* and *Richard II*, the effort is to dramatize national history moving through and beyond the disruptive fates of their protagonists, though as we have seen, the action of *Richard III* is not fully assimilated to the context of historical destiny the play announces as a way of understanding its own events. Without the experience of writing the histories, Shakespeare could not have written the major tragedies as we have them. For the tragedies (with the partial exception of *Othello*) are histories centered in a new, total way on their individual protagonists. In dramatizing the interplay of individual and national destiny in the English history plays, Shakespeare developed the concept of a hero whose personal fulfillment might also be the consummation of a whole society. In the major tragedies, such concretely felt heroic possibility contributes a crucial part of the substance of tragic loss. *Titus Andronicus* lacks this felt social possibility; without meaning to be only that, it is abortive domestic tragedy.

"O Sacred Receptacle of My Joys"

The young author of *Titus Andronicus* is self-consciously literary. Perhaps partly to show that he does not need to be beautified by borrowing the feathers of university-trained wits, he brings in more than fifty references to Roman literature and its handlings of Greek myth. But he does not succeed in projecting a Roman state, probably not because he could not have done so but because his focus is so intensely on family matters, exalted and outrageous. The first scene is before "the Senate house"; the "Tribunes and Senators" enter "aloft"; Titus is invested with a "palliament" as "candidatus"; his grave brother speaks with large gesture on behalf of "the people of Rome." But the action begins with a family fight between sons of the late Emperor, their factions on the verge of blows over the succession. Then comes solemn ceremonial action as Titus, who with his twenty-five sons has been the terror of the Goths in ten years of war, returns in triumph with the Queen of the Goths and her sons as prisoners. He brings the black coffin of two more sons who are to join twenty-one already buried in the tomb of the Andronici.

The tomb dominates the action and presumably the stage. As it is solemnly opened, Titus directs that his sons be laid in it by their brethren:

> O sacred receptacle of my joys,
> Sweet cell of virtue and nobility,
> How many sons hast thou of mine in store,
> That thou will never render to me more!
> (1.1.92–95)

To balance this, shall we say, "tenderness," the "proudest prisoner of the Goths," the captured Queen Tamora's oldest son, is dragged off for sacrifice "*Ad manes fratrum*" (96, 98), Titus blandly putting aside the passionate, eloquent protest of his mother. This sequence is an aggressive, aggrandizing ceremony, like Tamburlaine's ritual of white, red, and black tents on successive days of a siege, presented as though it were Roman custom, though it was in fact invented for the theater.

Like Lear's ceremony of dividing his territory in a contest of praise, the action progresses steadily, in the service of the egotism of a reverend, paternal protagonist, until it meets with an abrupt, devastating check. Where Lear is making the fatal mistake of giving up political authority, Titus, offered the empire, declines political power, also because of age, and makes the further error of choosing the former Emperor's cruel, weak son Saturninus to rule because he is the eldest. The sudden check in both plays comes over the issue of a daughter's independence. Saturnine, immediately after his election, announces that he will make Titus's daughter his empress. Titus at once agrees and his daughter complies; but Lavinia is already betrothed to Bassianus, the younger son of the former Emperor. When Bassianus steps forward to assert his right, Titus's noble brother, Marcus, and Titus's sons immediately support his claim to Lavinia. As they "convey her hence," the youngest son blocking the father's pursuit, Titus kills his son with a single blow: "What, villain boy, / Barr'st me my way in Rome?" (290–91). One could scarcely imagine a more complete exhibition of oblivious parental egotism buttressed with civic service, ceremony, and pride— nor a more rapid confrontation of it. The oldest son remonstrates, and is rebuked by Titus:

Nor thou, nor he, are any sons of mine,
My sons would never so dishonor me.
Traitor, restore Lavinia to the Emperor.
(294–96)

To cap it all, the new Emperor, who in asking for Lavinia seems to have tried to use his sudden new power merely to take away his brother's betrothed, no longer wants her:

Was none in Rome to make a stale
But Saturnine? Full well, Andronicus,
Agree these deeds with that proud brag of thine,
That saidst I begg'd the empire at thy hands.
(304–7)

Asserting his independence, he decides on the spot to marry the Queen of the Goths—a woman with grown sons, old enough to be his mother, as she makes clear in promising that she "will a handmaid be to his desires, / A loving nurse, a mother to his youth" (331–32). All the Andronici then plead with embittered Titus to let them bury in the sacred family tomb the son he has killed. His brother finally gains reluctant consent: "Well, bury him, and bury me the next" (386).

Up to this point, this opening scene is dramatically very well made, despite language that is frequently lame or merely ceremonial. Titus counting up sons dead in Rome's service is a male version of Volumnia counting up wounds on Coriolanus: "For two and twenty sons I never wept, / Because they died in honor's lofty bed" (3.1.10–11). His sons and the tomb provide for Titus a kind of family relationship that does without a wife as effectually as Volumnia's does without a husband. The tomb is in effect a womb of death—in which he takes deep satisfaction! The strongest poetry in the act is in these first lines addressed to the "sacred receptacle" and the liturgy of committal, which he speaks as the coffin is placed in it:

In peace and honor rest you here, my sons,
Rome's readiest champions, repose you here in rest,
Secure from worldly chances and mishaps!
Here lurks no treason, here no envy swells,
Here grow no damned drugs, here are no storms,
No noise, but silence and eternal sleep.
In peace and honor rest you here, my sons!
(1.1.150–56)

The only verbal remonstrance to the death-directed tendency in all this piety is given by Tamora as she pleads against the sacrifice of her son:

O, if to fight for king and commonweal
Were piety in thine, it is in these.
Andronicus, stain not thy tomb with blood!
Wilt thou draw near the nature of the gods?
Draw near them then in being merciful.
(114–18)

Titus overrules her eloquent and cogent protest with the blandness of an official explaining to a homeowner that the throughway must go through: "Patient yourself, madam, and pardon me" (121). It is clear that in a draft or earlier version the sacrifice was merely referred to as having happened; to dramatize it vividly enforces the motive for the Queen's later remorseless vengeance.[1]

It also opens up a perspective on Titus's ritual—"cruel, irreligious piety" (130), as she calls it—which the play completely fails to pursue. The ceremonial lynching of an enemy who might otherwise be a twin—an "enemy twin," as René Girard would phrase it—is necessary to maintain the crucial *difference* on which kinship ties are based.[2] The scapegoat ritual is necessary, the surviving sons must drag Alarbus off to "hew his limbs till they be clean consum'd" (129), to express potential hostility *among the Andronici*, which must be repressed if their total solidarity in family piety is to be maintained. But neither the opening scene nor the play reaches this latent motive—as *Macbeth* will later, where the violence of the heroic defender of Scottish society turns inward against its king.[3]

The opening scene abruptly leaves behind the division within the Andronici, by an exceedingly awkward transition. After all but Titus have joined in putting Mutius in the tomb, saying together, "He lives in fame, that died in virtue's cause," Marcus turns to Titus as if nothing had happened:

> *Marcus*: My lord, to step out of these dreary dumps,
>   How comes it that the subtile Queen of Goths
>   Is of a sudden thus advanc'd in Rome?
> *Titus*:   I know not, Marcus, but I know it is . . .
>   Is she not then beholding to the man
>   That brought her for this high good turn so far?
>   Yes, and will nobly him remunerate.
>   (390–94, 396–98)

---

[1] In the first quarto, Marcus's opening summary tells us that Titus has returned "bearing his valiant sons / In coffins from the field," and adds: "and at this day / To the monument of that Andronici / Done sacrifice of expiation, / And slain the noblest prisoner of the Goths." Sylvan Barnet comments in his edition (*The Signet Classic Shakespeare*): "These lines, omitted from the second and third quartos and from the Folio, are inconsistent with the ensuing action, in which Alarbus is sacrificed; perhaps Shakespeare neglected to cancel them in the manuscript after deciding to make Alarbus' execution part of the action."

[2] In *Violence and the Sacred*, tr. Patrick Gregory (Baltimore: Johns Hopkins University Press, 1977), René Girard argues that a society uses its ritual forms, most notably sacrifice and derivative rites that carry on the logic of sacrifice, to reconfirm the differences, within itself and between it and other societies, upon which it is founded. For the mythic mind, "Any violent effacement of differences, even if initially restricted to a single pair of twins, reaches out to destroy a whole society" (pp. 63–64). "Tragedy tends to restore violence to mythological themes. It in part fulfills the dire forebodings primitive men experience at the sight of twins. It spreads pollution abroad and multiplies the mirror images of violence. . . . If the tragic poet touches upon the violent reciprocity underlying all myths, it is because he perceives these myths in a context of weakening distinctions and growing violence. His work is inseparable, then, from a new sacrificial crisis" (p. 65).

[3] In "The Early Scenes of *Macbeth*: Preface to a New Interpretation," *ELH* 47 (1980): 1–31, Harry Berger, Jr., makes the telling point that this inward turning of violence is demanded by "the general psycho-structural dilemma of Scotland" as Shakespeare understands it in this play: " 'revolt against the king' is simply another name for Scottish policy, and the killing of the king may be a recurrent feature of the political process by which the kingdom periodically rids itself of the poison accumulating within it as a result of normal institutional functions" (pp. 30, 24).

Of course the queen, who remembers her dead son though Titus apparently does not, repays him, not nobly but in kind, thrice over and more. As the scene ends she smooths things over, dissuading her new, young husband from acting on his resentment against his younger brother, now married to Lavinia, and Titus. "Yield at entreats," she tells him in aside, "and then let me alone, / I'll find a day to massacre them all" (449–50). Her day comes immediately, in the extraordinary second act, during a hunt in a wood outside Rome, to which Titus has credulously invited the newly married couples.

Tamora and her illicit lover, Aaron the Moor, are now the villainous root of all evil, her two surviving sons the agents. By Aaron's contrivance and her encouraging presence, her sons Chiron and Demetrius stab the Emperor's brother and throw his body in a pit, then drag off Lavinia to rape her, cut out her tongue, and lop off her hands. Decoyed by Aaron, two of Titus's three remaining sons are brought to the edge of the pit; left alone, they fall into it in an inexplicable, half-mesmerized way. Then Aaron brings the Emperor to discover them in it and so convict them of the murder of his brother. Their execution follows in the next act. Titus pleads in vain for his sons and is tricked into sacrificing one of his hands, on the promise that they will be spared. When the mutilated Lavinia has been brought before grieving Titus by his brother Marcus, a messenger brings the heads of his two sons and "thy hand, in scorn to thee sent back" (3.1.237). Titus turns from remonstrance and complaint to ask "which way shall I find Revenge's cave?" (3.1.270).

One is tempted to dismiss all this bizarre violence as "mere melodrama." It is melodrama to the extent that the *particular circumstances and things done* are not motivated in such a way that we can understand them fully in social terms. A general motivation is provided in the injury done Tamora at the outset. But Aaron, the prime mover in these opening scenes, is a stock stage villain who tells us so with zest: "O how this villainy / Doth fat me with the very thoughts of it!" (3.1.202–3). We can understand what happens, however, when we see it as sexual potency conceived of only as violence and injury. On the one side, which the play from now on makes our side, there is family loyalty, centering on vertical relationship to Titus and, for a short time, on the chaste marriage of Lavinia and Bassianus, soon destroyed. On the other side, all the force is in illicit sexuality conceived and expressed as domination and violence. The sexually potent older couple forgo amorous delights proposed by Tamora to enjoy vicariously the sexual violence they abet in Demetrius and Chiron. Marcus and Titus, on their side, vicariously suffer the sexual violation of Lavinia.

The story Shakespeare seems to have dramatized sets up the situation in comprehensible historical and social terms as the infiltration of the Roman court by barbarians.[4] In the surviving eighteenth-century version of it, the opening chap-

---

[4]*The History of Titus Andronicus*, in *Sources*, vol. 6, pp. 34–44. "This work," Bullough judges, a chapbook "printed in mid-eighteenth century, probably goes back to the sixteenth-century original, . . . and may well represent a major source of the play" (p. 7).

ters describe how Titus and his twenty-five sons raised a siege of Rome, winning the gratitude of Emperor and people; how they fought continual wars and killed the King of the Goths. But "those barbarous People still encreasing in their Numbers," the Emperor, in order to make peace, marries the Queen of the Goths, with the condition that "in case he should die without Issue, her Sons might succeed in the Empire." Her hostility to Titus is *politically* motivated, for "he opposed this very much, as did many other; knowing, through the Emperor's weakness, that she being an imperious Woman, and of a hauty Spirit, would govern him as she pleased, and enslave the noble Empire to Strangers" (p. 38). She banishes Titus with the help of the Goths she puts in office, but when a rising of the people forces the recall of their "Deliverer," she must plot her revenge "more secretly" (p. 39).

Of course there may have been another version of the story, which Shakespeare used. But his omission of all the reasonable political motivation for the violence is consistent with his imaginative design. The prose tale has nothing about the rivalry of a dead Emperor's sons, no reference to a tomb of the Andronici (Titus is *saddened* by the loss of sons in battle), no marriage of a young, new-made Emperor to the older Queen. Lavinia there is betrothed to the son and natural heir of the Emperor by a former marriage, whom he dearly loves; the Queen arranges for her sons to kill him to protect their prospects of inheriting. The Queen in the story does have "a Moor as revengeful as herself." (When she gives birth to "a Blackmoor Child," she mollifies the aggrieved Emperor by "telling him it was conceived by Force of Imagination" [p. 39]!) The Moor and her two sons invite the Emperor's son to hunt in the forest, shoot him through the back with a poisoned arrow, and throw him into a deep pit dug for the purpose. Titus's sons soon join the murdered prince in the pit after Lavinia, "her heart misgiving her of some Treachery," has persuaded them to search for her husband (p. 40). The tricking of Titus out of his hand and sending it to him with his dead sons follows in the same brief chapter.

The rape and mutilation of Lavinia form a separate, subsequent episode. The Moor, observing that "she shunned all Company, retiring to Woods and Groves" to grieve the loss of her husband, informs "the Queen's two Sons, who, like the wicked Elders and the chaste Susanna, had long Time burned in Lust, yet knew her Virtues were proof against all Temptations, and therefore it could not be obtained but by Violence" (p. 42). There is no reference to Ovid or Philomela; the daughter reveals the identity of the ravishers without delay by writing with "a Wand between her Stumps" (p. 43). Titus's response is described, however, in a way that at once recalls Kyd's Hieronimo. Before he knows the villains' names, his "Grief . . . was so great, that no Pen can write or Words express; much ado they had to restrain him from doing Violence to himself" (p. 42). Afterwards he vowed revenge, "feigned himself distracted, and went raving about the City, shooting Arrows towards Heaven, as in Defiance, calling to Hell for Vengeance . . . ; and though his Friends required Justice of the Emperor against the Ravishers, yet could they have no Redress, he rather threatening them, if they insisted on it" (p. 43).

This description could suggest to a young dramatist that he had found material to match or outdo *The Spanish Tragedy*. *Titus Andronicus* dramatizes its
protagonist's responses as described here in the story, except that Titus does
not contemplate suicide, as Hieronimo does repeatedly, and there is no appeal
to the Emperor for justice. Perhaps because of the disciplined military character of Shakespeare's injured old man he could not be shown in the Cave of
Despair, toying with its dagger and noose; in any case, why reduplicate Kyd?
The void of legitimate political power, established at the outset by choosing to
open with sibling rivalry for the throne, excluded the possibility of dramatizing
appeals to a ruler for justice such as we get in "Justice, O justice for
Hieronimo," shouted out from the sidelines of the royal presence. Titus can
only shoot his arrows to Jove and Mars. But Shakespeare wholeheartedly takes
up the challenge to dramatize "grief so great, that no Pen can write or Words
express."

Marcus:	O brother, speak with possibility,
	And do not break into these deep extremes.
Titus:	Is not my sorrow deep, having no bottom?
	Then be my passions bottomless with them!
Marcus:	But yet let reason govern thy lament.
Titus:	If there were reason for these miseries,
	Then into limits could I bind my woes:
	When heaven doth weep, doth not the earth o'erflow?
	If the winds rage, doth not the sea wax mad,
	Threat'ning the welkin with his big-swoll'n face?
	And wilt thou have a reason for this coil?
	I am the sea; hark how her sighs doth blow!
	She is the weeping welkin, I the earth.

                                                        (3.1.214–26)

There is intense interest, as with Kyd, in turning passive suffering into active pressure of language on its limits as an agency through which the self negotiates relationship to the world. Shakespeare is more conscious of the process, as witness
Marcus's remonstrances here. The moderate brother makes a similar comment in
the next scene, where Titus mangles a dead fly after Marcus has suggested that,
being black, it is like black Aaron:

Titus:	Give me thy knife, I will insult on him,
	Flattering myself as if it were the Moor, . . .
	There's for thyself, and that's for Tamora.
	Ah, sirrah!
	Yet I think we are not brought so low,
	But that between us we can kill a fly
	That comes in likeness of a coal-black Moor.
Marcus:	Alas, poor man, grief hath so wrought on him,
	He takes false shadows for true substances.

                                                        (3.2.71–72, 74–80)

The self-conscious interest in displaced, projected images is like that of *A Midsummer Night's Dream*. Theseus's famous skeptical discussion of the process includes "the lunatic" as well as "the lover and the poet" among those whose "shaping fantasies . . . apprehend / More than cool reason ever comprehends" (5.1.5–6). Titus's distraction does not actually reach the point of lunacy—it is more under the control of "as if" than Hieronimo's in its deep extremes: "as if it were the Moor." Theseus's madman "sees more devils than vast hell can hold" (5.1.9). Titus does not need to imagine devils, provided as he is with Tamora and the Moor to stab at. *Titus Andronicus* makes subjective projection by its hero less necessary (the rationalist perspective of the whole is reflected in Aaron's saying "if there be devils, would I were a devil" [5.1.147]). But the interest in the process of taking fiction for fact and fact for fiction is carried to an extreme in Tamora's final charade, when she relies on Titus's lunacy to make him believe she is in fact "Revenge, sent from below / To join with him and right his heinous wrongs" (5.2.3–4). Titus is not taken in but pretends to be, reversing the way Kyd's finale works: where Hieronimo turns what is taken for playacting into actual killing of the villain, here the villains' playacting is seen through and made the means for actually trapping them. Tamora disguised as Revenge, and her two sons got up as Murder and Rapine, are utterly implausible, as Titus makes clear in sardonically pretending to be taken in:

> Good Lord, how like the Empress' sons they are!
> And you, the Empress! but we worldly men
> Have miserable, mad, mistaking eyes.
> (5.2.64–66)

It is great fun to take off into the wild blue yonder of literalized allegory, a fitting liberation of the previous pressure of Titus's invention trying to deal with the actual horror. It permits wit to have free play, however crude. When Tamora, incredibly credulous, leaves her allegorized sons behind, promising to return for a banquet of reconciliation, Titus can keep up the joke as his friends emerge to help him:

> *Titus*: Know you these two?
> *Publius*: The Empress' sons I take them, Chiron, and Demetrius.
> *Titus*: Fie, Publius, fie, thou art too much deceiv'd.
> The one is Murder, and Rape is the other's name.
> And therefore bind them, gentle Publius. . . .
> Oft have you heard me wish for such an hour,
> And now I find it, therefore bind them sure,
> And stop their mouths if they begin to cry. [*Exit.*]
> *Chiron*: Villains, forbear, we are the Empress' sons. . . .
> *Enter Titus Andronicus with a knife and Lavinia with a basin.*
> (5.2.153–57, 159–62, 165s.d.)

In the source, there is of course no imaginative charade: the sons are surprised in an ambush while hunting in the woods, "and binding them to a Tree, . . .

Andronicus cut their Throats whilst Lavinia, by his Command, held a Bowl between her Stumps to receive the Blood."[5]

"And Worse Than Progne I Will Be Reveng'd"

But what *is* the "reason for this coil"? In dropping all the political and dynastic considerations in the source, Shakespeare does without the sort of complex inter-penetration of social with family and sexual action which he could control so marvelously later. Instead he shapes his material in symbolic, mythopoeic ways that ask for understanding, on the deeper levels, *only* in poetic or symbolic terms. Titus has a long speech of recapitulation and justification as he prepares to kill Tamora's sons:

> You know your mother means to feast with me. . . .
> Hark, villains, I will grind your bones to dust,
> And with your blood and it I'll make a paste,
> And of the paste a coffin I will rear,
> And make two pasties of your shameful heads,
> And bid that strumpet, your unhallowed dam,
> Like to the earth swallow her own increase.
> This is the feast that I have bid her to,
> And this the banket she shall surfeit on,
> For worse than Philomel you us'd my daughter,
> And worse than Progne I will be reveng'd.
> (5.2.184, 186–95)

Titus's strongest line here echoes with Sonnet 19: "And make the earth devour her own sweet brood." Although there are constant references in the play to Ovid's Philomel and Procne and their revenge on Tereus, with a scene, on the whole quite effective, in which Lavinia dumbly takes up "Ovid's *Metamorphosis*" and "tosseth" it until she finds "the tragic tale" (4.1.41, 47), the outrageous revenge in the play is directed primarily at *maternal* sexuality, conceived and represented symbolically as a ruthless, devouring power.

In Ovid we have the revenge of two women against the ruthless *male* violation of femininity. Procne's decision to kill her son is not meditated but comes suddenly as she is thinking of other revenges: burning Tereus's palace with him in it, pulling out his tongue, putting out his eyes, castrating him:

> While *Progne* hereunto
> Did set hir minde, came *Itys* in, who taught hir what to doe.
> She staring on him cruelly, said, Ah, how like thou art
> Thy wicked father.[6]

The ensuing struggle between her maternal feeling and her overwhelming sense

---

[5] *Sources*, vol. 6, p. 43.
[6] Golding's translation, Bk. VI, lines 785–88; *Sources*, vol. 6, p. 56.

of outrage is very moving—and appalling. Looking right at the pleading child, she stabs him, Philomel cuts his throat, and the two women set about the women's work of preparing a solemn ritual meal for husband and wife alone together. The tale in Ovid is associated with women's ritual protest in the Bacchic rites. Informed of the outrage to her sister by the secret woven message, Procne frees her while running wild in the woods in animal disguise. The meal itself has a terrible immediacy in Ovid: Philomel reveals the boy's whereabouts by throwing Itys's bloody head in his father's face; Tereus screams, retches to cast his bowels out, seizes his sword, and pursues the women, only to find them turning into birds.

Shakespeare's handling of the final meal is ceremonial and theatrical: "Trumpets sounding, enter Titus like a cook, placing the dishes" (5.3.25s.d.), sets up the situation almost as a joke. The horror of the meal as it takes place is not in verbal focus, for as soon as Tamora has tasted the food, Titus kills Lavinia, invoking the precedent of Virginius; Tamora has not time to respond after she is told that she has fed on her sons, for Titus immediately kills her, and is killed in turn by Saturninus, and he by Titus's son Lucius. Not only does Titus, as vindictive father, destroy the sexually voracious, alien mother figure in a reversal of the sexual roles of the Philomel story; along with his extroverted revenge against Tamora, his introverted erotic investment in his disfigured daughter reaches a climax when he destroys Lavinia, whose care and feeding he has taken over since her rape and mutilation:

> Die, die, Lavinia, and thy shame with thee,
> And with thy shame thy father's sorrow die!
> (5.3.46–47)

The masculine tie to the feminine as a potential source of vulnerability is as vital to the play as is masculine fear and violence toward woman as aggressor.

What is at work in this strange action becomes clearer if, following the talion logic backwards, we consider the symbolic content of the injuries done to Titus and his family. Shakespeare concentrates in the second act what is strung out in separate episodes in the source story, to make one sustained sequence of horrors in the woods, around the pit as a central symbol. The Moor, who has been only a silent presence in Act 1, opens Act 2 with a triumphant salute to Tamora's elevation to power, and to his power through her and over her.

> Then, Aaron, arm thy heart, and fit thy thoughts,
> To mount aloft with thy imperial mistress,
> And mount her pitch, whom thou in triumph long
> Hast prisoner held, fett'red in amorous chains,
> And faster bound to Aaron's charming eyes
> Than is Prometheus tied to Caucasus.
> (2.1.12–17)

The assumption of these lines, that sexual potency is a cruel, dominating power, is to be acted out in what follows. Aaron goes on to relish the prospect that he will "wanton with this queen" while she in turn "will charm Rome's Saturnine, / And see his shipwrack and his commonweal's" (2.1.21, 23–24). The boy Emperor has married a woman not only old enough to be his mother, but one who comes equipped with a ruthless phallic lover intent with her on the young man's destruction. The play handles the infiltration of the Goths entirely in these sexual-family terms, with no suggestion of other barbarian qualities in them, and nothing of the "Roman" in Rome but military virtue and family loyalty.

Next in the wood, "Enter Chiron and Demetrius braving" (2.1.25s.d.). What they are braving about is which brother should have Lavinia—Shakespeare has moved their lusting after her up from the period after her husband's death in the story version to the morning after her wedding and made it over into a second dramatization of sibling rivalry! It is a very homey exchange:

Chiron:	Demetrius, thou dost overween in all, . . .
	'Tis not the difference of a year or two . . .
	I am as able and as fit as thou
	To serve, and to deserve my mistress' grace. . . .
Demetrius:	Why, boy, although our mother, unadvis'd,
	Gave you a dancing-rapier by your side.
	Are you so desperate grown to threat your friends?

They draw.
(2.1.29, 31, 33–34, 38–39)

Aaron steps forward, parts them, and brings up the little problem of how they plan to obtain Lavinia, to which Demetrius answers first in Richard III's machismo style, then in the idiom of *A Hundred Merry Tales!*

She is a woman, therefore may be woo'd,
She is a woman, therefore may be won,
She is Lavinia, therefore must be lov'd.
What, man, more water glideth by the mill
Than wots the miller of, and easy it is
Of a cut loaf to steal a shive. . . .
What, hast not thou full often strook a doe,
And borne her cleanly by the keeper's nose?
(82–87, 93–94)

This is the bragging talk of young men loitering about the village. Aaron picks it up as he intervenes, "Why then it seems a certain snatch or so / Would serve your turns" (95–96). He then moves up to greater intensity, using the doe image as he goes through his program for them during the coming hunt. The forest is built up by contrast with the court as a place "Fitted by kind for rape and villainy. / Single you thither then this dainty doe" (116–17).

There speak, and strike, brave boys, and take your turns, . . .
And revel in Lavinia's treasury.
(129, 131)

The young men's response almost ludicrously summarizes the assumption that—beyond poaching—sexual outrage proves manhood: "Thy counsel, lad, smells of no cowardice," says Chiron. The response of his older brother, Demetrius, is elevated into Senecan Latin: "Sit fas aut nefas, . . . Per Stygia, per manes vehor" (132–33, 135).[7]

The hunt in the woods opens with "a noise with hounds and horns" (2.2.o.s.d.) and poetry evoking the same dawn mood that ends the night's perplexities in *A Midsummer Night's Dream*. Hopeful, loyal Titus, urging his sons to "attend the Emperor's person carefully" (2.2.8), directs the huntsmen:

> Uncouple here and let us make a bay,
> And wake the Emperor and his lovely bride.
> (3–4)

In the comedy, Theseus, about to waken the lovers, says "Uncouple . . . / And mark the musical confusion / Of hounds and echo in conjunction" (*MND* 4.1.107, 110–11).[8] Tamora in the next scene, where she and Aaron are alone, tries to lead him to amorous delights "whilst the babbling echo mocks the hounds / . . . As if a double hunt were heard at once" (2.3.17, 19). She cites the example of "the wand'ring prince and Dido . . . curtain'd with a counsel-keeping cave" (22, 24). But enclosure will be different in this forest. Aaron brings her back to business:

> Madam, though Venus govern your desires,
> Saturn is dominator over mine:
> What signifies my deadly-standing eye. . . ?[9]
> (30–32)

The serious business of course is to do in the Andronici and Bassianus: Aaron has already hidden a bag of gold and written a letter to incriminate Titus's sons. But this elaborately and emphatically villainous plotting is really irrelevant to the actual dramatic development; what we watch is sexuality as violence. Bassianus and Lavinia, coming up as the Moor leaves Tamora, taunt her in an exchange that moves through Diana and Actaeon's horns to

> Under your patience, gentle Emperess,
> 'Tis thought you have a goodly gift in horning,
> And to be doubted that your Moor and you
> Are singled forth to try experiments. . . .
> *Bassianus*: The King my brother shall have note of this.
> (66–69, 85)

---

[7]Later on, Chiron recognizes verses in Latin sent as a veiled threat by Titus: "O, 'tis a verse of Horace, I know it well, / I read it in the grammar long ago" (4.2.22–23). Though the scene is immature art concerned with immaturity, it uses a remarkable range of social experience as well as style, with a sure sense of underlying attitudes. The sexual initiation Aaron is arranging for the boys, even though they have the intelligence and sensibility of village toughs, does involve breaking through inhibiting moral restraints, plunging through repressive ghosts and hellish anxieties.

[8]See also Howard Baker's observation that the poetry of the hunting scenes in *Titus* recalls the poetry of hunting in "Venus and Adonis," in *Induction to Tragedy* (Baton Rouge: Louisiana State University Press, 1939), pp. 135–37.

[9]"Faced with the underlying danger of Tamora's seductive sexuality, Aaron," David Willbern writes, "rejects her proposition while simultaneously affirming his own threatened phallic potency." "Rape and Revenge in *Titus Andronicus*," *English Literary Renaissance* 8 (Spring 1978): 166.

The chaste couple's self-righteousness is met by the entrance of Tamora's sons, for whom she concocts a vivid tale: "These two have 'ticed me hither to this place: / A barren detested vale you see it is" (92–93). The dreadful pit is first described as she develops a tall story of threats by Bassianus and Lavinia (in the play nobody digs the pit—it is just there):

> And when they show'd me this abhorred pit,
> They told me, here, at dead time of the night,
> A thousand fiends, a thousand hissing snakes,
> Ten thousand swelling toads, as many urchins,
> Would make such fearful and confused cries,
> As any mortal body hearing it
> Should straight fall mad, or else die suddenly.
>   (98–104)

Here, she says, they planned to bind her to a "dismal yew" to die, and called her "foul adulteress, / Lascivious Goth . . . / Revenge it, as you love your mother's life" (107, 109–10, 114). Demetrius and Chiron at once stab Bassianus: "This is a witness that I am thy son," says the elder, and the younger again announces that he is grown up, with "And this for me, struck home to show my strength" (116–17). As they prepare to drag Lavinia off despite her anguished pleas, Tamora backs them all the way. She will not consider saving another woman's honor by "a charitable murder," as Lavinia begs: "So should I rob my sweet sons of their fee. / No, let them satisfice their lust on thee" (179–80).

The two sons of Titus are next led on by Aaron and left at the brink of the pit. While the bad boys are raping Lavinia offstage, the good boys, onstage, are swallowed up. Their fall into the pit is ludicrous, viewed with detachment; but the author is working hard to keep it tragical:

> *Quintus*:   What, art thou fallen? What subtile hole is this,
>   Whose mouth is covered with rude-growing briers,
>   Upon whose leaves are drops of new-shed blood
>   As fresh as morning dew distill'd on flowers?
>   A very fatal place it seems to me.
>   (198–202)

The last line just asks, out of context, for the liberation of burlesque, such as we get in the clown's play of Pyramus and Thisbe: "I kiss the wall's hole / Not your lips at all" (*MND* 5.1.201). But there can be no such fun with the "subtile hole" in *Titus Andronicus*. Martius, down in it, finds Bassianus "like to a slaughtered lamb," visible by the light of his precious ring: "So pale did shine the moon on Pyramus, / When he by night lay bath'd in maiden blood" (223, 231–32). Quintus, "surprised with an uncouth fear," dares not look down: "ne'er till now / Was I a child to fear I know not what" (211, 220–21). Martius pleads that his brother help him "Out of this fell devouring receptacle, / As hateful as Cocytus' misty mouth."

> *Quintus*:   Reach me thy hand, that I may help thee out,
>   Or wanting strength to do thee so much good,

> I may be pluck'd into the swallowing womb
> Of this deep pit—
>
> (235–40)

which is exactly what happens, just in time for Aaron to arrive with the Emperor.

Now it obviously needs no Freud to tell Shakespeare what this hole is.[10] The difficulty is with the dramatic mode in which he is working. In a playful dramatic fantasy there would be no difficulty in developing such a symbol. In religious drama there was Hell's Mouth, which Marlowe could use effectively at the end of *Dr. Faustus*. Shakespeare here is developing a symbolism that *might* be religious, but in resolutely non-Christian terms (there is I think no Christian expression in the whole play); he is sticking strictly to a symbolism he can use ad hoc to express family and sexual relationships. Such symbolism in the mature tragedies, where it is placed in a fabric of familial and social action and characters, is comprehensible, whether or not we stop over its physiological reference. Lear in his mad alienation can be explicit:

> Down from the waist they are Centaurs,
> Though women all above;
> But to the girdle do the gods inherit,
> Beneath is all the fiends': there's hell, there's darkness,
> There is the sulphurous pit—
>
> (4.6.124–28)

and then go on in the next breath to recognize that his vision is unwholesome fantasy: "Give me an ounce of civet; good apothecary, / Sweeten my imagination" (130–31).

It is the coherence of such symbolism as the pit, albeit in this isolated, unaccounted-for way, which makes *Titus Andronicus* something besides melodrama—indeed the work of genius, albeit an artistic failure to the taste of later generations. It also explains, I think, why the play is not only unsuccessful but so painful that most criticism has turned a blind eye to much of its content. C. B. Young, for example, commenting on Ravenscroft's version (designed to improve what its redactor called "rather a heap of Rubbish than a Structure") found that one of the "small improvements" the late Restoration rendition did make was that in it, Quintus and Martius, "instead of senselessly tumbling into the pit, . . . are found gazing into it after having been decoyed into the spot more naturally."[11] Shakespeare, however, has *very* firm structure motivating that fall symbolically; but it is too unmediated and so too troubling for Young to recognize it. From the distance of the celibate friar's meditation in *Romeo and Juliet*, the key structural idea can be comfortably summarized: "The earth that's nature's mother is her

---

[10]"Here is Freud's plenty," as David Willbern proclaims in response to Tamora's account of the pit, which will "assume its central and over-determined symbolic significance as vagina, womb, tomb, and mouth, and all those 'snakes' and 'urchins' (hedgehogs or goblins) and 'swelling toads' may plausibly be imagined as grotesquely distorted phallic threats." "Rape and Revenge," p. 169.

[11]C. B. Young, "The Stage History of *Titus Andronicus*," in Cambridge ed., ed. J. Dover Wilson (Cambridge: Cambridge University Press, 1948), p. lxvii.

tomb; / What is her burying grave, that is her womb" (2.3.9–10). In *Titus,* the all-too-literal tomb-womb of Act 1 is matched by the devouring womb-tomb of Act 2 and the turning of the tables as Tamora devours her own sons in Act 5.

Our difficulties with such an episode as this need to be considered in the light of the fact that *Titus Andronicus* was a successful play in its time, as witnessed by the three quartos, 1594, 1600, 1611, and by Jonson's Induction to *Bartholomew Fair* (1614), which pairs *Titus* with *The Spanish Tragedy* as plays whose continued popularity demonstrated the irksome constancy of judgment among unsophisticated playgoers. The fact that the play has never been successful since, until our own violent and symbolically minded time, suggests that its success depended on habits of mind or sensibility that did not survive. Shakespeare in this case was clearly writing for an age, not for all time. The crucial difference is not that Elizabethans could tolerate more physical violence than later ages, though that must be a factor. There is just as much violence enacted on the stage in *Lear,* say, as in *Titus.* What we can infer from *Titus,* I think, is a greater habituation to seeing symbolic meaning in violence—or better, to feeling such meaning, consciously or not. Probably many of the play's first enthusiastic spectators came to demand more of the theater as it became more sophisticated; certainly those in later audiences who would still "swear *Ieronimo,* or *Andronicus,* are the best plays" drew Jonson's scorn. In Shakespeare's later work, the human meaning in social action of such violence is more clearly and compellingly conveyed, so that we accept it as we cannot easily accept the regressive erotic brutality in *Titus.*

Acceptance is partly a matter of aesthetic distance, partly the degree of intensity of the magnetic field of meaning established around the violence. The action that begins with Lavinia's entrance, taunted by the Empress's sons, "her hands cut off, and her tongue cut out, and ravish'd" (2.4.o.s.d.), can be contemplated comfortably from the distance of Theseus's poetry about paternal power in the opening of *A Midsummer Night's Dream*:

> What say you, Hermia? Be advis'd, fair maid.
> To you your father should be as a god;
> One that compos'd your beauties; yea, and one
> To whom you are but as a form in wax,
> By him imprinted, and within his power,
> To leave the figure, or disfigure it.
>
> (1.1.46–51)

There is a frisson for us here, even though "disfigure" is a witty pun, suggesting that a daughter is a trope, as well as a face and a bodily shape. Of course in the comedy the penalty of "the sharp Athenian law" is promptly mitigated from death to entering a nunnery. And in the end—when by the night's accidents in the wood Demetrius has returned to his first love, Helena—the stubborn insistence of Hermia's father on "my consent that she should be your wife" is simply overruled by Theseus. The whole play, meanwhile, has been about imaginative transformations. Helena has wished at the outset that she could be "translated" into Hermia (and in effect she is); Bottom has been "translated" into an ass; and when Snout comes to "disfigure, or to present," Wall, Wall is disfigured back into Snout. *A Midsummer Night's Dream* puts such imaginative process into particularly conscious focus.

Rosalie Colie, in *Shakespeare's Living Art,* shows how Shakespeare in his most successful works repeatedly translates metaphors back into enactment as events. She is particularly concerned with his use of traditional tropes: in *Romeo and Juliet* "the spectacular oppositions of the petrarchan rhetoric have been enlarged into plot, as well as into the emotional and social structure of the play." In her studies of that play, and notably also of *Othello* and *Antony and Cleopatra,* she shows how Shakespeare's process of "unmetaphoring" (an unhappily negative term) leads to the finding or refinding of relationships between language and experience, the "sinking of the conventions back into what, he somehow persuades us, is 'reality.' "[12] The pit in *Titus Andronicus* is a case where the common topos of womb and tomb (prominent of course in Christian iconography) does not persuade us that we are encountering reality. One can contrast Romeo's use of it as he forces his way into the tomb, the "womb of death" (5.3.45), of the Capulets.

Lavinia is an "unmetaphored" version of Theseus's trope, a daughter "disfigured" physically. The disfigurement is carried out, of course, not by the father who "composed her beauties," but by enemies, young brutes, and behind them, an overpowering, hostile maternal force. So Titus is put in a situation of emotional isolation with Lavinia in which he can experience her ravishment through grief and protest. The properly poetic and dramatic powers by which Shakespeare develops this situation are astonishing; in the enjoyment of them he can envisage extreme human and inhuman possibilities with a curious equanimity.

A great deal of Shakespeare's earliest work, when it deals with tragic material— the death of Adonis or the rape of Lucrece, or the outrages of *Titus Andronicus*— looks open-eyed at things from which inhibition would ordinarily flinch. In the different mode of his early histories, again we have situations worked up to poetic or rhetorical extremes with, one feels, a workmanlike detachment. Steadily increasing control of the overall design proves to be at work as we get to know these earliest productions, but developing from behind the surfaces rather than announcing itself with clear signposts, as it does later. In the histories there are thematic preoccupations, especially in the area of sexuality and family, for which he is only gradually finding public forms: *Richard III,* as we have seen, is a breakthrough. In the narrative poems he is freer, and to put it mildly, the subjects he chooses and the way he handles them are surprising. He is doing things of his own to traditional subjects and forms, and much of his autonomous artistic satisfaction must have been in that.

He shares with Ovid this equanimity in the enjoyment of active imaginative power. It is as though anything can be contemplated so long as it is being "translated" imaginatively into something else. Frequently in *Titus* the action halts as though it turned into a dumb show while the poetry elaborates it. As Stephen

[12]Rosalie Colie, *Shakespeare's Living Art* (Princeton: Princeton University Press, 1974), p. 145.

Lacey has shown, the poetry of *Titus Andronicus* frequently moves in this way out
from or around a static spectacle.[13] After Demetrius and Chiron have left Lavinia,
with cruel, crude taunts at her helplessness without tongue or hands, her uncle
Marcus comes on and for forty-seven lines gives voice to what is literally a dumb
show:

> Speak, gentle niece: what stern ungentle hands
> Hath lopp'd and hew'd, and made thy body bare
> Of her two branches, those sweet ornaments,
> Whose circling shadows kings have sought to sleep in,
> And might not gain so great a happiness
> As half thy love? Why dost not speak to me?
> Alas, a crimson river of warm blood,
> Like to a bubbling fountain stirred with wind,
> Doth rise and fall between thy rosed lips,
> Coming and going with thy honey breath.
>
> (2.4.16–25)

What is so troubling here is not only the violence but the loveliness presented with
it, the attraction along with revulsion, which is explicitly sexual attraction in the
image of the lost hands as "circling shadows kings have sought to sleep in," and
sexual also in a subliminal way in the imagery of the mouth as a rising and falling
fountain of warm blood.

In a similar but more explicit passage in *Venus and Adonis,* the shocking sight
of "the wide wound that the boar had trench'd / In his soft flank" (1052–53) is dealt
with at greater length and with more explicitly fanciful elaboration. At first,
Venus's eyes withdraw altogether, like the "tender horns" of a snail shrinking
"backward in his shelly cave with pain": "So at his bloody view her eyes are fled /
Into the deep-dark cabins of her head" (1033–34, 1037–38). The narrative mode
here permits a wonderfully flexible, compassionate control of aesthetic distance,
control of the *reception* of violence, as in this celebrated stanza where we feel for
Venus in feeling with the delicate vulnerability of the snail, "Long after fearing to
creep forth again" (1036). The narrative mode also permits imaginative suggestions to be left hanging in the neutrality of hypothesis, envisaged without being
asserted. So with Venus's fanciful development of the idea that, since wild creatures—lion, tiger, and wolf—all loved Adonis, the boar's violence was actually
intended as love:

> "But this foul, grim, and urchin-snouted boar,
> Whose downward eye still looketh for a grave,
> Ne'er saw the beauteous livery that he wore—
> Witness the entertainment that he gave.
>   If he did see his face, why then I know
>   He thought to kiss him, and hath kill'd him so.

[13]Stephen Wallace Lacey, "Structures of Awareness in Dante and Shakespeare" (Ph.D. diss., State
University of New York at Buffalo, 1972).

" 'Tis true, 'tis true, thus was Adonis slain:
He ran upon the boar with his sharp spear,
Who did not whet his teeth at him again,
But by a kiss thought to persuade him there;
    And nousling in his flank, the loving swine
    Sheath'd unaware the tusk in his soft groin."
                        (1105–16)

The tentativeness of Venus, trying on one conceit after another, permits the poet to present sexual fantasy shadowed by his poem—that such a late-maturing youth as Adonis is open to homosexual rape—without falsifying its status as fantasy. First the boar is entirely brutal, oblivious, and phallic, with his urchin snout and downward eye. Then his response is imagined as loving: he tries to dissuade Adonis with a kiss, but kills him because nature "pricked [him] out" with "one thing to [the] purpose nothing" (Sonnet 20). Then the aggressive goddess acknowledges: "Had I been tooth'd like him, I must confess, / With kissing him I should have kill'd him first" (1117–18). Yet these disturbing possibilities are presented in a way that is basically playful. A tidy couplet ends the excursus by describing an untidy fall that "stains her face with his congealed blood" (1122), and the poem is ready for another elaboration of the new static situation.

By comparison with the flexibility and control in such a passage, one feels that in *Titus* the dramatic medium, incompletely mastered, is getting in the way; or to put it the other way round, that Shakespeare in *Titus* is using this kind of aria di bravura in a way inappropriate to the dramatic mode. But *we* feel this difficulty to a degree that the original audiences well may not have felt it. The enthusiasm for elaborate complaints, or challenges, or vaunts, taking off from a static situation that demands expression, was part of the general excitement in the new theater for the new verse medium and for set speeches doing fine things. The Elizabethan audience was ready to listen to things like Hieronimo's "O eyes, no eyes, but fountains full of tears," or Marcus's leisurely description of Lavinia's missing hands. The dramatist had room for such rhetorical elaboration and for properly poetic development. The whole process is accepted as artificial, in a positive sense. In transforming disfigured Lavinia by figures or tropes, the play is taking imaginative action of the same kind that is eventually pressed beyond credibility altogether in Tamora's figuring herself and her sons as Revenge, Murder, and Rape, leaving Titus the opportunity to disfigure the two murderous rapists back into themselves, and then into a meat pie!

Titus Andronicus makes a special claim for such poetic elaboration of its materials by its emphatic use of classical precedents, especially Ovid.[14] Eugene Waith has suggested that its poetic development of horror has deep affinities to Ovid's imaginative transformations.[15] Violence, in Ovid, "is an emblem of the transformation," which "is itself transformed in the process into an object of interested but

---

[14]Howard Baker sets *Titus Andronicus* in a medieval and Renaissance English tradition of adapting Ovid in his *Induction to Tragedy*, pp. 121–26.

[15]Eugene Waith, "The Metamorphosis of Violence in *Titus Andronicus*," *Shakespeare Survey* 10 (1957): 39–49.

somewhat detached contemplation" (p. 43). Waith compares Marcus's description of Lavinia, "which has proved to be the most unpalatable passage in the play," to Ovid's descriptions of violence by extended comparisons: "In every case the visual image is exact and thus the horror more vivid, yet at the same time our minds are turned away from the individual as a whole to a minute contemplation of what has happened to one part of his body" (pp. 47, 42). A process of "abstracting and generalizing" eclipses the individuality of the body subjected to the violence, and "the suffering becomes an object of contemplation" (p. 47). The difficulty, as Waith sees it, is that this technique of description "is a narrative rather than a dramatic device." The change into a bird or a beast comes after "the unendurable emotional state robs the character of his humanity and the story ends, so to speak, with a point of exclamation" (p. 47). Although the special emphasis in *Titus* on situations beyond human endurance asks for "the full Ovidian treatment, . . . the final transformation cannot take place. We have the description which almost transforms Lavinia, but in the presence of live actors the poetry cannot perform the necessary magic. The action frustrates, rather than re-enforces, the operation of the poetry" (pp. 47–48).[16]

"Thou Map of Woe"

Waith's beautiful essay focuses on the play's formal virtues and problems. But the play's specific erotic content is also a main reason for its difficulty in going on from the symbolic action of the poetry. Violence, after all, is what sexuality turns into when it cannot go on, cannot find properly sexual consummation. As Ovid abundantly testifies, violence is sexuality metamorphosed. Marcus's description of Lavinia repeatedly emphasizes that she has been deprived, not simply of the capacity to communicate the identity of her ravishers, but of means of sexual expression by the use of the hands:

> O, had the monster seen those lily hands
> Tremble like aspen leaves upon a lute,
> And make the silken strings delight to kiss them.
> (2.4.44–46)

A similar image expresses the diffused eros of Cleopatra's barge:

> the silken tackle   ⋆
> Swell with the touches of those flower-soft hands,
> That yarely frame the office.
> (*Ant.* 2.2.209–11)

[16]Waith goes on to suggest that to attempt the kind of thing Shakespeare was after in *Titus Andronicus* was in line with sixteenth-century critics' emphasis on "admiration" as the proper effect of tragedy, in the sense of "wonder" or "astonishment." "Marlowe and Chapman each developed what might be called a rhetoric of admiration; one thinks of Marlowe's 'high astounding terms.'" From this perspective, "*Titus Andronicus* is Shakespeare's contribution to a special tragic mode. . . . The hero, in this respect like Tamburlaine or Bussy D'Ambois, is almost beyond praise or blame, an object of admiration" (p. 48).

When Marcus finally brings Lavinia to her father, Titus's first response is a rhapsody about her lost hands—and his hands:

> Speak, Lavinia, what accursed hand
> Hath made thee handless in thy father's sight? . . .
> Give me a sword, I'll chop off my hands too,
> For they have fought for Rome, and all in vain;
> And they have nurs'd this woe, in feeding life;
> In bootless prayer have they been held up,
> And they have serv'd me to effectless use.
> Now all the service I require of them
> Is that the one will help to cut the other.
>   (3.1.66–67, 72–78)

When Lucius asks, "Speak, gentle sister, who hath mart'red thee?" Marcus again describes her mouth, its tongue ripped out by hands as yet unknown to Titus's family:

> O, that delightful engine of her thoughts,
> That blabb'd them with such pleasing eloquence,
> Is torn from forth that pretty hollow cage,
> Where like a sweet melodious bird it sung
> Sweet varied notes, enchanting every ear!
>   (81–86)

David Willbern, writing from a rigorously psychoanalytic vantage point, observes that symbolically Lavinia's mouth is an upward displacement of the female genitals.[17] It is perhaps significant that the full descriptions of the mouth, here and later, are given to Marcus rather than to Titus.

It is striking that Titus anticipates, as a desperate wish, the cutting off of his hand, which follows, initiated by Aaron! Here it expresses a wish to identify with Lavinia, along with the feeling that all the dutiful things he has done with his hands have been ill rewarded. Perhaps subliminally there is also a wish for punishment of sexual misuse of the hands; a psychoanalytic commonplace is the link of the hand with guilt about masturbation associated with Oedipal fantasies centering on the mother. The scene is to end—after the heads of his sons have been presented to Titus, with his severed hand, sacrificed in the promise of saving them—in the almost intolerable grotesquery of

> Come, brother, take a head,
> And in this hand the other will I bear;
> And, Lavinia, thou shalt be employ'd [in these arms];[18]
> Bear thou my hand, sweet wench, between thy teeth.
>   (279–82)

---

[17]"Rape and Revenge in *Titus Andronicus*," pp. 171–72.

[18]The bracketed words are omitted by Evans in the *Riverside* text. The quartos read "in these Armes"; the Folio "in these things." Either version gives the line one foot too many; Dover Wilson omits the last word and substitutes "this" for "these" in the Cambridge edition. He explains that Aldis Wright "conjectured that 'the author, or some other corrector, to soften what must have been ludicrous

To put his severed hand in her mouth could be the enactment, in a dumb-show way, of sexual fantasy. It is a fantasy so deeply forbidden, yet so baldly and cryptically presented, that a coherent social response is difficult to manage.

One can contrast, in *King Lear,* the control of the subliminal meaning of Gloucester's blinding as castration. Whether one attends to it or not, it is there in the text: "Out, vild jelly!" (3.7.83). Earlier we have Lear lamenting his injustices with "Old fond eyes, / Beweep this cause again, I'll pluck ye out" (1.4.301–2), and calling on the storm to "crack nature's moulds, all germains spill at once / That makes ingrateful man!" (3.2.8–9). Later we have Edgar on his father and Edmund: "The dark and vicious place where thee he got / Cost him his eyes" (5.3.173–74). But Gloucester's blinding and death point to far more than the "dark and vicious place" of Edmund's begetting, including what Edmund feels to be the vicious familial and social place bequeathed to him by his father's transgression and which lies at the center of *his* motive. Similarly, Lear's rage against his own eyes and his violent denunciation of the procreative process, released in the barren world engendered by Cordelia's banishment, link the tabooed dimension of Lear's love for Cordelia to the whole context of his need for her and hence to the whole imaginative design of the play. In the later tragedy Gloucester cannot see how he has created the circumstances that will lead to his blinding, and Lear cannot recognize the connection between his need and the chaos he brings into the world. In *Titus Andronicus* it is Shakespeare who does not connect the play's abundantly eroticized violence with motives integral to the situation of his protagonist.

The pathos of Lavinia as a wounded human being, which is at times poignantly realized, is conveyed rarely by Titus, but rather by Marcus, or by the grandson Lucius, or by the pathetic pantomime called for from the actor as Lavinia weeps or gestures or seeks to hide herself, or tries by running after the frightened child, Lucius, to get Ovid's book from him. Titus in response to her keeps turning from her and her mutilated body, her sighs and tears, to himself, his body, his tears. Tears, especially, are made the medium of communication, in intense and elaborate developments of the familiar trope:

> She is the weeping welkin, I the earth . . .
> Then must my earth with her continual tears
> Become a deluge, overflow'd and drown'd.
> (3.1.226, 228–29)

Curiously grotesque but very imaginative passages center on tears as the only way open to the sufferers to act and so gain expression. The above passage continues from "overflow'd and drown'd" with the conceit that Lavinia's tears have become woes inside Titus:

---

in representation, wrote "armes" above "teeth" as a substitute for the latter'; that 'the printer of Q1 took "Armes" to belong to the first line'; and finally, that the scribe responsible for F 'made sense of the passage by substituting "things" for "Armes" ' " (p. 132). But "armes" can make sense as a conceit that the heads and hand have become the armorial insignia of the Andronici; and the extra syllable can go with a retard in the delivery. Editorial ingenuity is here frankly in the service of the embarrassment which is frequently expressed about this *outré* piece of business.

For why my bowels cannot hide her woes,
But like a drunkard must I vomit them.
Then give me leave, for losers will have leave
To ease their stomachs with their bitter tongues.
                          (230–33)

Sitting down at dinner in the next scene, Titus develops a series of conceits on hands, hearts, and tears, which start from the physical gestures of the actors. Marcus is sitting with arms folded in grief, not eating. Titus begins by saying they must eat just enough to preserve strength for revenge:

Marcus, unknit that sorrow-wreathen knot;
Thy niece and I, poor creatures, want our hands
And cannot passionate our ten-fold grief
With folded arms. This poor right hand of mine
Is left to tyrannize upon my breast,
Who, when my heart all mad with misery,
Beats in this hollow prison of my flesh,
Then thus I thump it down.
[*To Lavina.*] Thou map of woe, that thus dost talk in signs!
When thy poor heart beats with outrageous beating,
Thou canst not strike it thus to make it still.
Wound it with sighing, girl, kill it with groans.
                          (3.2.4–15)

This is effective, I think, in conveying compassion as well as an intolerable pressure of feeling that seeks to find an emblematic epiphany such as Waith speaks of. At the same time there is a submerged sexualization of death as an orgasmic consummation for the drowning, beating heart, projected as an auto-erotic rhapsody; a knife is envisaged now between her teeth, rather than the severed hand:

Or get some little knife between thy teeth,
And just against thy heart make thou a hole,
That all the tears that thy poor eyes let fall
May run into that sink, and soaking in,
Drown the lamenting fool in sea-salt tears.
                          (16–20)

When Marcus remonstrates at Titus's suggestion of violence—"teach her not thus to lay / Such violent hands upon her tender life"—he gives the dramatist, through Titus, another chance to deal in puns on hands:

How now! has sorrow made thee dote already?
Why, Marcus, no man should be mad but I.
What violent hands can she lay on her life?
Ah, wherefore dost thou urge the name of hands, . . .
O, handle not the theme, to talk of hands,
Lest we remember still that we have none.
Fie, fie, how franticly I square my talk,

As if we should forget we had no hands,
If Marcus did not name the word of hands!
(21–26, 29–33)

The verbal and rhythmical energy of this is remarkable; isolated, the punning is in bad taste—"O, *handle* not the theme"! But when read so that the iterative rhythms support it, there is a telling effect of near distraction in the circling repetition. The poetic energy is greater than anything in Kyd, and looks forward to the circling, anguished iteration and wordplay of *Richard II*. Dramatically, the difficulty is that the situation is so claustrophobic; Kyd devises richer social circumstances for Hieronimo to take up into his passioning. But this self-enclosed quality is essential to what Shakespeare is exploring. A scene of a family dinner, with only Titus, Marcus, Lavinia, and the grandson present, Titus then mauling a fly on his plate—this is part of an imaginative progress into domesticity that ends with him spoon-feeding Tamora.

After another domestic scene, in which the grandson and Lavinia move about with some scope, and the murderers' identity is learned, Shakespeare opens out his action by sending Titus, his brother, grandson, and friends out into the open with bows to shoot missives to the gods and to send an oration to the Emperor in a clown's basket of pigeons. He also develops a subplot about the "Blackmoor Child" who in the chapbook disappears after his conception has been so quaintly explained. The scenes in which Aaron defends his black "tadpole" are regularly praised: "Aaron's strange blend of villainy and engaging paternal affection" seems "beyond the reach of any of [Shakespeare's] contemporaries" to R. F. Hill.[19] The freedom of Aaron in his villainy is an immense relief after the conflictual constriction we have experienced, and his language is often wonderfully vital:

Nurse: O gentle Aaron, we are all undone! . . .
Aaron: Why, what a caterwauling dost thou keep!
          What dost thou wrap and fumble in thy arms?
                         (4.2.55, 57–58)

The two scenes in which Aaron protects his son from Chiron and Demetrius and, after he is captured, from Lucius and his army of Goths, show Shakespeare's sure feeling for opening out a tragic action before returning to its intense, deep-running channel—they are like the shift out of Scotland to the court of England toward the close of *Macbeth*. After so much displaced, submerged, and inhibited sexuality, it is delightful to have Aaron answer back to the moral indignation of the Queen's sons (of all people!):

Demetrius: Villain, what hast thou done?
Aaron: That which thou canst not undo.
Chiron: Thou hast undone our mother.
Aaron: Villain, I have done your mother.
                         (73–76)

---

[19]R. F. Hill, "The Composition of *Titus Andronicus*," *Shakespeare Survey* 10 (1957): 64. Hill's interesting essay assesses the play's blend of stylistic awkwardness and strength to suggest that it may be Shakespeare's earliest work.

The amoral mastery with which Aaron kills the nurse is a pleasure after so much self-righteous moral frustration: "Weeke, weeke!—so cries a pig prepared to the spit." "Shall she live to betray this guilt of ours, / A long-tongu'd babbling gossip?" (146, 149–50).

When captured, Aaron, with his gusty recitation of the villainies he has committed or directed, recapitulates what we have witnessed with fascinated horror, freeing us from our complicity in half enjoying outrage by *his* enjoying it so fully. Although he seems clearly designed to out-Ithamore Ithamore, there is something in him beyond Marlowe's Turk. He has a greater freedom to dip into the vernacular for free-spirited common expressions: "That codding spirit had they from their mother" (5.1.99). His outsider's relativism about religion is gayer than Barabas's: "for that I know / An idiot holds his bauble for a god" (5.1.78–79). To be sure, the whole thing is stagey, but so fitted to serve our emotional need here that it works very well indeed.

Aaron's "paternal affection" for his son also fits with the way family and sexuality are structured in the play as a whole. Here is frank sexual zest leading to unforced, committed parenting. But the condition for it is that father and son be "black," beyond "a thing . . . called conscience" (5.1.75), beyond, thanks to blackness, the "treacherous hue, that will betray with blushing":

> Here's a young lad fram'd of another leer:
> Look how the black slave smiles upon the father,
> As who should say, "Old lad, I am thine own."
>   (4.2.117, 119–21)

Aaron has plans for his son that anticipate Belarius with Guiderius and Arviragus in *Cymbeline*:

> I'll make you feed on berries and on roots,
> And feed on curds and whey, and suck the goat,
> And cabin in a cave, and bring you up
> To be a warrior and command a camp.
>   (177–80)

It is a pleasant pastoral vision—of nurturance without women.

Earlier, to Tamora's sons' objection to letting the child live and so betraying "thy noble mistress," Aaron has answered: "My mistress is my mistress, this myself" (4.2.106–7). A father who would care for his own son by himself, as an extension of himself, Aaron represents a vilified but actively potent version of Titus as a parent. Titus the dutiful warrior is the nurturing male parent whose curious nurture is, for him and for his family, all there is: he leads male children out to death and back into the family tomb; he cherishes a daughter made sexually safe yet suggestive by disfigurement, only finally to destroy her. After the engulfing Tamora is undone by making her swallow her own sons in a hideous parody of nurturance, we are led through farewells to the hero, not as a stern figure of authority, but as a tender, cherishing parent and grandparent. "Come hither, boy," Titus's surviving son urges his own son at the end,

> thy grandsire lov'd thee well.
> Many a time he danc'd thee on his knee,
> Sung thee asleep, his loving breast thy pillow;
> Many a story hath he told to thee,
> And bid thee bear his pretty tales in mind,
> And talk of them when he was dead and gone.
> (5.3.159–66)

Aaron's great power expresses a fantasy of manhood beyond the reach of what makes Titus vulnerable: the cruel power of a domineering woman, Tamora, and Titus's investment of self in a bond of intimacy with another woman, his daughter. Within Titus's sphere, free sexual energy and procreative power are villainy outside the family and directed at its destruction. Yet the villainous outsider, Aaron, we admire to the verge of sentimentality for his freedom and his loyalty to progeny, even as he is morally reviled. Aaron's misogynous logic in dismissing his mistress is echoed in the new Emperor's final command:

> As for that ravenous tiger Tamora,
> No funeral rite, no man in mourning weed, . . .
> But throw her forth to beasts and birds to prey.
> (5.3.195–96, 198)

But whereas Aaron's misogyny has been based in a fantasy that denies masculine vulnerability, the Emperor's instructions reflect the desperate trend of Titus's vengeful action against an overwhelming threat: let the omnivorous mother, having devoured her own children, be devoured in turn by other beasts of prey.[20]

Titus's concurrent need for the caring intimacy of a feminine presence is expressed early when he greets Lavinia as the "cordial of mine age to glad my heart!" (1.1.166), anticipating Lear's "I lov'd her most, and thought to set my rest / On her kind nursery" (1.1.123–24). Like Lear leading Cordelia off to prison, Titus will end his life in a cherishing, sublimated bond with his daughter: "Gentle Lavinia, let me kiss thy lips / Or make some sign how I may do thee ease" (3.1.120–21). Cordelia's death is the tragic outcome of Lear's demand that she love her father all; Titus kills Lavinia himself after an interim in which the mutually disabled couple have lived in an all-absorbing intimacy. But unlike *King Lear,* the early tragedy does not comprehend the suppressed link between the need the father seeks to fulfill in the child and the destructive development of an action that engulfs them both.

Titus and the revenge play by Kyd that seems to have inspired it both fail in a measure because they lack control of a social perspective on the protagonist, or lose it toward the end. *The Spanish Tragedy* seems to me a much better play,

---

[20]As Willbern notes, Aaron's final punishment—"Set him breast-deep in the earth, and famish him; / There let him stand and rave and cry for food"—derives from the same matrix of fantasy. Willbern writes: "He is indeed like a baby, half-born and half-buried and half-devoured by the earth, crying for food. Anyone who would serve him as a mother will be killed" ("Rape and Revenge in *Titus Andronicus,*" p. 181).

despite the lower level of properly poetic power, because there is so much more social experience and meaning in it, until the final rampage of Hieronimo. *Titus* defines its hero (and heroine) almost entirely in domestic terms, and its anti-heroes in antidomestic terms; there is no larger society, no larger human and social possibility, showing forth. And in trying to make extraordinary transpositions of usual family and antifamily roles and allegiances, the play tends to fall into sensationalism and sentimentality. The structure of the play substitutes paternal for maternal parenting and sentimentalizes Titus as it sensationalizes the malevolence of Tamora. In doing so it makes the destructiveness that is recognized as such all come from the outside—from Goths and their Moor—and does not acknowledge the destructiveness of Titus within his family, except in the moment, quickly passed over, of killing his youngest son. The revenge-play structure is used to avoid recognizing for what it is the underlying motive the play enacts.

Romeo and Juliet:
Comedy into Tragedy

Susan Snyder

Romeo and Juliet is different from Shakespeare's other tragedies in that it becomes, rather than is, tragic. Other tragedies have reversals, but in *Romeo and Juliet* the reversal is so radical as to constitute a change of genre: the action and the characters begin in familiar comic patterns, and are then transformed—or discarded—to compose the pattern of tragedy.

Comedy and tragedy, being opposed ways of apprehending the real world, project their own opposing worlds. The tragic world is governed by inevitability, and its highest value is personal integrity. In the comic world 'evitability' is assumed; instead of heroic or obstinate adherence to a single course, comedy endorses opportunistic shifts and realistic accommodations as means to an end of new social health. The differing laws of comedy and tragedy point to opposed concepts of law itself. Law in the comic world is extrinsic, imposed on society *en masse*. Its source there is usually human, so that law may either be stretched ingeniously to suit the characters' ends, or flouted, or even annulled by benevolent rulers. Portia plays tricks with the letter and spirit of Venetian law to save Antonio. The Dukes in *The Comedy of Errors* and *A Midsummer Night's Dream*, when the objects are family reunions and happily paired lovers, simply brush aside legal obstacles. Even deep-rooted social laws, like the obedience owed to parents by their children, are constantly overturned. But in the tragic world law is inherent: imposed by the individual's own nature, it may direct him to a conflict with the larger patterns of law inherent in his universe. The large pattern may be divine, as it generally is in Greek tragedy, or it may be natural and social, as in *Macbeth* and *King Lear*. Tragic law cannot be altered; it does no good to tell destruction to stop breeding destruction, or to tell gods or human individuals to stop being themselves.

In these opposed worlds our sense of time and its value also differs. The action of comedy may be quickly paced, but we know that it is moving towards a conclusion of 'all the time in the world'. The events of tragedy, on the other hand, acquire urgency in their uniqueness and their irrevocability: they will never happen again, and one by one they move the hero closer to the end of his

From *Essays in Criticism* 20 (1970), 391–402. Reprinted by permission of the editors of *Essays in Criticism*.

own time in death. In comedy short-term urgencies are played against a dominant expansiveness, while in tragedy a sense that time is limited and precious grows with our perception of an inevitable outcome.

In its inexorable movement and the gulf it fixes between the central figure and the others, tragedy has been compared to ritual sacrifice. The protagonist is both hero and victim, separated from the ordinary, all-important in his own being, but destined for destruction. That is the point of the ritual. Comedy is organized like a game. The ascendancy goes to the clever ones who can take advantage of sudden openings, plot strategies, and adapt flexibly to an unexpected move. But luck and instinct win games as well as skill, and comedy takes account of the erratic laws of chance that bring a Dogberry out on top of a Don John and, more basically, of the instinctive attunement to underlying pattern that crowns lovers, however unaware and inflexible, with final success.

Romeo and Juliet, young and in love and defiant of obstacles, are attuned to the basic movement of the comic game toward social regeneration. But they are not successful: the game turns into a sacrifice, and the favoured lovers become its marked victims. This shift is illuminated by a study of the play's two worlds and some secondary characters who help to define them.

If we divide the play at Mercutio's death, the death that generates all those that follow, it becomes apparent that the play's movement up to this point is essentially comic. With the usual intrigues and go-betweens, the lovers overcome obstacles in a move toward marriage. This personal action is set in a broader social context, so that the marriage promises not only private satisfaction but renewed social unity:

For this alliance may so happy prove
To turn your households' rancour to pure love.[1]

The state that requires this cure is set out in the first scene. The Verona of the Montague–Capulet feud is like the typical starting point of the kind of comedy described by Northrop Frye: 'a society controlled by habit, ritual bondage, arbitrary law and the older characters.'[2] Even the scene's formal balletic structure, a series of matched representatives of the warring families entering on cue, conveys the inflexibility of this society, the arbitrary division that limits freedom of action.

The feud itself seems more a matter of mechanical reflex than of deeply felt hatred. As H. B. Charlton has noted, its presentation here has a comic aspect.[3] The 'parents' rage' that sounds so ominous in the Prologue becomes in representation an irascible humour: two old men claw at one another only to be dragged back by their wives and scolded by their Prince. Charlton found the play flawed by this failure to plant the seeds of tragedy, but the treatment of the feud makes good sense if Shakespeare is playing on *comic* expectations.

[1]2.3.91–92. All Shakespeare references are to *The Complete Works*, ed. G. L. Kittredge (Boston, 1936).

[2]*Anatomy of Criticism* (Princeton, 1957), p. 169. Although the younger generation participates in the feud, they have not created it; it is a legacy from the past.

[3]*Shakespearian Tragedy* (Cambridge, 1948), pp. 56–57.

Other aspects of this initial world of *Romeo and Juliet* suggest comedy. Its characters are the minor aristocracy and servants familiar in comedies, concerned not with wars and the fate of kingdoms but with arranging marriages and managing the .kitchen. More important, it is a world of possibilities, with Capulet's feast represented to the young men as a field of choice. 'Hear all, all see', says Capulet to Paris, 'And like her most whose merit most shall be' (1.2.30–31). 'Go thither', Benvolio tells Romeo, 'and with unattainted eye/ Compare her face with some that I shall show . . .'⁴ and Rosaline will be forgotten for some more approachable beauty. Romeo rejects the words, of course, but in action he soon displays a classic comic adaptability, switching from the impossible love to the possible just as Proteus, Demetrius, Phoebe, and Olivia do in their respective comedies.

Violence and disaster are not absent, of course, but they are unrealized threats. The feast yields a kind of comic emblem when Tybalt's potential violence is rendered harmless by Capulet's festive accommodation.

> Therefore be patient, take no note of him.
> It is my will; the which if thou respect,
> Show a fair presence and put off these frowns,
> An ill-beseeming semblance for a feast.
>   (1.5.73–76)

This overruling of Tybalt is significant, for Tybalt is a recognizably tragic character, the only one in this part of the play. He alone takes the feud seriously: It is his inner law, the propeller of his fiery nature. He speaks habitually in the tragic rhetoric of honour and death:

>   What, dares the slave
> Come hither, cover'd with an antic face,
> To fleer and scorn at our solemnity?
> Now by the stock and honour of my kin,
> To strike him dead I hold it not a sin.
>   (1.5.57–61)

Tybalt's single set of absolutes cuts him off from a whole rhetorical range available to the other young men of the play: lyric love, witty fooling, friendly conversation. Ironically, his imperatives come to dominate the play's world only when he himself departs from it. While he is alive, Tybalt is an alien.

In a similar manner, the passing fears of calamity voiced by Romeo, Juliet, and Friar Laurence are not allowed to dominate this atmosphere. If the love of Romeo and Juliet is already imaged as a flash of light swallowed by darkness (an image invoking inexorable natural law), it is also expressed as a sea venture, which suggests luck and skill set against natural hazards, chance seized joyously as an opportunity for action. 'Direct my sail', Romeo tells his captain Fortune;⁵ but soon he feels himself in command:

⁴1.2.89–90.
⁵1.4.113.

I am no pilot; yet, wert thou as far
As that vast shore wash'd with the farthest sea,
I should adventure for such merchandise.
                                        (2.2.82–84)

The spirit is Bassanio's as he adventures for Portia, a Jason voyaging in quest of the Golden Fleece.[6] Romeo is ready for difficulties with a traditional lovers' stratagem, one that Shakespeare had used before in *Two Gentlemen of Verona*: a rope ladder 'which to the high topgallant of my joy/Must be my convoy in the secret night' (2.4.201–202).

But before the ladder can be used, Mercutio's death intervenes to transform this world of exhilarating venture. Mercutio has been almost the incarnation of comic atmosphere. He is the best of game-players, endlessly inventive, full of quick moves and counter-moves. Speech for him is a constant play on multiple possibilities: puns abound because two or three meanings are more fun than one, and Queen Mab brings dreams not only to lovers like Romeo but to courtiers, lawyers, parsons, soldiers, maids. These have nothing to do with the case at hand—Romeo's premonition—but Mercutio is not bound by events. They are merely points of departure for his expansive wit. In Mercutio's sudden, violent end, Shakespeare makes the birth of a tragedy coincide exactly with the symbolic death of comedy. The element of freedom and play dies with him, and where many courses were open before, now there seems only one. Romeo sees at once that an irreversible process has begun:

This day's black fate on moe days doth depend
This but begins the woe others must end.
                                        (3.1.124–125)

It is the first sign in the play's dialogue pointing unambiguously to tragic causation. Romeo's future action is now determined: he *must* kill Tybalt, he *must* run away, he is fortune's fool.

This helplessness is the most striking quality of the second, tragic world of *Romeo and Juliet*. That is, the temper of the new world is largely a function of onrushing events. Under pressure of events, the feud turns from farce to fate, from tit for tat to blood for blood. Lawless as it is in the Prince's eyes, the feud is dramatically the law in *Romeo and Juliet*. Previously external and avoidable, it has now moved inside Romeo to become his personal law. Fittingly, he takes over Tybalt's rhetoric of honour and death:

Alive in triumph, and Mercutio slain?
Away to heaven respective lenity,
And fire-ey'd fury be my conduct now!
Now, Tybalt, take thy 'villain' back again
That late thou gavest me.
                                        (3.1.127–131)

---

[6] *Merchant of Venice*, 1.1.166–174.

Even outside the main chain of vengeance, the world is suddenly full of imperatives: against his will Friar John is detained at the monastery, and against his will
the Apothecary sells poison to Romeo. Urgency becomes the norm as nights run
into mornings in continuous action and the characters seem never to sleep. The
new world finds its emblem not in the aborted attack but in the aborted feast. As
Tybalt's violence was out of tune with the Capulet feast in Act 2, so in Acts 3 and 4
the projected wedding is made grotesque when Shakespeare insistently links it
with death.[7] Preparations for the feast parallel those of the first part, so as to
underline the contrast when

> All things that we ordained festival
> Turn from their office to black funeral—
> Our instruments to melancholy bells,
> Our wedding cheer to a sad burial feast.
> (4.5.84–87)

I have been treating these two worlds as consistent wholes in order to bring
out their opposition, but I do not wish to deny dramatic unity to *Romeo and
Juliet*. Shakespeare was writing one play, not two, and in spite of the prominence of the turning point we are aware that premonitions of disaster precede
the death of Mercutio and that hopes for avoiding it continue until near the
play's conclusion. The world-shift that converts Romeo and Juliet from
instinctive winners into sacrificial victims is thus a gradual one. In this connection the careers of two secondary characters, Friar Laurence and the Nurse,
are instructive.

In being and action these two belong to the comic vision. Friar Laurence is
one of a whole series of Shakespearean manipulators and stage-managers,
those wise and benevolent figures who direct the action of others, arrange
edifying tableaux, and resolve intricate public and private problems. Notable
in the list are Oberon, Friar Francis in *Much Ado*, Helena in the latter part of
All's Well, Duke Vincentio and Prospero. Friar Laurence shares the religious
dress of three of this quintet and participates to some extent, by his knowledge of herbs and drugs, in the magical powers of Oberon and Prospero. Such
figures are frequent in comedy but not in tragedy, where the future is not
manipulable. The Friar's aims are those implicit in the play's comic movement, an inviolable union for Romeo and Juliet and an end to the families'
feud.

The Nurse's goal is less lofty, but equally appropriate to comedy. She
wants Juliet married—to anyone. Her preoccupation with marriage and
breeding is as indiscriminate as the life force itself. But she conveys no sense
of urgency in all this. Rather, her garrulity assumes the limitless time that
frames the comic world but not the tragic. In this sense her circumlocutions
and digressions are analogous to Mercutio's witty flights and to Friar

[7]3.4.23–28; 3.5.202–203; 4.1.6–8; 4.1.77–86; 4.1.107–108; 4.5.35–39; 5.3.12.

Laurence's counsels of patience. The leisurely time assumptions of the Friar and the Nurse contrast with the lovers' impatience, creating at first the normal counterpoint of comedy[8] and later a radical split that points us, with the lovers, directly to tragedy.

For what place can these two have in the new world brought into being by Mercutio's death, the world of limited time, no effective choice, no escape? In a sense, though, they define and sharpen the tragedy by their very failure to find a place in the dramatic progress, by their growing estrangement from the true springs of the action. 'Be patient', Friar Laurence tells the banished Romeo, 'for the world is broad and wide' (3.3.16). But the roominess he assumes in both time and space simply does not exist for Romeo. His time has been constricted into a chain of days working out a 'black fate', and he sees no world outside the walls of Verona (3.3.17).

Comic adaptability again confronts tragic integrity when Juliet is faced with a similarly intolerable situation—she is ordered to marry Paris—and turns to her Nurse for counsel as Romeo does to the Friar. The Nurse replies with the traditional worldly wisdom of comedy. Romeo has been banished and Paris is very presentable. Adjust yourself to the new situation.

> Then, since the case so stands as now it doth,
> I think it best you married with the County.
> O, he's a lovely gentleman!
> (3.5.218–220)

She still speaks for the life force. Even if Paris is an inferior husband, he is better than no husband at all.

> Your first is dead—or 'twere as good he were
> As living here and you no use of him.
> (226–227)

But such advice has become irrelevant, even shocking, in this context. There was no sense of jar when Benvolio, a spokesman for accommodation like the Nurse and the Friar, earlier advised Romeo to substitute a possible for an impossible love. True, the Nurse is urging violation of the marriage vows; but Romeo was also sworn to Rosaline, and for Juliet the marriage vow is a seal on the integrity of her love for Romeo, not a separate issue. The parallel points up the progress of tragedy, for while Benvolio's advice sounded sensible and was in fact unintentionally carried out by Romeo, the course of action outlined by the Nurse is unthinkable to the audience as well as Juliet. The memory of the lovers' dawn parting that began this scene is too strong. Juliet and the Nurse no longer speak the same language, and estrangement is inevitable. 'Thou and my bosom henceforth shall be

---

[8]Clowns and cynics are usually available to comment on romantic lovers in Shakespeare's comedies, providing qualification and a widened perspective without real disharmony. A single character, like Rosalind in *As You Like It*, may incorporate much of the counterpoint in her own comprehensive view.

twain', Juliet vows privately.[9] Like the death of Mercutio, Juliet's rejection of her old confidante has symbolic overtones. The possibilities of comedy have again been presented only to be discarded.

Both Romeo and Juliet have now cast off their comic companions and the alternate modes of being that they represented. But there is one last hope for comedy. If the lovers will not adjust to the situation, perhaps the situation can be adjusted to the lovers. This is usual comic solution, and we have at hand the usual manipulator to engineer it.

The Friar's failure to bring off that solution is the final definition of the tragic world of the play. Time is the villain. Time in comedy generally works for regeneration and reconciliation, but in tragedy it propels the protagonists to destruction; there is not enough of it, or it goes wrong somehow. The Friar does his best: he makes more than one plan to avert catastrophe. The first, typically, is patience and a broader field of action. Romeo must go to Mantua and wait

> till we can find a time
> To blaze your marriage, reconcile your friends,
> Beg pardon of the Prince, and call thee back . . .
> (3.3.150–152)

It is a good enough plan, for life if not for drama, but it depends on 'finding a time'. As it turns out, events move too quickly for the Friar, and the hasty preparations for Juliet's marriage to Paris leave no time for cooling tempers and reconciliations.

His second plan is an attempt to *gain* time, to create the necessary freedom through a faked death. This is, of course, another comic formula; Shakespeare's later uses of it are all in comedies. It is interesting that the contrived 'deaths' of Hero in *Much Ado*, Helena in *All's Well*, Claudio in *Measure for Measure*, and Hermione in *The Winter's Tale*, unlike Juliet's, are designed to produce a change of heart in other characters.[10] Time may be important, as it is in *The Winter's Tale*, but only as it promotes repentance. Friar Laurence, less ambitious and more desperate than his fellow manipulators, does not hope that Juliet's death will dissolve the families' hatreds but only that it will give Romeo a chance to come and carry her off. Time in the comic world of *The Winter's Tale* co-operates benevolently with Paulina's schemes for Leontes' regeneration; but for Friar Laurence it is both prize and adversary. Romeo's man is quicker with the news of Juliet's death than poor Friar John with the news of the deception. Romeo himself beats Friar Laurence to the Capulets' tomb. The onrushing tragic action quite literally outstrips the slower steps of accommodation before our eyes. The Friar arrives too

---

[9]3.5.242. Later, in the potion scene, Juliet's resolve weakens temporarily, but she at once rejects the idea of companionship. The effect is to call attention to her aloneness:

> I'll call them back again to comfort me.
> Nurse!—What should she do here?
> My dismal scene I needs must act alone.
> (4.3.17–19)

[10]The same effect, if not the plan, is apparent in Imogen's reported death in *Cymbeline*.

late to prevent one half of the tragic conclusion, and his essential estrangement is only emphasised when he seeks to avert the other half by sending Juliet to a nunnery. It is the last alternative to be suggested. Juliet quietly rejects the possibility of adjustment and continuing life: 'Go, get thee hence, for I will not away' (5.3.160).

The Nurse and the Friar illustrate a basic principle of the operation of comedy in tragedy, which might be called the principle of irrelevance. In tragedy we are tuned to the extraordinary. *Romeo and Juliet* gives us this extraordinary centre not so much in the two individuals as in the love itself, its intensity and integrity. Our apprehension of this intensity and integrity comes gradually, through the cumulative effect of the lovers' lyric encounters and the increasing urgency of events, but also through the growing irrelevance of the comic characters.

De Quincey perceived in the knocking at the gate in *Macbeth* the resumption of normality after nightmare: 'the re-establishment of the going-on of the world in which we live, which first makes us profoundly sensible of the awful parenthesis that has suspended them.'[11] I would say rather that the normal atmosphere of *Macbeth* has been and goes on being nightmarish, and that it is the knocking at the gate that turns out to be the contrasting parenthesis, but the notion of a sharpened sensitivity is valid. As the presence of alternate paths makes us more conscious of the road we are in fact travelling, so the Nurse and the Friar makes us more 'profoundly sensible' of Romeo's and Juliet's love and its true direction.

After *Romeo and Juliet* Shakespeare never returned to the comedy-into-tragedy formula, although the canon has several examples of potential tragedy converted into comedy. There is a kind of short comic movement in *Othello*, encompassing the successful love of Othello and Desdemona and their safe arrival in Cyprus, but comedy is not in control even in the first act. Iago's malevolence has begun the play, and our sense of obstacles overcome (Desdemona's father, the perils of the sea) is shadowed by his insistent presence. The act ends with the birth of his next plot.

It is not only the shift from comedy to tragedy that sets *Romeo and Juliet* apart from the other Shakespeare tragedies. Critics have often noted, sometimes disapprovingly, that external fate rather than character is the principal determiner of the tragic outcome. For Shakespeare, tragedy is usually a matter of both character and circumstance, a fatal interaction of man and moment. But in this play, although the central characters have their weaknesses, their destruction does not really stem from these weaknesses. One may agree with Friar Laurence that Romeo is rash, but it is not his rashness that propels him into the tragic chain of events but an opposite quality. In the crucial duel between Mercutio and Tybalt, Romeo tries to make peace. Ironically, this very intervention contributes to Mercutio's death.

[11]'On the Knocking at the Gate in *Macbeth*,' *Shakespeare Criticism: A Selection*, ed. D. Nichol Smith (Oxford, 1916), p. 378.

Mer: Why the devil came you between us? I was hurt
         under your arm.
Rom: I thought all for the best.

(3.1.108–109)

If Shakespeare wanted to implicate Romeo's rashness in his fate, this scene is handled with unbelievable ineptness. Judging from the resultant effect, what he wanted to convey was an ironic dissociation between character and the direction of events.

Perhaps this same purpose dictated the elaborate introduction of comic elements before the characters are pushed into the opposed conditions of tragedy. Stress on milieu tends to downgrade the importance of individual temperament and motivation. For this once in Shakesperian tragedy, it is not what you are that counts, but the world you live in.

Romeo and Juliet:
A Formal Dwelling

James L. Calderwood

As an indirect entry to *Romeo and Juliet* let me dwell for a moment on Shakespeare's management of vows, since vows are especially good indices of a dramatist's conception of language in addition to having a strong bearing on character, motive, even dramatic form. In *Titus Andronicus* Shakespeare saw in the vow a formal principle of Senecan revenge tragedy. Out of the chaos of his material the dramatist contrives a teleology in which the vow serves as a structural promise to be redeemed by a culminating act of vengeance. The strangest vow in that strange play, however, is not Titus's vow of vengeance but Lucius's vow of mercy (in 5.1), which results from Aaron's insistence that unless his child goes free he, like his descendant Iago, "never will speak word." Shakespeare makes much of this contract between Lucius and Aaron partly because it introduces an element of mercy into a drama whose zestful cruelty makes Antonin Artaud's pronouncements on that subject seem saccharine by comparison but partly too because like so many other bizarre encounters in the play it figures his dramatic problem of uniting words and actions. The contract involves the exchange of Lucius's "word" for Aaron's "plot," and that is precisely the kind of contract Shakespeare has himself been trying without success to negotiate in *Titus Andronicus*. By spinning out the implications of Lucius's vow one might arrive at a fairly good notion of the central dramatic problem of the play.

Vows are equally significant in *Love's Labour's Lost*. In vowing themselves to the life of Academe the scholars rely on the autonomy of words, not as they function in society but as defined, purified, and sworn to by themselves. So constituted, words will suppress nature in the form of the scholars' own "affections" and "the huge army of the world's desires" (primarily women). Since a purely private verbal world is impossible, their fragile fortress of words collapses before the assaulting army of the world's desires marching in petticoats from France. The scholars then scatter a second set of vows during their Muscovite wooing scene, each to the wrong lady, the disastrous effect of which suggests that if words may be overvalued through private hoarding they

From *Shakespearean Metadrama* (Minneapolis: University of Minnesota Press, 1971), 85–119. Copyright © 1971 by the University of Minnesota. Reprinted by permission.

may also be undervalued through promiscuous spending. Behind the surface plight of laboring lovers hiding behind words and then distributing them wildly in all directions stands the poet's metadramatic plight as he tries to arbitrate between the individual and private needs of his art on the one hand and the all-too-public and debased nature of the language in which his art must be cast. No solution to that problem is arrived at in *Love's Labour's Lost*. Neither by trying to virginize the universal whore language nor by trailing her about the streets and risking contamination himself can the playwright achieve the elusive and mysterious marriage of language and art that will make him whole.

It is generally supposed that *Titus Andronicus* preceded *Love's Labour's Lost,* and if so then the comedy may be seen as a reaction to the would-be tragedy, a recoiling from violent action, contrived plots, and stage sensationalism. The result is a purely verbal, plotless, essentially nondramatic work. Since it is also generally supposed that *Love's Labour's Lost* preceded *Romeo and Juliet* perhaps the latter can be considered in some degree at least as a response to the issues dealt with in the comic play. The marriage of the hero and heroine for instance would seem to acquire special significance in view of the conspicuous non-marriage of the lovers in the earlier play. In *Love's Labour's Lost* marriage was conceived of as the proper terminus of dramatic form, where the play ought to but perversely refuses to end, and as the product of a true language. Neither form nor language is discovered, however, and we are left with a mannered, courtly play of words illustrating its author's astonishing virtuosity but also, as he himself underscores by thrusting Mercade into the nonaction, a certain glib and glittering superficiality. The truth of the feelings is first suppressed by words and later distorted and obscured by them. As the purgative punishments of the scholars imply, the poet's language must somehow incorporate inner truth and outer reality, the mystery of love and such bleak facts of nature as time, suffering, death.

II

These then are the major metadramatic issues, at least on the side of language, confronting Shakespeare as he turns to *Romeo and Juliet*. From the problem of language he moves on in this play to the problem of dramatic form. But first let us focus on language and particularly on the balcony scene of 2.2 where vows again come into prominence. The place to begin is of course Juliet's famous complaint against the tyranny of names:

'Tis but thy name that is my enemy;
Thou art thyself though not a Montague.
What's Montague? It is nor hand nor foot
Nor arm nor face nor any other part

Belonging to a man. O be some other name!
What's in a name? That which we call a rose
By any other word would smell as sweet.
So Romeo would, were he not Romeo called,
Retain that dear perfection which he owes
Without that title. Romeo, doff thy name,
And for thy name, which is no part of thee,
Take all myself.

(2.2.38–49)

Here and more widely throughout the play, brilliantly figured in the implicit metaphor of family and relatives, verbal nominalism is equated with a kind of social personalism. That is, in her anxiety to circumvent the opposition of their relatives Juliet would reject all relations and find ultimate truth in the haecceity, thisness, or as she puts it "dear perfection" of a totally unaffiliated Romeo. In the same way nominalism rejects the family or tribal relations of words in their more universal and abstract forms and situates verbal truth in the concrete and particular terms that seem most closely tied to the unique, unrelated, and hence true objects of which reality is composed. Juliet's nominalism here is a position with which the poet can readily sympathize,[1] because words come to the poet as Romeo comes to Juliet, trailing dark clouds of a prior public identity. Romeo comes to Juliet not merely from the streets of Verona and the house of Montague but from the shallows of Petrarchan love dotage as well, since he begins this play as Berowne ended his, an unrequited wooer of "Rosaline" (who is appropriately no more than a "name" in *Romeo and Juliet*). Juliet's verbal program is roughly analogous to that of the scholars of Navarre when they sought to establish their Academe. Where they tried to seal themselves off from the outside world by founding an elite society on a private lan-

---

[1]It is a position with which we can all sympathize, for that matter, since it reflects a recurrent human urge to scour our modes of apprehending experience, to brighten up a world that has been sicklied over by the pale cast of thought and drab expression. Anxious to purify Romeo of his family connections and meet him in all his shining individuality, Juliet might well approve of Husserl's desire for philosophy to return to things themselves, to let phenomena speak for themselves without the mediating and therefore presumably falsifying intervention of the mind with all its presuppositions (of which genus, or family, is surely a major meddler). However, the Hopkinsean "inscape" of man—the unique Romeo freed of his Montague associations—was less attractive to Renaissance moral philosophers, usually registered Platonists, who distinguished between two aspects of human nature—general and specific, genus and differentia—and felt that although the differentia made men interesting it was the genus that kept them civilized (see for instance Cicero's *Offices*, chapters 30 and 31). Juliet might want Romeo to be able to say "I am myself alone," but the man who actually says it is Richard Crookback at a major moment in a long and uniquely inhuman career (*3 Henry VI*, 5.6.83). In "The King's Language: Shakespeare's Drama as Social Discovery," *Antioch Review*, 21 (1961):369–387, Sigurd Burckhardt has some brief but shrewd remarks about Juliet's nominalism; and for an excellent equation of nominalism and personalism see Murry Krieger's "The Existential Basis of Contextual Criticism" in *The Play and Place of Criticism* (Baltimore, 1967), pp. 239–251. In his interesting article "The Rose and Its Name: On Denomination in *Othello, Romeo and Juliet, Julius Caesar*," *Texas Studies in Literature and Language*, 11 (1969): 671–686, Manfred Weidhorn discusses the bondage of verbal categories from which the lovers are liberated by virture of their meeting without introductions.

guage, Juliet seeks to go even further, to rename or even "de-name" in the interests of purifying a Romeo who has been abroad with his pseudo–love.[2] (Of course Juliet does not know about Rosaline, but Shakespeare does, and thus has Juliet repudiate Petrarchan "form," "strangeness," and "cunning" a bit further on.)

Romeo is more than willing to be renamed—

Call me but love and I'll be new baptized;
Henceforth I never will be Romeo
                    (2.2.50–51)

—but his language throughout the scene betrays him. Like Berowne, who prematurely thought himself cured of the Petrarchan style, Romeo still has "a trick/Of the old rage" (*LLL*, 5.2.416-417). It reveals itself most obviously when he begins keening vows:

	Lady, by yonder blessed moon I vow
	That tips with silver all these fruit-tree tops—
Juliet.	O swear not by the moon, the inconstant moon
	That monthly changes in her circled orb,
	Lest that thy love prove likewise variable.
Romeo.	What shall I swear by?
Juliet.	Do not swear at all.
	Or, if thou wilt, swear by thy gracious self,
	Which is the god of my idolatry,
	And I'll believe thee.
Romeo.	If my heart's dear love—
Juliet.	Well, do not swear. Although I joy in thee,
	I have no joy of this contract tonight.
	It is too rash, too unadvised, too sudden,
	Too like the lightning, which doth cease to be
	Ere one can say it lightens. Sweet, goodnight.
	This bud of love, by summer's ripening breath,
	May prove a beauteous flower when next we meet.
	Goodnight, goodnight! As sweet repose and rest
	Come to thy heart as that within my breast.
Romeo.	O wilt thou leave me so unsatisfied?
Juliet.	What satisfaction canst thou have tonight?
Romeo.	The exchange of thy love's faithful vow for mine.
	(2.2.107–127)

Like the scholars of Navarre in their wooing phase ("O who can give an oath?") Romeo is a ready spender of words and, also like them, naively trustful that vows can trace around lovers a magic circle to hold the devilish world at bay. But like the French ladies Juliet has a maturer conception of the laws of

---

[2]The walled orchard that isolates the lovers from the harsh realities of Veronese life is very much akin to the park of the scholars in *Love's Labour's Lost*, which was so rigorously declared off limits to foreign speech and female bodies.

verbal contract and the power of their magic. Her rejection of the "inconstant moon" as a third party to the contract and her apprehensions about the rash, unadvised, and oversudden enlarge the more immediate threat of the feuding families to include all that is dangerously unstable beyond the periphery of private feeling. But she is also unsure of Romeo's love, which is available to her only as it is given shape in his language. Instinctively she distrusts his *style*, as Shakespeare forces us to notice by having her twice interrupt him as he cranks up his rhetorical engines in preparation for Petrarchan flights. Throughout this scene, and the play for that matter, it is Romeo's speech that soars airily and often vacuously. Juliet's, though hardly leaden, is more earthbound. She is not opposed to vows entirely—though her nominalism inevitably tends in that direction—but seeks a true language in which they may be expressed. Thus when Romeo selects the moon as a symbol of purity to swear by, she, recognizing the pseudo-purity of his own Petrarchan style, reminds him that the moon is also a symbol of inconstancy. Not the purling phrases rising easily to the lips of a thousand dandies with well-hinged knees but the genuine custom-made article is what she seeks:

> O gentle Romeo,
> If thou dost love, pronounce it faithfully.
> Or if thou think'st I am too quickly won
> I'll frown and be perverse and say thee nay—
> So thou wilt woo; but else, not for the world.
> In truth, fair Montague, I am too fond,
> And therefore thou mayst think my 'haviour light.
> But trust me, gentleman, I'll prove more true
> Than those that have more cunning to be strange.
> (2.2.93–101)

"Pronounce it faithfully"—unfortunately Romeo, who would forge a binding verbal contract, is himself bound to the book of form. Like Paris, whom Lady Capulet lengthily describes as a "fair volume" (1.3.79ff), and Tybalt, whom Mercutio despises as an "antic, lisping, affecting fantastico" who stands "much on the new form" (2.4.29–37) and "fights by the book of arithmetic" (3.1.105), Romeo not only kisses "by the book" (1.5.112) but trumpets vows by the book of Petrarchan form. Juliet admits that she *could* play at Petrarchanism and that to do so might even invest her behavior with an appearance of mature reserve that her forthrightness of feeling makes her seem without. But even if a bit fondly, she specializes in truth, not form, and so concludes "but farewell compliment!/ Dost thou love me?" (2.2.89–90). Truly virginal, she recoils from the potential contamination of vows loosely and grandiloquently untethered: "Well, do not swear." Do not swear, do not even speak—that is the end of the nominalistic line because even at their best words cannot perfectly reflect the autonomous individuality of objects, or in this case of genuine love. Seeking an ideal communion of love at a level beyond idle breath, Juliet would purify words quite out of existence and reduce dialogue to an exchange of intuition and sheer feeling—a marriage of true minds accomplished without the connective medium of language.

III

If we set Juliet's remarks on names in a literary perspective instead of a general nominalistic one they might be taken to suggest an extreme toward which the lyric impulse sometimes tends, that is an ineffable purity. Here it is an ineffable purity of love, but its counterparts elsewhere would include the "unexpressive nuptial song" mentioned by Milton in "Lycidas," that etherealized music in Keats's "Ode on a Grecian Urn"—

> Heard melodies are sweet, but those unheard
> Are sweeter; therefore, ye soft pipes, play on;
> Not to the sensual ear, but, more endeared,
> Pipe to the spirit ditties of no tone

—and the dumb eloquence of lips in Hopkins's "The Habit of Perfection":

> Shape nothing, lips; be lovely-dumb:
> It is the shut, the curfew sent
> From there where all surrenders come
> Which only makes you eloquent.

Such scattered examples remind us of how its recurrent attraction to the pure and ideal leads lyric toward seclusion from the ruck and reel of time, action, and the world. Etymologically, though not always in practice, lyric aspires to the condition of music, seeking to purify noise into melody and sometimes even, as expressed in the examples above, to a point beyond sound, to stillness. Similarly as regards time and motion, lyric would discover a terminal rest, a retreat from the hurly-burly of action and consequences where thought and feeling crystallize in an expressive stasis. Murray Krieger has demonstrated the apt ambiguity of the word "still" to express in terms of motion the ever-moving fixity of poetry as it sets progressive experience within a transfixing form or, in Yeatsian language, unites the dancer with the dance.[3] In talking about *Romeo and Juliet*, however, we need to enlarge on the ambiguities of stillness by adding silence to the ever-neverness of motion since Juliet, as we have seen, would reduce love's dialogue to a silent communion of unique, inexpressible feeling.

Shakespeare, it is time to say, is abundantly aware how foolish such a *reductio ad silentium* must be from the standpoint of the poet. However intense his own longing to attain a purity out of the swing of speech—and it seems to me considerably so—he knows with Mallarmé that poetry is written with words, not ideas, and especially not ideas before which the poet must become breathless with adoration.

---

[3]See "The Ekphrastic Principle and the Still Movement of Poetry; or *Laokoön* Revisited" in *The Play and Place of Criticism*, pp. 105–128.

If Juliet's view were to prevail the play would turn mute and time stand still, or at least slow down to the point where nine o'clock tomorrow takes twenty years to arrive (2.2.168–170). Drama would dissolve into lyric and lyric would dissolve into a silent center of inexpressible love surrounded by the cacophony of the street scenes, the nurse's babble and Mercutio's bawdry, the expostulations of Capulet, and the intoned sententiae of Friar Laurence.

The plight of the poet who would retreat within lyric to a purer wordlessness is humorously illustrated when Juliet, after appropriately hearing "some noise within" and retiring briefly to investigate, returns to the balcony and cannot momentarily locate Romeo:

> *Juliet.* Hist! Romeo, hist! O for a falconer's voice
> To lure this tassel-gentle back again!
> Bondage is hoarse, and may not speak aloud,
> Else would I tear the cave where Echo lies
> And make her airy tongue more hoarse than mine
> With repetition of my Romeo's name.
> Romeo!
>
> (2.2.159–165)

If "Necessity" as Berowne said could make the scholars "all forsworn/Three thousand times within this three years' space" (*LLL,* 1.1.150–151), it can also make a sorely frustrated Juliet acknowledge the indispensability of names within a little more than a hundred lines of her great protest against them. In that brief space the tyrannous "bondage" of verbal categories (locking the free spirit of reality into claustrophobic linguistic cells) metamorphoses into its opposite, the "bondage" that prevents Juliet from giving full free voice to that most useful category "Romeo." For the lovers and for the poet Shakespeare the notion of establishing communion on a plane of feeling transcending the imperfections of speech is "but a dream/Too flattering-sweet to be substantial" (2.2.140–141). Not only must the lovers rely on names for the rudiments of communication, but their love itself becomes a great name-singing celebration:

> *Romeo.* It is my soul that calls upon my name.
> How silver-sweet sound lovers' tongues by night,
> Like softest music to attending ears!
>
> (2.2.165–167)

> *Juliet.* . . . and every tongue that speaks
> But Romeo's name speaks heavenly eloquence.
>
> (3.2.32–33)

That Juliet somewhat humorously belies herself in this last quotation, finding a "heavenly eloquence" in the name she earlier thought inimical to their love, is in keeping with a play that seems founded on the principle of the oxymoron: she wants, it seems, a "nameless naming." The paradox metadramatically reflects the difficulty of Shakespeare's own situation as he wrestles in this play with the slipperiest of antagonists, verbal purity, against whom even he may be overmatched.

It is a contest waged between every poet and language, and it ends for better or worse in a compromise somewhere between the private dream and the public fact. The contest is the more arduous for being conducted within the ring of drama where the impulse to verbal purity takes the form of lyric, which retards, as opposed to action, which impels. I'll get back to this particular issue later; for the moment I need to isolate the linguistic problem from the more embracing dramatic one.

If one charted the private/public range of language in *Romeo and Juliet*, at the furthest private extreme would come "silence," a nominalistic tendency so rigorous as to still speech entirely. Obviously since we do have a script for the play this extreme does not become manifest, except at those moments during performances when the lovers exchange prolonged glances and wordless sighs. Still at this end of the chart would appear the lovers' language within the orchard—self-cherishing, insular, answerable only to private feeling. At the extreme public end of the chart opposite silence is noise, disturbance, disquiet—the "airy word" of the opening scene which the Prince says has "thrice disturbed the quiet of our streets" with civil brawls. (The Prince is significantly more concerned with "peace" as quiet than as cessation of hostilities; the greatest threat to the play is sheer noise, its consistent goal harmonic sound.) Also at this end of the scale despite its affectation of privacy and purity is Romeo's Petrarchan language, full of sighs, show, and manner, and far too "airy" in its own way, as Juliet instantly perceives, to substantialize love in any genuine form. Here too, though antagonistic to Romeo's Petrarchanism, is Mercutio's ribald wordplay, as amusingly impure verbally as the sensuality it dotes on is in comparison to Romeo and Juliet's love.

One would also expect to place Friar Laurence's "holy words" within the public sphere since it is through the public institutions of church and marriage, by having "Holy Church incorporate two in one," that the friar hopes to reunite the oppugnant families. That would seem an ideal union, the private bond of love becoming a public bond of marriage sealing the families, because although love itself may be a fine and private thing marriage is by nature public. Its function is to translate private feeling into the received language of society and so give public residence to what may otherwise be simply emotional vagrancy—unpropertied, subjective, and strange. This love, we know, transcends all that. But nonetheless the wedding *is* private, and the marriage it begets remains so. Consecrated by holy words, the lovers' vows bind them to one another (suggesting that the language of love's communion so absent from *Love's Labour's Lost* has been discovered) but in this private union they remain divorced from the wider social context into which genuine marriage would incorporate them.

Their love then is translated into a language that goes unheard beyond the narrow circle formed by themselves, the friar, and later the nurse. Alone in the privacy of his cell Friar Laurence can celebrate the sacrament of Communion, can give quiet voice to *the* Word (Logos), and have its spiritual benefits circulate among all men. But he cannot do so with the sacrament of marriage. If marriage is to be the medium of a secular, familial communion, its sacramental language must be heard by the fallen families it would save, and in that regard the friar's words are as inaudible as those of the lovers. The most obvious symbol of the friar's inability to give public circulation to his own and the lovers' language is his short-circuited letter to Romeo in Mantua. Like Romeo when he leaves the orchard haven for the brawling streets, the friar's words—surrogates for the lovers' words—run afoul of the "infectious pestilence" of the outside world (5.2.10). (Mercutio's curse "A plague o' both your houses" is thus most literally fulfilled by the plague that detains Friar John.) Despite his intentions then Friar Laurence is less a mediator between private and public spheres than a religious version of the private—his rather monastic celibacy suggesting an analogue to the withdrawn lyric adoration of the lovers. Only when the lovers are dead and he, Horatio-like, tells their story does the friar finally marry them to the social order and bind the families as he had hoped.

Through neither family nor church can love make its way into the social context, nor through a third major institution, the state. As a political entity the Veronese state is elusive to the vanishing point; its dramatic form is simply the voice of the Prince, quite literally his sentences. In the opening scene ("hear the sentence of your moved prince") he decrees death to anyone who breaks the peace, and in 3.1 he pronounces sentence on Romeo ("A gentler judgment vanished from his lips," the friar reports, "Not body's death but body's banishment"—3.3.10–11). From one standpoint the princely word is not good since the peace it ordained is subsequently broken and the banished body returns; from another it is, since Mercutio and Tybalt die for their offense and Romeo for his (the Prince had said "when [Romeo's] found that hour is his last," and so it is—3.1.200). The political word clearly has its limits—as when the citizen, unaware that Tybalt is dead, cries "Up, sir, go with me./I charge thee in the Prince's name, obey" (3.1.144–145)[4]—but it also has its sovereignty, as Juliet laments:

"Romeo is banishèd!" To speak that word
Is father, mother, Tybalt, Romeo, Juliet,
All slain, all dead. "Romeo is banishèd!"
There is no end, no limit, measure, bound,
In that word's death; no words can that woe sound.
                                        (3.2.122–126)

If the Prince's word cannot spring the dead to life and duty as the citizen demanded, it can afflict the living with death.

The major emphasis in 3.2 and 3.3, in which the word "banished" is repeated nineteen times, is to force on the lovers the antinominalist realization that although as Juliet said a name is "nor hand nor foot/Nor arm nor face nor any

---

[4]In performances of the play it is sometimes assumed that the citizen addresses a kneeling Benvolio rather than a dead Tybalt. But Benvolio has just said "There lies that Tybalt," not "here" as he would if he were kneeling over him. The citizen, greatly concerned to take Tybalt in, is inattentive to matters such as death, Hamlet's "fell sergeant" who is more "strict in his arrest" even than vigilante citizens.

other part/Belonging to a man," even so airily universal a verb as "banishèd" can permanently still all those moving parts:

> *Juliet.*   That "banishèd," that one word "banishèd,"
>   Hath slain ten thousand Tybalts.
>   (3.2.113–114)

> *Juliet.*   To speak that word
>   Is father, mother, Tybalt, Romeo, Juliet,
>   All slain, all dead.
>   (3.2.122–124)

> *Romeo.*   Calling death "banishment"
>   Thou cut'st my head off with a golden axe.
>   (3.3.21–22)

If the language of love is inaudible to society, the language of society is deafening to the lovers. From such clangor the only final escape is to the quiet of the grave.

IV

"Banishèd" is the severing word that immediately threatens and finally destroys the communion of love since because of it the lovers are forced to communicate through society by means of the friar's message, and that is precisely what they cannot do. Only in a state of lyric seclusion hermetically sealed off from the plague-stricken world outside can their language retain its expressive purity. But the lovers cannot remain forever in the orchard, much as they would like to, and the poet cannot escape the fact that whereas his art is private, wrought in his own stylistic image and even given that personal signature that Shakespeare laments in Sonnet 76, his linguistic medium itself is intransigently public. As part of the vulgar tongue the words he would adopt are contaminated by ill usage, by an ever-present epidemic of imprecision, banality, lies, false rhetoric, jargon, true rhetoric, sentimentality, and solecisms, and by more localized historical plagues such as Petrarchanism, Euphuism, inkhorn neologisms, television commercials, social scientese, and beat or hippie nonspeak. Like Juliet on first confronting Romeo, the poet wants to compel words to abandon their corrupt public identities and submit to his cleansing rebaptism. Or again, to use another of the play's metaphors, like Romeo words as public identities must die ("He heareth not, he stirreth not, he moveth not" Mercutio says of Romeo; "The ape is dead"—2.1.15–16) so that they may be reborn within the context of the poem ("Call me but love and I'll be new baptized;/ Henceforth I never will be Romeo"—2.2.50–51).

This account of things is perhaps unduly metaphoric and a bit confusing as regards Romeo, whose verbal status is rather ambiguous. His Petrarchan style is impure, as underscored by Juliet's stylistic objections, because in the context of the play it comes from that extramural world outside the orchard. That is not to say that the sonnets of Wyatt, Sidney, Spenser, or Petrarch himself exhibit corrupt language. It is to say that the Petrarchan *style* has a public existence outside individual Petrarchan poems and that in Shakespeare's time—and certainly in his own view, as Sonnet 130 makes clear—it stood for a debased literary currency. Paradoxically at least some of this impurity derives from the fact that the Petrarchan style aspires to pure poetry and in so aspiring becomes an airy, hyperbolic, mechanically artificial expression of unfelt and undiscriminating feelings. In this sense it is too pure ("Virtue itself turns vice, being misapplied"—2.3.21), and when the too pure becomes too popular it turns impure, an infectious blight on the literary landscape.

From this excessive purity excessively available, Juliet recoils, seeking like Shakespeare a more individual style, a more genuine purity. But neither Juliet nor Shakespeare fully succeeds in the attempt to forge a new and authentic idiom. We are clearly asked to regard the movement from Romeo-Rosaline to Romeo-Juliet as an advance from Petrarchan dotage to true romantic love. And surely in large degree it is—after all, this love seals its bond in marriage and bears it out even to and beyond the edge of doom. Granted, and yet I doubt that either we or Shakespeare can rest fully at ease with the lovers' style. The trouble is that the old Romeo is imperfectly killed off; the ape is not really dead—too much of his Petrarchan manner and language live on in him; and Juliet, despite her anti-Petrarchan bias, too readily quickens to the invitations of his style. Her better speeches are resistance pieces that gain eloquence in the process of denying the power of speech itself, most notably in the balcony scene. She scores well off Romeo's verbal extravagance:

> *Romeo.* Ah Juliet, if the measure of thy joy
> Be heaped like mine, and that thy skill be more
> To blazon it, then sweeten with thy breath
> This neighbour air and let rich music's tongue
> Unfold the imagined happiness that both
> Receive in either by this dear encounter.
> *Juliet.* Conceit, more rich in matter than in words,
> Brags of his substance, not of ornament.
> They are but beggars that can count their worth,
> But my true love is grown to such excess
> I cannot sum up sum of half my wealth.
> (2.6.25–34)

But if the worth of private feeling cannot be assessed in the crude countinghouse of language, Juliet seems not always aware of it. This is most noticeable when on learning that Romeo has killed Tybalt her feelings swing from love to dismay:

> O serpent heart hid with a flowering face!
> Did ever dragon keep so fair a cave?
> Beautiful tyrant! Fiend angelical!
> Dove-feathered raven! Wolvish ravening lamb!
> Despised substance of divinest show!
> (3.2.73–77)

The distinction in the last line between substance and show invites our recollection of the distinction between substance and ornament in her speech just quoted (2.6.3–31) and urges on us the stylistic reversal that has occurred. It is wonderfully fitting that Juliet should register the shock to private feeling by adopting Romeo's Petrarchan oxymorons (cf. 1.1.181–188) at the exact moment when her loyalties turn in the antinominalist direction of "family" (she grieves not for Tybalt the unique but for Tybalt the cousin). She quickly recovers from this style and feeling, as does their love in general, but in the remainder of the scene her style (like Romeo's in 3.3) keeps shrilling upward into a mannered hysteria in which conceit, less rich in matter than in words, brags of its ornament, not its substance. Bathos is now their medium, and their verbal excesses are defended on the authority of unique feeling:

> *Romeo.*   Thou canst not speak of that thou dost not feel.
> Wert thou as young as I, Juliet thy love,
> An hour but married, Tybalt murdered,
> Doting like me and like me banishèd,
> Then mightst thou speak, then mightst thou tear thy hair
> And fall upon the ground as I do now,
> Taking the measure of an unmade grave.
>
> (3.3.64–70)

Such claims disarm criticism—ours I suppose as well as that of the friar, who must be wincing at the amount of hypothesis required to put him in the position of youth and love. No one denies the validity and intensity of the feeling, but of course a riot of feeling need not necessitate a riot of language and premature measurements of graves that look suspiciously like cribs. Romeo rejects all discipline that originates beyond self, whether moral, social, or stylistic. In effect he repudiates the world, and so hastens logically on to the notion of suicide. When Friar Laurence, harried back and forth across the room by the banging of the world at his door and the blubbering of a Romeo who would dissolve all connections with the world, cries in exasperation "What simpleness is this!" (3.3.77) his choice of the noun is perfect, for in the unblended simpleness of Romeo the man of unique feelings there is indeed at this point great silliness. However, Romeo is not altogether as pure in his simpleness as he would like, and radical purgation is called for:

> O tell me, friar, tell me
> In what vile part of this anatomy
> Doth my name lodge? Tell me, that I may sack
> The hateful mansion.
>
> (3.3.105–108)

To become pure "Romeo" and extirpate his connections with everything beyond self he would destroy "Montague," the "vile part" of him in which the world has staked its claim. But as the friar points out, the dagger that pierces Montague pierces Romeo as well:

Why rail'st thou on thy birth, the heaven, and earth?
Since birth and heaven and earth all three do meet
In thee at once, which thou at once wouldst lose.
                                            (3.3.119–121)

So far as I can see there is small evidence that Romeo absorbs much of the friar's lesson. For him there remains no world beyond the walls of Juliet's garden, where the lovers still strive to meet with all the nominalistic singularity of their Edenic forebears. Their lamentations in 3.2 and 3.3 are only a more strident stylistic version of their speech in 3.5. In this the last scene in which they engage in genuine dialogue before the destructive force of the word "banishèd" takes its full toll, we see the lyric imagination desperately seeking to impose its own truth on the world of fact and sunrise:

Juliet. Wilt thou be gone? It is not yet near day.
      It was the nightingale and not the lark
      That pierced the fearful hollow of thine ear.
      Nightly she sings on yond pomegranate tree.
      Believe me, love, it was the nightingale.
                                            (3.5.1–5)

And again:

Juliet. Yond light is not daylight, I know it, I—
      It is some meteor that the sun exhales
      To be to thee this night a torchbearer
      And light thee on thy way to Mantua.
                                            (3.5.12–15)

In line with her nominalistic "A rose by any other word" Juliet would rebaptize Nature, transforming lark and daylight into nightingale and meteor to the end that time stand still. Romeo allows himself to be persuaded that "it is not day," but as soon as he does so Juliet's lyric preoccupation is gone: "It is, it is! Hie hence, be gone, away!" (3.5.25–26). As it operates in the wide world, language may be less pure than the lovers would wish, but it stands for a view of reality that neither lover nor poet can safely ignore. Time, light, larks, and the usual terms for them remain intransigently themselves, answerable to their public definitions. The lover who withdraws entirely from the world into an autistic domain of feeling must pay for his pleasure with his life, as Romeo would were he to remain in the orchard. By the same token the poet who reshapes language in the exclusive light of his own designs, turning his back on his audience and creating not a truly individual but merely a unique style, must pay for his eccentric pleasures with his poetic life. There is no great danger of that here since the trouble with the lovers' style is not eccentricity but conventionality. The purity it aspires to, like that of the Petrarchanism to which it is uncomfortably akin, is too easily come by. And judging their language this way, I should be quick to add—that is, grading it down for poetic diction and a superabundance of rhetorical figures—is not to impose on the play a modern bias against rhetoric but to accept the implications of the play itself and to honor Shakespeare's own standards, which are implicit in his gradual estrangement over the years from an enameled, repetitive, lyrical style in favor of one that is concentrated, complex, and dramatic.

V

It would seem then that in *Romeo and Juliet* Shakespeare has encountered but by no means resolved the poet's dilemma. No doubt he must often have known perfectly well where he wanted poetically to go and yet could not get there, and knew that too. On the authority of the play's structure we can assume that he wanted to get from Rosaline to Juliet, from pure poetry to a viable poetic purity, but that he did not complete the journey in satisfactory style. That he realized this seems evident from the care he has taken to protectively enclose the lovers' poetic purity. Robert Penn Warren has shrewdly argued that the "impure poetry" of Mercutio and the nurse—poetry, that is, that reflects the impurity of life itself by means of wit, irony, logical contradictions, jagged rhythms, unpoetic diction, and so forth—provides a stylistic context in which we can more readily accept the too pure poetry of the lovers.[5] Warren assumes in other words that the impure poetry in the play functions much as William Empson claims comic subplots function, as lightning rods to divert the audience's potentially dyslogistic reactions away from the vulnerable high seriousness of the main plot (main style).[6] The implication is that Shakespeare is trying to have it both ways at once, that like Juliet asking for an "unnamed naming" in the balcony scene he asks us to accept the authenticity of a style that he himself knows is too pure and therefore needful of protection. From this perspective one sees that in stacking the literary deck against the lovers—by providing the stylistic opposition of Mercutio and the nurse and the environmental opposition of the feuding families, of fate, coincidences, and mistimings—Shakespeare has actually stacked it in their favor. The obvious contrast is with *Antony and Cleopatra*, and we might note that whereas the impure poetry of Enobarbus functions like that of Mercutio and the nurse, by that time Shakespeare has mastered his own stylistic problems and can imbue those lovers' language with an impurity of its own. If the later technique risks more, it stands to gain more too, and as we all know does.

The argument made here in terms of style can be extended to character and genre also, for the lovers themselves, no less than their style, are too pure and they acquire in the minds of too many readers an unearned tragic stature. Even though

---

[5]In his famous article "Pure and Impure Poetry" originally printed in the *Kenyon Review*, 5 (Spring 1943):228–254, and since reprinted in many collections of critical essays.

[6]Empson's remarks on subplots appear in *Some Versions of Pastoral*, pp. 25–84 of the New Directions paperback edition (New York, 1960).

the play rejects uniqueness Shakespeare has nominalistically bleached from Romeo and Juliet most of the impurities that rub off on man by virtue of his public contacts. They simply have no public contacts. Despite the importance of family, they are essentially unrelated, meeting as isolated individuals rather than (like Antony and Cleopatra) as complex human beings with social, political, religious, and even national allegiances and responsibilities to contend with. Insufficiently endowed with complexity, with the self-division that complexity makes possible, and with the self-perceptiveness that such division makes possible, they become a study in victimage and sacrifice, not tragedy. Their experience portrays not the erosion within but the clash without, and the plot harries them toward lamentation instead of vision. One of the major ironies of the final scene in the tomb is that for all its imagery of radiance the illumination is entirely outside Romeo, kindled by torches and Juliet's beauty, not by a self-reflective consciousness. On the stylistic failure as it relates to tragedy Maynard Mack says "Comic overstatement aims at being preposterous. Until it becomes so, it remains flat. Tragic overstatement, on the other hand, aspires to be believed, and unless in some sense it is so, remains bombast."[7]

In Shakespeare's protection of the lovers Mercutio plays a crucial role, for although Juliet rejects the false purity of Romeo's Petrarchan style she never has to encounter the rich impurity of Mercutio's speech. And it is Mercutio who seems the genuine threat. The nurse's style is abundantly impure, but that is all it is, whereas Mercutio can deliver pure poetry impurely. In his much-admired, much-maligned Queen Mab speech, which looks so suspiciously and conspicuously irrelevant to the main issues of the play, Mercutio turns pure poetry back on itself. Even while presenting a lengthy illustration of pure poetry he defines it as a product of fancy and foolishness airily roaming like Queen Mab herself through dreaming minds, to which it offers substitute gratifications that have no direct bearing on reality—on real courtier's real curtsies and suits, on lawyer's stunning fees, ladies' kisses, parsons' benefices, soldiers' battles. "Peace, Mercutio, peace!" Romeo cries. "Thou talk'st of nothing." But because Mercutio can talk of something as well as nothing, because he can deal in both pure and impure styles, he is given a tough and enduring eloquence that makes the nurse, mired in the language of sensual expedience, seem gross and Romeo callow. (Romeo to be sure can vie with Mercutio in the lubricities of street speech, but Romeo-with-Juliet is another man altogether; Shakespeare keeps the two scrupulously discrete.)

Entering the orchard where felt experience is sovereign, Romeo can dismiss Mercutio's extramural ribaldry about Rosaline with a famous line—"He jests at scars that never felt a wound" (2.2.1). When the wound is in the other chest though, Romeo must play straight man to more famous lines:

[7]Maynard Mack, "The Jacobean Shakespeare: Some Observations on the Construction of the Tragedies," in *Jacobean Theatre*, vol. I of Stratford-upon-Avon Studies, ed. John Russell Brown and Bernard Harris (New York, 1960), p. 15.

> *Romeo.*   Courage, man, the hurt cannot be much.
> *Mercutio.* No, 'tis not so deep as a well nor so wide as a
>   church door, but 'tis enough, 'twill serve.
>   (3.1.98–100)

This asks to be compared to the lovers' style. They repeatedly claim that language is too shallow a thing to reach into the deeps of private feeling, but their own verbal practice is hardly consistent with such a claim. Whenever their feelings are touched, torrents follow. Hence the bristling oxymorons of the stricken Romeo in 1.1—

> Why then O brawling love! O loving hate!
> O anything, of nothing first create!
> O heavy lightness, serious vanity,
> Misshapen chaos of well-seeming forms!
> Feather of lead, bright smoke, cold fire, sick health!
> Still-waking sleep that is not what it is!
> This love feel I, that feel no love in this.
>   (1.1.182–188)

Hence the same oxymorons from Juliet's lips in 3.2 ("Beautiful tyrant! fiend angelical!" etc.) and the bathos of Romeo in 3.3, for example—

> Heaven is here
> Where Juliet lives, and every cat and dog
> And little mouse, every unworthy thing,
> Live here in heaven and may look on her,
> But Romeo may not.
>   (3.3.29–33)

It is in this context of grotesque verbal posturing, where convulsions of speech coalesce with tantrums of feeling, that, Mercutio's words on death acquire a quiet and sustained eloquence. It is those words ironically that best fulfill the stylistic requirements of Juliet's early nominalism. The uniquely felt inner "hurt" Mercutio does not try directly to define, thus avoiding the risks of hyperbole and general verbal inflation that prey on the speech of the lovers when they reflect on *their* wounds. The private feeling that's past the size of speech is suggested only obliquely, in terms of the size of the physical "hurt," and even then by saying not what it is but what it is not. Here in the plain style is functional language, language that like the wound itself is content to be "enough," to "serve" rather than run riot. In general then it is the mixed tones of Mercutio's speech that the lovers most need to incorporate into their own style. But Shakespeare has kept Mercutio permanently stationed on the outer side of the orchard wall, as oblivious to the existence of their love as they are to him.

   The public world is too crass and bellicose to assimilate the private truth of love, and Mercutio is a good instance of the fact that there are public truths that the lovers cannot assimilate. Given two such disjunctive languages, only mutual injury remains possible. The lovers' language fails when it seeks to make its way by means of Father John through the plague-ridden world beyond the orchard.

Love's feelings hold constant, but during the reunion in the tomb the dialogue of love dissolves into lyric monologues heard only by the speaker. One further step remains. The purity of their love (figured after Romeo's departure in Juliet's resistance to marrying Paris) is reasserted in a second marriage ceremony that is even more private than the first:

> Romeo. Arms, take your last embrace. And lips, O you
> The doors of breath, seal with a righteous kiss
> A dateless bargain to engrossing death!
> (5.3.113–115)

In this final contract the breath of lyric speech and the breath of life are simultaneously expended to seal an endless bond with silence. So too with Juliet, who retreats into a remoter stillness as the noise of the outside world rushes toward her:

> Yea, noise? Then I'll be brief. O happy dagger!
> This is thy sheath. There rest and let me die.
> (5.3.169–170)

As the *Liebestod* stressed by Denis de Rougemont and others, Romeo and Juliet's love has been a flight from the frustrations of life toward the consummations of the grave. Similarly, as *Liebestille* their linguistic style has been a flight from noise toward a silence beyond speech. The silence is at last achieved and with it an expressiveness that extends their own bond of feeling outward. For embraced in and by death their still figures bespeak the truth of their love to the wondering representatives of the social order gathered in the tomb, and do so with such persuasiveness that it transforms those random and rancorous individuals into a genuine community united in sorrow and sympathy. The cost, however, runs high. What is purchased is in the Prince's apt phrase a "glooming peace"—peace as public amity has been bought by the sacrifice of the lovers to the peace of an enduring but eloquent stillness.

VI

Neither in life nor through language then do the lovers make connections with their social order or the wide world beyond the orchard. Self-engrossed to the end, their speech admits no impediments, not even death. Death in fact is less an impediment than a goal, a terminal value whose stillness, privacy, and endlessness sum up the character of their love. In this final marriage to death they divorce the world.

It goes without saying that there is a sentimentality about the ending of the play that goes down hard—the bravura notes of Romeo's final speeches, the pathetic suicides, the stagy recognition scene that seems framed to fulfill the child's morbidly gratifying wish to be present at his own imagined funeral. But Shakespeare is not merely pumping up the pathos in order to celebrate the absoluteness of a fine and constant love done in by a crass society; he is also attempting to negotiate between private and public values. In comedy such negotiations are fulfilled in weddings that incorporate private love into the larger social context. In tragedy the division between private and public values is normally bridged by sacrifice: the hero's alienating uniqueness becomes through his sacrificial death the instrument that binds his survivors to one another and to his now lost and lamented value. So it is with Romeo and Juliet. Though divorced from the world, as "poor sacrifices" they bring about the marriage of the divided society they leave behind. With this wider social marriage the play finds its formal resolution, and so it is ultimately to Shakespeare's maturing concept of dramatic form that the lovers are sacrificed.

Before turning to the question of dramatic form, though, let me note briefly how the statues to be erected by the bereaved fathers confirm the success of sacrifice in bringing about fulfillment in both private and public spheres:

> *Montague.* But I can give thee more.
> For I will raise her statue in pure gold,
> That whiles Verona by that name is known
> There shall no figure at such rate be set
> As that of true and faithful Juliet.
> *Capulet.* As rich shall Romeo's by his lady's lie,
> Poor sacrifices of our enmity.
> (5.3.298–304)

The statues become the final emblem of that expressive stillness to which the lovers' language has been implicitly devoted since the balcony scene. However, the nominalistic purity to which they had aspired is now transcended since the private meaning and value of their love, as given expression in the silent gold figures, will be made permanently public.

The verbal recoil of the play from noise toward expressive stillness is the more apparent if we analyze the play in terms of an economic or commercial motif that also culminates in the statues. Briefly, the lovers' self-valuation stresses pricelessness, the impossibility of "selling" their love to the two families or the public—especially to Juliet's father, who feudalistically regards marriage as a business transaction. To Romeo Juliet is a "jewel" precious beyond price (the nurse at one point, incidentally, calls her "Jule"): "Beauty too rich for use, for earth too dear" (1.5.48–49). To Capulet she is "the hopeful lady of my earth" (1.2.15)—his *fille de terre*, or "heiress"—who, however, because she is an unmarketable commodity by virtue of prior commitment to Romeo will finally inherit only enough of his land to make a grave (5.3.297). And Juliet says of herself:

> They are but beggars that can count their worth;
> But my true love is grown to such excess
> I cannot sum up sum of half my wealth.
> (2.6.32–34)

Paradoxically then Montague "will raise her statue in pure gold" (5.3.299). The effect of doing so will be on the one hand to reduce Juliet to the base metal of public commerce but on the other hand to cast that metal in an unnegotiable form. As pure gold statuary the lovers retain a pricelessness that transcends commercial distribution even while their value is "sold" in the sense of its being publicly shared. This selling of a priceless commodity is an exact equivalent in commercial terms to the "expressive stillness" we spoke of on the linguistic plane.

So much for the verbal-commercial aspects of the statues' nonverbal expressiveness—though their very nonverbalness is an issue to which we will return in the next section. I have so far dealt with the stillness of the statues as "silence," but to give the analysis a turn toward dramatic form I need to stress the motionlessness of stillness. The gold that was so much the object of commercial voyages in Shakespeare's time and that once discovered and minted went its endless voyage from pocket to pocket finds in the shape of the statues a permanent rest. So does Romeo, who says more than he knows when he prepares for his suicide:

> O here
> Will I set up my everlasting rest
> And shake the yoke of inauspicious stars
> From this world-wearied flesh.
> (5.3.109–112)

Romeo's experience in the play is depicted among other things as a voyage.[8] Setting off for what will become his first meeting with Juliet he says

> But He that hath the steerage of my course
> Direct my sail!
> (1.4.112–113)

Again in the balcony scene:

> I am no pilot, yet wert thou as far
> As that vast shore washed with the farthest sea
> I should adventure for such merchandise.
> (2.2.82–85)

And finally after his "O here/Will I set up my everlasting rest":

> Come, bitter conduct, come, unsavoury guide!
> Thou desperate pilot, now at once run on
> The dashing rocks thy sea-sick weary bark.
> (5.3.116–118)

Thus Romeo voyages through the play to the final port of everlasting rest, which is

---

[8]Moody Prior was the first, I think, to point out the pattern of this voyaging imagery, in *The Language of Tragedy* (New York, 1947), pp. 69–70.

both the grave and the gold statue commissioned by Capulet. In the form of the statue he embodies the paradox of motionless movement, a dynamic illusion of life artistically arrested—always moving and never moving in the same sense that an "everlasting rest" is both intransitive and ceaseless, a restless rest.[9]

However, motion is more pervasive in the play than this. There is the violent motion or commotion, the street fighting, with which everything begins; there is the balcony scene contract that Juliet calls

> too rash, too unadvised, too sudden,
> Too like the lightning which doth cease to be
> Ere one can say it lightens
>
> (2.2.118–120)

and the quick clandestine wedding that Romeo ("O let us hence; I stand on sudden haste") forces against the friar's counsels of moderation ("Wisely and slow—they stumble that run fast"—2.3.93–94). There are also Mercutio itching for action, and the pell-mell Tybalt anxious for a grave; the immediacy of Romeo's banishment by the Prince ("Let Romeo hence in haste,/ Else when he's found that hour is his last"); the relentless rush of time as the Thursday of Juliet's enforced marriage to Paris is tolled on by Capulet the perpetual-motion matchmaker—

> Day, night, hour, tide, time, work, play,
> Alone, in company, still my care hath been
> To have her matched;
>
> (3.5.178–180)

the speed of Romeo's return from Mantua; and finally the death-dealing liveliness of the poisons ("O true apothecary!/ Thy drugs are quick"—5.3.119–120).[10]

The world at large rushes and the lovers haste toward one another, but when they are united, especially within the orchard, time and motion cease. Given the contrasting principles of movement and stasis, the form of the play might be diagrammed as a horizontal line interrupted by several circles indicating the times (in 1.5, 2.2, 2.6, 3.5, and 5.3) when Romeo and Juliet are together. For in each of these five scenes the primary tension is between staying and departing, and in each scene the lovers are called out of stillness by the exigencies of time and motion. In 1.5 they have been stilled in a kiss ("Then move not while my prayer's effect I take"—108) but are interrupted by the nurse calling Juliet to her mother. In 2.2 Romeo starts to leave but is called back by Juliet, who then forgets why she did so; their next lines play on stillness in time and space:

[9]"Stillness" as figured in the statues thus takes on the oxymoronic ever-neverness of Keats's urn and the other instances of literary ekphrasis analyzed by Murray Krieger in "The Ekphrastic Principle and the Still Movement of Poetry; or *Laokoön* Revisited."

[10]This generalized haste of time and action has been frequently noted, perhaps most significantly in Brents Stirling's chapter "They Stumble That Run Fast" in *Unity in Shakespearean Tragedy* (New York, 1956).

> *Romeo.*   Let me stand here till thou remember it.
> *Juliet.*   I shall forget, to have thee still stand there,
>   Remembering how I love thy company.
> *Romeo.*   And I'll still stay, to have thee still forget,
>   Forgetting any other home but this.
>   (2.2.172–176)

But at their backs they always hear the nurse's voice clucking Juliet in and Romeo away (2.2.136, 149, 151). In 2.6 they are so transfixed by one another that the friar must pun heavily on leaving and staying even to get them to their own wedding:

> Come, come with me, and we will make short work,
> For, by your leaves, you shall not stay alone
> Till Holy Church incorporate two in one.
>   (2.6.35–37)

And in 3.5 a world of clocks and irreversible sunrises tolls for Romeo, who "must be gone and live or stay and die" (11).

Staying a moment ourselves, we should observe that Shakespeare has here reversed the situation in *Love's Labour's Lost* in which the faint linear thrust of dramatic action was constantly diverted and absorbed into the circular eddies of lyric. If one of the things Shakespeare learned in that play is the inability of lyric speech to substitute for dramatic action, the effects of that lesson on *Romeo and Juliet* are apparent in the way the linear current of action repeatedly overcomes lyric retardations. Though enraptured by a stillness beyond time and motion, the lovers, particularly Romeo, have larger obligations to fulfill outside the orchard walls where Mercutio and Tybalt are impatient to die, the Prince to deliver his banishment speech, the apothecary to lay out his quick drugs. With all the play and players waiting for Romeo (and metadramatically for Shakespeare) he can hardly linger forever with Juliet.

Though all the scenes mentioned earlier are lyric in their attempts to set up self-sustaining moments of expressive feeling, the surrender of lyric to drama is especially evident in 3.5. We considered this scene earlier as an instance of the lyric style desperately seeking and failing to impose love's longings on nature and time. In the present connection I would stress the lyric *form* of this lovers' parting since in it Shakespeare scrupulously observes all the conventions of the aubade.[11] Thus when the lovers are compelled to part, a traditional lyric form is "parted" also—in the sense both of being interrupted and more important of being relegated from a lyric whole to a dramatic part. The clear implication is that lyric cannot remain sufficient unto itself in drama but like the lovers themselves must be sacrificed to a larger conception of form.

---

[11] These conventions are conveniently listed by R. E. Kaske in "The Aube in Chaucer's *Troilus*," which appears in *Chaucer Criticism: Troilus and Criseyde and the Minor Poems*, ed. Richard J. Schoeck and Jerome Taylor (South Bend, Ind., 1961), pp. 167–179. However, the conventions are perfectly exemplified in the first sixty-five lines of the present scene, to which I therefore refer the curious reader insufficiently up on his aubes.

VII

Yet there is a sense in which Shakespeare has tried to give with one hand and take with the other, which after all is the nature of a sacrifice, something won through losing. What he loses, it would appear, is the permanence, fixity, and still-ness of lyric; but what he gains is perhaps a greater stillness, that of dramatic form. This is the rushing stasis, the ever-never species of stillness. For all the rush and bustle of action, the hasty mistimings, the voyaging to eternity are locked perpetually in what is at this stage of his career Shakespeare's most care-fully plotted and symmetrically patterned play. As if in reaction to the formless-ness of *Love's Labour's Lost*, where he invented a plot that was little more than a series of verbal events brought to an abrupt and frustrate conclusion, he next turned to the preestablished plot of Arthur Brooke's *Tragical Historye of Romeus and Juliet*. Though he trimmed most of the suet from Brooke's plump poem of some 6000 lines, compressing the action and tightening the time scheme, he nonetheless followed the main course of its plot with considerable fidelity.

In *Romeo and Juliet* then Shakespeare knew exactly where he was going. No doubt he did so in other plays too—but here he takes pains to announce his formal mastery of his materials and sense of direction, as for instance in the unusual (at this stage of his career) device of the sonnet prologues to Acts 1 and 2, both of which sum up and forecast action. Take the opening prologue:

> Two households, both alike in dignity,
>> In fair Verona where we lay our scene,
> From ancient grudge break to new mutiny
>> Where civil blood makes civil hands unclean.
> From forth the fatal loins of these two foes
>> A pair of star-crossed lovers take their life,
> Whose misadventured piteous overthrows
>> Doth with their death bury their parents' strife.
> The fearful passage of their death-marked love
>> And the continuance of their parents' rage
> Which, but their children's end, nought could remove,
>> Is now the two hours' traffic of our stage;
> The which if you with patient ears attend,
>> What here shall miss, our toil shall strive to mend.

The journey metaphor later to be associated primarily with Romeo is here assigned to both lovers in "misadventured," perhaps in "children's end," clearly in "the fearful passage of their death-marked love." Some of that metaphor's linear movement carries over into the following line—"And the continuance of their parents' rage"—so that "continuance" evokes spatial motion as well as temporal duration. Children's love and parental hate both voyage through the play toward the terminal port of death. Then finally the metaphor expands to encompass the presentation of the play itself, fusing temporal and spatial progress in the "two hours' traffic of our stage" figure. For two hours audience and actors are stationed in one theatrical place, and yet as the prologue to Act 3 of *Henry V* puts it—

> our swift scene flies
> In motion of no less celerity
> Than that of thought.

More important than this kind of stationary movement in the theater are the implications of Shakespeare's metadramatic merger of the play's internal fiction, the voyage of the lovers, and the play itself, the traffic of drama ("traffic" appropriately smuggling a commercial connotation into the concept of voyaging). The lovers' voyage occurs under the stars (it is most fittingly a disaster, *dés* + *astre*), which may be considered as both astrological and astronomical influences. Astrologically the stars are equivalent to fate, the fore-plotted journey of star-crossed lovers. And indeed the course of the lovers' voyage and of Shakespeare's play (dramatic traffic) has been pre-plotted in Arthur Brooke's tragical historye. Appropriately, since *fatum* means the "sentences" of the gods, fate has here a literary dimension, and Romeo is quite right to address the dead Paris as "One writ with me in sour misfortune's book" (5.3.82). His journey and that of all the other characters are fated not merely by "inauspicious stars" (5.3.111) but by their literary analogue, an inauspicious plot adopted from Brooke.

From a metadramatic as opposed to thematic standpoint then the repeated references throughout the play to stars, fate, fortune, the curse of birth, the charted journey, all the deterministic forces bearing on the lovers, testify to the sovereignty not merely of cosmic design in human affairs but of plot and form in the construction of *Romeo and Juliet*.[12] And here too is stationary movement. The great haste of the play, the fractious encounters, the stumbling of those who run fast, the recurrent thrusting of the lovers out of the still stasis of lyric, the ramrodding of time—all this activity is necessitated by a plot that demands movement to perfect its design, to complete the voyage of which it is the chart. As chart or plot the dramatic voyage is still, yet nevertheless contains sequences of evolving actions. Its correlative in the fictional world within the play is the fixed pattern of stars that astrologically "moves" the lovers whose unalterable destiny is to advance to the destination of death.[13]

---

[12]Stressing the metadramatic implications of fate is in line with the last paragraph of chapter 9 of *The Poetics* where Aristotle (as Kenneth Burke notes in *Language as Symbolic Action*, Berkeley, Calif., 1966, p. 30) "seems to be saying in effect: The way to make a plot effective is to make it seem inevitable, and the way to make it seem wonderful is to make its imitation of inevitability seem fate-driven." Fate, free will, necessity, and other crucial matters of belief about reality are from the standpoint of poetics merely so much grist for the dramatist's mill.

[13]In the ambiguousness of these astrological/astronomical stars we may also see figured the paradox of fatality and free will in dramatic characters. Astrologically the lovers are fated to do what they indeed do, to make their dramatic voyage from *a* to *z*, as any literary character is fated to comply with the dictates of the plot in which he finds himself. But if on the other hand we think of the stars as astronomical guides to navigation, they point up the appearance of self-determination in the characters since as navigator man uses stars instead of being astrologically used by them. Combining the two con-

Not only does Shakespeare forecast his control of dramatic form in the sonnet prologues; he reaffirms it at the end of the play when Friar Laurence, a major manipulator of plot, recapitulates all that has happened (5.3.229–269). At the corresponding point in *Love's Labour's Lost* Shakespeare advertised a failure of dramatic form by allowing Mercade his destructive entrance. Now, however, the friar presents us with a scrupulously detailed forty-line synopsis that accounts for each phase of the action in terms of a governing literary design. In effect the friar pleads his case on the grounds of a coherent plot—not of course his own plot, which failed, but Shakespeare's plot, which succeeds by means of the friar's failure and the lovers' misfortune.

VIII

Shakespeare's success in *Romeo and Juliet* is impressive by comparison with past failures but by no means total. His concentration on, almost celebration of, dramatic form imparts to the play a highly rigid structure based on the division between Montagues and Capulets and between lovers and society. As Sigurd Burckhardt has observed, the play has "a symmetry which, even though it is a symmetry of conflict, is comforting."[14] For despite the family feud the social order is in no real danger of collapse. What turbulence there is gets expressed within a stabilizing framework formed by the Prince and the friar, the one devoted to civil order, the other all reason and moderation. The virulence of the conflict between families is mitigated by the principals themselves, the spindle-shanked and slippered old men who allow the feud to continue less from rancor than from apathy. And the lovers are themselves untainted by the enmities abroad; they are not at odds with an antagonistic society so much as they are simply apart from it—hurt by ricochet rather than direct intent, by a secret that always could be made public but never is. Hence there is a strong sense of the arbitrary about the play and the lovers' fate, which with all its dependence on accident, coincidence, and sheer mistiming seems imposed and gratuitous. Finally at the end there is a too easy resolution both of the social problem of uniting the families and of the dramatic dilemma of finding a style in which the private and public dimensions of language are happily joined.

For the dramatic or more precisely linguistic dilemma is resolved at the end not stylistically but symbolically, by means of the emblematic statues in which Shakespeare has sought to comprise both private and public values. If the lovers'

---

cepts in one symbol as Shakespeare has done gives us man the navigator using the stars to maintain a pre-charted course from which he cannot deviate. Metadramatically the playwright seeks to maintain the appearance of freedom in his characters, to present them to us as free agents who choose the plot (character issuing in action, as A. C. Bradley put it) that has in literary fact chosen them. "Is it even so?" Romeo says on hearing of Juliet's supposed death, "Then I defy you, stars!" And then on the authority of private feeling and personal volition he rushes back to Verona to keep an appointment in the tomb that Shakespeare's plot had long ago "prescribed" for him.

[14] In "The King's Language: Shakespeare's Drama as Social Discovery."

nominalistic conception of speech implies a verbal purity bordering on nonspeech, here in the silence of the statues is that stillness; and if their love has aspired to a lyric stasis, here too in the fixity of plastic form is that stillness. But by being publicly available—representing the lovers and their value but representing them for the Veronese audience—the statues surpass the aspirations and expressive aims of the lovers. The communicative gap between the private secret love and the social order oblivious to the existence of that love is bridged—and this seems the major significance of the statues—by *artistic form*. Cast in such form, the worth of unique experience is popularized without being cheapened. By shifting from a verbal to a visually symbolic plane Shakespeare ingeniously makes the most of his stylistic liabilities while acknowledging silently that the too pure language of the lovers could not in itself effect such a union.[15] For the dual stillness of the statues, their silence and motionlessness, reflects not merely the poetic tendencies of the lovers but in a large sense the formal properties of Shakespeare's play. The statues materialize at the conclusion, that is, precisely at the point at which the play as temporal experience materializes into spatial form for its audience, the point at which form completes itself on stage and crystallizes in our memories. If language has not linked the public and private world, then form does. And seen in the perspective of dramatic form, the division between lovers and social order is not divisive because the principle of division itself, the playing off of the two worlds in opposition, gives rise to the form of *Romeo and Juliet*. The paradox of form is like that of love in "The Phoenix and the Turtle":

> Two distincts, division none:
> Number there in love was slain.

So the most fruitful coalescence of divided worlds is not to be found in the verbal paradoxes of the oxymoron but in the dramatic paradoxes of the play as shaped entity. As symbols of that shaping the statues of the closing scene reflexively comment on Romeo's oxymorons of the opening scene (1.1.181ff). Those oxymorons clashingly connect the two divided spheres of the opening scene, the public quarrel in the streets and Romeo's private dotage on Rosaline. Hence they are uttered just at the moment when Romeo and Benvolio, who have been talking of Romeo's private problems in love, arrive at the place where the street violence occurred. The "airy word" that bred the "civil brawls" (1.1.96) now expresses in the discordance of Romeo's oxymorons the inner brawling of Petrarchan dotage and unites the two spheres of experience, public and private, as versions of a kind of linguistic noise. In both areas the word has gone bad. Though somewhat redeemed by the speech of the lovers later on, the word never gets placed in public circulation.

---

[15]In Brooke's poem there are no statues and no gold, only a tomb raised aloft on every side of which in memory of the lovers "were set and eke beneath/ Great store of cunning epitaphs." That Shakespeare has eliminated mention of the epitaphs further emphasizes the nonverbal expressiveness of the statues and hence aligns them with the plastic or spatial aspects of Shakespeare's dramatic art. Brooke's poem incidentally appears in volume I of Geoffrey Bullough's *Narrative and Dramatic Sources of Shakespeare* (London and New York, 1957) and somewhat abridged in Alice Griffin's *The Sources of Ten Shakespearean Plays* (New York, 1966).

It is left for the statues to symbolize in form an ideal but dramatically unrealized social and verbal union. "Fain would I dwell on form" Juliet told Romeo; but it is really Shakespeare who has dwelt on form in this play, and by doing so has enabled Romeo and Juliet to dwell permanently *in* form.

One final point. I spoke earlier about the nominalistic impulse behind Shakespeare's creation of lovers from whom all family or universal relationships have been deleted—nominalistic because we are asked to confront the lovers as unique particulars. The fact, however, that the lovers are less singular in language and character than we might wish suggests that this deletion of universals is actually antinominalistic, less Aristotelean or Scotist than Platonic. Uniqueness, Shakespeare seems to have realized by the end of this play, is not the condition of being free from universal ties and tendencies; it is not a kind of pure essence left behind after we have burned off all accidental impurities. Distillation of that sort, in fact, leaves us with something very like Platonic universals themselves. But this seems to have been the process by which the lovers were created—a purification by dramatic fiat, giving us a Platonic conception of pure love cast in the role of particulars. At the end of the play, however, Shakespeare seems to sense that with men as with poems uniqueness resides in the form or contextual organization of non-unique qualities—a form sufficiently complex in its internal relations to defy reductive abstraction. Is this not part of the meaning of the statues also? Only by destroying the formal context of the statues can one commercialize the gold of which they are made. Detached though they are from their fictional surroundings, Romeo and Juliet, like the gold in the statues, are permanently embedded in the context of *Romeo and Juliet*, where presumably not even the critic's chisels can get at their priceless worth.

Romeo and Juliet
and the Problematics of Love

Rosalie L. Colie

It was not altogether easy to make a tragedy of a love story, traditionally the stuff of comedy. We are so accustomed to *Romeo and Juliet*, for instance, and to *Othello* and *Antony and Cleopatra*, that we tend to forget that there were technical problems for the playwright in making sufficiently serious as tragedies the domestic problems of love. "Love" existed in the Renaissance in important literary shapes, but on the whole these were not tragic—indeed, if anything, the conjunctive powers of love were regarded, in drama, as suited rather to comic solutions than to high tragic decisiveness. Further, love itself is an unstable element: it is flighty, and as such a proper subject for farce, not for tragedy—at best, romantic comedy, ending in beautiful conciliations, offered a proper generic habitat for tales of love.

Outside of drama, literary love tended to take two major shapes,[1] one of them, the romance, was closely related to comedy, its organization owing much to comic conventions and feeding back into Renaissance comic formulations. The other, the love-lyric, presents quite a different world of love: from Dante's forceful presentation onward, love in lyric form seemed to be of a higher sort than the love presented in either comedy or romance, a private experience in a world—as opposed to the world of comedy or romance—sparsely populated, with a few figures all enjoying notably intense emotions.[2] In the lyric poetry of love, poets began all kinds of explorations into themselves, so that in literature if not in life, psychological self-exploration and self-description were normally practised, and a vast reservoir of *topoi* of self-

[1]Though there are many more than those I cite, some studies of "literary love" have been very useful to me: John Bayley, *The Characters of Love* (London, 1961), especially Chapter 3, on *Othello*; Maurice Valency, *In Praise of Love* (New York, 1961), for the "courtly" background, as well as C. S. Lewis' classic (and classically-disputed) *Allegory of Love* (Oxford, 1936). For *Romeo and Juliet*, see H. A. Mason, *Shakespeare's Tragedies of Love* (London, 1970), Chapters One to Three, as well as Karl-Heinz Wenkel, *Sonettstrukturen in Shakespeares Dramen*, Linguistica et Litteraria, I (1968); Inge Leimburg, *Shakespeares Romeo und Julia*, Beihefte zu *Poetica*, IV (1968), stresses the "romance" associations of the play.

[2]For the development of sonnets and sonnet-theory, see [Walter] Moench, *Das Sonett* [(Heidelberg, 1955)]; for petrarchanism, [Leonard] Forster, *The Icy Fire* [(Cambridge, 1969)]; and Cynthia Grant Tucker's forthcoming work.

inspection became the inheritance of the great Renaissance writers of songs and sonnets.

In particular, the sonnet cycle offered possibilities for developing the lyric themes of love.[3] Dante set the tone and Petrarca confirmed it, to influence writers of lyric cycles and sonnet cycles throughout the long Renaissance, who in turn added their own variations and contributed their own insights to a genre elevated by those Italian models to something far beyond the ordinary love-lyric. By the time Shakespeare tried his hand at a love-tragedy, he had already worked in several of the major literary love-forms of the Renaissance. His sonnets are a major document in the lyric tradition, and several early comedies served him as preparations for his major love-tragedies, *Romeo and Juliet* and *Othello: Two Gentlemen of Verona* offered one kind of pre-study for *Romeo and Juliet, Much Ado* is in part a comic dress-rehearsal for *Othello*. Without *Romeo and Juliet*, I think, Shakespeare would have had greater difficulties with the problems raised by *Othello*.

It is, then, with that early play that I wish to deal first. With *Romeo and Juliet*, its plot deriving from a sad and rather sordid novella, Shakespeare attempted his first love-tragedy. How did an ambitious and experimental author go about this task? First of all, he drew upon types officially "comic,"[4] types which had already colonized the prose narratives of the Renaissance. He peopled his play in a perfectly familiar way, with figures from the comic cast: the young girl; her suitor (*adulescens amans*), whom her father does not favor; another *adulescens* (County Paris), whom the father approves; a father, *senex*, who becomes, naturally, *senex iratus* when crossed by his daughter; a nurse, not only the customary *nutrix* but a particular subtype, *nutrix garrula*. Our hero is accompanied by a friend, indeed by two friends, Benvolio and Mercutio; in a comedy, for symmetry, presumably Juliet would have had two school-fellows with her, to be disposed of at the play's end to the two young men. Here, though, she is unaccompanied; and because the play is a tragedy, Mercutio can be killed off and Benvolio fall out of the play without our wondering why or lamenting the absence of appropriate girls to be given away to Romeo's "extra" friends.

Comedies take place in cities; this tragedy is very city-bound; even Friar Lawrence's cell is within walking distance of the famous two houses. When Romeo flees Verona, he does not take to the woods, as a proper romance-hero might have been expected to do (and as Orlando does), but settles in nearby Mantua, to out-wait, as he hopes, his troubles. As befits a comic city-scene, we have splendid servants of different sorts, baiting each other and irritating as well as serving their betters, providing relief for what turns out to be a very grim sequence of actions.

---

[3]Evidently, the sonnet-sequence was particularly important in the development of self-preoccupation and introspection, and was its main literary vehicle, as Mrs. Tucker's work makes plain.

[4]Comic personages are discussed in [Julius Caesar] Scaliger, *Poetices* [*Libri Septem*], [(Lyon, 1561)] pp. 20–22; and see John Vyvyan, *Shakespeare and the Rose of Love* (London, 1960).

So far, so good; but how to turn the play into a tragedy of love? What language, for example, to use? From the first spoken words of *Romeo and Juliet*, the Chorus' speech in sonnet-form, we are directed to a major source for the play's language, the sonnet tradition, from which, as we see at once, Romeo had drunk deep; like the young men at Navarre's court, Romeo knew the literary modes of the Renaissance young gentleman. Critics of the play speak again and again of the sonnets in the play itself,[5] sometimes even a full fourteen lines spoken by a speaker alone or by two speakers in consort—the great sonnet exchange between Romeo and Juliet at their meeting is a sign both of their rhetorical sophistication and of their union with one another. Some of the sonnets have an extra quatrain or even sestet; once an octave stands alone, several times a sestet stands alone. All this sonnet-formality must draw our attention to what the playwright was up to—that is, his deepening of events by a language habitually associated with a particular kind of high-minded and devoted love. By his borrowing of devices and language from another genre for his tragedy, he cues us to the kind of love involved in his play. Of all the lyric forms, indeed of all the literary forms, of love, the sonnet-sequence honors the profound seriousness of the emotion: love is central to the life and existence of the sonnet-persona, who gives himself over to the delicious exigencies of his condition, which he celebrates with all the force of his soul and of his poetical powers. As more transitory love-lyrics do not, the sonnet-sequence also provides opportunities for deep and faceted self-examination, as the sonneteer considers and reconsiders his ever-changing emotional state, recording as carefully as possible his perceptions of his own shifting progress and regress along his path.

We are introduced to Romeo, typed as a melancholy lover before he appears onstage, who enters speaking "distractedly" in the proper Petrarchan rhetoric of oxymoron. He runs through the rhetorical exercises of the love-poet with extraordinary facility. He sets his own text—"Here's much to do with hate, but more with love" (1.1.173)—and amplifies it:

> Why then, O brawling love! O loving hate!
> O anything, of nothing first create!
> O heavy lightness! serious vanity!
> Mis-shapen chaos of well-seeming forms!
> Feather of lead, bright smoke, cold fire, sick health!
> Still-waking sleep, that is not what it is!
> This love feel I, that feel no love in this.
>
>   (1.1.174–80)

Shortly after this comical though splendid display of his reading in Petrarchan fig-

---

[5]See Nicholas Brooke's excellent *Shakespeare's Early Tragedies* (London, 1968), pp. 80–106 (on sonnets and sonnet-likeness, especially pp. 87–88); and [James] Calderwood, *Shakespearean Metadrama*, [(Minneapolis, 1970)] Chapter Four.

ure, Romeo defines love, in the manner, says one French theorist, of the *blason*, or (as English critics tended to say) of the definition:[6]

> Love is a smoke rais'd with the fume of sighs;
> Being purg'd, a fire sparkling in lovers' eyes;
> Being vex'd, a sea nourish'd with loving tears.
> What is it else? A madness most discreet,
> A choking gall, and a preserving sweet.
>   (1.1.188–92)

He runs through the repertory—the oxymora, so casually tossed off, the variations upon a hundred sonnets in the official mode. His *epideixis* is clear—"Why then," and "What is it else?" introduce a spate of words in the right key, uttered by an energetic youth creating his own role according to the best literary models.

Romeo's Rosaline, always invisible to us, is made up of whole cloth, the texture of which is classical reference:

>   she'll not be hit
> With Cupid's arrow. She hath Dian's wit.
> And in strong proof of chastity well arm'd.
> From Love's weak childish bow she lives unharm'd.
> She will not stay the siege of loving terms,
> Nor bide th'encounter of assailing eyes.
> Nor ope her lap to saint-seducing gold.
> O she is rich in beauty; only poor
> That, when she dies, with beauty dies her store.
>   (1.1.206–14)

Romeo's clichés play upon the Epicurean argument for love, using the themes of *carpe diem* and productivity so familiar from love-lyrics (and the second familiar from Shakespeare's own remarkable sequence of sonnets). Romeo continues in language remarkably close to those sonnets:

> For beauty, starv'd with her severity,
> Cuts beauty off from all posterity.
>   (1.1.217–18)

The next couplet points to its own artificiality, with its ostentatious opposition of bliss and despair, again a sonnet-cliché. That couplet then leads to a familiar paradox:

> She is too fair, too wise, wisely too fair,
> To merit bliss by making me despair.
> She hath forsworn to love, and in that vow
> Do I live dead that live to tell it now.
>   (1.1.219–22)

---

[6]Note also Romeo's reference to *fel* and *mel* here, repeated at 1.5.90, and the adverse criticism of Romeo as a poet in Joseph Chiang, "The Language of Paradox in *Romeo and Juliet*." *S. Stud.*, III (1967), 22–42.

Even in the familiar self-denial of the sonneteer, self-critical and self-indulgent at once, Romeo the lover maintains decorum.[7]

Decorum or no, what we are asked to see in this Romeo is the lover by the book, the lover *too* decorous, who adopts the Petrarchan role and lives it to the utmost—in his rhyme, in his solitary nightlife, in the moping melancholy that so worries his mother. And Romeo sticks to the rules of his loving: when Benvolio urges him to Capulet's feast, hoping that he will there find another lady to fall in love with, Romeo is shocked—but in a sestet:

> When the devout religion of mine eye
> Maintains such falsehood, then turn tears to fires:
> And these, who, often drown'd, could never die,
> Transparent heretics, be burnt for liars!
> One fairer than my love! The all-seeing sun
> Ne'er saw her match since first the world begun.
> (1.2.88–93)

Romeo's hyperbolical fidelity leaves much to be desired, since he falls in love with Juliet the instant he claps eye on her and rhymes his new love at once, in familiar language most beautifully disposed:

> O, she doth teach the torches to burn bright!
> It seems she hangs upon the cheek of night
> As a rich jewel in an Ethiop's ear . . .

and on and on, to

> Did my heart love till now? Forswear it, sight:
> For I ne'er saw true beauty till this night.
> (1.5.42–44, 50–51)

Both Romeo and Juliet are quick at this kind of language: their sonnet, with its "extra" quatrain at the end, spoken in turn by the two of them, is a marvelous sublimation of the witty exchange of young people meeting and trying each other out. Romeo speaks the first quatrain, Juliet the second; they divide the sestet, Juliet setting the rhyme and Romeo matching it. As Juliet notes, Romeo knows the rules of love—"You kiss by the book"—and so does she, certainly, for she is capable of very conventional wit in terms of love, as, it turns out later, she is also capable of conventional comment on hate.

Mercutio offers a critical voice against Romeo's softer one: as the young men go to the dance, Mercutio teases Romeo, challenging him to exchanges of wit much like those to which Benvolio had earlier challenged Romeo. All three young men knew their rhetorical alternatives and chose their styles freely: Mercutio mocks Romeo in terms of his love-learned language:

---

[7]For some discussion of this, see [Rosalie Colie] *Paradoxia* [*Epidemica*, (Princeton, 1966)], Chapter Two; and Cynthia Grant Tucker's ["Studies in Sonnet Literature"] (unpublished dissertation, University of Iowa, 1967).

> Romeo! humours! madman! passion! lover!
> Appear thou in the likeness of a sigh;
> Speak but one rhyme and I am satisfied;
> Cry but "Ay me!" pronounce but "love" and "dove" . . . ,
>
> (2.1.7–10)

to pass on to a wonderfully punning salaciousness about the true purpose of loving. Mercutio provides at these points an Ovidian voice, that of the high-spirited libertine whose awareness of the physical delights of love balance the sweetness, the near-nambypambyness of the Petrarchan traditional language. In his later exchange with Mercutio, Romeo answers in kind, thereby convincing his friend that he is once more "sociable," which is to say, out of love and a sane man again. Romeo has altered his decorum, as Mercutio notes—"Thy wit is a very bitter sweeting; it is a most sharp sauce"—from his melancholy sonneteering to the man-about-town, man-among-men style of the epigrammatist: he sharpens Mercutio's Ovidian voice to something nearer Martial's tone. And this of course is what fools Mercutio into believing that his friend has fallen out of love, for no man in the lover's pose can make the jests of 2.4 about sexuality. We of course know better: Romeo is finally and at last in love—and, dutiful to convention, has fallen in at first sight. This prescription of love's proper origin is written into the action, given reality, unmetaphored, in the scene at the feast: both young people recognize, too, what is happening to them, though they obey the rules of courteous wordplay, which detonates their passion, as well as observing the rules of courtly loving.

Romeo by no means abandons sonnet-language because he has in fact fallen truly in love—again and again in his speeches to and about Juliet, conventional sonnet-topics turn up. To his new love, seen at her window, he offers the conventional likeness of eyes to stars:

> Two of the fairest stars in all the heaven,
> Having some business, do entreat her eyes
> To twinkle in their spheres till they return.
> What if her eyes were there, they in her head?
> The brightness of her cheek would shame those stars.
> As daylight doth a lamp; her eyes in heaven
> Would through the airy region stream so bright
> That birds would sing, and think it were not night.
>
> (2.2.15–22)

Which is to say, her eyes are not like stars, but like suns; Romeo is a conceited poet, who draws out his conceits to utter hyperbole—as we shall see, his Juliet can do the same. He borrows other stock-elements from the sonneteer: in the orchard he wishes to be a glove on her hand to feel her cheek leaning against that hand, in Mantua he wishes to be a mouse, the humblest beast about the house, so as to catch sight of Juliet in Verona. Again, he combines two common sonnet-images, that of the lover as skipper and that of the lady as merchandise, in three pretty lines:

I am no pilot; yet, wert thou as far
As that vast shore wash'd with the farthest sea,
I should adventure for such merchandise.
                    (2.2.82–84)

As critics are fond of saying, Juliet's language is less artificial than Romeo's, which seems to point to her greater simplicity in love than his, to her greater realism about their situation than his.[8] But she too has had her training in the love-rhetoric: her Romeo will "lie upon the wings of night/ Whiter than new snow on the raven's back" (3.2.18–19). She too can pursue a conceit to its ultimate, absurd conclusions:

                    when he shall die,
Take him and cut him out in little stars,
And he will make the face of heaven so fine
That all the world will be in love with night,
And pay no worship to the garish sun.
                    (3.2.21–25)

It is worth noting that Juliet's metaphoric daring is greater than Romeo's: she solves the sun-stars problem firmly and defiantly in favor of her image, while his imagery was less committed, less precise, and less extreme: he speaks, more than she, by the book. Her conceit of "little stars," which shall translate Romeo to classical immortality in a constellation, sends us back to his likeness of her to the sun. Her language honors the darkness in which her love is conceived, and its ugliest, most forceful image ("cut him out in little stars") forebodes that love's violent end.

When the Nurse comes in with the news of Tybalt's death at Romeo's hands, Juliet bursts into oxymoron, violently denouncing her lover in a passage as rhetorically extreme as anything Romeo had uttered in his period of self-persuaded, false love:

O serpent heart, hid with a flow'ring face!
Did ever dragon keep so fair a cave?
Beautiful tyrant! fiend angelical!
Dove-feather'd raven! wolfish-ravening lamb!
Despised substance of divinest show!
                    (3.2.73–77)

On she goes, in this language, until her reason returns to remind her that of the two, she would far rather have lost Tybalt than Romeo. With that realization, she returns to the simpler poetry more characteristic of her utterance. It may be, as Levin has suggested, that Juliet's linguistic extravagance marks her estrangement from Romeo—certainly it marks her loss of herself in passionate outrage; on the other hand, the images she uses in this passage are linked both to those she had earlier used to try to express her large love for Romeo, and to those he used of her. Even here, the conjunction between the lovers is maintained in their language.

[8]Harry Levin, "Form and Formality in *Romeo and Juliet*," *SQ*, XI (1961), 3–11; Calderwood, pp. 87ff.

As we look back over the lovers' utterance, we can see very plainly the problem of expression: petrarchan language, *the* vehicle for amorous emotion, can be used merely as the cliché which Mercutio and Benvolio criticize; or, it can be earned by a lover's experience of the profound oppositions to which that rhetoric of oxymoron points. When Romeo and Juliet seek to express their feelings' force, they return constantly to petrarchanisms hallowed with use—but, having watched their development as lovers, an audience can accept as valid the language upon which they must fall back. When Romeo readies himself to die, he does so in the proper sonnet-imagery, to which he has earlier had recourse—

> Thou desperate pilot, now at once run on
> The dashing rocks thy sea-sick weary bark.
>   (5.3.117–18)

After this crisis and the acknowledgment that ends it, the love of Romeo and Juliet resumes its course, to express itself in the familiar dawn-song of medieval tradition, a song which the lovers speak in dialogue. At this point, one might note a general feature of this play, of which the *aubade* is a splendid example: it is full of set pieces of different kinds. Lady Capulet and the Nurse speak a duet about the County Paris's charms; at Juliet's supposed death, Lord and Lady Capulet, the Nurse, and Paris utter a quartet. There are many double exchanges—Juliet's sonnet-exchange with Romeo at the dance, Romeo's exchanges with Benvolio and Mercutio, Juliet's stichomythy with Paris at Friar Lawrence's cell. Arias as well: Juliet's great prothalamic invocation to night, with its Ovidian echoes, "Gallop apace, you fiery-footed steeds"; her schematic meditation on death and the charnel-house just before she takes the drug; Mercutio's inventions on the subject of dreams. The effect of these passages is greatly to draw our attention to the poetry of this play, to the evocativeness of its language, but also to do something else, risky in a play though ideal in a lyric, to arrest the action for the sake of poetic display.

When we look at the play from some distance and in terms of fairly stock rhetorical patterns, we can see how formalized, how static, much of its organization is, how dependent upon tableaux and set-pieces. The Chorus begins the play with his sonnet, then one party enters, then the other (from, we presume, "houses" demarcated in the stage-architecture). The two parties engage in a mock-version of the vendetta which, with Tybalt's entrance onstage, quickly transforms the action into real violence, and ends with the Prince's order for the maintenance of peace. At the play's end, one party enters to lament the death of a child, then the other, lamenting the death of the other child; both parties stand to hear Friar Lawrence's unraveling of the plot and the Prince's strictures. Each bereaved father promises the other, appropriately, a sepulchral statue of his child in commemoration of child, of love, and of the ultimate sad settlement of the long feud.[9] With a final moralizing sestet, the Prince, a dignified *deus ex machina*, ends the

---

[9]For something of this "fixing" at a work's end, see Francis Berry, *The Shakespearean Inset* (London, 1965); and Murray Krieger, "The Ekphrastic Principle and the Still Movement of Poetry," in *The Play and Place of Criticism* (Baltimore, 1967).

action altogether. The lyric interludes, so important to the tone and psychology of the whole play, are of a piece with the pageant-like dramaturgy. Though they reveal the conditions of the speaker's mind, they do so in language rather dictated by the situation than obedient to the complexity of the plot, character, or action. The language loosens itself in many ways from the sonnet-substance from which it draws so much, but in *Romeo and Juliet* it is never so free as in *Othello,* where the same body of conventional language is managed to fit the characters' and the plots' needs without drawing undue attention to itself.

Romeo and Juliet is in many ways an apprentice-play: there the poet first met the real problems involved in turning lyrical love into tragedy. The Chorus must tell us at the outset that these lovers are star-crossed, and, in case we should forget that this is so, Romeo says later, rather awkwardly, "my mind misgives / Some consequence, yet hanging in the stars, / Shall bitterly begin his fearful date / With this night's revels" (1.4.106–109). Friar Lawrence's *sententiae* reinforce the notion of rash haste, but they do not increase our sense of tempo—rather, in the way of *sententiae,* they do just the opposite. Rash haste and star-crossing are the rigid *donnée* of the action, which we are not invited to question or to consider. Love is unhappy, deeply-felt, beautifully expressed; youth is wasted at the behest of irrational old age, but the involvements of tragic behavior have not found their language in this play, although the spectacular oppositions of the petrarchan rhetoric have been enlarged into plot, as well as into the emotional and social structure of the play.

All the same, *Romeo and Juliet* makes some marvelous technical manipulations. One of the most pleasurable, for me, of Shakespeare's many talents is his "unmetaphoring" of literary devices, his sinking of the conventions back into what, he somehow persuades us, is "reality," his trick of making a verbal convention part of the scene, the action, or the psychology of the play itself. Love-at-first-sight is here made to seem entirely natural, set against the artificiality and unreality of Romeo's self-made love for Rosaline; its conventionality is forgotten as it is unmetaphored by action. Again, the *aubade* is indeed a dawn-song sung after a night of love, when the lovers must part, but a dawn-song of peculiar poignancy and relevance because of the way in which these lovers must part on this particular day. Another brilliant, natural unmetaphoring is the *hortus conclusus,* which by metaphoric convention a virgin is, and where also pure love naturally dwells, according to the Song of Songs and a host of subsequent poems and romances. Juliet's balcony simply opens upon such an orchard, a garden enclosed, into which Romeo finds out the way. The virgin is, and is in, a walled garden: the walls of that garden are to be breached by a true lover, as Romeo leaps into the orchard.

Still more important is the much-noticed manipulation of light and dark in the play; for Romeo and Juliet, ordinary life is reversed, with darkness the only safe time, when love between them is really possible. They meet at night, their marriage lasts one night, until light parts them. When they finally come together, it is at night in a tomb, which becomes their tomb in actuality. Their second night together is *nox perpetua una dormienda.* A conventional figurative setting in lyric tradition becomes the "real" setting, carrying with it a specific symbolic significance for the play.

The common juxtaposition and contrast of love and war are also involved in *Romeo and Juliet,* though not as simile merely. In Verona, love emerges as involved with warfare: the love of Romeo and Juliet is set in contrast to brawling and feud, but its poignancy comes from the bitterness of the unexplained vendetta. In their lives the lovers speak for peace and reconciliation and at their death are turned into symbols of that reconciliation, into sepulchral statues. Love and war are both real enough, but they do not and cannot coexist in this play's world: the one destroys the other. The conjunction of love and death, commonly linked in the metaphors of lyrical tradition, make this play unmistakably non-comic; death is the link between the love-theme and the war-theme, the irreversible piece of action that stamps the play as tragic. Still, Romeo and Juliet die as much by accident as Pyramus and Thisbe do, to whose story the narrative of their death owes much. Indeed, the lovers are preserved in a nearly Ovidian way, not as plants, but in an *ecphrasis,* as memorial statues exemplifying a specific lesson to future generations.

Romeo and Juliet:
The Meaning of a Theatrical Experience

Michael Goldman

Everything in *Romeo and Juliet* is intense, impatient, threatening, explosive. We are caught up in speed, heat, desire, riots, running, jumping, rapid-fire puns, dirty jokes, extravagance, compressed and urgent passion, the pressure of secrets, fire, blood, death. Visually, the play remains memorable for a number of repeated images—street brawls, swords flashing to the hand, torches rushing on and off, crowds rapidly gathering. The upper stage is used frequently, with many opportunities for leaping or scrambling or stretching up and down and much play between upper and lower areas. The dominant bodily feelings we get as an audience are oppressive heat, sexual desire, a frequent whiz-bang exhilarating kinesthesia of speed and clash, and above all a feeling of the keeping-down and separation of highly charged bodies, whose pressure toward release and whose sudden discharge determine the rhythm of the play.

The thematic appropriateness of these sensations to Shakespeare's first great tragedy of the unsounded self is obvious enough, perhaps too obvious. Shakespeare's tragic heroes usually pass from isolation to isolation. Romeo cannot be one of the boys or Hamlet one of his northern world's competent, adaptable young men. At the beginning the isolation is that of the unsounded self, some form of self-sufficiency, remoteness, or withdrawal. The hero strikes us as a kind of closed structure. He very clearly carries a packaged energy; on first meeting him we recognize the container and the seal. (Think of Romeo or Hamlet for swift opening indications of these.) The ultimate isolation comes in the rupture of the package, the energy's discharge. The drama marks the change. Romeo and Juliet are isolated by the sudden demands of love returned, and the world of their play reflects the violence of the transformation.

The type of outline just given is useful but treacherous. It is useful because it sharpens our sense of the Shakespearean dramatic situation and gives us a reasonably pertinent norm by which to measure individual developments. But to follow it out in detail, to translate each tragedy back into the outline, to tell it like a story for any of the plays would be to lose exactly what makes the idea of the unsounded self important—that it is basic to drama, something far different

From Goldman, Michael; *Shakespeare and the Energies of Drama.* Copyright © 1972 by Princeton University Press. Reprinted by permission of Princeton University Press.

from story or subject or theme. This is what is wrong with thinking about theatrical impressions in terms of thematic appropriateness, as a kind of varnish over the poetry and plot.

What ideally has to be done and is perhaps more easily attempted for *Romeo and Juliet* than for later plays is to talk about what the experience of the whole amounts to. The impression is strong and distinctive; why do we mark it as we do? The problem is to take all the elements that affect us in the theater and examine them as they arrange themselves in our response, asking what relevance this configuration bears to our lives.

If we try to see what the deep effect of the combination of these elements is, the crucial question is that of the relation that connects the plot, the visual spectacle, and the wordplay. Clearly they share a common busyness, suddenness, and violence. "These violent delights have violent ends" is enough to explain their congruence at least superficially. But it does not account for the richness of our response to the elaborate detail of the drama. Nor does it account for the peculiar aptness we sense in certain kinds of detail. Why are there so many puns and such obscene ones? Why should Mercutio and the Nurse be given long, digressive bravura speeches? Why is the balcony stressed, and the athleticism it entails? Why should certain lines like "Wherefore art thou Romeo?" or "What's in a name?" or "A feasting presence full of light" stick in the memory? The last may be explained by its "beauty out of context"—always a doubtful procedure—but the other lines resist even that easy question-begging method, and consequently give us a good place to begin.

"Wherefore art thou Romeo?"

Romeo's name presents a problem to others besides Juliet but she characteristically sees more deeply into the difficulty. For it is not enough to decide whether Romeo should be called humors, madman, passion, lunatic, villain, coward, boy, Capulet, Montague, or even Romeo. The question is really why he must have a name at all. *Romeo and Juliet* is a tragedy of naming, a tragedy in which at times Romeo's name seems to be the villain:

> As if that name,
> Shot from the deadly level of a gun,
> Did murder her, as that name's cursed hand
> Murder'd her kinsman. O, tell me, friar, tell me,
> In what vile part of this anatomy
> Doth my name lodge? Tell me, that I may sack
> The hateful mansion.
>
> (3.3.102–08)

But though this echoes Juliet's other famous question and her insistence that a name is after all "nor hand, nor foot,/ Nor arm, nor face," it is far different from "What's in a name?" in even its immediate implications. The trouble with Romeo's name here is not that it is a trivial attribute that raises accidental difficulties, but that "Romeo" now has a history, an inescapable reality of its own. It is the name of the man who has killed Tybalt; it is attached to a past and Romeo is responsible for it. It is Romeo who is banished for what Romeo has done. His anguish, though emotionally an intensification of Juliet's in the balcony scene, is logically an answer to her question. This, among other things, is what's in a name.

Not only do names have a peculiar substantiality in the play (they can murder, die, be torn; every tongue that speaks "But Romeo's name speaks heavenly eloquence") but words themselves take on a namelike intensity. That is, they take on, usually by repetition, the importance and attributes of persons:

> Say thou but "I"
> And that bare vowel "I" shall poison more
> Than the death-darting eye of cockatrice.
> I am not I, if there be such an I;
> Or those eyes shut, that makes thee answer "I."[1]
>
> ". . . banished"
> That "banished," that one word "banished,"
> Hath slain ten thousand Tybalts.
>   (3.2.45–49, 112–14)

Here, as with "day" in 4.5,[2] the effect in the theater is not to deepen the meaning of the word but at once to strip the meaning away through endless repetition and to give it a namelike life of its own.

As these examples suggest, naming is characteristically associated with separation in the play. It is no accident that at the time of painful separation on the morning after their marriage the lovers' aubade turns on the name of a bird:

> It was the nightingale, and not the lark . . .
> It was the lark, the herald of the morn,
> No nightingale.
>   (3.5.2–7)

They are passing from a night of sensual union to a day of exile. Night, as Mercutio has observed, is a time of free association, of fantastic invention, but day makes stricter demands upon our consciousness. When Romeo agrees to call the bird by some other name, Juliet must quickly admit that it is indeed the lark. The lovers relinquish the right to rename the world as they please; they must know the world's names for things if they wish to stay alive in it.

The play's everpresent thrust toward punning heightens our sense of the accepted meaning of words and of the rampant psychic energy that rises to

---

[1] Restoring the Q_2 reading of "I" for "ay" in ll. 45, 48, and 49.
[2] Most lamentable day, most woeful day,
   That ever, ever, I did yet behold!
   O day! O day! O day! O hateful day!
   Never was seen so black a day as this.
   O woeful day, O woeful day!
              (50–54)

break the meanings down. The wordplay makes its contribution as much by its quantity and irrepressibility as by its content. The puns are rapid and raw, emphasizing the suddenness and violence that is part of all punning, while the very process of punning raises issues that are central to the play. A pun is a sudden exchange of names, uniting objects we are not ordinarily allowed to unite, with a consequent release of energy, often violent and satisfying, and always satisfying to the extent that it is violent. It is something both terrible and lovely; we say "That's awful," when we mean "That's good." Romeo and Juliet themselves are like the components of a particularly good pun—natural mates whom authority strives to keep apart and whose union is not only violent but illuminating, since it transforms and improves the order it violates, though it is necessarily impermanent.

The fury of the pun is the fury of our submerged innocence; we play with words as Romeo and Juliet play with the lark and nightingale. Punning restores to us—under certain very narrow conditions, and for a brief interval—our freedom to change names and to make connections we have been taught to suppress, to invent language, to reconstitute the world as we please. *Romeo and Juliet* begins with a series of puns leading to a street brawl culminating in a dangerous mistake (Benvolio, intending to restore order, draws his sword) that spreads the conflict to include nearly the entire company. The sequence is significant, for the energy of the pun, fully released in an organized society where names and rules are important, tends to be disastrous. Capulet and Montague lackeys lurk around the stage like forbidden meanings looking for an opportunity to discharge themselves. And at the level of responsible authority, the equivalent of the lackeys' idle brawling (or the overwhelming passion of the young lovers) is the capacity for instant and mistaken decision. From Benvolio's intervention in the opening street brawl to Romeo's suicide in the tomb, the play is a tissue of precipitous mistakes. Capulet hands a guest list to a servant who cannot read and the tragedy is initiated (significantly it is a list of names—all of which are read out—that is the villain). Mercutio's death is a mistake; and Romeo's error, like Capulet's and Benvolio's, enacts itself as a backfiring gesture, an action that—like a pun—subverts its manifest intention. Romeo's pathetic "I thought all for the best," rings in our ears when we see Lawrence and Capulet stricken by the lovers' death.

Counter to all the hasty and disastrous action of the play, there runs a surge of simple authoritative confidence, voiced at different times by almost every major character. The first scene ends with Romeo's assertion that he will always love Rosaline. As Romeo goes off, Capulet enters insisting that it will be easy to keep the peace. The juxtaposition of these two errors goes beyond simple irony; the encounter between confident assumption and the sudden event is one of the play's important motifs, just as the disparity between principle and practice is one of its recurrent themes. The Friar's first speech, for example, is often seen as a moralization of the action of *Romeo and Juliet,* and indeed there is a clear and effective dramatic connection between his homily and the action that surrounds it. The contrast between the night-time intensity of the scene immediately preceding, and the complacent tranquillity of Lawrence's reflections is obviously intended, and to further enforce the connection, he begins by moralizing the contrast:

> The grey-ey'd morn smiles on the frowning night . . .
> And flecked darkness like a drunkard reels
> From forth day's path.
>
> (2.3.1–4)

As he goes on, he seems to anticipate events that are to follow, but on closer inspection, his remarks are not precisely appropriate:

> Virtue itself turns vice, being misapplied;
> And vice sometime's by action dignified.
> (21–22)

The first of these lines fits the lovers and much else in the play, but the second, though on the surface equally fitting, turns out to be harder to apply. Romeo is apparently acting in accordance with its teaching when he buys forbidden poison to use on himself, as is Capulet when he decides that a hasty marriage (which he has earlier roundly denounced) will rouse Juliet from her sorrows, or as the Nurse is when she advises Juliet to marry Paris. And Friar Lawrence certainly imagines he is taking a virtuous course when he offers poison to Juliet. By the play's end, of course, Lawrence's intervention has proved an example of virtue misapplied. The very confidence of his assertions becomes a source of disaster when he acts, and the very ease of his rhetoric is part of the texture of his actions. Friar Lawrence makes a strong bid to be the moral center of the play, but it is his bid that finally interests us more than his vision. Just as he shares a penchant for confidently interpreting events with Capulet, the Nurse, and Romeo, among others, like them he has a disturbing capacity for guessing wrong.

At the end of the play Lawrence is pardoned. "We still have known thee for a holy man." The Friar deserves his reputation, and it is as necessary to society that he have his name for holiness as that he utter his sound and inappropriate *sententiae*. If he were not capable of making terrible mistakes, there would be no need of him. We must have friars and fathers, and all the system of responsibility that goes with naming, for the very reason that these figures fail in their responsibility: there is an energy in life that changes names, that breaks down the rules of language, of law, and even of luck.[3]

---

[3]The play is famous for its long arias, of which there are two kinds. The speeches of the lovers are expressions of their isolation and desire; separated from each other, they speak at length. The Nurse, Mercutio, and Capulet, however, are given great bursts of speech in company; and the reaction of those around them is important. Their set-pieces are met with outcry; but they are carried away and will not stop. Each is a force in nature breaking into the expected or permissible flow of things; each imitates the impulsive action of the play, "of nothing first create"; each adds to the prevailing sense of impatience and irrepressible energy.

Romeo and Juliet bear the brunt of discovering this energy, and, like all tragic victims, they are isolated—even from each other—before they are destroyed. Characteristically, we remember them as separated: the drug comes between them in the final scene, earlier the balcony divides them; in the nightingale-lark scene they are together only at the moment of leave-taking. On all three occasions, the probable use of the stage serves to underline the strain that the effort toward contact demands of them—in Romeo's yearning upward toward the balcony, the perilous rope-ladder descent, the torches and crowbars breaking into the tomb. And of course there are always insistent voices—Mercutio and his friends, the Nurse, Paris, the watch—calling them away, repeating their names, threatening to interrupt them.

It is not fanciful to see their last scene in the tomb as suggestive of sexual union and of the sexual act. A battle takes place at the door, it is torn open—and on stage the barrier is finally only a curtain that gives easily enough after some bloodshed. It is also almost certainly the same inner stage or pavilion where Juliet has gone to bed on the eve of her wedding to Paris, and so it must remind the audience of that innocent chamber. (The curtains close as she falls on the bed, are opened in 4.5 to show her apparently dead, and only open again, revealing her still prostrate, as Romeo breaks into the tomb.) The identification is given force by the new stream of wordplay that has entered since Tybalt's death, reversing the dominant pun of the play. Up to that point the language of combat has been transformed by punning into suggestions of sexual encounter ("Draw thy tool"); but in the concluding scenes, violent death is repeatedly described in terms of sex and the marriage festival. Romeo vows, "Well, Juliet, I will lie with thee tonight," meaning he will die; the lovers toast each other with poison ("Here's to my love," "This do I drink to thee"); and, in one of the great condensing images of the play, Juliet's beauty makes the "vault a feasting presence full of light." This last phrase catches up the play's repeated impressions of light and fire illuminating the night and suffuses the death of the lovers with a suggestion of their long-denied marriage banquet.

Romeo and Juliet, with its emphasis on language, young love, and the affectations and confusions of both, has clear affinities with the Shakespearean comedies of its period. Except for its fatalities, it follows the standard form of New Comedy. The two lovers are kept apart by a powerful external authority (some form of parental opposition is of course typical), and much of the action concerns their efforts to get around the obstacles placed in their path. Their ultimate union—in a marriage feast—results in a transformation of the society that has opposed them.

Like Romeo, Juliet, as she moves toward tragedy, is sometimes treated in a manner familiar from the early comedies: a sense of the "real" is produced by contrasting serious and superficial versions of the same situation or event. As Romeo progresses in seriousness from Rosaline to Juliet, so Juliet advances through at least three stages to her waking in the tomb. Lawrence sends her on her way with his usual cheery assurance, and even Romeo approaches his descent into the grave with a kind of boyish eagerness, but Juliet goes beyond them. Originally she shares their confident reading of the scene:

> . . . bid me go into a new-made grave
> And hide me with a dead man in his shroud,—
> Things that, to hear them told, have made me tremble;
> And I will do it without fear or doubt.
>
> (4.1.84–87)

But her anticipatory vision of the tomb in 4.3 powerfully forecasts her actual fate:

> What if it be a poison, which the friar
> Subtly hath minist'red to have me dead . . .
> How if, when I am laid into the tomb,
> I wake before the time that Romeo
> Come to redeem me? . . .
> The horrible conceit of death and night,
> Together with the terror of the place,—
> As in a vault, an ancient receptacle,
> Where, for this many hundred years, the bones
> Of all my buried ancestors are pack'd;
> Where bloody Tybalt, yet but green in earth,
> Lies fest'ring in his shroud. . .
>
> (24–43)

"Fear and doubt" do afflict her, but it is even more notable that Juliet is the only one in the play who begins to guess what the final scene will be like.

In the tomb itself, Juliet continues to display her distinctive isolation and awareness. Her fate is given a final impressiveness by a gesture that carries on the special violence of the play. Shakespeare follows his source, Brooke's *The Tragical History of Romeus and Juliet,* in having Juliet commit suicide with Romeo's knife. But his Juliet, unlike Brooke's, first canvasses other ways to die—the poisoned cup, a kiss. These deaths, like Romeo's, are elegant, leave no mark upon the body, and have the comforting theatrical import of an easy transcendence of death—but they are not available to her; the impulsive pace of the action will not allow it. The watch is heard. She reaches for the dagger instead:

> This is thy sheath; there rust, and let me die.
>
> (5.3.170)

The death is messy, violent, sexual. It is interesting that Romeo's is the more virginal, and that Juliet's is the first in the play that has not been immediately caused by a misunderstanding.

Against the play's general background, its rapidly assembling crowds, its fevered busyness, its continual note of impatience and the quick violence of its encounters, the image that remains most strongly in our minds is not of the lovers as a couple, but of each as a separate individual grappling with internal energies that both threaten and express the self, energies for which language is inadequate but that lie at the root of language, that both overturn and enrich society. Touched by adult desire, the unsounded self bursts out with the explosive, subversive, dangerous energy of the sword, gunpowder, the plague; and every aspect of our experience of *Romeo and Juliet* in the theater engages us in this phenomenon—from the crude rush of the brawling lackeys to the subliminal violence of the puns. We undergo, in a terrible condensation like the lightning-flash, the self-defining, self-immolating surge with which adolescence is left behind. As Juliet swiftly outgrows the comforts of the family circle, so Romeo moves far from the youthful packs that roam the streets of Verona, so many Adonises hunting and scorning. The lovers remain in the audience's minds in a typical pose and atmosphere, lights burning in the darkness, their names called, their farewells taken, each isolated in a moment of violent and enlightening desire.

Language and Sexual Difference in *Romeo and Juliet*

Edward Snow

Introduction

Romeo and Juliet is about an experience that transcends "a common bound." The play emphasizes the opposition between the imaginative vision its protagonists bear witness to in love and the truth of a world whose order must be enforced at passion's expense. And though events bring Romeo and Juliet together in this experience, language suggests how radically they share it. When they first meet "palm to palm" at the Capulet's ball, for instance, their antiphonal responses generate a perfectly formed sonnet. The moment is emblematic of the erotic relationship as the play views it: two exposed, vulnerably embodied selves reaching out tentatively across sexual difference and social opposition, while their imaginations mingle in an intersubjective privacy that weaves its boundaries protectively around them. And later, when Romeo is admiring Juliet from below her balcony, still hidden from her view, her first words appear inside one of his lines of blank verse, as if his imaginative response to her were the generative matrix from which her own desiring self emerges:

Romeo:	See how she leans her cheek upon her hand!
	O that I were a glove upon that hand,
	That I might touch that cheek!
Juliet:	Ay me!
Romeo:	She speaks!
	O, speak again, bright angel . . .
	(2.2.23–26)[1]

Juliet's language, in turn, once it acquires a momentum of its own, conjures up Romeo's actual physical presence, even though she herself is absorbed in purely subjective imaginings:

Juliet:	What's in a name? That which we call a rose
	By any other word would smell as sweet;

From *Shakespeare's "Rough Magic": Renaissance Essays in Honor of C. L. Barber*, ed. Peter Erickson and Coppélia Kahn (Newark: University of Delaware Press, 1985), 168–192. Reprinted by permission. Some of the original footnotes for this essay have been shortened.

[1]All quotations are from *The Riverside Shakespeare*, ed. G. B. Evans et al. (Boston, 1974).

> So Romeo would, were he not Romeo call'd,
> Retain that dear perfection which he owes
> Without that title. Romeo, doff thy name,
> And for thy name, which is no part of thee,
> Take all myself.
>
> Romeo: *(appearing to her)* I take thee at thy word.
> Call me but love, and I'll be new baptiz'd;
> Henceforth I never will be Romeo.
>
> (2.2.43–51)

The play is full of tricks like these that make Romeo and Juliet's language seem like a medium in which their relationship takes form as well as an instrument for bringing it about. The most pervasive of these devices are the elaborately matched images and turns of phrase that link their separate speeches. Romeo tells Juliet that he has "night's cloak" to hide him from her kinsmen (2.2.75); a few moments later she informs him that "the mask of night" is on her face (2.2.85). The effect is of two imaginations working in the same idiom, in touch not so much with each other as with similar experiences of self and world. Juliet's "Come, night, come, Romeo, come, thou day in night" (3.2.17) communicates with Romeo's "It is the east, and Juliet is the sun" (2.2.3) at a purely transcendental level: both responses are spoken in isolation, yet they are tuned to the same imaginative frequency, and imply the existence of a single world of desire encompassing the two lovers' separate longings. This sense of communication taking place at a level beyond conscious awareness, and bridging distances that desire itself is helpless to overcome, is especially powerful in the final scene, where the phrases of Juliet's grief for Romeo echo and uncannily transform those of his for her.

These subliminal correspondences do more, I think, to convince us that Romeo and Juliet are appropriately fitted to each other than anything which passes directly between them. Yet the matched speeches that create this sense of fit also measure the differences it subsumes. The very devices which implicate Romeo and Juliet in a shared experience, that is, also focus our attention on a difference in the way each experiences that experience. The boundary between Romeo and the cloak of night he draws around him to hide himself from men's eyes is not the same as the one between Juliet and the mask of night she looks out from in a spirit of uninhibited self-disclosure: the shared metaphoric experience embraces two very different habits of being. In one sense, these differences are purely idiosyncratic: they are what make Romeo Romeo and Juliet Juliet. But they also have to do with what makes one male and the other female. Such, at least, is what I hope to suggest in this study of the separate worlds of desire that appear within the union between Romeo and Juliet. Though I will be dwelling in what follows on differences, I don't mean by doing so to call the relationship itself into question; indeed, it seems to me that the more acutely we become aware of them, the less vulnerable the play's romanticism becomes to the charges of sentimentality, immaturity, or rhetorical superficiality that are often brought against it. And though I will be claiming that these differences consistently favor Juliet's imaginative world, I don't mean to suggest that the critical perspective they imply belittles Romeo: on the contrary, his experience in love now seems to me poignant and phenomenologically complex where once it seemed merely facile and self-indulgent. What I *would* like to suggest, however, is that the language of *Romeo and Juliet* is most intricately concerned not with the opposition between passion and the social order but with the difference between the sexes: and that its subtler affirmations have to do not with romantic love but female ontology.

I

The imaginative universe generated by Romeo's desire is dominated by eyesight, and remains subject to greater rational control than Juliet's. His metaphors assemble reality "out there," and provide access to it through perspectives that tend to make him an onlooker rather than a participant. There is a kind of metonymic fascination in his language with parts and extremities, especially when viewed from a distance, against a backdrop that heightens the sensation of outline and boundary. Juliet "hangs upon the cheek of night / As a rich jewel in an Ethiop's ear" (1.5.45–46); he swears "by yonder blessed moon . . . That tips with silver all these fruit-tree tops" (2.2.107–8); a ladder of rope will convey him to "the high top-gallant" of his joy (2.4.190); he looks out of Juliet's window to see that "jocund day / Stands tiptoe on the misty mountain tops" (3.5.9–10). Contact with Juliet tends to be a matter of reaching out, and gently touching, while the idea of union with her generates imagery of parts securely fitted to each other rather than wholes merging and boundaries dissolving: "See how she leans her cheek upon her hand! / O that I were a glove upon that hand, / That I might touch that cheek!" His imagination fixes objects in stable Euclidean space, and keeps them separate and distinct, even when entertaining fantasies of metamorphosis. In the world it generates, change can occur when two things exchange places, or when one thing displaces another, but places and things themselves do not seem to be subject to alteration: "Two of the fairest stars in all the heaven, / Having some business, do entreat her eyes / To twinkle in their spheres till they return. / What if her eyes were there, they in her head?" (2.2.15–18). The sense this metaphor betrays of transformation as something temporary and provisional haunts Romeo's world, and makes (as we shall see) the growth he experiences in love problematical in a way that Juliet's is not.

Direct apprehensions of process are thus difficult to come by in the world of Romeo's metaphors. If Juliet appears to be alive in the tomb, it is because "beauty's ensign yet / Is crimson in thy lips and in thy cheeks, / And death's pale flag is not advanced there" (5.3.94–96). "Poeticizing" beauty and death in this way keeps them separate and masks the erotic and generative links between them. It also transforms them from realities known in the flesh to "ensigns" that signal conventionally encoded meanings to a distant viewer. Romeo tends to hypostatize feelings in much the same way. When he does imagine himself in the world rather than "looking on" (1.4.38), it is usually by picturing himself as an object in space that is "moved" by external forces. At one point he may "sink" under love's heavy burden (1.4.22), and at another "o'erperch" walls with the help of "love's light wings" (2.2.66), but in both instances the metaphors make him an object that remains separate from and unchanged by disembodied emotional forces acting on him from without. Even time becomes in his language a spatial dimension he moves through as an essentially unchanging object. His favorite metaphor is the sea-journey, with himself more often the ship than the pilot ("He that hath the steerage of my course, / Direct my sail" [1.4.112–13]; "Thou desperate pilot, now at once run on / The dashing rocks thy sea-sick weary bark" [5.3,117–18]). Time can move him from place to place, bring him near his goal or buffet him about, but (so at least his language implies) it rarely works any inner transformation on him, and it remains (again, in his language) the enemy rather than the element of his will.

This is not to deny that Romeo changes during the course of the play, nor that he has several positive experiences of time along the way. The issue here is not so much what happens to him as the way in which his language admits what does happen to him into consciousness. One thing that haunts Romeo throughout the play is a certain disjunction between life and the forms in which he is able to make it present to himself. Thus while his language tends to make him an onlooker to the world, the plot and *mis-en-scéne* stress his kinetic involvement in it—leaping and climbing the Capulet walls, fighting with Tybalt, making love to Juliet, riding back and forth between Verona and Mantua, forcing his way into Juliet's tomb, and always, it seems, on his way to or from somewhere when we encounter him.[2] (With Juliet, as we shall see, it is just the opposite: her freedom of movement in the actual world is severely restricted, yet her imagination places her at the center of a dynamic, expanding universe, and seizes uninhibitedly on the sources of gratification that come within reach.) His dream of Juliet—one of his "happiest" temporal experiences—is an example of how the present-at-hand is changed into something remote and elusive when his language reaches out to possess it:

> If I may trust the flattering truth of sleep,
> My dreams presage some joyful news at hand.
> My bosom's lord sits lightly in his throne,
> And all this day an unaccustom'd spirit
> Lifts me above the ground with cheerful thoughts.
> I dreamt my lady came and found me dead—
> Strange dream, that gives a dead man leave to think!—
> And breath'd such life with kisses in my lips
> That I reviv'd and was an emperor.

---

[2] For an acute discussion of the kinesthetic dimension in *Romeo and Juliet*, and on bodies in general in Shakespeare, see Michael Goldman, *Shakespeare and the Energies of Drama* (Princeton, 1972).

> Ah me, how sweet is love itself possess'd,
> When but love's shadows are so rich in joy!
>   (5.1.1–11)

In reflecting on a present happiness, Romeo translates it into an anticipation of future joy. (Juliet does exactly the opposite: when she anticipates the future—most notably while awaiting Romeo and before drinking the Friar's potion—her imagination makes it present, and she rushes in to fill it.) A change he experiences in the here and now becomes imaginatively intelligible to him as the harbinger of something still "at hand" in a future mystified by desire. His interpretation of the dream's content repeats this process. The dream itself is a beautiful expression of the revivification Romeo has already undergone in his relationship with Juliet. But he interprets it as an auspicious "sign" of what the future holds in store for him. And projecting it out of the present into the imminent future transforms it from a metaphor of the consummated relationship into an ironic foreshadowing of its tragic conclusion ("I will kiss thy lips, / Haply some poison yet doth hang on them, / To make me die with a restorative" [5.3.164–66]).[3]

Even when Romeo embraces the happiness which the presentness of Juliet's love bestows on him, he does so in terms of a potentially tragic future: "but come what sorrow can, / It cannot countervail the exchange of joy / That one short minute gives me in her sight. / Do thou but close our hands with holy words, / Then love-devouring death do what he dare, / It is enough I may but call her mine" (2.6.3–8). This tendency to think of love as moments of satisfaction rather than a process of growth, and hence to experience happiness within it against a backdrop of apocalyptic loss, is something Romeo shares with the male protagonists in Shakespeare's darkest treatments of love and sexual desire. Compare, for instance, Othello's joy at being reunited with Desdemona on Cyprus, especially in the light of her reaction to his expression of it:

Othello: If it were now to die,
'Twere now to be most happy; for I fear
My soul hath her content so absolute
That not another comfort like to this
Succeeds in unknown fate.
Desdemona: The heavens forbid
But that our loves and comforts should increase
Even as our days do grow!
                        (2.1.189–94)

---

[3]Other critics have interpreted this dream differently. Norman Holland offers a traditional psychoanalytic reading that stresses the mechanism of "reversal" in "Romeo's Dream and the Paradox of Literary Realism," *Literature and Psychology* 13 (1963): 97–103; for a summary see his *Psychoanalysis and Shakespeare* (New York, 1964), pp. 265–67. Majorie Garber discusses an evolution within the dream from simple prediction to metaphorical or mythic truth in *Dream in Shakespeare: From Metaphor to Metamorphosis* (New Haven, 1974), pp. 44–47. Both critics, like Romeo, interpret the dream by referring it to future events.

It doesn't follow from the similarity that Romeo's love for Juliet is just another manifestation of the masculine pathology Othello acts out in his marriage with Desdemona: indeed, the example of Othello should make us appreciate all the more the positive significance of Romeo's unthreatened responsiveness to the energies sexual desire releases in Juliet, and his continued devotion to her after their relationship has been consummated. But there *is* a suggestion that Romeo is a "carrier" of attitudes that are agents of tragedy in Shakespeare, and that Juliet's love only partially redeems him from them.

II

Juliet, however, is the locus of affirmative energies that can't be contained within a tragic frame of reference. Her imaginative universe, in contrast to Romeo's, is generated by all the senses, and by a unity of feeling that is more than just the sum of their parts. Her desire generates images of whole, embodied selves, and extravagant gestures of giving and taking: "Romeo, doff thy name, / And for thy name, which is no part of thee, / Take all myself" (2.2.47–49); "That runaways' eyes may wink, and Romeo / Leap to these arms untalk'd of and unseen!" (3.2.6–7). She manages to be both subject and object in love without inner conflict or contradiction: "O, I have bought the mansion of a love, / But not possess'd it, and though I am sold, / Not yet enjoy'd" (3.2.26–28). The imagination that formulates desire this way tends to produce images of inwardness and depth rather than distance ("My bounty is as boundless as the sea, / My love as deep" [2.2.133–34]). Thus where Romeo tells her to "look" out her window at the "envious streaks" that "lace the severing clouds in yonder east," she in turn tries to convince him it is the nightingale that "pierc'd the fearful hollow" of his ear (3.5.1–10).[4]

Juliet's sensations tend in general to be more "piercing" and ontologically dangerous than Romeo's. Her imagination inhabits a Blakean universe, where perceptual experience spontaneously invades and emanates from the self, instead of becoming the structuring activity it is for Romeo, even when he is most enraptured. Even vision is for her an armed faculty that penetrates the field of perception instead of gazing into it from a wistful distance: "But no more deep will I endart mine eye / Than your consent gives strength to make it fly" (1.3.98–99). One of the things that makes Juliet so formidable is the almost eager willingness with which she is able to give herself over to the dynamic, shelterless force-field of emotions and sensations into which desire

---

[4]Here, as elsewhere in this texture of contrasts, a difference between distant objects and inner depths also involves a difference between seeing and hearing. Even the larger dramatic structures that shape the plot contribute to the impression of different hierarchies of the senses operating in the two central characters. Thus in both their first two encounters, at the Capulet ball and in the balcony scene, Juliet is for Romeo first an *object* that then speaks, while he is for her first a *voice* that then becomes manifest.

plunges her, and experience herself as both the object and the generative source of its metamorphic energies. (In this she is the opposite of Blake's Thel.) Submission to its imperatives becomes for her a "prodigious" coming-into-selfhood: "My only love sprung from my only hate! / Too early seen unknown, and known too late! / Prodigious birth of love it is to me / That I must love a loathed enemy" (1.5.138–41). Out of the self experienced as object ("Prodigious birth of love it is *to me*") an "I" springs, impelled by the necessity that is also its motive force. (In the Nurse's recollection of Juliet's weaning, she is similarly an "it" from which an "I" emerges, again through an assent to sexual necessity. The generative imagery is, as we shall see, a defining characteristic of Juliet's world.) Her language makes love and hate particularized emotions that both possess and are possessed by her ("*my* only love," "*my* only hate"), and characterizes the relation between them as an irreversible transformation that locates the place where the self gives birth. In Romeo's parallel utterance, however, they remain abstract tokens that can be manipulated from a distance, in conventional Petrarchan fashion: "Here's much to do with hate, but more with love. / Why then, O brawling love! O loving hate! / O any thing, of nothing first create! / O heavy lightness, serious vanity, / . . . / This love feel I, that feel no love in this" (1.1.176–82). The result is a kind of objectified "I," adrift in an experience its language can't specify (". . . that feel no love *in this*"), and lacking the imperative that moves Juliet.

In a sense this comparison is unfair to Romeo, since his speech occurs before he has fallen in love with Juliet. Yet the counterpoint between the passages seems to insist on it. The Petrarchan side of Romeo it emphasizes, moreover, never entirely disappears from the play. His response to the revelation that Juliet is a Capulet contrasts similarly to hers that he is a Montague: "Is she a Capulet? / O dear account! my life is my foe's debt" (1.5.117–18). His language of reckoning counterpoints her generative imagery; she speaks of imperatives springing from within while he refers to a life held in thrall. Even at the end of the play it is still basically his old self that grieves for Juliet, though with a depth of feeling he would have been incapable of before falling in love with her. His language there, as we have seen, manipulates the opposition between death and beauty in much the same way it did the one between love and hate earlier. And there is the same note (though more poignantly sounded) of a self adrift in experience, partially baffled in its attempts to make received ideas and conventional language express what it is feeling: "How oft when men are at the point of death / Have they been merry, which their keepers call / A lightning before death! O how may I / Call this a lightning?" (5.3.88–91).

Romeo's and Juliet's "I"s are in fact elaborately contrasted in the course of the play, largely through a series of matched passages that explore the relationship between vision, will, and instinct. In the opening scene Romeo and Benvolio together bemoan (as if it were a shared male attitude) the fact that desire is not subject to rational, visual control, and that the actual experience of love involves a turmoil and violence at odds with one's views of it:

Benvolio:	Alas that love, so gentle in his view,
	Should be so tyrannous and rough in proof!
Romeo:	Alas that love, whose view is muffled still,
	Should, without eyes, see pathways to his will!
	(1.1.169–72)

Romeo tends in general to regard vision as an instrument controlled by the conscious will, and hence as the faculty that locates the place of the "I" ("When the devout religion of mine eye / Maintains such falsehood, then turn tears to fires" [1.2.88–89]; "Eyes, look your last!" [5.3.112]). His language tends to make perceptions into possessions and assertions of will: "I'll go along no such sight to be shown, / But to rejoice in splendor of mine own" (1.2.100–101). At the same time it allegorizes instinctual promptings so that they become external to the self— either a blind, alien will or a friendly "counsellor" to whom Romeo lends his own eyes (2.2.80–81).

Juliet's "I," however, is linked more closely by the play of the text with a capacity for assent than with the organs Othello will later term the "speculative and offic'd instruments" of rational will:

Nurse:	"Yea," quoth my husband, "fall'st upon thy face?
	Thou wilt fall backward when thou comest to age,
	Wilt thou not, Jule?" It stinted and said "Ay."
Juliet:	And stint thou too, I pray thee, nurse, say I.
	(1.3.55–58)

As Juliet's character unfolds, it becomes evident that this capacity to say "Ay" to necessity involves more than just a woman's learning to "bear" male oppression (1.4.93). It also signals a willingness to surrender the conscious self to the impersonal forces that stir within it. Her "falling backward" will likewise involve a kind of ontological trust in sexual experience and the world which opens with its relinquishments. Against connotations of guilt, subjection, and tragic punishment, it poses the idea of a fall backward into innocence, the reversal or undoing of an original fall.

Juliet's capacity to answer to imperatives that address her from realms beyond the reach of the individual will is central to Shakespeare's conception of her. The motif is asserted in her first entrance: "How now, who calls?"; "Madam, I am here, / What is your will?" (1.3.5–6). On the surface she expresses a deference to parental will that her own erotic willfulness will replace, and hence provides us with a touchstone for measuring her growth during the course of the play. But her words also suggest a capacity to hear the forces that call to the self from beyond it, and paradoxically to become *manifest* in answering to their demands. Even when Juliet aligns herself obediently with her parent's wishes, her words manage to articulate a more enigmatic relation between self and will: "I'll look to like, if looking liking move" (1.3.97). It hardly matters whether looking moves liking or liking moves looking in this elusive reply: it seems to regard the willing self as a spontaneous interaction between rational, premeditated intentions and instinctual reactions, rather than associating it with one or the other. (In Blake's terms, she looks *through* her eyes, while Romeo looks *with* his.) As a result she is less susceptible to the conflict Romeo articulates between what is experienced *in* love and what is known *as* love. She is able to accept the blindness of love as proper to its element ("if love be blind, / It best agrees with night" [3.2.9–10]), and welcome the disruptive energies in which it engulfs the self. Her apostrophe to night, with its intense anticipation of the sexual act, is addressed as much to the impersonal force of Eros as it is to Romeo: "Come, gentle night, come, loving, black-brow'd night, / Give me my Romeo" (3.2.20–21). This capacity to embrace sexual experience in all its strangeness (cf. 3.2.15), and still admit it into the self as something intimate and gentle, makes Juliet not only a potentially redemptive figure for Romeo but a touchstone for Shakespeare's subsequent explorations of the polarities of erotic love.

Juliet's desire, then, functions as an *erotic* reality-principle that counteracts a wistfulness ingrained in Romeo. The images generated by Romeo's desire tend to wind up in a subjunctive, conditional space ("What if her eyes were there, they in her head?"; "O that I were a glove upon that hand, / That I might touch that cheek"), and a part of him always seems more interested in entertaining them as figures of the imagination than in realizing them. Juliet's images, however, exist in an urgently desired future, and are charged with an erotic energy that makes the experience they invoke present and actual in her imagination. It seems no paradox that the desire for Romeo she expresses in her apostrophe to night should culminate in an image that sublimates an experience of orgasm, even though she is anticipating her first sexual encounter: "Come, gentle night, come, loving, black-brow'd night, / Give me my Romeo, and, when I[5] shall die, / Take him and cut him out in little stars" (3.2.20–22).[6]

Even when Juliet's language seems to place her in the same imaginative world with Romeo, there is often a contrast between the tendency of his metaphors to keep love distant and remote, and hers to bring it up close, and make it possible.[7] Romeo's preoccupation with the light of beauty, for instance, isolates the object of his desire, and mystifies the distance that separates him

[5]Although Q2 and F both read "when *I* shall die," many editors substitute Q4's "when *he* shall die," usually on the grounds that "I" makes Juliet sound inappropriately selfish. But "he" deprives the image of its orgasmic connotations (which are anything but egocentric), and in doing so eliminates the climax toward which the erotic energy of the entire speech builds. . . .

[6]Here again Romeo's imaginative impulses are at odds with his physical actions. In the events of the play, it is he rather than Juliet who most often acts to close the physical distance between them—approaching her at the ball and touching her hand, returning to the Capulet house and climbing the garden wall outside her balcony, scaling a ladder of rope to consummate their marriage in her bedroom, riding back to Verona when he hears of her death, and breaking open her tomb to be with her there.

[7]Lady Macbeth, whose invocation to Night is a twisted recollection of Juliet's, operates similarly *within* her husband's mental universe: pressing for the realization of the deed his imagination conjures up as a *possibility*, and dwells on at arm's length in compulsively subjunctive terms.

from it ("It seems she hangs upon the cheek of night," "What light through yonder window breaks?"). When Juliet has recourse to the idea, however, beauty's light becomes an enabling force that emanates from the consummated relationship: "Lovers can see to do their amorous rites / By their own beauties" (3.2.8–9). Their matching images of black-white contrasts differ in much the same way. Romeo's evoke a purely visual experience—a stable figure-ground relationship that again defines an *object* of desire, and isolates it in the distance: "Beauty too rich for use, for earth too dear! / So shows a snowy dove trooping with crows, / As yonder lady o'er her fellows shows" (1.5.47–49). Juliet's, on the other hand, is a sensually experienced image, and it sublimates the physical contact of an achieved sexual relationship: "Come, night, come, Romeo, come, thou day in night, / For thou wilt lie upon the wings of night, / Whiter than new snow upon a raven's back" (3.2.17–19).

Finally, as this last example suggests, Juliet's language of desire is more extravagantly metamorphic than Romeo's. Even when Romeo s imagination plays with the idea of cosmological change, it operates within the grid of the mundane world, and according to its logic: "It is the east, and Juliet is the sun" (2.2.3). Juliet's images, however, loosen the boundaries that fix the rational universe in place, and draw it into a state of continual flux: Romeo is both night and day in night, she both waits for him in the night as he wings his way toward her and is herself the winged night on whose back he lies like new snow—all in the space of two lines. The boundaries between self and world, subject and object, active and passive, male and female become similarly fluid in her imagination, as we shall see in more detail later in this essay. Her figures also (to use a Nietzschean term) transvalue the world more radically than Romeo's. When he places Juliet's eyes in the vacancies left in the heavens by two truant stars, he imagines that they "Would through the airy region stream so bright / That birds would sing and think it were not night" (2.2.21–22). The reversal effected within this characteristically subjunctive fantasy is temporary, and grounded in illusion: the birds sing in the night not because Juliet's brightness has caused them to change allegiances but because it deceives them into thinking night is day, and in doing so triggers their normal routine. In Juliet's companion image, however, the world is permanently transfigured, and the inversion of values that accompanies the change is a matter of conscious erotic commitment: "Give me my Romeo, and when I shall die, / Take him and cut him out in little stars, / And he will make the face of heaven so fine / That all the world will be in love with night, / And pay no worship to the garish sun" (3.2.21–25).

III

The impression, then, is of two distinct modes of desire—one reaching out, the other unfolding—exquisitely fitted to each other, but rarely meeting in the same phenomenological universe. Wherever the language the two lovers exchange most emphatically suggests a sharing of experience, close inspection reveals difference and often, in Romeo's case, poignant estrangement. Always, it seems, there is a lack in Romeo that corresponds to an overflowing in Juliet. Consider the parting remarks that Shakespeare has so carefully fitted together across separate moments near the end of the balcony scene:

> *Juliet:*   Good night, good night! as sweet repose and rest
>   Come to thy heart as that within my breast.
>   (2.2.123–24)
>
> *Romeo:*   Sleep dwell upon thine eyes, peace in thy breast!
>   Would I were sleep and peace, so sweet to rest!
>   (2.2.186–87)

Juliet wishes for Romeo (as both the lover who desires him and the "saint" who intercedes for him) out of her own sense of well-being—with an intuition, perhaps, that what is "within" her must somehow "come to" him. When she parts from Romeo, she takes with her a love that is a source of "sweet repose and rest," and her instinct is to wish for him the same inner experience in her absence. Romeo, however, can only take this as being left "unsatisfied" (2.2.125). Superficially this may be a joke by the Mercutio in Shakespeare: it suggests that Romeo's idealized romanticism masks ordinary sexual desire. But in a deeper sense Romeo really doesn't seem to know what he wants, and when pressed by Juliet to specify what *would* satisfy him, has to fall back on the notion of an exchange of "vows." His desire seems to originate in a need that is prior to Juliet, and it has to be sustained in language rather than in some burgeoning inner place. In Juliet's case, however, love intrudes into a waiting latency of self and will ("I am here, / What is your will?"; "I'll look to like if looking liking move"), and she experiences it as a "prodigious birth" that once engendered grows of its own accord, and thrives as much on Romeo's absence as on his presence. When she prepares to part from Romeo before her first exit in the balcony scene, her images evoke the generative rhythms of nature ("This bud of love, by summer's ripening breath, / May prove a beauteous flow'r when next we meet" [2.2.121–22]); they anticipate not "satisfaction" but the flowering of what will have been gestating during the interim. Shakespeare suggests just how prodigious this birth in Juliet is going to be by having her "next meet" Romeo only three lines later, when she returns to inform him of feelings that have already grown from images of ripening buds and beauteous flowers into a desire for marriage conceived as a radically *human* form of commitment and risk-taking:

> Three words, dear Romeo, and good night indeed,
> If that thy bent of love be honorable,
> Thy purpose marriage, send me word to-morrow,
> By one that I'll procure to come to thee,
> Where and what time thou wilt perform the rite,
> And all my fortunes at thy foot I'll lay,
> And follow thee my lord throughout the world.
>   (2.2.142–48)

But where Juliet experiences genesis and gestation, Romeo is haunted by a sense of emptiness and unreality. While Juliet's love is ripening offstage, Romeo stands alone, anxiously luxuriating in the dreamlikeness of what is happening to him: "O blessed, blessed night! I am afeard, / Being in night, all this is but a dream, / Too flattering-sweet to be substantial" (2.2.139–41). And when Juliet exits again after sharing with him "their" plans for marriage, he again becomes "one too many by [his] weary self":[8]

Juliet: A thousand times good night! (*Exit*)
Romeo: A thousand times the worse, to want thy light.
               Love goes toward love as schoolboys from their books,
               But love from love, toward school with heavy looks.
                                                                                       (2.2.154–57)

His metaphor describes love as relief from a state of boredom and oppression that returns when the loved object is "withdrawn" (2.2.130). Unlike Juliet's passion for Romeo, which becomes a reality-principle of its own capable of generating value and direction, Romeo's for Juliet remains to some extent an attempt to escape from a reality he finds oppressive, and it is attended (so, at least, his language here would suggest) by feelings of truancy as well as resolve.

It is thus characteristic of Romeo that his attempt to wish Juliet the kind of "good night" she earlier wished him should turn into a longing to be where she is (ontologically as well as physically) that simultaneously expresses his own unrest ("Would I were sleep and peace, so sweet to rest"). In the process he turns one phenomenological universe into something very like its opposite. Her world of whole selves and embodied feelings ("as sweet repose and rest / Come to thy heart as that within my breast") becomes in his language a realm of personifications and part objects that he gazes into from a wistful distance. More importantly, the "repose and rest" that Juliet experiences *within,* as the very condition of her desire for Romeo, becomes a state of quiescence lying passively "upon" her. Juliet's own imagination later adapts itself to this transformation as she anticipates their sexual union: "Come night, come, Romeo, come, thou day in night, / For thou wilt lie upon the wings of night / Whiter than new snow upon a raven's back" (3.2.17–21). But in doing so she activates Romeo's images: concrete, tactile sensations take the place of personified abstractions, and his quietly fitted surfaces are drawn into a ceaselessly metamorphic flux. The death Juliet inflicts upon herself is likewise a violently erotic consummation of his wish to "rest" quiescently in her breast: "O happy dagger, / This is thy sheath; there rest,[9] and let me die" (5.2.169–70). This last transformation is, as we shall see, paradigmatic of the exchange of loves that takes

[8]This is Benvolio's description of the feeling of his own by which he "measured" the "affections" of a solitary, retiring Romeo (1.1.128). The behavior that introduces us to Romeo's idiosyncracies, then, is something by which one adolescent male recognizes himself in another.

[9]I have departed from the Riverside text which, following Q2 and F, reads "There *rust,* and let me die." Q1 has "Rest in my bosom.". . . .

place between Romeo and Juliet: his gentle desire to be "pillowed for ever" (to use Keats' Romeo-like language) on a breast he associates as much with maternal comfort as sexual desire becomes "in" her a violent thrust aimed at the quick of being.

These differences are present in every scene between Romeo and Juliet, and culminate in their separate, elaborately linked deaths. When Romeo forces his way into Juliet's tomb, he is still seeking through union with her the "rest" that eludes him: "Here, here, will I remain / With worms that are thy chambermaids; O, here / Will I set up my everlasting rest" (5.3. 108–10). This conjuring with the word "here" echoes his complaint at the beginning of the play of being "out" of the place where he is "in" love: "I have lost myself; I am not here; / This is not Romeo, he's some other where" (1.1.197–98). It also recalls his decision after leaving the Capulets' ball to "turn back" to Juliet in order to "find out" the "centre" of his "dull earth" (2.1.2). His language in the tomb is like a final incantation designed to overcome whatever it is that enforces this distance from himself as well as Juliet. He seems to want to conjure up with words the experience of being in place, the simple "I am here" (1.3.5) that Juliet begins with, and Romeo instinctively associates with her.

Juliet, however, emerges from the experience Romeo wishes to arrive at. (Weaning structures her desire in the same figurative way that search for the peace-giving breast does Romeo's.) By the time she returns to consciousness in the tomb, her initial "I am here" has grown through time into something fuller and more complex: "I do remember well where I should be, / And there I am" (5.3.149–50). And though she wakes effortlessly into the experience of self-coincidence Romeo labors to attain in death, her voice locates it not "here" but "there." She is already "some other where," though in a very different sense than Romeo. Her awakening in the tomb is one of the rare instances, in fact, when her words "turn back" toward their center. Usually the "here" is for her imagination a backing for ventures outward, into the world and across ontological thresholds—not, as it is for Romeo, a goal in which to "set up" an "everlasting rest." Her similarly self-referential "there" when she kills herself a few moments later—"O happy dagger, / This is thy sheath; there rest, and let me die"—unlooses the voice that says "me" from the body that houses it (like a final weaning), and launches it toward an altogether mysterious silence. When she does use "here" in the final scene, the word refers not to where she is but to what's "out there": "What's here? A cup clos'd in my true love's hand? / Poison, I see, hath been his timeless end" (5.3.161–62). It thus becomes an index of both her openness to the present-at-hand and her access to things that happen in her absence.

Romeo can never quite manage to make Juliet and the situation in which he finds her "here" in this way during the final scene, in spite of his conjurings with the word. He remains incapable of the kind of seeing that *grasps* things as hers does. He is too self-conscious in his grief, and too anxious (in both senses of the word) to materialize in language a death that feels "unsubstantial" to him, to risk the spontaneous responsiveness that comes naturally to her: "Eyes, look your last! / Arms, take your last embrace! and lips, O you / The doors of breath, seal with a righteous kiss / A dateless bargain to engrossing death!" (5.3.112–15). Juliet, on the contrary, merely says "I will kiss thy lips," and then does so (a far cry from her initial "What is your will?"), and registers her surprise with "Thy lips are warm"—a simple tactile observation that goes straight to the heart of grief.

IV

Juliet's "I do remember well where I should be, / And there I am" is a response to an immediate dramatic situation; but the total fabric of the play's language, concerned as it is with constitutive interchanges between the speaking self and the world in which it finds itself, lends the utterance an epigrammatic clarity and resonance.[10] Like a combination of the Cartesian *cogito* and the Freudian *wo es war, soll ich werden,* it articulates an experience of self-coincidence that is both arrival and return—in the present moment, to the body—from a realm closed to consciousness. And the pattern of motifs that it consummates suggests that it is something Juliet grows into during the course of the play. We have already seen how it complicates her initial "Here I am"; it also expands the "Ay me" she first utters in the balcony scene. There she is an unelaborated self (and self-affirmation) on the brink of the experience of sexual desire that will cause it to flower. By the final scene it has been filled out by a "remembering well" that enables her to venture over the threshold between life and death, consciousness and unconsciousness, the self and the non-self, and find herself where she "should be" when she returns.[11] (Cleopatra's "I have / Immortal longings in me" is another "I me" filled out with temporal experience that allows it to cross over and internalize this threshold.)

Though it is Romeo who triggers this flowering in Juliet—the Nurse tells her in their first scene together that "women grow bigger by men" (1.3.95)—echoes in the language of the play suggest that this "remembering well" is an ability she inherits from the Nurse herself: "That shall she, marry, I remember it well . . . I never shall forget it . . . I warrant, and I should live a thousand years, / I never should forget it" (1.3.22–47). It involves what seems in *Romeo and Juliet* a uniquely female capacity to "grow bigger" in the element of time—to assimilate, nurture, and in Juliet's case prodigiously transform the happenings of life.

[10]A gnomic quality tends to attach to the language of location and self-assertion in other plays by Shakespeare more or less directly concerned with ontological "world" and its possession / dispossession. *King Lear*, especially, is insistent in its epigrammatic use of such language: cf. France's "Thou losest here, a better where to find" (addressed to Cordelia), Edmund's "The wheel has come full circle, I am here," and Cordelia's own "And so I am; I am," followed immediately by her gnomic "No cause, no cause."

[11]In doing so she passes effortlessly from the subjunctive realm where Romeo's imagination characteristically languishes ("should be") into the present indicative where hers flourishes ("There I am").

The repetitions of the Nurse's reverie about Juliet's weaning issue from an involuntary memory conceived in female rather than male terms—not a chamber of sealed vessels inaccessible to consciousness (this Proustian notion of the past is congruent with Romeo's sense of life as a series of "encounters" [cf. 2.5.29] that pass him by) but a vast interconnectedness in which the self peacefully dwells. Her recollections circle around a natural cataclysm and around human separation and loss—an earthquake, Juliet's weaning, the deaths of "Susan" and her husband—yet they open on an interior space where no real harm can come to the self or the things it cherishes. (Its opposite is the partially repressed realm of phallic violence that haunts the soldier's dream and Mercutio's reverie: "Sometime she driveth o'er a soldier's neck, / And then dreams he of cutting foreign throats, / Of breaches, ambuscadoes, Spanish blades, / Of healths five fadom deep; and then anon / Drums in his ear, at which he starts and wakes, / And being thus frighted, swears a prayer or two, / And sleeps again" [1.4.82–88].) Her daughter and her husband are alive in her memory, not mourned but loved. The tremors of an earthquake survive as the shaking of a dove-house wall, bidding her to "trudge." Juliet's "fall" becomes an occasion for merriment, and though the crude male jest is at her expense ("Thou wilt fall backward when thou comest to age"), the man who makes it "takes her up," and tenderly reassures her.[12]

The Nurse's memory weaves[13] all this eventfulness into a matrix of primary female experience (birth, lactation, weaning, marriage, maidenheads and their loss) from which Juliet emerges, standing high-lone and saying "Ay." Juliet will be weaned again in the course of the play, this time from the fate the Nurse holds out to her as a woman as well as the one Lady Capulet urges upon her as a wife.[14] Her initial weaning ushers her into a world of "day" the Nurse seems to think of as hers and Juliet's privileged domain, even though she happily acknowledges the presence of her husband and Juliet's parents at its periphery, the latter away at Mantua, the former there to take up Juliet when she falls.[15]

---

[12]See Barbara Everett's beautiful essay, *"Romeo and Juliet:* The Nurse's Story," *Critical Quarterly* 14 (1972): 129–39.

[13]I use the term "weaves" advisedly. The Nurse's reverie allows us to observe what a Jungian would call "the anima" at work processing the raw material of life, creating from an inchoate jumble of events the illusion of a continuous fabric of experience. Even at the level of language itself there is an impulse to take compounds apart in order to weave them more securely into the ongoing flow: "I'll lay fourteen of my teeth— / And yet, to my teen be it spoken, I have but four— / She's not fourteen" (1.3.12–14). Mercutio's Queen Mab speech, which is in so many ways a complement of the Nurse's reverie, exhibits a similar delight in creating wholes out of disparate components, yet its fragile constructions exist in a "Time out a' mind," and cannot altogether conceal the authorial presence of a destructive, arbitrarily malicious "animus": "Her waggon-spokes made of long spinner's legs, / The cover of the wings of grasshoppers, / Her traces of the smallest spider web . . ." (1.4.62–64).

[14]The language of the play suggests, in fact, that it is the Nurse who has to be weaned from Juliet: "Go, counsellor, / Thou and my bosom henceforth shall be twain" (3.5.239–40).

[15]Juliet assimilates this beneficent "taking up" as a kind of ontological constant in the background of her own essentially anti-tragic capacity for risk-taking. Romeo, on the other hand, knows it only as an "unaccustomed" feeling brought on by dreams and implemented by "thoughts": "If I may trust the flattering truth of sleep, / My dreams presage some joyful news at hand. / My bosom's lord sits lightly on his throne, / And all this day an unaccustom'd spirit / Lifts me above the ground with cheerful thoughts."

The Nurse's reverie conjures up the idea of a woman's life as a vast biological cycle, a succession of archetypal experiences so intimately in touch with natural, generative time ("Sitting *in* the sun under the dove-house wall") that it really does seem plausible to think of living a thousand years. Sexuality is for her a source of pleasure, and the thought of it presides over her happy acquiescence to this realm and the woman's lot Verona prescribes for her. But for Juliet it becomes a *passion*—the source of a willfulness and a metaphysical desire that from the point of view of society and perhaps even nature are essentially transgressive. Her element will prove to be the night, and she herself the epitome of things violent and brief. Yet we are made to feel, I think, that Juliet's link with the primary realm of the Nurse continues unimpaired beneath her movement away from it during the course of the play. The Nurse's temporal rootedness and uncomplicated belief in the *goodness* of sexual experience are incorporated by Juliet's radical will as a voice prompting and giving its blessing to her ventures into the unknown: "Go, girl, seek happy nights to happy days" (1.3.105).[16]

Indeed, the notion of a "voice within" that summoms and directs Juliet develops into a full-scale motif during the course of the play, and the Nurse is intricately associated with it. The Nurse first "calls her forth" from offstage, and when she appears, asking "Who calls?" the Nurse replies, "Your mother." Later, at the end of the Capulet ball, when Juliet and the Nurse remain alone together onstage, an anonymous offstage voice calls Juliet's name (Q2's stage direction reads, "One calls within, 'Juliet' "), and it is the Nurse who answers with "Anon, anon!" By the time of the balcony scene, the original situation has come full circle: Juliet, alone onstage with Romeo, hears the Nurse's voice summoning her from offstage, and refers to it as "some voice within" that *she* now says "anon" to. (Later in the scene this offstage summons and Juliet's response break into her address to Romeo, and are in turn assimilated by it.) This sequence appears to establish the Nurse as the generative "mother" of Juliet, and as a transmitter of the voices that call to her both from "within" and "beyond."[17] It also implies

---

Here, especially, the difference doesn't so much criticize Romeo as underscore the poignancy of his situation: having to invent and sustain at the level of fantasy and consciousness what is given to Juliet as the stable ground of experience.

[16]This discussion of the Nurse's and Juliet's connectedness owes much to the current feminist appropriation of psychoanalytic object-relations theory: Nancy Chodorow's *The Reproduction of Mothering* (Berkeley and Los Angeles, 1978), especially, should be felt in the background of my argument. It must be added, however, that although this perspective provides a rich context within which to understand what Juliet assimilates from the Nurse, it has practically nothing to tell us about the forces that propel Juliet *away* from the Nurse, into individuality and the undomesticatable "strangeness" of the erotic. Indeed, Shakespeare's portrayal of Juliet brings into focus the limitations of both sides of the current argument within psychoanalytic theory between models of the psyche that privilege object-relations and libido respectively.

[17]The convergence of the two "withins"—the one beyond the world of the stage and the one beneath the conscious self—in Juliet's experience, and their manifestation to her as *voice*, suggest the nature of her extraordinary strength of will. (One might contrast Hamlet's equally auspicious summons from these two realms, and the confusion that the Ghost's offstage voice generates from "beneath.") Romeo, on the other hand, must *suppose* controlling forces whose transcendent will remains silent and undisclosed ("But He who hath the steerage of my course, / Direct my sail").

an identification or symbiosis between them that Juliet is in the process of growing away from. Its severance appears to be complete when Juliet dismisses the Nurse from *her* breast ("Thou and my bosom henceforth shall be twain"), and then fails to respond to her voice as it attempts to wake her for her marriage with Paris. (The Nurse's increasingly panicky address is a medley of all the calls Juliet has previously answered: "Mistress! . . . Juliet! . . . Why, lamb! why, lady! . . . Why, love, I say! madam! . . . I needs must waken her. . . .") Yet there are suggestions that this apparent repudiation of the Nurse is really a sign that her mediating function of waking Juliet to the voices within has been fulfilled. Thus Juliet, abandoned to her own resources when the Friar deserts her in the tomb, is able to hear the offstage "noise" that frightens him away as if it were personally calling to her,[18] and answers "Yea" (rather than "anon") to it—another convergence of obedience and affirmation in her that issues in an impulsive act of will.

Juliet thus seems to enjoy a smooth passage from the realm of the "good Nurse" (2.5.21, 28, 54) directly into the strangeness of sexual experience. The Nurse's free associations, her husband's jest, and the play of coincidences combine to weave a background for her in which sex is connected with weaning and saying "I." And sexuality does seem a matter of individuation for Juliet—individuation that is instinctively connected with affirmation. She *emerges into* sexual desire (in her two balcony scenes, literally standing "high-lone"), and experiences it as a means of action and a source of bounty, not, as it tends to be for Romeo, the longing for a lost self or distant object.

Needless to say, this is not how the patriarchal order that urges marriage on Juliet intends things to turn out. Marriage for a woman, as Lady Capulet's presence throughout the Nurse's reverie reminds us, is supposed to be a passage from daughter to wife and maid to mother that elides the realm of autonomous female sexuality and the powers associated with it. The notion of the sexual initiation legitimized by the institution of marriage as an unsexing of women is punningly suggested by a series of remarks about the "making" and "marring" of mothers and maids;[19] it is blatantly underscored by Sampson's equation of deflowering and capital punishment: " 'Tis all one; I will show myself a tyrant: When I have fought with the men, I will be civil with the maids; I will cut off their heads." Some editors follow Q4 in emending Q2F's "civil" to "cruel," on the grounds that the act of violence Sampson describes is scarcely a civil one. But the same male logic that makes the taking of a woman's maidenhead a beheading makes it the civil act *par excellence* (as we see in the case of

[18]The Nurse's own voice, first trying to wake Juliet and then calling for help upon discovering that she is "dead," had earlier prompted Lady Capulet to inquire, "What *noise* is here?" (4.5.17).

[19]Cf. Lady Capulet: "younger than you . . . Are made already mothers. By my count, / I was your mother much upon these years / That you are now a maid" (1.3.69–73); also Paris, "Younger than she are happy mothers made," answered by Capulet, "And too soon marr'd are those so early made" (1.2.12–13). The spoken language here labors to insinuate an *identity* of "mother" and "maid" (through the agency of a "making" that is also a "marring")—as if by being "made" a mother a woman were "made" into a "maid."

Desdemona): by it her autonomy and her sexual will are taken from her, and she is positioned within the social order, subject to her husband and the rules of married chastity.

The Nurse's and Lady Capulet's counsels come from opposite realms, then, one where women grow by men, the other where a woman is marred by being "made" matron and maid at once. (Lady Macbeth, in taking upon herself her husband's ambitions, makes herself into a diabolical version of what Lady Capulet represents by negating in herself what the Nurse embodies: "Come, you spirits / That tend on mortal thoughts, unsex me here, / . . . Come to my woman's breasts, / And take my milk for gall. . . .") Yet both counsel the same thing, and there is a sense of collusion between them as they do so. Their very presence together before Juliet is emblematic of a social arrangement that contrives to divorce the sexual aspect of motherhood from the figure of the wife, and confine it to a domestic sphere where it will serve rather than threaten the male order that depends on it. But precisely because the female "knowledge" the Nurse embodies is excluded from the realm of male power, there is a sense that Juliet can inherit it in some magically direct way ("were not I thine only nurse, / I would say thou hadst suck'd wisdom from thy teat" [1.3.67–68]), free of the divisions which found that realm and the repressions that maintain it. Her sexuality seems to issue spontaneously from a core of primary identifications, and in a form more potentially disruptive to the male order of things than the anxious phallic assertiveness ("My naked weapon is out") which produces "rebellious subjects" (1. 1.81) within it.

Romeo and Juliet is full of a sense of how social prerogatives based on the oppression of women place the men who enjoy them at a disadvantage in the realm of primary experience. Sampson reasons that since "women, being the weaker vessels, are ever thrust to the wall," he will "push Montague's men from the wall, and thrust his maids to the wall" (1.1.15–18), even though he himself has just admitted that the place nearest the wall is the superior position. And the image of the maid thrust against the wall by Sampson's gross assaults, the object not even of sexual lust but deflected male rivalry, is somehow balanced by that of the Nurse "Sitting in the sun under the dove-house wall," alone with Juliet in the world of women, enjoying there the backing of an elemental realm whose existence Sampson, with his insecure phallic readiness to give and take offence, will never even remotely intuit. Mercutio, for whom the "sociable" is an antidote to "groaning for love" (2.4.88–89), likewise perceives woman's position in love as analogous to her position in the civil order, and the sexual act as a means of subduing her to it: "This is the hag, when maids lie on their backs, / That presses them and learns them first to bear, / Making them women of good carriage" (1.4.92–94). Yet the bearing women are expected to endure in society is matched in the realm of ontological experience by a *power* to bear, and bear fruit, that men are denied by a code that regards submission as "dishonorable [and] vile" (as Mercutio terms Romeo's "calm" reaction to Tybalt's challenge), and defines freedom as a matter of keeping one's neck "out of collar" (1.1.4–5).

Juliet's apostrophe to night suggests, moreover, that woman's sexual place is where the imagination thrives. The climax of her speech sublimates an intoxicating sensation of floating weightlessly in a void that encompasses the sexual act, while at the same time being oneself its ground and bearing the whole of it ("for thou wilt lie upon the wings of night / Whiter than new snow upon a raven's back"), that seems accessible only from beneath. She is the one in a position to take in sexual experience, and witness the epiphany that occurs at the moment of relinquishment: "Give me my Romeo, and, when I shall die, / Take him and cut him out in little stars, / And he will make the face of heaven so fine . . ." Romeo's imagination, by contrast, does not seem open to the sexual act in the way Juliet's is, and though his experience in love can't be reduced to Mercutio's travesty of it as "a great natural that runs lolling up and down to hide his bauble in a hole" (2.4.91–93), its horizons do seem limited by his desire to rest in Juliet's breast.

Similar ironies govern the socially instituted discrepancy between Romeo's and Juliet's approaches to love. We first encounter Romeo not being addressed by the "intergenerational"[20] will of the Montague family (as we might expect had Shakespeare wished either to portray the love relationship as symmetrical or explore it primarily within the division between the two families),[21] but adrift in the unsupervised realm of male adolescence. Yet the liberty to "inquire" he enjoys there has resulted in a mind full of knowledge about love (obviously acquired, as Juliet remarks, "by th' book") that betrays the absence of any felt connection with the source of instinctual wisdom Juliet draws from. He also enjoys a freedom of movement and the company and support of friends, while she is confined within the family places (hall, bedroom, tomb) and isolated from anyone with whom she might share her experiences as a young woman. But as a result she is the one who seems most capable and at home in the solitude that is love's element ("My dismal scene I needs must act alone"), and the one who provides the impetus and inner direction of their relationship once Romeo initiates it. His social advantages also create transitional conflicts that Juliet is spared. The male bonds that form in adolescence involve phallic allegiances against women and the threats of impotence, emasculation, and effeminacy posed by the actual sexual relation—hence Mercutio's almost compul-

---

[20]The term is from Nancy Chodorow, "Family Structure and Feminine Personality," in *Women, Culture, & Society*, ed. Michelle Zimbalist Rosaldo and Louise Lamphere (Stanford, 1974), p. 57.

[21]Such assumptions (or conclusions) govern most criticism of the play's alleged dramatic immaturity or limitations. James L. Calderwood, for instance, attributes the play's less-than-total success to a "concentration on, almost celebration of, dramatic form [that] imparts to the play a highly rigid structure based on the division between Montagues and Capulets and lovers and society" (*Shakespearean Metadrama* [Minneapolis, 1971], p. 116), while Sigurd Burckhardt finds it limited by "a symmetry which, even though it is a symmetry of conflict, is comforting" (*Shakespearean Meanings* [Princeton, 1968], p. 264). It has been the contention of this essay, on the contrary, that Shakespeare establishes these conventional dramatic symmetries (in the opening prologue, for instance), only to move within and beyond them to asymmetries that are the "true ground" (5.3.180) not only of the play's "woe" but its generative energies as well. The story of the two "star-cross'd lovers" we are introduced to in the beginning has by the end become that of "Juliet and her Romeo."

sive eagerness to generate collective sexual ridicule of the Nurse, and his mockery of a "fishified" Romeo ("without his roe, like a dried herring") who is only "Romeo" (Mercutio insists) when he is "sociable" and not "groaning for love." These attitudes persist, moreover—as the opening scene makes clear—in the adult world, and hence make the conflict Mercutio articulates between social identity and sexual relatedness not just a passing adolescent stage but a permanent male dilemma.[22] Romeo is of all Shakespeare's romantic or tragic heroes the one least inhibited by these male bonds and the cultural values that reinforce them. When the play opens he is already disaffected with society, and too narcissistically self-absorbed to feel the *pull* of friendship. And when he falls in love with Juliet, he positively relishes the submissive role of fitting himself to her will. Yet Mercutio has to die (so the plot seems to tell us) before Romeo and Juliet's relationship can be sexually consummated, and Mercutio himself blames his death on Romeo's betrayal—for "coming between" Mercutio and Tybalt, to be sure, but also, one feels, for allowing something to come between the two of them. Shakespeare thus manages to make the presence of a bad conscience about sexual love that is endemic to masculinity felt in the background of Romeo's experience, and the one short moment that Romeo falls back into it plunges him and the entire play into tragedy: "O sweet Juliet, / Thy beauty hath made me effeminate, / And in my temper soft'ned valor's steel" (3.1.113–15).

V

It is not surprising, then, that Romeo lacks Juliet's temporal and positional assurance (Mercutio's "Where the devil should this Romeo be?" matches her "I do remember well where I should be, / And there I am"), considering what his male background provides for him. Even the Friar, whose place in Romeo's life corresponds to that of the Nurse in Juliet's, can only provide the counsel of someone who has abdicated from the flow of human experience and the disruptions that mark it. His presence as a "ghostly confessor" (2.6.21) introduces into the background of Romeo's love the idea of male celibacy, with its reservations about the legitimacy of sexuality ("So smile the heavens upon this holy act, / That afterhours with sorrow chide us not!" [2.6.1–2]), and its attempt to avoid the alternations of love and grief and attachment and separation which the Nurse's memory transforms into a steady state of well-being. The Nurse, remembering "Sitting in the sun under the dove-house wall," evokes a nature in which earthquakes and weanings magically correspond; the Friar speaks from his "cell" of a nature permanently arrested at the maternal breast, and elides all the "partings" through which life passes on its way from birth to death: "The earth that's nature's mother is her tomb; / What is her burying grave, that is her

[22]See Coppélia Kahn, *Man's Estate: Masculine Identity in Shakespeare* (Berkeley and Los Angeles, 1981), for a seminal discussion of the importance of this conflict throughout Shakespeare's work.

womb; / And from her womb children of divers kind / We sucking on her natural bosom find" (2.3.9–12). The Nurse's reverie evokes the feeling of being immersed in temporal process, and suggests an ability to communicate with the impersonal forces that dictate the "times" of human life ("Shake, quoth the dovehouse; 'twas no need, I trow, / To bid me trudge"). The Friar, on the other hand, thinks of time as the "plot" of an unknowable, otherworldly will, and his actions embody a half-guilty attempt to manipulate its "accidents" ("A greater power than we can contradict / Hath thwarted our intents").[23]

Romeo and Juliet mirror these differences, in death as well as life. The noise that frightens the Friar from the tomb triggers, as we have seen, Juliet's final "Yea": it seems to signal her to "be brief" much as the earthquake bid the Nurse to "trudge." Romeo, however, resolves to "defy" the "stars" when he hears of Juliet's death, and must force an unwilling death to take him: "Thou detestable maw, thou womb of death, / Gorg'd with the dearest morsel of the earth, / Thus I enforce thy rotten jaws to open, / And in despite I'll cram thee with more food" (5.3.45–48). Buried in these metaphors of grief is a fantasy of oral retaliation against the withdrawn, depriving maternal breast. It does not so much enter Romeo's psyche as take its place in the haunted male background which the gentleness of his own love stands out against but never entirely exorcises. When he enters the tomb, he similarly leaves behind him troubled images of sexual experience like those that will later possess Othello's deranged imagination: "Alack, alack, what blood is this, which stains / The stony entrance of this sepulchre? / What mean these masterless and gory swords / To lie discolor'd by this place of peace?" (5.3.140–43).

Once inside the tomb, where a few moments later Juliet will wake into a remembering well, Romeo grows forgetful, and reality begins to feel dreamlike to him: "What said my man, when my betossèd soul / Did not attend him as we rode? I think / He told me Paris should have married Juliet. / Said he not so? Or did I dream it so? / Or am I mad, hearing him talk of Juliet, / To think it was so?" (5.3.76–81). Grief may be the immediate cause of this distraction, but the feeling of being adrift in a temporal element that undermines the will and robs consciousness of its experience is deeply characteristic of Romeo. Even when he is happiest in love he tends to regard what is happening to him as a series of winged, half-unreal moments, and reaches out for them with language in an attempt to hold and lengthen them. For Juliet, however, time is a metamorphic principle that animates her from within. The goals Romeo aims for as havens from temporal flux and the "weariness" it causes are for her charged thresholds of being. Even her impatience for their love's future is that of the bud for the flower, not, as it is for Romeo, that of a schoolboy for recess.[24]

These differences are especially pointed in the images with which Romeo and

---

[23]For a related distinction between the Nurse and the Friar as "mediators," see Richard Fly, *Shakespeare's Mediated World* (Amherst, 1976), p. 19.

[24]I am indebted to Howard Tharsing for this formulation of Romeo and Juliet's temporal differences.

Juliet conjure up ideas of the life-in-death that persists in the tomb. His personifications of the "state" of death are a denial of time, process, and substance: death
becomes a jealous lover (or would-be lover) who "keeps" Juliet in thrall, while
worms attend on her as chambermaids. The unhappy imagination that creates this
image is, in spite of the love that charges it, an enemy of the will in Juliet that tells
Romeo's "happy" dagger to "there rest, and let me die." Juliet, on the contrary,
anticipating the future into which the friar's potion will cause her to wake, thinks
of the tomb as a place of real, historical time, where physical process continues in
the absence of life: "an ancient receptacle, / Where for this many hundred years
the bones / Of all my buried ancestors are pack'd, / Where bloody Tybalt, yet but
green in earth, / Lies fest'ring in his shroud" (4.3.39–43). Her imagination then
proceeds to enliven this place with a scenario that makes crossing over into it all
the more urgent: "O, look! methinks I see my cousin's ghost / Seeking out Romeo,
that did spit his body / Upon a rapier's point. Stay, Tybalt, stay! / Romeo, Romeo,
Romeo! Here's drink—I drink to thee." (4.3.55–58). Romeo's subsequent "Here's
to my love!" (5.3.119) is, by contrast, nostalgic, not directional. It is a static gesture
with which he fixes himself in the scene of his own death, not a crossing over to
Juliet.

The language of the final scene measures these differences in minute detail.
Romeo's resolve to "remain" in the tomb ("here, here will I remain, / With
worms that are thy chambermaids") is, again, an attempt to conjure up the
scene of his death, and prolong it into eternity; Juliet's is an active refusal to
"come away" with the friar, who "dare[s] no longer stay." And Romeo's emphasis on *staying* with Juliet ("I still will stay with thee, / And never from this palace
of dim night / Depart again") is undercut when a few moments later she tenderly chides him for having left no poison to help her "after." He thinks of
death as an "everlasting rest," but she perceives it as a "timeless end," and
resolves in her own death to "be brief." In these last instances, especially,
Juliet's language is both more realistic and metaphysically resonant than
Romeo's. "Timeless end" is a ruthless tautology spoken by someone for whom
life *is* time; yet it simultaneously evokes an afterlife more mysterious and sub-
lime than the eternity Romeo's consciousness is equipped to understand.
"After" is a spatio-temporal pun: it refers both to Juliet's crossing-over to
Romeo and the situation in which he has "left" her. Both meanings gently
underscore the limits of Romeo's imagination: able only to die into the scene of
consciousness, not cross over or escape by extinguishing it, and unable to make
room or provision there for a *live* Juliet, in spite of his concern for her. His
desire to *remain* forever and hers to *be* brief epitomizes the difference between
them, a difference that in spite of their fit assigns them separate meanings and
destinations. The gold statues erected at the end of the play might almost be
symbolic realizations of the state Romeo aspires to in death, but they fail utterly
to capture Juliet. Though he sees her in the end as a beauty that makes the
tomb "a feasting presence full of light," she associates herself in death with the
sudden illumination of the lightning, that active principle "which doth cease to

be / Ere one can say it lightens." Romeo leaves behind a letter that acknowledges the audience present at the scene of his death, and its attempt to avoid being misunderstood evokes the problematical, compromised endings of such characters as Lucrece, Hamlet, and Othello. Juliet, however, is content, regardless of how we measure her, to "measure [us] a measure and be gone" (1.4.10). In doing so she becomes a rare unquestioned center of value in the otherwise turbulent world of Shakespeare's tragedies.

Coming of Age in Verona

Coppélia Kahn

Romeo and Juliet is about a pair of adolescents trying to grow up. Growing up requires that they separate themselves from their parents by forming an intimate bond with one of the opposite sex which supersedes filial bonds. This, broadly, is an essential task of adolescence, in Renaissance England or Italy as in America today, and the play is particularly concerned with the social milieu in which these adolescent lovers grow up—a patriarchal milieu as English as it is Italian. I shall argue that the feud in a realistic social sense is the primary tragic force in the play—not the feud as agent of fate,[1] but the feud as an extreme and peculiar expression of patriarchal society, which Shakespeare shows to be tragically self-destructive.[2] The feud is the deadly *rite-de-passage* which promotes masculinity at the price of life. Undeniably, the feud is bound up with a pervasive *sense* of fatedness, but that sense finds its objective correla-

From *Modern Language Studies* 8 (1977–1978), 5–22. Reprinted by permission of *Modern Language Studies*. Some of the original footnotes for this essay have been shortened.

[1]A long-standing interpretation of *Romeo and Juliet* holds that it is a tragedy of fate. F. S. Boas, *Shakespeare and His Predecessors* (New York, 1896), p. 214; E. K. Chambers, *Shakespeare: A Survey* (London, 1929), pp. 70–71; E. E. Stoll, *Shakespeare's Young Lovers* (Oxford, 1937), pp. 4–5; and G. L. Kittredge, ed., *Sixteen Plays of Shakespeare* (New York, 1948), p. 674 are the most prominent of the many critics who have shared this view. Stopford Brooke, *On Ten Plays of Shakespeare* (London, 1905, pp. 36, 65) held the quarrel between the houses to be the cause of the tragedy, but saw the quarrel in moral rather than social terms as an expression of any "long-continued evil". More recently, H.B. Charlton, "Shakespeare's Experimental Tragedy," in his *Shakespearian Tragedy* (Cambridge, England, 1948), pp. 49–63, calls the feud the means by which fate acts, but objects to it as such on the grounds that it lacks convincing force and implacability in the play. For an orthodox Freudian interpretation of the feud as a regressive intrafamilial, narcissistic force which prevents Romeo and Juliet from seeking properly non-incestuous love objects, see M. D. Faber, "The Adolescent Suicides of Romeo and Juliet," *Psychoanalytic Review*, 59 (1971), 169–182.

[2]As usual, Shakespeare portrays the milieu of his source in terms with which he and his audience are familiar; he is not at pains to distinguish the Italian family from the English. Here I accept Lawrence Stone's definition of the patriarchal family:

> This sixteenth-century aristocratic family was patrilinear, primogenitural, and patriarchal: patrilinear in that it was the male line whose ancestry was traced so diligently by the genealogists and heralds, and in almost all cases via the male line that titles were inherited; primogenitural in that most of the property went to the eldest son, the younger brothers being dispatched into the world with little more than a modest annuity or life interest in a small estate to keep them afloat; and patriarchal in that the husband and father lorded it over his wife and children with the quasi-absolute authority of a despot.

Lawrence Stone, *The Crisis of the Aristocracy: 1558–1660* (London: Oxford University Press, 1971), abridged edition, p. 271.

tive in the dynamics of the feud and of the society in which it is embedded. As Harold Goddard says,

> The fathers are the stars and the stars are the fathers in the sense that the fathers stand for the accumulated experience of the past, for tradition, for authority, and hence for the two most potent forces that mold and so impart 'destiny' to the child's life . . . heredity and training. The hatred of the hostile houses in *Romeo and Juliet* is an inheritance that every member of these families is born into as truly as he is born with the name Capulet or Montague.[3]

That inheritance makes Romeo and Juliet tragic figures because it denies their natural needs and desires as youth. Of course, they also display the faults of youth; its self-absorption and reckless extremism, its headlong surrender to eros. But it is the feud which fosters the rash, choleric impulsiveness typical of youth by offering a permanent invitation to and outlet for violence.

The feud is first referred to in the play as "their parents' strife and their parents' rage" and it is clear that the fathers, not their children, are responsible for its continuance. Instead of providing social channels and moral guidance by which the energies of youth can be rendered beneficial to themselves and society, the Montagues and the Capulets make weak gestures toward civil peace while participating emotionally in the feud as much as their children do. While they fail to exercise authority over the younger generation in the streets, they wield it selfishly and stubbornly in the home. So many of the faults of character which critics have found in Romeo and Juliet are shared by their parents that the play cannot be viewed as a tragedy of character in the Aristotelian sense, in which the tragedy results because the hero and heroine fail to "love moderately."[4] Rather, the feud's ambiance of hot temper permeates age as well as youth; viewed from the standpoint of Prince Escalus who embodies the law, it is Montague and Capulet who are childishly refractory.

In the course of the action, Romeo and Juliet create and try to preserve new identities as adults apart from the feud, but it blocks their every attempt. Metaphorically, it devours them in the "detestable maw" of the Capulets' monument, a symbol of the patriarchy's destructive power over its children. Thus both the structure and the texture of the play suggest a critique of the patriarchal attitudes expressed through the feud, which makes "tragic scapegoats" of Romeo and Juliet.[5]

---

[3]Harold Goddard, *The Meaning of Shakespeare* (2 vols.), Chicago: The University of Chicago Press, 1951, I, 119.

[4]This is a more recent critical tendency than that referred to in note 1, and is represented by Donald A. Stauffer, *Shakespeare's World of Images* (New York, 1949), pp. 55–57; Franklin M. Dickey, *Not Wisely But Too Well* (San Marino, 1957), pp. 63–117; and Roy W. Battenhouse, *Shakespearean Tragedy: Its Art and Christian Premises* (Bloomington and London, 1969), pp. 102–129. However, Dickey and Paul N. Siegel, "Christianity and the Religion of Love in *Romeo and Juliet*," *Shakespeare Quarterly* XII (1961), p. 383, see the lovers' passion, flawed though it is, as the means by which divine order based on love is restored to Verona.

[5]Paul N. Siegel (cited in note 4) uses this phrase, but in a moral rather than social context; he sees them as scapegoats through whom their parents expiate their sins of hate and vengefulness.

Specifically, for the sons and daughters of Verona the feud constitutes social-ization into patriarchal roles in two ways. First, it reinforces their identities as sons and daughters by allying them with their paternal household against another paternal household, thus polarizing all their social relations, particu-larly their marital choices, in terms of filial allegiance. They are constantly called upon to define themselves in terms of their families and to defend their families. Second, the feud provides a "Psycho-sexual moratorium" for the sons,[6] an activity in which they prove themselves men by phallic violence on behalf of their fathers, instead of by courtship and sexual experimentation which would lead toward marriage and separation from the paternal house. It fosters in them the fear and scorn of women, associating women with effeminacy and emascu-lation, while it links sexual intercourse with aggression and violence against women, rather than pleasure and love. Structurally, the play's design reflects the prominence of the feud. It erupts in three scenes at the beginning, middle, and end (1.1, 3.1, 5.3) which deliberately echo each other, and the peripateia, at which Romeo's and Juliet's fortunes change decisively for the worse, occurs exactly in the middle when Romeo kills Tybalt, an action which poses the two conflicting definitions of manhood between which Romeo must make his tragic choice.

It has been noted that *Romeo and Juliet* is a domestic tragedy but not that its milieu is distinctly patriarchal as well as domestic. Much of it takes place within the Capulet household and Capulet's role as *paterfamilias* is apparent from the first scene in which his servants behave as members of his extended family, as *famuli* rather than employees. That household is a charming place: protected and spacious, plentiful with servants, food, light, and heat, bustling with festiv-ity, intimate and informal even on great occasions, with a cosy familiarity between master and servant. In nice contrast to it stands the play's other domi-nant milieu, the streets of Verona. It is there that those fighting the feud are defined as men, in contrast to those who would rather love than fight, who in terms of the feud are less than men. Gregory and Sampson ape the machismo of their masters, seeking insults on the slightest pretext so that they may prove their valor. In their blind adherence to a groundless "ancient grudge," they are parodies of the feuding gentry. But in Shakespeare's day, as servants they would be regarded as their master's "children" in more than a figurative sense, owing not just work but loyalty and obedience to their employers as legitimate mem-bers of the household ranking immediately below its children.[7] As male servants their position resembles that of the sons bound by their honors to fight for the families' names. Most importantly, their obvious phallic competitiveness in being quick to anger at an insult to their status or manhood, and quick to draw their swords and fight, shades into phallic competitiveness in sex as well:

---

[6]The term is Erik Erikson's, as used in "The Problem of Ego Identity," *Psychological Issues* I, no. 1 (1959), 103–105. . . .

[7]See Gordon Schochet, "Patriarchalism, Politics, and Mass Attitudes in Stuart England," *The Historical Journal* XII, 3 (1969), 413–441.

I strike quickly, being moved . . . A dog of the house of Montague moves me . . .
Therefore I will push Montague's men from the wall and thrust his maids to the wall . . .
Me they shall feel while I am able to stand.

(1.1.6, 9, 12–14, 18–20, 30)[8]

In this scene and elsewhere, the many puns on "stand" as standing one's ground in fighting and as erection attest that fighting in the feud demonstrates virility as well as valor. Sampson and Gregory also imply that they consider it their prerogative as men to take women by force as a way of demonstrating their superiority to the Montagues:

. . . women, being the weaker vessels, are ever thrust to the wall. Therefore I will push Montague's men from the wall and thrust his maids to the wall . . . When I have fought with the men, I will be civil with the maid—I will cut off their heads . . . the heads of the maids or their maidenheads. Take it in what sense thou wilt.

(1.1.16–20, 24–25, 27–28)

As the fighting escalates, finally Capulet and Montague themselves become involved, Capulet calling for a sword he is too infirm to wield effectively, simply because Montague, he claims, "flourishes his blade in spite of me." With the neat twist of making the masters parody the men who have been parodying them, the fighting ends as the Prince enters. At the cost of civil peace, all have asserted their claims to manhood through the feud.

Tybalt makes a memorable entrance in this first scene. Refusing to believe Benvolio's assertion that his sword is drawn only to separate the fighting servants, he immediately dares him to defend himself. To Tybalt, a sword can only mean a challenge to fight, and peace is just a word:

What, drawn and talk of peace? I hate the word
As I hate hell, all Montagues, and thee.
Have at thee, coward!

(1.1.72–74)

In the first two acts, Shakespeare contrasts Tybalt and Romeo in terms of their responses to the feud so as to intensify the conflict Romeo faces in Act 3 when he must choose between being a man in the sanctioned public way, by drawing a sword upon an insult, or being a man in a novel and private way: by reposing an inner confidence in his secret identity as Juliet's husband.

In Act 3, the fight begins when Tybalt is effectively baited by Mercutio's punning insults; from Mercutio's opening badinage with Benvolio, it is evident that he too is spoiling for a fight, though he is content to let the weapons be words. But words on the hot mid-day streets of Verona are effectively the same as blows which must be answered by the drawing of a sword. When Romeo arrives, Tybalt calls him "my man," "a villain," and "boy," all terms which simultaneously impugn his birth and honor as well as his manhood. Mercutio makes

[8]This and all subsequent quotations are taken from *The Complete Signet Classic Shakespeare*, ed. Sylvan Barnet (New York: Harcourt, Brace, Jovanovich, 1963, 1972). Where relevant I have noted variant readings.

words blows, but Romeo tries to do just the opposite, by oblique protestations of love to Tybalt, which must seem quite mysterious to him if he listens to them at all: "And so, good Capulet, whose name I tender / As dearly as mine own, be satisfied" (3.1.72–73). Romeo's puns of peacemaking fail where Mercutio's puns of hostility succeeded all too well. Only one kind of rigid, simple language, based on the stark polarities Capulet-Montague, man-boy, is understood in the feud. No wonder Mercutio terms Romeo's response a "calm, dishonorable, vile submission" and draws on Tybalt: Romeo has allowed a Capulet to insult his name, his paternal heritage, his manhood, without fighting for them. Like Tybalt, Romeo owes a duty to "the stock and honor of his kin." When Mercutio in effect fights for him and dies, the shame of having allowed his friend to answer the challenge which according to the code of manly honor, he should have answered, overcomes Romeo. He momentarily turns against Juliet, the source of his new identity, and sees her as Mercutio sees all women:

> O sweet Juliet,
> Thy beauty hath made me effeminate,
> And in my temper softened valor's steel!
> (3.1.111-117)

In that moment, caught between his radically new identity as Juliet's husband, which has made him responsible (he thinks) for his friend's death, and his previous traditional identity as the scion of the house of Montague, he resumes the latter and murders Tybalt. As Ruth Nevo remarks,

> Romeo's challenge of Tybalt is not merely an instance . . . of a rashness which fatally flaws his character . . . on the contrary, it is an action first avoided, then deliberately undertaken, and it is entirely expected of him by his society's code.[9]

As much as we want the love of Romeo and Juliet to prosper, we also want the volatile enmity of Tybalt punished and the death of Mercutio, that spirit of vital gaiety, revenged, even at the cost of continuing the feud. Romeo's hard choice is also ours. Though the play is constantly critical of the feud as the medium through which criteria of patriarchally-oriented masculinity are voiced, it is just as constantly sensitive to their association of those criteria with more humane principles of filial loyalty, loyalty to friends, courage, and personal dignity.

Among the young bloods serving as foils for Romeo, Benvolio represents the total sublimation of virile energy into peace-making, agape instead of eros; Tybalt, such energy channelled directly and exclusively into aggression; and Mercutio, its attempted sublimation into fancy and wit. (Romeo and Paris seek manhood through love rather than through fighting, but are finally impelled by the feud to fight each other.) That Mercutio pursues the feud though he is neither Montague nor Capulet suggests that feuding has become the normal social pursuit for young men in Verona. Through his abundant risqué wit, he suggests its psychological function for them, as a definition of manhood. Love is only

[9]Ruth Nevo, "Tragic Form in *Romeo and Juliet*," *SEL* IXX, 241–258.

manly, he hints, if it is aggressive and violent and consists of subjugating, rather than being subjugated by women:

If love be rough with you, be rough with love;
Prick love for pricking and you beat love down.
(1.4.27–2)

Alas, poor Romeo, he is already dead: stabbed with a white wench's black eye; run through the ear with a love song; the very pin of his heart cleft with the blind bow-boy's butt-shaft; and is he a man to encounter Tybalt?

(2.4.14–1)

The conflict between his conception of manhood and the one which Romeo learns is deftly and tellingly suggested in Romeo's line, "He jests at scars that never felt a wound." Juliet is a Capulet, and Romeo risks death to love her; the trite metaphor of the wound of love has real significance for him. Mercutio considers love mere folly unworthy of a real man, and respects only the wounds suffered in combat. Ironically, Mercutio will die of a real wound occasioned partly by Romeo's love, while Romeo, no less a man, will die not of a wound but of the poison he voluntarily takes for love.

Mercutio mocks not merely the futile, enfeebling kind of love Romeo feels for Rosaline, but all love. Moreover, his volley of sexual innuendo serves as the equivalent of both fighting and love. In its playful way, his speech is as aggressive as fighting, and while speech establishes his claim to virility, at the same time it marks his distance from women. As Romeo says, Mercutio is "A gentleman . . . that loves to hear himself talk and will speak more in a minute than he will stand to in a month" (2.4.153–155). Mercutio would rather fight than talk, but he would rather talk than love, which brings us to his justly famed utterance, the Queen Mab speech. Like so much in this play, it incorporates opposites. While it is surely a set-piece set apart, it is also highly characteristic of Mercutio, in its luxuriant repleteness of images and rippling mockery. While it purports to belittle dreamers for the shallowness of the wishes their dreams fulfill, it sketches the world of which the dreamers dream with loving accuracy, sweetmeats, tithe pigs, horses' manes and all. In service to the purest fancy, it portrays Mab's coach and accoutrements with workmanlike precision. It pretends to tell us dreams are "nothing but vain fantasy" but this pose is belied by the speaker's intense awareness that real people do dream of real things.[10] In short, Mercutio's defense against dreams gives evidence of his own urge to dream, but it also reveals his fear of giving in to the seething nighttime world of unconscious desires associated with the feminine; he prefers the broad daylight world of men fighting and jesting.

---

[10]Robert O. Evans, *The Osier Cage: Rhetorical Devices in Romeo and Juliet* (Lexington, Ky: University of Kentucky Press, 1966), argues that the Queen Mab speech deals with the real subjects of the play—money and place, the main reasons for marriage—and in the extended treatment of the soldier which concludes its catalogue of Mab's victims, "presents what in the milieu of Romeo and Juliet was a principal destructive force—violence" (p. 79).

Significantly, his catalogue of dreamers ends with a reference to the feminine mystery of birth, and an implied analogy between the birth of children from the womb and the birth of dreams from "an idle brain." He would like to think that women's powers, and desires for women, are as bodiless and inconsequential as the dreams to which they give rise, and to make us think so too he concludes his whole speech with the mock-drama of a courtship between the winds. For him the perfect image of nothingness is unresponsive and inconstant love between two bodies of air. But Mercutio protests too much; the same defensiveness underlies his fancy as his bawdy. Puns and wordplay, the staple of his bawdy, figure prominently in dreams, as Freud so amply shows; relying on an accidental similarity of sound, they disguise a repressed impulse while giving voice to it.[11]

II

In the feud names, the signs of patriarchal authority and allegiance, are calls to arms, and words are blows. As Romeo and Juliet struggle to free themselves from the feud, their effort at first takes the form of creating new names for themselves to reflect their new identities. When they learn each other's names, they attend only to surnames, which signify the social constraints under which their love must exist. Romeo says, "Is she a Capulet? / O dear account! My life is my foe's debt" (1.5.119–120), and the Nurse tells Juliet, "His name is Romeo, and a Montague, / The only son of your great enemy" (1.5.138–139). Juliet's extended meditation on Romeo's name in the balcony scene begins with her recognition that for Romeo to refuse his name—to separate himself from the feud—he would have to deny his father (2.233–4), and moves from this unlikely alternative to her own fanciful effort to detach the man from the name, and their love from the social reality in which it is embedded: "'Tis but thy name that is my enemy. / Thou art thyself, though not a Montague" (2.1.38–39). Through the irony of Juliet's casual "but thy name," Shakespeare suggests both that it is impossible for Romeo to separate himself from his public identity as a Montague, and that his public identity is nonetheless extraneous and accidental, no part of what he really is. The Romeo already transfigured by his love for Juliet is a different person and his name should reflect it. The exchange which Juliet proposes hints at this:

---

[11]Norman Holland, "Mercutio, Mine Own Son the Dentist," in *Essays on Shakespeare*, ed. Gordon Ross Smith, University Park, Pa.: Pennsylvania State University Press, 1965, pp. 3–14, comments suggestively on the contrast between Mercutio and Romeo in this respect:

He jests at scars that fears to feel a wound—a certain kind of wound, the kind that comes from real love that would lay him low, make him undergo a submission like Romeo's. Mercutio's bawdry serves to keep him a non-combatant in the wars of love . . . . Not for Mercutio is that entrance into the tomb or womb or maw which is Romeo's dark, sexual fate. (p. 12)

> Romeo, doff thy name,
> And for thy name, which is no part of thee,
> Take all myself.
>
> (2.2.47–49)

In fact, his new identity as a man is to be based on his allegiance to her as her husband, and not on his allegiance to his father. In the wedding scene,
Romeo says with his desperate faith, "It is enough I may but call her mine" (2.6.8),
an ironic allusion to the fact that though she now has taken his surname in marriage, all he really can do is "call" her his, for the feud will not allow their new identities as husband and wife to become publicly known, as is all too apparent when
Romeo's veiled references to Tybalt's name as one which he tenders as dearly as
his go uncomprehended in Act 3.

Later, bemoaning his banishment in Friar Lawrence's cell, Romeo curses his
name and offers literally to cut it out of his body as though it were merely physical and its hateful consequences could be amputated. Symbolically, he is trying
to castrate himself; as a consequence of the feud he cannot happily be a man
either by fighting for his name and family or by loving Juliet. Banished and
apart from her, he feels, he will have no identity, and nothing to live for. His
obsession with his name at this point recalls Juliet's " 'Tis but thy name that is
my enemy." In the early moments of their love, both of them seek to mold
social reality to their changed perceptions and desires by manipulating the verbal signifiers of that reality. But between Romeo's banishment and their death,
both learn in different ways that not the word but the spirit can change reality.
Juliet becomes a woman and Romeo a man not through changing a name but by
action undertaken in a transformed sense of the self requiring courage and
independence.

Unmanned in the friar's cell by the thought of life without Juliet, Romeo
hurls himself to the floor in tears and petulantly refuses to rise. The significance
of this posture is emphasized by the Nurse's exclamation, "O, he is even in my
mistress' case, / Just in her case!" (3.3.84–85). Echoing the sexual innuendo of
the play's first scene in a significantly different context, the Nurse urges him
vigorously,

> Stand up, stand up! Stand, and you be a man.
> For Juliet's sake, for her sake, rise and stand!
> Why should you fall into so deep an O?
>
> (3.3.88–90)

Friar Lawrence's ensuing philosophical speech is really only an elaboration of the
Nurse's simple, earthy rebuke. The well-meaning friar reminds him that he must
now base his sense of himself as a man not on his socially sanctioned identity as a
son of Montague, but on his love for Juliet, in direct conflict with that identity—a
situation which the friar sees as only temporary. But this conflict between manhood as aggression on behalf of the father, and manhood as loving a woman, is at
the bottom of the tragedy, and not to be overcome.

In patriarchal Verona, men bear names and stand to fight for them; women, "the weaker vessels," bear children and "fall backward" to conceive them, as the Nurse's husband once told the young Juliet. It is appropriate that Juliet's growing up is hastened and intensified by having to resist the marriage arranged for her by her father, while Romeo's is precipitated by having to fight for the honor of his father's house. Unlike its sons, Verona's daughters have, in effect, no adolescence, no sanctioned period of experiment with adult identities or activities. Lady Capulet regards motherhood as the proper termination of childhood for a girl, for she says to Juliet,

> Younger than you,
> Here in Verona, ladies of esteem
> Are already made mothers.
> (1.3.69–71)

and recalls that she herself was a mother when she was about her daughter's age. Capulet is more cautious at first: "Too soon marred are those so early made" (1.2.13), he says, perhaps meaning that pregnancies are more likely to be difficult for woman in early adolescence than for those even slightly older. But the pun in the succeeding lines reveals another concern besides this one:

> Earth hath swallowed all my hopes but she;
> She is the hopeful lady of my earth.
> (1.2.14–15)

Fille de terre is the French term for heiress, and Capulet wants to be sure that his daughter will not only survive motherhood, but produce healthy heirs for him as well.

Capulet's sudden determination to marry Juliet to Paris comes partly from a heightened sense of mortality which, when it is introduced in the first act, mellows his character attractively:

> Welcome, gentlemen! I have seen the day
> That I have worn a visor and could tell
> A whispering tale in a fair lady's ear,
> Such as would please. 'Tis gone, 'tis gone, 'tis gone.
> (1.5.23–26)

But he cannot give up claim on youth so easily as these words imply. When he meets with Paris again after Tybalt's death, it is he who calls the young man back, with a "desperate tender" inspired by the thought that he, no less than his young nephew, was "born to die." Better to insure the safe passage of his property to an heir now, while he lives, than in an uncertain future. Even though decorum suggests but "half a dozen friends" as wedding guests so hard upon a kinsman's death, he hires "twenty cunning cooks" to prepare a feast, and stays up all night himself "to play the housewife for this once," insisting against his wife's better judgment that the wedding be celebrated not a day later. For him, the wedding constitutes the promise that his line will continue, though his own time end soon. Shakespeare depicts Capulet's motives for forcing the hasty marriage with broad sympathy in this regard, but he spares the anxious old man no tolerance in the scene in which Juliet refuses to marry Paris.

In Shakespeare's source, Arthur Brooke's versification of an Italian novella, the idea of marriage with Paris isn't introduced until after Romeo's banishment. In the play, Paris broaches his suit (evidently, not for the first time) in the second scene, and receives a temperate answer from Capulet, who at this point is a model of fatherly tenderness and concern:

> My child is yet a stranger in the world
> She hath not seen the change of fourteen years.
> Let two more summers wither in their pride
> Ere we may think her ripe to be a bride.
>
> But woo her, gentle Paris, get her heart;
> My will to her consent is but a part.
> And she agreed, within her scope of choice
> Lies my consent and fair according voice.
> (1.2.8–11, 16–19)

Significantly, though, this scene begins with Capulet acting not only as a father but also as the head of a clan; alluding to the recent eruption of the feud and the Prince's warning, he says lightly, ". . . 'tis not hard, I think, / For men so old as we to keep the peace." Only when his failure to exert authority effectively over the inflammatory Tybalt results in Tybalt's death, an insult to the clan, does Capulet decide to exert it over his daughter, with compensatory strictness. Thus Shakespeare, by introducing the arranged marriage at the beginning and by making Capulet change his mind about it, shows us how capricious patriarchal rule can be, and how the feud changes fatherly mildness to what Hartley Coleridge called "paternal despotism."[12] After Tybalt's death, the marriage which before required her consent is now his "decree," and his anger at her opposition mounts steadily from an astonished testiness to brutal threats:

> And you be mine, I'll give you to my friend:
> And you be not, hang, beg, starve, die in the streets,
> For, by my soul, I'll ne'er acknowledge thee.
> Nor what is mine shall ever do thee good.
> (3.5.193–196)

Perhaps Shakespeare got the inspiration for these lines from Brooke's poem, where Capulet cites Roman law allowing fathers to "pledge, alienate. and sell" their children, and even to kill them if they rebel.[13] At any rate, it is clear that

---

[12]*Romeo and Juliet: A New Variorum Edition*, ed. Horace Howard Furness, Philadelphia: Lippincott and Co., 1871, p. 200.

[13]Arthur Brooke, *The Tragicall Historye of Romeus and Juliet in Narrative and Dramatic Sources of Shakespeare*, ed. Geoffrey Bullough, London: Routledge, Kegan and Paul, 1966, I, p. 336, 1951–1960.

Capulet's anger is as violent and unreflective as Tybalt's though he draws no sword against Juliet, and that the emotional likeness between age and youth in this instance is fostered by different aspects of the same system of patriarchal order.

Romeo finds a surrogate father outside that system, in Friar Lawrence, and in fact never appears onstage with his parents. Juliet on the other hand, always appears within her father's household until the last scene in the tomb. Lodged in the bosom of the family, she has two mothers, the Nurse as well as her real one. With regard to Juliet, the Nurse is the opposite of what the Friar is for Romeo—a surrogate mother within the patriarchal family, but one who is, finally, of little help in assisting Juliet in her passage from child to woman. She embodies the female self molded devotedly to the female's family role. The only history she knows is that of birth, suckling, weaning, and marriage; for her, earthquakes are less cataclysmic than these turning points of growth. She and Juliet enter the play simultaneously in a scene in which she has almost all the lines and Juliet less than ten, a disproportion which might be considered representative of the force of tradition weighing on the heroine.

The Nurse's longest speech ends with the telling of an anecdote (35–48) which she subsequently repeats twice. It is perfectly in character: trivial, conventional, full of good humor but lacking in wit. And yet it masterfully epitomizes the way in which woman's subjugation to her role as wife and mother, in the patriarchal setting, is made to seem integral with nature itself:

> And then my husband (God be with his soul!
> 'A was a merry man) took up the child.
> "Yea," quoth he, "dost fall upon thy face?
> Thou wilt fall backward when thou hast more wit;
> Wilt thou not, Jule?" and by my holidam,
> The pretty wretch left crying and said, "Ay."
> (1.3.39–44)

The story is placed between the Nurse's recollections of Juliet's weaning and Lady Capulet's statements that girls younger than Juliet are already mothers, as she herself was at Juliet's age. This collocation gives the impression of an uninterrupted cycle of birth and nurturance carried on from mother to daughter, under the approving eyes of fathers and husbands. The Nurse's husband, harmlessly amusing himself with a slightly risqué joke at Juliet's expense, gets more than he bargains for in the child's innocent reply. The Nurse finds the point of the story in the idea that even as a child, Juliet had the "wit" to assent to her sexual "fall;" she takes her "Ay" as confirmation of Juliet's precocious fitness for "falling" and "bearing." But in a larger sense than the Nurse is meant to see, "bearing" implies that it will be Juliet's fate to "bear" her father's will and the tragic consequences of her attempt to circumvent it. And in a larger sense still, all women, by virtue of their powers of bearing, are regarded as mysteriously close to the Earth which, as Friar Lawrence says is "Nature's mother", while men, lacking these powers, and intended to rule over the earth, rule over women also. As the Nurse says, "Women grow by men" (1.3.95).

Against this conception of femininity, in which women are married too young to understand their sexuality as anything but passive participation in a vast biological cycle through childbearing, Shakespeare places Juliet's unconventional, fully conscious and willed giving of herself to Romeo. Harry Levin has pointed out how the lovers move from conventional formality to a simple, organic expressiveness which is contrasted with the rigid, arbitrary polarization of language and life in Verona.[14] Juliet initiates this departure in the balcony scene by answering Romeo's conceits, "love's light wings," "night's cloak," with a directness highly original in the context:

> Dost thou love me? I know thou wilt say "Ay";
> And I will take thy word.
> (2.2.90–91)

Free from the accepted forms in more than a stylistic sense, she pledges her love, discourages Romeo from stereotyped love-vows, and spurs him to make arrangements for their wedding. As she awaits their consummation, the terms in which she envisions losing her virginity parody the terms of male competition, the sense of love as a contest in which men must beat down women or be beaten by them:

> Come, civil night,
> Thou sober-suited matron all in black,
> And learn me how to lose a winning match,
> Play'd for a pair of stainless maidenhoods.
> (3.210–13)

She knows and values her "affections and warm youthful blood" but she has yet to learn the cost of such blithe individuality in the tradition-bound world of Verona. When the Nurse tells her that Romeo has killed Tybalt, she falls suddenly into a rant condemning him, in the same kind of trite oxymorons characteristic of Romeo's speech before they met (see especially 1.1.178–186); such language in this context reflects the automatic thinking of the feud, which puts everything in terms of a Capulet-Montague dichotomy. But she drops this theme when a word from the Nurse reminds her that she now owes her loyalty to Romeo rather than to the house of Capulet:

> *Nurse*:   Will you speak well of him that killed your cousin?
> *Juliet*:   Shall I speak ill of him that is my husband?
> Ah, poor my lord, what tongue shall smooth thy name,
> When I, thy three-hours' wife, have mangled it?
> (3.2.96–99)

Romeo's "name" in the sense of his identity as well as his reputation now rests not on his loyalty to the Montagues but on Juliet's loyalty to him and their reciprocal identities as husband and wife apart from either house.

Juliet's next scene (3.5), in which she no sooner bids farewell to Romeo than

[14]Harry Levin, "Form and Formality in *Romeo and Juliet*," in *Twentieth Century Interpretations of Romeo and Juliet*, ed. Douglas Cole, Englewood Cliffs, N.J.: Prentice-Hall, 1970, 85–96.

learns that she is expected to marry Paris, depicts another crucial development in her ability to use language creatively to support her increasing independence. As the scene opens, it is Juliet who would use words as a pretty refuge from harsh reality, re-naming the lark a nightingale, the sunrise a meteor, as though words could stop time from passing, and Romeo who gently insists that they accept their painful separation for what it is. But when her mother enters with bitter expressions of hatred toward Romeo, Juliet practices a skillful equivocation which allows her to appear a loyal Capulet while also speaking her heart about Romeo.

When her father's rage erupts moments later, however, Juliet is unable to say more than a few words on her own behalf. Seeking comfort and counsel from the Nurse, the only advice she receives is expediency. The Nurse is so traditionally subservient to her master that she cannot comprehend a loyalty to Romeo which would involve opposing Capulet, and she has no idea of Juliet's growing independence of her father and commitment to Romeo. Juliet's disbelieving "Speak'st thou from thy heart?," and the Nurse's assurance that she does, underscore the difference between them as women. The Nurse has no "heart" in the sense that she has no self-defined conception of who she is or to whom she owes her fidelity; for her, affection and submission have always been one. As Coleridge said, she is characterized by a "happy, humble ducking under."[15] Whereas Juliet, now inwardly placing fidelity to Romeo above obedience to her father and thus implicitly denying all that family, society, and the feud have taught her, utters a lie in perfect calm to end her conversation with the Nurse. There is no way for her to speak the truth of her heart in her father's household, so she may as well lie. Though she will again employ equivocation in her stilted, stichomythic conversation with Paris later, her closing line, "If all else fails, myself have power to die," bespeaks a self-confidence, courage, and strength no longer dependent on verbal manipulations.

III

In this play ordered by antitheses on so many levels, the all-embracing opposition of Eros and Thanatos seems to drive the plot along.[16] The lovers want to live in union; the death-dealing feud opposes their desire. The tragic conclusion, however, effects a complete turnabout in this clearcut opposition between love and death, for in the lovers' suicides love and death merge. Romeo and Juliet die as an act of love, in a spiritualized acting out of the ancient pun. Furthermore, the final scene plays off against each other two opposing views of the lovers' death: that they are consumed and destroyed by the feud, and that

[15]*Coleridge's Writings on Shakespeare*, ed. Terence Hawkes, New York: Capricorn Books, 1959, p. 118, Coleridge adds to this phrase "yet resurgence against the check," but he is referring to the Nurse's garrulity in the first scene, when she persists in repeating her story against Lady Capulet's wishes.
[16]Levin, p. 90. He does not develop this point.

they rise above it, united in death. I shall now explore the ambivalence of this conclusion in an attempt to show how it reflects the play's concern with coming of age in the patriarchal family.

It cannot be denied that, through the many references to fate, Shakespeare wished to create a feeling of inevitability, of a mysterious force stronger than individuals shaping their courses even against their will and culminating in the lovers' deaths. Yet it is also true that, as Gordon Ross Smith says, the play employs fate not as an external power, but as a subjective feeling on the parts of the two lovers.[17] And this subjective feeling springs understandably from the objective social conditions of life in Verona. The first mention of fate, in the Prologue's phrase "fatal loins," punningly connects fate with feud and antici- pates the rhyme uttered by Friar Lawrence, which might stand as a summary of the play's action:

The Earth, that's Nature's mother, is her tomb;
That which we call her burying grave, that is her womb.
(2.3.9–10)

The loins of the Montagues and the Capulets are fatal because the two families have established a state of affairs whereby their children are bound, for the sake of family honor, to kill each other. It is hardly necessary to recall how Romeo's first sight of Juliet is accompanied by Tybalt's "Fetch me my rapier, boy!," or how (as I have shown) their very names denote the fatal risk they take in loving each other. Romeo's premonition, as he sets off for the Capulets' ball, that he will have "an untimely death," or Juliet's, as his banishment begins, that she will see him next in a tomb, are not hints from the beyond, but expressions of fear eminently realistic in the circumstances.

The setting and action of the final scene are meant to remind us of the hos- tile social climate in which the lovers have had to act. It begins on a bitter- sweet note as the dull and proper Paris approaches to perform his mangled rites, recapitulating wedding in funeral with the flowers so easily symbolic of a young and beautiful maiden, and reminiscent of her expected defloration in marriage. By parallelling the successive entrances of Paris and Romeo, one who has had no part in the feud, the other who has paid so much for resisting it, both of whom love Juliet, Shakespeare suggests the feud's indifferent power over youth. Each character comes in with the properties appropriate to his task, and enjoins the servant accompanying him to "stand aloof." Their ensuing sword-fight is subtly designed to recall the previous eruptions of the feud and to suggest that it is a man-made cycle of recurrent violence. Paris' challenge to Romeo,

Stop thy unhallowed toil, vile Montague!
Can vengeance be pursued farther than death?

[17]Gordon Ross Smith, "The Balance of Themes in *Romeo and Juliet*," *Essays on Shakespeare*, ed. Gordon Ross Smith, University Park, Pa.: The Pennsylvania State University Press, 1965, p. 39.

Condemnèd villain, I do apprehend thee.
Obey, and go with me; for thou must die.
(5.3.54–57)

recalls Tybalt's behavior at the Capulets' ball, when he assumed Romeo's very
presence to be an insult, and in Act 3, when he deliberately sought Romeo out to
get satisfaction for that insult. Romeo responds to Paris as he did to Tybalt, first by
hinting cryptically at his true purpose in phrases echoing those he spoke in Act 3:

By heaven, I love thee better than myself,
For I come hither armed against myself . . . .
(5.3.64–65)

Then once more he gives in to "fire-eyed fury" when Paris continues to provoke
him, and in a gesture all too familiar by now, draws his sword.

Shakespeare prepares us well before this final scene for its grim variations on
the Friar's association of womb and tomb. Juliet's moving soliloquy on her fears of
waking alone in the family monument amplifies its fitness as a symbol of the power
of the family, inheritance, and tradition over her and Romeo. She ponders "the
terror of the place—"

. . . a vault, an ancient receptacle
Where for many hundred years the bones
Of all my buried ancestors are packed;
(4.3.38–41)

In a "dismal scene" indeed, she envisions herself first driven mad by fear, dese-
crating these bones by playing with them, and then using the bones against herself
to dash her brains out. This waking dream, like all the dreams recounted in this
play, holds psychological truth; it bespeaks Juliet's knowledge that in loving
Romeo she has broken a taboo as forceful as that against harming the sacred relics
of her ancestors, and her fear of being punished for the offense by the ancestors
themselves—with their very bones.

As Romeo forces his way into the monument, he pictures it both as a monstrous
mouth devouring Juliet and himself and as a womb:

Thou detestable maw, thou womb of death,
Gorged with the dearest morsel of the earth,
Thus I enforce thy rotten jaws to open,
And in despite I'll cram thee with more food.
(5.3.45–49)

When the Friar hastens toward the monument a few minutes later, his exclamation further extends the meanings connected with it:

Alack, alack, what blood is this, which stains
The stony entrance to this sepulchre?
(5.3.140–141)

The blood-spattered entrance to the tomb which has been figured as a womb recalls both a defloration or initiation into sexuality, and a birth. Juliet's wedding bed is her grave, as premonitions had warned her, and three young men, two of them her bridegrooms, all killed as a result of the feud, share it with her. The birth which takes place in this "womb" is perversely a birth into death, a stifling return to the tomb of the fathers, not the second birth of adolescence, the birth of an adult self, which the lovers strove for.[18]

But the second part of the scene, comprising Romeo's death-speech, the Friar's entrance and hasty departure, and Juliet's death-speech, offers a different interpretation. Imagery and action combine to assert that death is a transcendent form of sexual consummation, and further, that it is rebirth into a higher stage of existence—the counterpart of an adulthood never fully achieved in life. That Shakespeare will have it both ways at once is perfectly in keeping with a play about adolescence in that it reflects the typical conflict of that period, which Bruno Bettelheim describes as "the striving for independence and self-assertion, and the opposite tendency, to remain safely at home, tied to the parents."[19] It is also similar to the ambivalent ending of *Venus and Adonis*, another work about youth and love, in which Venus' long-striven-for possession of Adonis takes the form of the total absorption of each person in the other, at the price of Adonis' death.[20]

It might be argued that Romeo and Juliet will their love-deaths in simple error, caused by the mere chance of Brother John's failure to reach Romeo with the news of Juliet's feigned death, and that chance is fate's instrument. But the poetic consistency and force with which their belief in death as consummation is carried out, by means of the extended play of words and actions on dying as orgasm, outweighs the sense of chance or of fate. The equation of loving with dying is introduced early, and most often dying is linked to the feud, for instance in Juliet's reference to grave and wedding bed in Act 1, scene 5, restated in the wedding scene. Romeo's banishment produces an explosion of remarks linking wedding bed with tomb and Romeo as bridegroom with death.[21] The Friar's potion inducing a simulated death on the day of Juliet's wedding with Paris titillates us further with ironic conjunctions of death and marriage. But when Romeo declares, the instant after he learns of Juliet's supposed death, "Is it e'en so? Then I defy you, stars!" (5.1.24),[22] the context in which we have been led to understand and expect the lovers' death is transformed. Romeo no longer conceives his course of action as a way of circum-

---

[18]In "The 'Uncanny,' " Freud remarks that the fantasy of being buried alive while appearing to be dead is a fantasy of intra-uterine existence (*Standard Edition*, Vol. XVII, p. 244). The conflation of womb and tomb, birth and death throughout the play lends weight to this interpretation of the deaths and their setting.

[19]Bruno Bettelheim, *The Uses of Enchantment: The Meaning and Importance of Fairy Tales*, New York: Knopf, 1976, p. 91.

[20]See my article, "Self and Eros in *Venus and Adonis*," *The Centennial Review*, XX, 4 (Fall, 1976), 351–371.

[21]See III.2.136–137; III.5.94–96; 141; 201–203.

[22]The second quarto prints ". . . then I denie you starres," which, though it offers a different shade of meaning, still expresses Romeo's belief that he acts independently of fate.

venting the feud, which now has no importance for him. Rather, he wills his
death as a means to permanent union with Juliet. When he says, in the same
tone of desperate but unshakable resolve, "Well, Juliet, I will lie with thee
tonight," as her lover and bridegroom he assumes his role in the love-death so
amply foreshadowed, but that love-death is not merely fated; it is willed. It is
the lovers' triumphant assertion over the impoverished and destructive world
which has kept them apart. Romeo's ensuing conversation with the apothecary
is full of contempt for a merely material world, and his confidence that he alone
possesses Juliet in death is so serene that he indulges in the mordantly erotic
fantasy that amorous Death keeps Juliet in the tomb "to be his paramour"
(5.3.102–105), recalling and dismissing the earlier conception of death as
Juliet's bridegroom.

Shakespeare fills Romeo's last speech with the imagery of life's richness: the
gloomy vault is "a feasting presence full of light," and Juliet's lips and cheeks are
crimson with vitality. His last lines, "O true apothecary! / Thy drugs are quick.
Thus with a kiss I die." (5.3.120), bring together the idea of death as sexual consummation and as rebirth. Similarly, Juliet kisses the poison on his lips and calls it
"a restorative." They have come of age by a different means than the rites of passage, phallic violence and adolescent motherhood, typical for youth in Verona.
Romeo's death in the Capulets' (not his own fathers') tomb reverses the traditional
passage of the female over to the male house in marriage and betokens his refusal
to allow the code of his fathers, while it is Juliet, not Romeo, who boldly uses his
dagger, against herself.[23]

---

[23]In an illuminating essay which stresses the importance of the family, "Shakespeare's Earliest
Tragedies: *Titus Andronicus* and *Romeo and Juliet*," *Shakespeare Survey* 27 (1974), pp. 1–9, G.K.
Hunter offers a different though related interpretation:

> It is entirely appropriate that the 'public' wedding bed of Romeo and Juliet (as against their private
> bedding) should be placed in the Capulet family tomb, for it is there that Romeo may most effec-
> tively be seen to have joined his wife's clan, where their corporate identity is most unequivocally
> established. (p. 8)

The Modernity of *Julius Caesar*

Maynard Mack

1

In a tribute composed to introduce the collection of plays that we now call the *First Folio*, Shakespeare's fellow playwright Ben Jonson spoke of his colleague's work as not of an age but for all time. Though the compliment was something of a commonplace in Renaissance funerary rhetoric, it has proved to be remarkably clairvoyant, at least up to the present hour. And of no play, perhaps, has the continuing relevance been more striking than that of *Julius Caesar*, which again and again twentieth-century directors and producers have successfully presented as a parable for our days.

Among the many aspects of the play that contribute to its modernity, one in particular, to my mind, stands out, and it is to this exclusively, leaving out much, that I want to call attention here. The place to begin is the second scene.

We have just learned from scene 1 of Caesar's return in triumph from warring on Pompey's sons. We have seen the warm though fickle adulation of the crowd and the apprehension of the tribunes. Now we are to see the great man himself. The procession enters to triumphal music; with hubbub of a great press of people; with young men stripped for the ceremonial races, among them Antony; with statesmen in their togas: Decius, Cicero, Brutus, Cassius, Casca; with the two wives Calphurnia and Portia; and, in the lead, for not even Calphurnia is permitted at his side, the great man. As he starts to speak, an expectant hush settles over the gathering. What does the great man have on his mind?

Caesar:	Calphurnia.
Casca:	Peace, ho! Caesar speaks.
Caesar:	Calphurnia.
Calphurnia:	Here, my lord.
Caesar:	Stand you directly in Antonius' way When he doth run his course. Antonius.
Antony:	Caesar, my lord?
Caesar:	Forget not in your speed, Antonius,

From *Everybody's Shakespeare: Reflections Chiefly on the Tragedies* (Lincoln: University of Nebraska Press, 1993), 91–106. Reprinted by permission of the author.

> To touch Calphurnia; for our elders say,
> The barren, touched in this holy chase,
> Shake off their sterile curse.
> *Antony:*   I shall remember.
> When Caesar says, "Do this," it is performed.
>   (1.2.1)

What the great man had on his mind, it appears, was to remind his wife, in this public place, that she is sterile; that there is an old tradition about how sterility can be removed; and that while of course he is much too sophisticated to accept such a superstition himself—it is "our elders" who say it—still, Calphurnia had jolly well better get out there and get tagged!

Then the procession takes up again. The hubbub is resumed, but once more an expectant silence settles as a voice is heard.

> *Soothsayer:* Caesar!
> *Caesar:* Ha! Who calls?
> *Casca:* Bid every noise be still. Peace yet again!
> *Caesar:* Who is it in the press that calls on me?
>   I hear a tongue shriller than all the music
>   Cry "Caesar!" Speak. Caesar is turned to hear.
> *Soothsayer:* Beware the ides of March.
> *Caesar:*   What man is that?
> *Brutus:* A soothsayer bids you beware the ides of March.
> *Caesar:* Set him before me; let me see his face.
> *Cassius:* Fellow, come from the throng; look upon Caesar.
> *Caesar:* What say'st thou to me now? Speak once again.
> *Soothsayer:* Beware the ides of March.
> *Caesar:* He is a dreamer. Let us leave him. Pass.
>   (1.2.13)

It is easy to see from even these small instances, I think, how a first-rate dramatic imagination works. There is no hint of any procession in Plutarch, Shakespeare's source. "Caesar," says Plutarch, "*sat* to behold."[1] There is no mention of Calphurnia in Plutarch's account of the Lupercalian race, and there is no mention anywhere of her sterility. Shakespeare, in nine lines, has given us an unforgettable picture of a man who would like to be emperor, pathetically concerned that he lacks an heir, and determined, even at the cost of making his wife a public spectacle, to establish that this is owing to no lack of virility in him. The first episode thus dramatizes instantaneously what I take to be the oncoming theme of the play: that a man's will is not enough; that there are other matters to be reckoned with, like the infertility of one's wife, or one's own affliction of the falling sickness that spoils everything one hoped for just at the instant when one had it almost in one's hand. Brutus will be obliged to learn this lesson too.

[1] *Shakespeare's Plutarch*, ed. C. F. Tucker Brooke, 2 vols. (Haskell House reprint, New York, 1966), 1:92.

In the second episode the theme develops. We see again the uneasy rationalism that everybody in this play affects; we hear it reverberate in the faint contempt—almost a challenge—of Brutus's words as he turns to Caesar: "A soothsayer bids you beware the ides of March." Yet underneath, in the soothsayer's quiet defiance as he refuses to quail under Caesar's imperious gaze, and in his soberly reiterated warning, Shakespeare allows us to catch a hint of something else, something far more primitive and mysterious, from which rationalism in this play keeps trying vainly to cut itself away: "He is a dreamer. Let us leave him. Pass." Only we in the audience are in a position to see that the dreamer has foretold the path down which all these reasoners will go to their fatal encounter at the Capitol.

Meantime, in these same two episodes, we have learned something about the character of Caesar. In the first, it was the Caesar of human frailties who spoke to us, the husband with his hopeful superstition. In the second, it was the marble superman of state, impassive, impervious, speaking of himself in the third person: "Speak! Caesar is turned to hear." He even has the soothsayer brought before his face to repeat the message, as if the thought that somehow, in awe of the marble presence, the message would falter and dissolve: how can a superman need to beware the ides of March?

We hardly have time to do more than glimpse here a man of divided selves, then he is gone. But in his absence, the words of Cassius confirm our glimpse. Cassius's description of him exhibits the same quality that we had noticed earlier. On the one hand, an extremely ordinary man whose stamina in the swimming match was soon exhausted; who, when he had a fever once in Spain, shook and groaned like a sick girl; who even now, as we soon learn, is falling down with epilepsy in the market place. On the other hand, a being who has somehow become a god, who "bears the palm alone," who "bestrides the narrow world Like a colossus" (1.2.135). When the procession returns, no longer festive but angry, tense, there is the same effect once more. Our one Caesar shows a normal man's suspicion of his enemies, voices some shrewd human observations about Cassius, says to Antony, "Come on my right hand, for this ear is deaf" (1.2.213). Our other Caesar says, as if he were suddenly reminded of something he had forgotten, "I rather tell thee what is to be feared Than what I fear, for always I am Caesar" (1.2.211).

Wherever Caesar appears hereafter, we shall find this distinctive division in him, and nowhere more so than in the scene in which he receives the conspirators at his house. Some aspects of this scene seem calculated for nothing other than to fix upon our minds the superman conception, the Big Brother of Orwell's *1984*, the great resonant name echoing down the halls of time. Thus at the beginning of the scene:

> The things that threatened me
> Ne'er looked but on my back. When they shall see
> The face of Caesar, they are vanishèd.
>
> (2.2.10)

And again later:

> Danger knows full well
> That Caesar is more dangerous than he.
> We are two lions littered in one day,
> And I the elder and more terrible.
>
> (2.2.44)

And again still later: "Shall Caesar send a lie?" (2.2.65). And again: "The cause is in my will: I will not come." (2.2.71)

Other aspects of this scene, including his concern about Calphurnia's dream, his vacillation about going to the senate house, his anxiety about the portents of the night, plainly mark out his human weaknesses. Finally, as is the habit in this Rome, he puts the irrational from him that his wife's intuitions and her dream embody; he accepts the rationalization of the irrational that Decius skillfully manufactures, and, as earlier at the Lupercalia, hides from himself his own vivid sense of forces that lie beyond the will's control by attributing it to her:

> How foolish do your fears seem now, Calphurnia!
> I am ashamèd I did yield to them.
> Give me my robe, for I will go.
>
> (2.2.105)

2

So far we have looked at Caesar, the title personage of the play and its historical center. It is time now to consider Brutus, the play's tragic center, whom we also find to be a divided man—"poor Brutus," to use his own phrase, "with himself at war" (1.2.46). That war, we realize as the scene progresses, is a conflict between a quiet, essentially domestic and loving nature, and a powerful integrity expressing itself in a sense of honorable duty to the commonweal. This duality is what Cassius probes in his long disquisition about the mirror. The Brutus looking into the glass that Cassius figuratively holds up to him, the Brutus of this moment, now, in Rome, is a grave studious private man, of a wonderfully gentle temper as we shall see again and again later on; very slow to passion, as Cassius's ill-concealed disappointment in having failed to kindle him to an immediate response reveals; a man whose sensitive nature recoils at the hint of violence lurking in some of Cassius's speeches, just as he has already recoiled at going with Caesar to the market place, to witness the mass hysteria of clapping hands, sweaty nightcaps, and stinking breath. This is the present self that look into Cassius's mirror.

The image that looks back out, that Cassius wants him to see, the potential other Brutus, is the man of public spirit, worried already by his uncertainty about Caesar's intentions, lineal descendant of an earlier Brutus who drove a would-be monarch from the city, a republican whose body is visibly stiffening in our sight at each huzza from the Forum, and whose anxiety, though he makes no reply to Cassius's inflammatory language, keeps bursting to the surface: "What means this shouting? I do fear the people choose Caesar for their king" (1.2.79). The problem at the tragic center of the play, we begin to sense, is the tug of private versus public, the individual versus a world he never made, any citizen anywhere versus the selective service greetings that history is always mailing out to each of us. And this problem is to be traversed by the other tug this scene presents, between the irrational and the rational, the destiny we imagine we can control and the destiny that sweeps all before it.

Through 1.2, Brutus's patriotic self, the self that responds to these selective service greetings, is no more than a reflection in a mirror, a mere anxiety in his own brain, about which he refuses to confide, even to Cassius. In 2.1, we see the public self making further headway. First, there is Brutus's argument with himself about the threat of Caesar, and in his conclusion that Caesar must be killed we note how far his private self—he is, after all, one of Caesar's closest friends—has been invaded by the self of public spirit. From here on, the course of the invasion accelerates. A letter comes, tossed from the public world into the private world, into Brutus's garden, addressing, as Cassius had, the patriot image reflected in the mirror: "Brutus, thou sleep'st. Awake, and see thyself!" (2.1.46). Then follows the well-known brief soliloquy (which Shakespeare was to expand into the whole play of *Macbeth*), showing us that Brutus's mind has moved on from the phase of decision to the inquietudes that follow decision:

Between the acting of a dreadful thing
And the first motion, all the interim is
Like a phantasma, or a hideous dream.
(2.1.63)

Brutus anticipates here the dreamlike mood and motion with which Macbeth moves to the murder of Duncan. What is important to observe, however, is that these lines again stress the gulf that separates motive from action, that which is interior in man and controllable by his will from that which, once acted, becomes independent of him and moves with a life of its own. This gulf is a no man's land, a phantasma, a hideous dream.

Finally, there arrives in such a form that no audience can miss it the actual visible invasion itself, as this peaceful garden-quiet is intruded on by knocking, like the knocking of fate in Beethoven's Fifth Symphony, and by men with faces hidden in their cloaks. Following this, a lovely interlude with Portia serves to emphasize how much the private self, the private world, has been shattered. There is something close to discord here—as much of a discord as these gentle people are capable of—and though there is a reconciliation at the end and Brutus's promise to confide in her soon, this division in the family is an omen. So is the knock of the latecomer, Caius Ligarius, which reminds us once again of the exactions of the public life. And when Ligarius throws off his sick man's kerchief on learning that there is an honorable exploit afoot, we may see in it an epitome of the whole scene, a graphic visible renunciation, like Brutus's (or like Prince Hal's at about the same time in Shakespeare's career) of the private good to the public; and we may see this also in Brutus's own exit a few lines later, not into the inner house where Portia waits for him, but out into the thunder and lightning of the public life of Rome. It is not without significance that at our final glimpse of Portia, two scenes later, she too stands outside the privacy of the house, her mind wholly occupied with thoughts of what is happening at the Capitol, trying to put on a public self for Brutus's sake: "Run, Lucius, and commend me to my lord; Say I am merry . . ." (2.4.44).

3

Meantime, at the Capitol, the tragic center and the historical center meet. The suspense is very great as Caesar, seeing the Soothsayer in the throng, reminds him that the ides of March are come, and receives in answer, "Ay, Caesar, but not gone" (3.1.2). More suspense is generated as Artemidorus presses forward with the paper that we know contains a full discovery of the plot. Decius, apprehensive, steps quickly into the breach with another paper, a petition from Trebonius. More suspense still as Popilius sidles past Cassius with the whisper, "I wish your enterprise today may thrive" (3.1.13), and then moves on to Caesar's side, where he engages him in animated talk. But they detect no tell-tale change in Caesar's countenance; Trebonius steps into his assignment and takes Antony aside; Metellus Cimber throws himself at Caesar's feet; Brutus gives the signal to "Press near and second him" (3.1.29), and Caesar's "Are we all ready?" (3.1.31) draws every eye to Caesar's chair. One by one they all kneel before this demigod—an effective tableau which gives a coloring of priest-like ritual to what they are about to do. Caesar is to bleed, but, as Brutus has said, they will sublimate the act into a sacrifice:

Let's kill him boldly but not wrathfully;
Let's carve him as a dish fit for the gods,
Not hew him as a carcass fit for hounds.
(2.1.172)

In performance, everything in the scene will reflect this ceremonial attitude to emphasize the almost fatuous cleavage between the spirit of the enterprise and its bloody result.

The Caesar we are permitted to see as all this ceremony is preparing will be almost entirely the superman, for obvious reasons. To give a color of justice to

Brutus's act, even if we happen to think the assassination a mistake as many members of an Elizabethan audience emphatically would, Caesar must be seen in a mood of super-humanity at least as fatuous as the conspirators' mood of sacrifice. Hence Shakespeare makes him first of all insult Metellus Cimber: "If thou dost bend and pray and fawn for him, I spurn thee like a cur" (3.1.45), and then comment with intolerable pomposity—in fact, blasphemy—on his own iron resolution, which he alleges to be immovable even by prayer and thus superior to the very gods. Finally, Shakespeare puts into his mouth one of those supreme arrogances that can hardly fail to remind us of the ancient adage "Whom the gods would destroy they first make mad." "Hence!" Caesar cries, "Wilt thou lift up Olympus?" (3.1.74). It is at just this point, when the colossus Caesar drunk with self-importance is before us, that Casca strikes. Then they all strike, with a last blow that brings out for the final time the other, human side of this double Caesar: "*Et tu, Brute?*" (3.1.77).

And now this little group of men has altered history. The representative of the evil direction it was taking toward autocratic power lies dead before them. The direction to which it must be restored becomes emphatic in Cassius's cry of "Liberty, freedom, and enfranchisement!" (3.1.81). Solemnly, and again like priests who have just sacrificed a victim, they kneel together and bathe their hands and swords in Caesar's blood. Brutus exclaims:

> Then walk we forth, even to the market place,
> And waving our red weapons o'er our heads,
> Let's all cry, "Peace, freedom, and liberty!"
>   (3.1.108)

If the conjunction of those red hands and weapons with this slogan is not enough to give an audience a start, the next passage will; for now the conspirators explicitly invoke the judgment of history on their deed. On the stages of theaters the world over, so they anticipate, this lofty incident will be re-enacted, and

> So oft as that shall be,
> So often shall the knot of us be called
> The men that gave their country liberty.
>   (3.1.116)

We in the audience, recalling what actually did result in Rome—the civil wars, the long line of despotic emperors—cannot miss the irony of their prediction, an irony that insists on our recognizing that this effort to control the consequences of an act is doomed to fail. (It is a theme that Shakespeare will touch again in *Macbeth* and *Lear*.) Why does it fail?

One reason why is shown us in the next few moments. The leader of this assault on history, like many another reformer, is a man of high idealism, who devoutly believes that the rest of the world is like himself. It was just to kill Caesar—so he persuades himself—because he was a threat to freedom. It would not have been just to kill Antony, and he vetoes the idea. Even now, when the consequence of that decision has come back to face him in the shape

of Antony's servant kneeling before him, he sees no reason to reconsider it. There
are good grounds for what they have done, he says; Antony will hear them, and be
satisfied. With Antony, who shortly arrives in person, he takes this line again:

> Our reasons are so full of good regard
> That were you, Antony, the son of Caesar
> You should be satisfied.
>
> (3.1.224)

With equal confidence in the reasonableness of human nature, he puts by
Cassius's fears of what Antony will do if allowed to address the people: "By your
pardon; I will myself into the pulpit first And show the reason of our Caesar's
death" (3.1.236). Here is a man so much a friend of Caesar's that he is still
speaking of him as "our Caesar," so capable of rising to what he takes to be his
duty that he has taken on the leadership of those who killed him, so trusting of
common decency that he expects the populace will respond to reason, and
Antony to honor the obligation laid on him by their permitting him to speak. At
such a man, one hardly knows whether to laugh or cry.

The same mixture of feelings is likely to be stirring in us as Brutus speaks to
the people in 3.2. As everybody knows, this is a speech in what used to be called
the great liberal tradition, which assumes that men in the mass are reasonable.
It has therefore been made a prose oration, spare and terse in diction, tightly
patterned in syntax so that it requires close attention, and founded, with respect
to its argument, on three elements: the abstract sentiment of duty to the state
(because he endangered Rome, Caesar had to be slain); the abstract sentiment
of political justice (because he had delusions of grandeur, Caesar deserved his
fall); and the moral authority of the man Brutus.

As long as that moral authority is concretely before them in Brutus's presence,
the populace is impressed. But since even trained minds do not always respond
well to abstractions, they quite misunderstand the content of his argument, as
one of them indicates by shouting, "Let him be Caesar!" (3.2.41). What moves
them is the obvious sincerity and the known integrity of the speaker; and when he
finishes, they are ready to carry him off on their shoulders on that account alone,
leaving Antony a vacant Forum. The fair-mindedness of Brutus is thrilling but
painful to behold as he calms this triumphal surge in his favor, urges them to stay
and hear Antony, and then, in a moment very impressive dramatically as well as
symbolically, walks off the stage, alone. We see then, if we have not seen before,
a possible first answer to the question why the effort to take control of history
failed as it so often does, blinkered by its own idealism.

4

When Antony takes the rostrum, we sense a possible second answer. It has
been remarked that in a school for demagogues this speech should be the whole
curriculum. Antony himself describes its method when he observes in the preced-

ing scene, apropos of the effect of Caesar's dead body on the messenger from Octavius, "Passion, I see, is catching" (3.1.283). A statement that cannot be made about reason, as many of us learn to our cost.

Antony's speech differs from Brutus's as night from day. Brutus formulates from the outset positive propositions about Caesar and about his own motives on no other authority than his own. Because of his known integrity, Brutus can do this. Antony takes the safer alternative of concealing propositions in questions, by which the audience's mind is then guided to conclusions which seem its own:

> He hath brought many captives home to Rome,
> Whose ransoms did the general coffers fill.
> Did this in Caesar seem ambitious?
>
> (3.2.88)

> You all did see that on the Lupercal
> I thrice presented him a kingly crown,
> Which he did thrice refuse: Was this ambition?
>
> (3.2.95)

How well Shakespeare knew crowds becomes clear in the replies to Antony. Brutus, appealing to reason, is greeted with wild outbursts of emotion: "Let him be Caesar!" Antony appeals only to emotion and pocketbooks, but now they say, "Methinks there is much reason in his sayings," and chew upon it seriously.

With equal skill, Antony stirs up impulses only to thwart them. He appeals to curiosity and greed in the matter of the will, but then withholds it teasingly. In the same manner, he stirs up rage against the conspirators while pretending to dampen it (3.2.151): "I fear I wrong the honorable men Whose daggers have stabbed Caesar; I do fear it." Finally, he rests his case, not, like Brutus, on abstractions centering in the state and political justice, but on emotions centering in the individual listener. The first great crescendo of the speech, which culminates in the passage on Caesar's wounds, appeals first to pity and then to indignation. The second, culminating in the reading of Caesar's will, appeals first to curiosity and greed, then to gratitude.

His management of the will is particularly cunning: it is an item more concrete than words, an actual tantalizing document that can be flashed before the eye, as in many a modern political TV sound byte. He describes it at first vaguely, as being of such a sort that they would honor Caesar for it. Then, closer home, as something which would show "how Caesar loved you" (3.2.141). Then, with an undisguised appeal to self-interest, as a testament that will make them his "heirs." The emotions aroused by this news enable him to make a final test of his ironical refrain about "honorable men," and finding the results all that he had hoped, he can come down now among the crowd as one of them, and appeal directly to their feelings by appealing to his own: "If you have tears, prepare to shed them now" (3.2.169).

The power of this direct appeal to passion can be seen at its close. Where formerly we had a populace, now we have a mob. As a mob, its mind can be sealed against later recoveries of rationality by the insinuation that all reasoning is simply a surface covering up private grudges, like the "reason" they have heard from Brutus; whereas from Antony himself, the plain, blunt friend of Caesar, they are getting the plain, blunt truth and (a favorite trick) only what they already know.

So they are called back to hear the will. Antony no longer needs this as an incentive to riot; the mingled rage and pity he has aroused will take care of that. But, after the lynching when the hangover comes, and you are remembering how that fellow looked, swaying a little on the rope's end, with his eyes bugging out and the veins knotted at his temples, then it is good to have something really reasonable to cling to, like seventy-five drachmas (or thirty pieces of silver) and some orchards along a river.

By this point, we can fully understand that a further ground for the failure of the effort to control history is what has been left out of account—what all these Romans from the beginning, except Antony, have been trying to leave out of account: the phenomenon of feeling, one of many nonrational factors in the life of men, in the life of the world, in the processes of history itself—of which this blind infuriated mob is one kind of exemplification. Too secure in his own fancied suppression of this influence, Brutus has failed altogether to reckon with its power. Thus he could seriously say to Antony in the passage quoted earlier: Antony, even if you were "the son of Caesar You should be satisfied," as if the feeling of a son for a murdered father could ever be "satisfied" by reasons. And thus, too, urging the crowd to hear Antony, he could walk off the stage alone, the very figure of embodied "reason," unaware that only the irrational is catching.

Meantime, the scene of the mob tearing Cinna the Poet to pieces simply for having the same name as one of the conspirators (3.3) confirms the victory of unreason and gives us our first taste of the chaos invoked by Antony when he stood alone over Caesar's corpse. Now, reconsidering that prediction and this mob, we recognize a third reason why attempts to direct the course of history have usually failed. We have seen already that history is only minimally responsive to noble motives, only minimally responsive to rationality. Now we see clearly what was hinted in the beginning by those two episodes with Calphurnia and the soothsayer—that it is only minimally responsive to conscious human influence of any sort. With all their reasons, the conspirators and Caesar only carried out what the soothsayer foreknew. There is, in short—at least as this play sees it—a degree of determinism in history, whether we call it cultural, fatal, or providential, which *helps* to shape our ends, "Roughhew them how we will" (*Ham.*, 5.2.11). One of the alternative names of that factor in this play is Caesarism, cult of the ever regenerating Will to Power. Brutus puts the point, all unconsciously, when the conspirators are gathered at his house:

> We all stand up against the spirit of Caesar,
> And in the spirit of men there is no blood.
> O that we then could come by Caesar's spirit,

And not dismember Caesar! But, alas,
Caesar must bleed for it.

(2.1.167)

Then Caesar does bleed for it; but his spirit, as Brutus's own remark might have
told him, proves invulnerable. It is simply set free by his assassination, and now, as
Antony says, "ranging for revenge, . . . Shall in these confines with a monarch's
voice Cry 'Havoc' and let slip the dogs of war" (3.1.270).

5

The rest of the play is self-explanatory. It is clear all through Acts 4 and 5 that
Brutus and Cassius are defeated before they begin to fight. Antony knows it and
says so at 5.1. Cassius knows it too. Cassius, an Epicurean in philosophy and therefore one who has never heretofore believed in omens, now mistrusts his former
rationalism: he suspects there may be something after all in those ravens, crows,
and kites that wheel overhead. Brutus too mistrusts *his* rationalism. As a Stoic, his
philosophy requires him to repudiate suicide, but he admits to Cassius that if the
need comes he will repudiate philosophy instead. This, like Cassius' statement, is
an unconscious admission of the force of the non-rational in human affairs, a non-
rational influence that makes its presence felt again and again during the great battle. Cassius, for instance, fails to learn in time that Octavius "Is overthrown by
noble Brutus' power" (5.3.52), becomes the victim of a mistaken report of
Titinius's death, runs on his sword crying, "Caesar, thou art revenged" (5.3.45),
and is greeted, dead, by Brutus, in words that make still clearer their defeat by a
power unforeseen: "O Julius Caesar, thou art mighty yet! Thy spirit walks
abroad and turns our swords In our own proper entrails" (5.3.94). In the same
vein, when it is Brutus's turn to die, we learn that the ghost of Caesar has reappeared, and he thrusts the sword home, saying, "Caesar, now be still" (5.5.50).

Among the many topics on which Shakespeare casts a cold eye in this short
play—among them the nature of heroism, the toll that public life exacts, the
legitimacy of power, the danger of violent change (this last especially relevant
in 1599 because of the growing concern for the succession after the aging
Queen should die)—the aspect that seems to me to account best for its hold on
audiences in our totalitarian century of putsches, coups, and assassinations is its
stress on the always ambiguous relation between humankind and history.
During the first half of the play, what we are chiefly conscious of is the human
will as a force in history—men making choices, controlling events. Our typical
scenes are 1.2, where a man is trying to make up his mind; or 2.1, where a man
first reaches a decision and then, with his fellows, lays plans to implement it; or
2.2, where we have Decius Brutus persuading Caesar to decide to go to the senate house; or 3.1 and 3.2, where up through the assassination, and even up
through Antony's speech, men are still, so to speak, impinging on history,
moulding it to their conscious will.

But then comes a change. Though we still have men in action trying to mould their world (or else we would have no play at all), one senses a real shift in the direction of the impact. We begin to feel the insufficiency of noble aims, for history is also consequences; the insufficiency of reason and rational expectation, for the ultimate consequences of an act in history are unpredictable, and usually, by all human standards, illogical as well; and finally, the insufficiency of the human will itself, for there is always something to be reckoned with that is nonhuman and inscrutable—Nemesis, Moira, Fortuna, the Parcae, Providence, Determinism: men have had many names for it, but it is always there. Accordingly, in the second half of the play, our typical scenes are those like 3.3, where Antony has raised something that is no longer under his control or anyone's. Or like 4.1, where we see men acting as if, under the thumb of expediency or necessity or call it what you will, they no longer had wills of their own but prick down the names of nephews and brothers indiscriminately for slaughter. Or like 4.3 and all the scenes thereafter, where we are constantly made to feel that Cassius and Brutus are in the hands of something bigger than they know.

In this light, we can see readily enough why it is that Shakespeare gives Julius Caesar a double character. The dilemma in all violence is that the human Caesar who has human ailments and is a human friend is the Caesar who can be killed. Whereas the marmoreal Caesar, the everlasting Big Brother, must repeatedly be killed but never dies because he lurks in each of us and all together. Any political system is a potential Rome, and there is no reason for the citizen of any country, when he reads or watches a production of *Julius Caesar*, to imagine that this is ancient history.

How Not to Murder Caesar

Sigurd Burckhardt

I

It has been true of Shakespeare critics—as it has been of others supposedly in pursuit of knowledge—that they have felt pretty free to speculate about what Shakespeare "was really like" or "really believed"—or even whether he was real at all—and then to interpret the plays to fit their speculations. As regards *Julius Caesar*, they have argued for better than a century and a half about its political meaning. There are what we may call the republican critics, who believe that Shakespeare's political sympathies are with Brutus, the republican idealist, who is defeated by the very nobility of his ideals. There are, on the other side, the monarchist critics, who cite authorities from Dante to Hooker to prove that Shakespeare's age considered Caesar the founder of the monarchical order in Rome, and Brutus, for all his fine speeches, as no better than a regicide, who is justly punished for his terrible crime. Still other critics try to find a compromise solution; and finally there are those—usually gentlemen of the theatre, with a no-nonsense attitude toward ideas—who are sure that Shakespeare didn't care one way or the other, as long as he came up with a play that filled the house and the cash box.

Another preconception about Shakespeare took root even in his own lifetime and grew so sturdy that today it is still hard to eradicate. I mean the notion that Shakespeare was a "natural genius," somehow directly in touch with the Muse, without the intervening benefit of a solid education. Hence, he wrote splendid poetry, to be sure, and had an unerring instinct for what goes on in men's souls, but he also, alas! committed some sad boners. Not that anyone is pedant enough to hold these boners against him. But still, there they are; and since a critic of this persuasion, though he may be a little short on genius, has at least got a degree from an institution of higher learning, he does note the boners and treats himself to a few moments of complacent condescension.

The striking clock in *Julius Caesar* is Shakespeare's most notorious boner. Everyone knew it for an anachronism—everyone, that is, except Shakespeare, who was out poaching and seducing Anne Hathaway when he should have been at school parsing his Latin. So it is that all annotated editions of the play carry a note to Act 2, Scene 1, line 192, duly explaining that Shakespeare erred at this

From *The Centennial Review* 11:2 (Spring 1967), 141–156. Reprinted by permission.

point. What I propose to do is simply this: I shall assume that Shakespeare did know that he was committing an anachronism—and see what follows from this assumption.

One thing follows immediately: if he did know, he must have intended his readers—and most particularly his learned critics, i.e. those most certain to notice the anachronism—to be struck by it. And beyond that he must have expected his learned critics to divide into two groups: those who would promptly, in the assurance of their prior learning, charge him with an error, and those who would submit to the facts as given by him and say: "How odd! Let's see if we can discover what Shakespeare may have had in mind."

The latter group, instead of writing a condescending note, will start looking carefully, not just at the line in question, but for other instances of time-telling in the play. And they won't have far to look: the scene itself is rich in such instances. It is the so-called "Orchard Scene." It opens with Brutus alone in his garden, late at night, talking to himself about his decision to join the conspiracy. A little later the conspirators enter, led by Cassius, and confer with Brutus on the details of the murder plan. But throughout, the scene is punctuated with time references. In the very first line Brutus lets us know that he is unsure of the time of *day*:

> I cannot by the progress of the stars
> Give guess how near to day.

Forty lines later he shows himself equally unsure of the time of *month:*

> Is not tomorrow, boy, the first of March?

and his servant boy has to inform him that he is off by a full fourteen days. Another forty lines, and Cassius enters with the conspirators. And now something odd happens: while Brutus and Cassius withdraw immediately to the background and confer in inaudible whispers, the secondary conspirators take the center of the stage and engage in a seemingly pointless dispute over the points of the compass, the point of the sun's rising, and the time of *year.* Only after some ten lines of this do Brutus and Cassius come forward, and the main business of planning the assassination is taken up. As soon as the plan is agreed on, the clock strikes three times and is carefully taken note of.

The mere facts of the matter prove design; clearly Shakespeare had something in mind. The time references progress from time of day to time of month to time of year; they are thrust into the foreground when much more important business is relegated to the background; and they all testify to confusion and uncertainty—until the fateful decision has been made, when suddenly these groping guesses yield to the countable precision of a novel chronometric device. So the first result of my assumption has been the discovery of a design; the obvious next question—much more difficult, of course—is: what does the design signify?

Here we need to recall two historical circumstances, which Shakespeare and his audience had reason to be very concretely aware of. One is that Caesar's fame rested in good part on his institution of the Julian calendar. Plutarch— Shakespeare's source—praises this great reform and mentions it as one of the reasons why Caesar was hated: the Roman conservatives felt it to be an arbitrary and tyrannical interference with the course of nature. The second circumstance is that in 1582 Pope Gregory had decreed the reform of the Julian—that is to say, of the traditional Christian—calendar, which in the meantime had drifted almost ten days out of phase. This reform had immediately become an issue in the bitter politico-religious struggles of the age; the Catholic countries accepted it and so adopted the so-called "New Style," while the Protestant countries rejected it and clung to the "Old Style." Thus at the turn of the century—Shakespeare wrote *Julius Caesar* in 1599—a situation existed in Europe exactly analogous to that of Rome in 44 B.C. It was a time of confusion and uncertainty, when the most basic category by which men order their experience seemed to have become unstable and untrustworthy, subject to arbitrary political manipulation.

With these facts in mind, we return to the Orchard Scene. The scene's core is the planning of the conspiracy. Three proposals are made and, on Brutus' insistence, rejected; the third of these is to kill Mark Antony along with Caesar. The rejection—which, of course, soon proves to be a fatal mistake—is based, not so much on grounds of expediency or even morality, but on grounds of *style*. Indeed, under Brutus' influence the planning generally becomes a stylistic question. The plot as such is already decided on, the actors are chosen, the parts in the main assigned; but what still needs to be determined, at least in Brutus' view, is the style in which the action is to be carried out. And on this he has firm opinions; Antony must be spared because otherwise

> Our course will seem too bloody, Caius Cassius,
> To cut the head off and then hack the limbs,
> Like wrath in death and envy afterwards . . .
> Let us be sacrificers but not butchers, Caius . . .
> Let's kill him boldly, but not wrathfully;
> Let's carve him as a dish fit for the gods,
> Not hew him as a carcass fit for hounds . . .
>   This shall make
> Our purpose necessary, and not envious;
> Which so appearing to the common eyes,
> We shall be call'd purgers, not murderers.

And later, when it is a question of whether or not to let Antony speak, Brutus repeats:

> Though now we must appear bloody and cruel,
> As by our hands and this our present act
> You see we do, yet see you but our hands
> And this the bleeding business they have done.
> Our hearts you see not; they are pitiful;

And pity to the general wrong of Rome—
As fire drives out fire, so pity pity—
Hath done this deed on Caesar.

In speaking of the conspiracy I have slipped into the metaphor of the drama: I have talked of plot, action, actors, and style. There is ample warrant for the use of this metaphor in the play itself; Brutus and Cassius employ it repeatedly—most explicitly right after the murder, when in fact it ceases to be a metaphor:

How many ages hence
Shall this our lofty scene be acted over
In states unborn and accents yet unknown.

Let us think of Cassius and Brutus as manifestly they think of themselves: plotters in the dramatic sense, men who have decided to author and produce a tragedy entitled "Julius Caesar." Really it is Cassius who has had the idea for the plot; but he feels the need of a co-author—Brutus—to give the production the kind of prestige and styling that will make it a hit with the audience, the Roman populace. Somewhat to Cassius' distress, Brutus takes his function very seriously and overrules his partner on a number of points which later turn out to be crucial. Evidently we must look a little more closely at the style Brutus has in mind.

What he wants is not a bare assassination, but a tragedy of classical, almost Aristotelian purity. There is to be no wholesale slaughter, with the curtain coming down, as in *Hamlet*, on a heap of corpses. Only the tragic hero is to be killed, and the killing itself is to be a ritual, a sacrifice, formal and even beautiful. Nor is there to be any unseemly vilification: the victim is to be presented, not as a villain like Claudius of Denmark, but as a great and noble man, who falls because he has one tragic flaw: ambition. And his killers, the authors, must not act from personal motives; they must be as priests and physicians, performing their solemn duty of purging the commonwealth. Everything Brutus says and does—most particularly his permitting Antony to speak and his own speech in justification of his act—is informed by this determination to make the tragedy a classical one: noble, purgative, impersonal, inevitable.

He is only too successful. The classical style has disastrous consequences, because Brutus is utterly mistaken about the audience for whom the tragedy is intended. He is thinking of an audience of noble, sturdy republicans, capable of the moral discrimination and public spirit which classical tragedy demands. But *we* know from the opening scenes that the actual audience is very different: eager to be led, easily tricked, crude in their responses. The people insist on having their good guy and their bad guy; they are perfectly ready to accept Brutus as their good guy, provided he lets them have Caesar for their bad guy. But this, Brutus' ideal of style forbids. Brutus is most irretrievably damned, not when the mob is ready to stone him, but when it acclaims him: "Let him be Caesar!" Nothing shows so clearly as this shout of applause how totally the audience has missed Brutus' point, and how totally Brutus has misjudged his audience.

That is why Shakespeare makes the clock strike at the very moment when Brutus has persuaded the conspirators to adopt the classical style for their performance. The political point of the play is not that the monarchical principle is superior to the republican—nor the reverse—but that the form of government, the style of politics, must take account of the time and the temper of the people, just as the dramatist's style must. Brutus is not guilty of treachery, nor of having embraced an inherently wrong political philosophy; he is guilty of an anachronism. The clock, striking as soon as he has irrevocably committed himself to the Old Style, signifies to us—though not to him—that time is now reckoned in a new, Caesarean style.

There were in Shakespeare's day, as there are always, those who retreated from a confused and turbulent present to older forms, older certainties. In literature they preached the return to the great classical models, on their knowledge of which they naturally prided themselves, and in the name of which they felt confident they could judge their own day. Ben Jonson, Shakespeare's contemporary and competitor, was of this faction. With an irony so gentle that it is almost a salute, Shakespeare shows not only the fate of such retreats but the way to diagnose them. The striking clock is not only a metaphor; it is a touchstone. Proud classicists, sure of their learning, will mark it as evidence that Shakespeare had, in Ben Jonson's words, "small Latin and less Greek." But in the very act of doing so they betray their blindness, their refusal fully to surrender to the actually *given*—in this case to the carefully wrought pattern of time references by which Shakespeare defines the precise meaning of his anachronism. Instead of first submitting to the present, the given, and trying to discover its inner structure and meaning, they judge and condemn it by pre-established standards. And so they are blind not only to the present but even to the past they know so well.

Very few of us have read Ben Jonson's Roman tragedies. And probably none of us has seen them performed; they have long since vanished from the stage and into the stacks. On the other hand, most of us have read *Julius Caesar;* most of us have seen it—or at least had the opportunity to see it; and all of us have, at some time or other, quoted phrases from it. If we ever have occasion to look at an edition of Ben Jonson's *Catiline* or *Sejanus,* we find the margins covered with references—supplied by Jonson himself—to his classical sources. Every line is buttressed with classical authority; one would have to be very learned indeed to catch Jonson in an anachronism. The only trouble is that the plays in their entirety are anachronisms—while Shakespeare's work is as alive as ever. Why? Not because Jonson was the lesser "creative genius," in the vague, inspirational sense in which that term is commonly understood; but because, though he knew very well that no clock ever struck in ancient Rome, he did not know what the clock had struck in his own day. Hence, while *Sejanus* gathers dust on library shelves, Caesar's death and Brutus' fall, as Shakespeare has taught us to see them, and as he confidently predicted, are acted over in states unborn and accents yet unknown.

That is the point of his anachronism—precisely defined, exactly calculated, and placed with shrewd irony so that it would serve as an acid test for his critics. It proves, not his ignorance, but his incredible capacity for laying himself open to the tumultuous realities of his age and situation and experience—and his extraordinary ability to penetrate them and embody them in metaphors so true, so carefully wrought that they have remained valid ever since. We often hear it said that Shakespeare still lives because he had the genius to penetrate beneath the temporary and superficial to what is permanently and immutably true. But this, though perhaps not wrong, is a dangerously misleading way of stating the case. It is the classicists, the Brutuses, who believe they are in possession of the eternal verities; and we have seen what happens to them. Shakespeare knew that the truths that last are painfully purchased by those who without reserve expose themselves to reality in all its confusion and still preserve within it the will to order, the will to form.

It's not so difficult to kill Caesar, to kill the ruler; once you get close enough, a bare bodkin will serve. Like Hamlet, one could do it pat. What *is* difficult is to discover how to kill him. For however corrupt, however tyrannical the ruler may be, he does, as of that moment, represent what order there is; do away with him, and you do away with order. That is why the style of killing Caesar is of such importance; the style must embody the vision of order—presumably better, truer, stabler—that will take the place of the order embodied in Caesar. And because that style is necessarily an embodiment, an incarnation of vision in the flesh-and-blood realities and corporealities of the moment, it stands under the judgment of those realities and of that moment.

II

There is a line by Emily Dickinson which catches, better than anything else I know, the essence of what we loosely call the "creative experience," which I take to mean the experience of anyone—artist, scientist, scholar, statesman, philosopher—who tries to create shapes truer than those existing. The line reads: "After great pain a formal feeling comes." What sets the great creators apart from ordinary men is not so much the capacity for inspiration, for vision— though of course these too play a part—as the ability to sustain, often for a long time and without let-up, the pain of disorder. Aware of the inadequacy, the falsity, the injustice of the existing orders, the creator must wish to demolish them—that is what it means to murder Caesar—without as yet knowing what orders will take their place; he must suffer the confrontation with an unstructured reality—a reality that refuses, in its chaotic multiplicity, to yield to man's need of form, of intelligible shape. Modern critics often speak of creative tension; in the last analysis, I believe, this is the tension between the surrender to the raw substance of experience, the given, and the will to order. Brutus is aware of this tension and has felt this pain:

> Since Cassius first did whet me against Caesar,
> I have not slept.
> Between the acting of a dreadful thing
> And the first motion, all the interim is
> Like a phantasma or a hideous dream.

But he cannot sustain the pain long enough to forge a new style, a new mode of order. To gain the blessed release of the "formal feeling," he flees to an old style. Judged in terms of beauty, of purity and nobility, there is no fault to be found with this style. Listen to Brutus rejecting the proposal that the conspirators bind themselves by an oath:

> No, not an oath! . . .
> What need we any spur but our own cause
> To prick us to redress? What other bond
> Than secret Romans that have spoke the word
> And will not palter? and what other oath
> Than honesty to honesty engag'd
> That this shall be, or we will fall for it? . . .
>   Do not stain
> The even virtue of our enterprise . . .
> To think that or our cause or our performance
> Did need an oath; when every drop of blood
> That every Roman bears, and nobly bears,
> Is guilty of a several bastardy
> If he do break the smallest particle
> Of any promise that hath pass'd from him.

Even in Shakespeare's own work we will search a long time before we find another speech of such purity: so free of all verbal and metaphorical trickery, so simple, and yet so nobly eloquent. And if we compare these lines to those of Hamlet when the Prince makes his comrades swear—not just once but three times over—not to divulge what they have seen, we have some measure of the sheer beauty of the form Brutus retreats to.

But it is a retreat all the same; the pain has not been great enough, nor deep enough. This is the pain Hamlet suffers and breaks under and finally hands on to his friend Horatio as his bitter legacy:

> Absent thee from felicity a while
> And in this harsh world draw thy breath in pain
> To tell my story.

In fact, Hamlet is the exact counterpart to Brutus. Like Brutus he accepts the task to kill the ruler, to fashion a tragedy; and like Brutus he botches the job. But he botches it for the opposite reason; instead of settling too quickly for a ready-made form, he despairs of the very possibility of form. The corruption of the world he is supposed to purge enters into his very soul, so that he spends his energy probing the infection, in himself as well as in everyone about him. He is so overwhelmed by his discovery of monstrous disorder that his great enterprise loses, in his words, "the name of action," and the initiative passes to the king. Unlike Brutus, he knows only too well that the clock has struck upon the old style:

> The time is out of joint. O cursed spite
> That ever I was born to set it right!

But he sees, from the depth of his loathing and self-loathing, no possibility of forging a new style, of passing through the great pain to a formal feeling, a truer, more valid shaping of reality. In the end he settles for a stoic resignation which is moving and impressive, but which nevertheless signifies an abdication from his task to discover a new order:

> If it be now, 'tis not to come; if it be not to come, it will be
> now; if it be not now, yet it will come: the readiness is all.

For in the meantime there are corpses lying about of people—most tragically Ophelia—who might have lived but for his inability to rise above his pain.

A tragedy—to define it very simply—is a *killing poem;* it is designed toward the end of bringing a man to some sort of destruction. And the killer is, quite literally, the poet; it is he, and no one else, who devises the deadly plot; it is he, therefore, who must in some sense accept responsibility for it. Even if the events of the plot are drawn from history—as with *Julius Caesar* they obviously are—what is the poet's purpose in re-enacting them and shaping them as he does, at that particular time and place? Why does he not leave history to the historians? Why, and how, does he represent as a living reality what is, or seems to be, a dead past? In other words, what is he, the plotter, *doing* when he has Caesar killed?

These questions are not simply speculative. It is always true that a poem—especially a dramatic poem—is an act, not just a report; but this truth used to be felt more concretely in Shakespeare's day than it is in ours. When the Essex faction was preparing an armed uprising in 1601, they induced Shakespeare's company to put on a performance of *Richard II,* to serve as a prelude to the revolt. And after the uprising had collapsed, Shakespeare and his colleagues were summoned by the authorities to be questioned about their possible implication in the plot. Queen Elizabeth knew very well that the plotting of playwrights and that of rebels may have more in common than merely the name: "I am Richard II, know ye not that?" I am not suggesting that anyone producing a play by Bertolt Brecht should be subpoenaed to testify before the Un-American Activities Committee. But I am suggesting that Shakespeare had pressingly concrete reasons to know that when he was plotting a tragedy—even a historical tragedy—he was not just retelling a story in dramatic form; he was committing an act—the action of his play—in the full moral and social sense of the word "act."

Not that he needed the reminder; he was poet enough—proud poet enough—to claim the responsibility he incurred by this kind of action. That is why, in so many of his plays he has a part for himself as *deviser of the plot,* and why again and again he probes the problem: what am I doing when I invent, or re-invent, a mechanism designed to bring about a man's destruction? In the name of what, for the sake of what, do I do this? And even assuming the necessity of doing it, how well do I do it? Is my aim so sure that there is no unnecessary killing, or is it so uncertain that all Italy is plunged into civil war, or that Ophelia and Gertrude, Polonius and Laertes, Rosencrantz and Guildenstern must die along with the king?

III

It may be, of course, that the tragic poet does not worry about this kind of accountability, but takes the position that after all he is only the poet, trying to write as perfect a tragedy as he knows how. This role also Shakespeare watched himself playing and wrote into a play. His "perfect tragedy," in this sense of the term, is *Othello*, by general agreement the most flawlessly structured of all his tragedies. In it he devises a plot so beautifully tooled, so accurately deadly that, once set going, it seems of its own momentum to bring about the destruction for which it is designed. But into it he writes his own part as the deviser of a perfect tragedy—and the part is Iago's. Iago it is who composes the tragedy called "Othello"; he stands at the footlights and tells us, step by step, how he shapes it, from the first most general idea through the overall scheme down to the specific devices of plotting. And beyond that he lets us share the keen joy of mastery, of subtle skill and power, that he derives from this enterprise. If Othello is a great tragedy and not just a perfect one, this self-portrait of the "pure" tragic poet is the reason. The play shows what manner of man he is who creates art for art's sake, or at least tragedy for tragedy's sake.

This kind of tragedy was real enough for Shakespeare to have done it once, in full awareness of what he was doing; but it was not, on the whole, his kind. He admits, in Iago, to the sense of triumph which every craftsman is bound to feel when he fashions a perfect instrument, no matter what the ultimate end. But the triumph is sterile. None of Shakespeare's plotters—not even the well-intentioned ones—are presented as fathers; Brutus and Hamlet as well as Macbeth and Richard III are childless. But the most childless of all, if so illogical a superlative is permitted—the man whom we cannot even imagine as being a father, the way we *can* imagine Brutus and do imagine Macbeth—is Iago. There is, as it were, no blood in him—hardly even that which boils with hatred or is fired by ambition. He is a perfect craftsman.

Permit me, at this point, a brief parenthetical digression. I cannot think of any more devastating revelation of how we today feel and see reality than the fact that we accept—without revulsion and even without a sense of incongruity—a metaphor such as "father of the H-bomb." It's not the H-bomb as such that I have in mind, terrifying though it is. Mankind has always invested a good part of its ingenuity in devising more perfect engines of destruction. But I doubt that any previous age has called the devisers of such engines by the name of "father." "Father of poison gas," "father of the machine gun," "father of the electric chair"—these, it seems to me, would have been impossible. The mere phrase "father of the H-bomb" betrays more of what we truly are than a thousand pages of the Congressional Record can conceal. For we speak the truth about ourselves, not in our pious sentiments but in the metaphors we find for them.

It was not, I am convinced, Shakespeare's ambition to write perfect tragedies; my guess is that the very term would have made him shudder, as Iago makes us shudder. It is no mere paradox to say that Shakespeare wrote great tragedies because he thought it monstrous to think of them as perfect. Murder is, at best, a bleeding or strangling business; we are dangerously deceived if we believe that it can be styled into beauty. That is Brutus' illusion. True, he does not enjoy his work, as Iago does; he feels driven to it in the service of a higher cause. So, for that matter, does Othello, another sacrificial killer who thinks he must and can purge the world and goes about his work with noble pity. But Othello is never so deluded as when he is most priestly; and Brutus, after his fine words about not being a butcher and not hewing Caesar as a carcass fit for hounds, stands on the stage, his arms bloody to the elbows and at his feet Caesar's pitifully mangled carcass.

The eighteenth century felt squeamish about Shakespeare's tragedies and preferred to pretty them up a little—especially *King Lear,* the end of which was rewritten so that Cordelia was saved to marry Edgar and live happily ever after. Today we smile condescendingly at such prettifying; we pride ourselves on being able to take our Shakespeare straight. But I am not at all sure that this pride is in Shakespeare's spirit. I think he meant the end of *King Lear* to be as Samuel Johnson found it: unbearable.

We take our Shakespeare straight; but our critics supply us with chasers. There are various comforting theories about the nature of tragedy—theories which sound disconcertingly like those of Brutus and Othello. A tragedy, we are told, is a kind of sacrifice brought to purge the world of some disorder and restore it to its natural harmony. To be sure, we pity the victim; we feel terror at the price that has to be paid for the restoring of order. But in the end we feel rather as Brutus does:

As fire drive out fire, so pity pity—
And pity for the general wrong of Rome
Hath done this deed on Caesar.

It is this comforting theory that the clock tolls into an irrecoverable past. For it rests on a no longer tenable faith in an underlying universal order—an order that may be temporarily disturbed but can, by the proper purgatives properly administered, be reestablished. This faith Shakespeare felt compelled to abandon. Measured by Caesar's time, the Caesarean system is not a general wrong but a true order, however it may look measured by another time. The natural order cannot be known, or at least not be known certainly enough to legitimize the murder of Caesar in the classical style. Once the time is out of joint, sacrificial tragedy is no longer possible—or rather, it is an illusion by which we deceive ourselves, if not about our motives, at least about the consequences of our action.

All this is not to say that Shakespeare gave up the quest for order and subsided into a flaccid relativism. Rather, he found that he had to accept undiminished responsibility for his failures to create order—for his tragedies, in other words. Order, for him, was not something that only needed to be restored; it had to be continually created. And the great metaphor for his vision of order is not something grand and cosmic like the harmony of the spheres or the chain of being; it is something modest, earthly, human—marriage. He does see his function as that of a priest—only not the sacrificial priest who protests that the victim must have, like Caesar, "all true rites and lawful ceremonies," but the priest performing the sacrament of marriage. What he has to learn is the true rite of this sacrament—the words which will make the marriage of true minds truly binding, stable and fruitful. There are fearful impediments to this kind of marriage; and once Shakespeare can no longer refuse to admit these—as he still does in his famous sonnet—he engages in a series of fierce attempts to remove them. These attempts are his tragedies, ending in separation, death—failure. But they are all directed toward the same ultimate end: the creation of new order, new unions. And being that, they are redeemed, in retrospect, as necessary steps, necessary failures. In *The Tempest*, Shakespeare as Prospero shows us how all the chaos and turbulence, the separation and loss and grief and madness, were but means to the one true end: the joining of two young people who would, except for the tempest, have remained apart. When all is said and done, the poet's job has been to learn, as Shakespeare puts it in his twenty-third sonnet, "the perfect ceremony of love's rite"—not of murder, not of sacrifice, but of marriage:

As an unperfect actor on the stage
Who with his fear is put besides his part,
Or some fierce thing replete with too much rage,
Whose strength's abundance weakens his own heart,
So I, for fear of trust, forget to say
The perfect ceremony of love's rite,
And in my own love's strength seem to decay,
O'ercharg'd with burden of my own love's might.
O, let my books be then the eloquence
And dumb presagers of my speaking breast,
Who plead for love and look for recompense
More than that tongue that more hath more express'd.
   O, learn to read what silent love hath writ:
   To hear with eyes belongs to love's fine wit.

Dream and Interpretation: *Julius Caesar*

Marjorie Garber

In the final act of *Julius Caesar*, Cassius, fearful of defeat at Philippi, dispatches Titinius to discover whether the surrounding troops are friends or enemies. He posts another soldier to observe, and when the soldier sees Titinius encircled by horsemen and reports that he is taken, Cassius runs on his sword and dies. Shortly afterward, Titinius reenters the scene bearing a "wreath of victory" from Brutus. When he sees the dead body, he at once understands Cassius's tragic mistake. "Alas, thou has misconstrued everything!" (5.3.84), he cries out, and he too runs on Cassius's sword.

That one cry, "thou hast misconstrued everything!", might well serve as an epigraph for the whole of *Julius Caesar*. The play is full of omens and portents, augury and dream, and almost without exception these omens are misinterpreted. Calpurnia's dream, the dream of Cinna the poet, the advice of the augurers, all suggest one course of action and produce its opposite. The compelling dream imagery of the play, which should, had it been rightly interpreted, have persuaded Caesar to avoid the Capitol and Cinna not to go forth, is deflected by the characters of men, making tragedy inevitable. For *Julius Caesar* is not only a political play, but also a play of character. Its imagery of dream and sign, an imagery so powerful that it enters the plot on the level of action, is a means of examining character and consciousness.

Much of the plot of *Julius Caesar*, like that of *Richard III*, is shaped by the device of the predictive dream or sign. The two plays also have another point of similarity, not unrelated to the device of dream: each divides men into two camps, those who attempt to control dream and destiny and those who are controlled by it. In *Richard III* only Gloucester thinks himself able to master dream and turn it to his own purposes; Edward, Clarence, and Hastings are its helpless victims. *Julius Caesar*, on the other hand, presents a number of characters who declare themselves indifferent to dream or contemptuous of its power: Cassius, who so firmly places the fault not in our stars but in ourselves; Decius Brutus, who deliberately misinterprets Calpurnia's prophetic dream to serve his own ends; Octavius, in whom the whole dimension of emotion seems lacking; and

From Marjorie Garber, *Dream in Shakespeare* (New Haven: Yale University Press, 1974), 47–58.

Caesar himself. Caesar's conviction, however, is notably wavering as the play begins. As Cassius points out to the conspirators,

> he is superstitious grown of late,
> Quite from the main opinion he held once
> Of fantasy, of dreams, and ceremonies.
>   (2.1.195–97)

Caesar struggles against this tendency, repeatedly invoking his public persona to quell his private fears: "Danger knows full well," he boasts, "That Caesar is more dangerous than he" (2.2.44–45). Yet he protests too much.

In his susceptibility to dream and introspection he stands midway between the coldness of Decius Brutus and the blind self-preoccupation of Brutus, for Brutus is in a way the least self-aware of all these characters, because he thinks of himself as a supremely rational man. Again and again he confronts his situation and misinterprets it, secure in his own erroneous sense of self. His frequent solitary ruminations have a certain poignancy about them; they approach a truth and reject it through lack of self-knowledge. Thus he meditates,

> Between the acting of a dreadful thing
> And the first motion, all the interim is
> Like a phantasma, or a hideous dream:
> The genius and the mortal instruments
> Are then in council; and the state of man,
> Like to a little kingdom, suffers then
> The nature of an insurrection.
>   (2.1.63–69)

Yet in the next moment he turns his back on this foreboding and welcomes the conspirators to his house. It is Brutus who sees the ghost of Caesar and is indifferent to him; Brutus who is afflicted with a revealing insomnia: "Since Cassius first did whet me against Caesar," he says, "I have not slept" (2.1.61–62). Like Gloucester, Macbeth, and Henry IV, all similarly blind to self, he bears his crime on his conscience and cannot sleep, though he is visited by an apparition which seems to come from the dream state. There is a poignant moment after the ghost's first appearance, when he tries in vain to convince his servants and soldiers that they have cried out in the night:

Brutus:	Didst thou dream, Lucius, that thou so criedst out?
Lucius:	My lord, I do not know that I did cry.
Brutus:	Yes, that thou didst. Didst thou see anything?
Lucius:	Nothing, my lord.
Brutus:	Sleep again, Lucius. Sirrah Claudius!
	(*To Varro*). Fellow thou, awake!
Varro:	My lord?
Claudius:	My lord?
Brutus:	Why did you so cry out, sirs, in your sleep?
Both:	Did we, my lord?

Brutus:	Ay. Saw you anything?
Varro:	No, my lord, I saw nothing.
Claudius:	Nor I, my lord.

(4.3.291–301)

Nowhere is the quintessential loneliness of the conscience-stricken man more forcefully portrayed. "Nothing, my lord." Brutus, too, has misconstrued everything, and his tragedy is that he suspects it. Trapped by his high-minded vanity and his inability to function in the world of action—trapped, that is, by his own character—he sees the Rome he tried to rescue in ruins as a result of his act.

Caesar's ghost appears to Brutus in the source for *Julius Caesar*, Plutarch's *Lives of the Noble Grecians and Romans*. Its presence is also related to the Senecan theatrical tradition we have discussed above. Psychologically, it can be seen as an extension of Brutus's guilt feelings; like Richard III's Bosworth dream or the appearance of Banquo's ghost, the apparition here presents itself to one man only and is not sensed by the others present. Such visionary dream figures are found in Shakespeare only in plays which are directly concerned with the psychological condition of the characters; the disappearance of the ghost as a type in the plays following *Macbeth* is a sign, not merely of dramaturgical sophistication, but also of a shift in emphasis. For *Julius Caesar* is, in a way, the last play of its kind. The uses of dream, vision, and omen will change sharply in the plays that follow.

The motif of the misinterpreted dream in this play becomes a main factor in the dramatic action, demonstrating, always, some crucial fact about the interpreter. In the second scene of the play the soothsayer's warning goes unheeded, though in the same scene Caesar betrays his superstitious cast of mind. The contrast is adeptly managed: Antony is reminded to touch Calpurnia in the course of his race on the Lupercal, to remove her "sterile curse" (1.2.9). But when the soothsayer cautions Caesar to "beware the ides of March" (18), he rejects the intended warning out of hand;

He is a dreamer, let us leave him. Pass.
(1.2.24)

The inference is that dreams, like omens, are of no value; "dreamer" is a pejorative dismissal, akin to "madman." Calpurnia may have need of supernatural aid, but not the public Caesar. Already in this early scene we see him assuming a position closer to that of gods than men, a thoughtless hubris which is in itself dangerous. The omen, intrinsically a kind of dramatic device, is chiefly significant because it indicates his lack of self-knowledge.

The next scene, like much of the play, is in part at least a landscape of the mind. Casca, who is to be one of the conspirators, apprehensively reports to Cicero the strange events of the day. The heavens are "dropping fire" (1.3.10), a slave's hand flames but does not burn, a lion walks in the Capitol, an owl sits in the marketplace at noon. These omens are all reported by Plutarch,[1] but

Shakespeare turns them to dramatic purpose, making them mirror the conspirators' mood. "When these prodigies / Do so conjointly meet," says Casca,

> let not men say,
> "These are their reasons, they are natural,"
> For I believe they are portentous things
> Unto the climate that they point upon.
> (1.3.28–32)

To this superstitious view Cicero has a wise and moderate reply.

> Indeed, it is a strange-disposèd time:
> But men may construe things after their fashion,
> Clean from the purpose of the things themselves.
> (33–35)

This is Titinius's lament: "Thou hast misconstrued everything." Like all the quasi-oracular pronouncements in this play, it is two-edged. Men may construe things as they like for their own purposes; just so Cassius plays on Brutus's fears of monarchy to enlist his help. And men may also misconstrue through error; so Caesar misreads the signs which might have kept him from death. But if Cicero's answer is apposite, it is also bloodless and dispassionate. What he does not consider is the element of humanity, the energy of men's passions inflamed by supposed signs. He is outside the tragedy, a choric figure who does not reenter the drama.

More and more it becomes evident that signs and dreams are morally neutral elements, incapable of effect without interpretation. By structuring his play around them, Shakespeare invites us to scrutinize the men who read the signs—to witness the tragedy of misconstruction. The two senses of Cicero's maxim, the willful deceiver and the willingly deceived, are the controllers of dream and the controlled. Decius Brutus, perhaps the coldest in a play replete with cold men, states the position of the former unequivocally. No matter how superstitious Caesar has lately become, he, Decius Brutus, is confident of his ability to manipulate him.

> I can o'ersway him; for he loves to hear
> That unicorns may be betrayed with trees,
> And bears with glasses, elephants with holes,
> Lions with toils, and men with flatterers;
> But when I tell him he hates flatterers,
> He says he does, being then most flattered.
> Let me work;
> For I can give his humor the true bent,
> And I will bring him to the Capitol.
> (2.1.203–11)

¹"The Life of Julius Caesar," trans. Thomas North (1579), in *Shakespeare's Plutarch*, ed. C. F. Tucker Brooke (New York: Haskell House, 1966) II, 95–96.

Willful misconstruction is his purpose and his art. And, fulfilling his promise, it is Decius Brutus who artfully misinterprets Calpurnia's dream and coaxes Caesar to the scene of his death.

Calpurnia's dream is one of the play's cruxes. By this time in the course of the drama an internal convention has been established regarding dreams and omens: whatever their source, they are true, and it is dangerous to disregard them. Shakespeare's audience would certainly have been familiar with the story of Julius Caesar, and such a collection of portents and premonitions would have seemed to them, as it does to us, to be infallibly leading to the moment of murder. Calpurnia herself adds to the catalogue of unnatural events:

> A lioness hath whelped in the streets,
> And graves have yawned, and yielded up their dead;
> Fierce fiery warriors fought upon the clouds
> In ranks and squadrons and right form of war,
> Which drizzled blood upon the Capitol;
> The noise of battle hurtled in the air,
> Horses did neigh and dying men did groan,
> And ghosts did shriek and squeal about the streets.
>   (2.2.17–24)

This is in fact an apocalypse of sorts, the last judgment of Rome. Unlike the events narrated by Casca, those reported by Calpurnia are not specified in Plutarch; it is noteworthy how much more *Shakespearean* they are, and how economically chosen to foreshadow, metaphorically, the later events of the play. The lioness is Wrath, and from her loins will spring forth "ranks and squadrons and right form of war," while the ghost of Caesar appears solemnly in the streets. Shakespeare was to remember this moment soon again, upon the appearance of the most majestic of all his ghosts.

> In the most high and palmy state of Rome,
> A little ere the mightiest Julius fell,
> The graves stood tenantless, and the sheeted dead
> Did squeak and gibber in the Roman streets.
>   (*Ham.* 1.1.113–16)

Calpurnia's *bona fides* as a prophetess is thus firmly established by the time we hear her dream, and so too is the blind obstinacy of Caesar. He willfully misinterprets a message from his augurers, who advise him to stay away from the Capitol, alarmed by the sacrifice of a beast in which they found no heart. "Caesar should be a beast without a heart," he declares, "If he should stay at home today for fear" (2.2.42–43), thus completely reversing the message of the haruspices. In this mood he is interrupted by Decius Brutus, whose wiliness outlasts his own more heedless cunning. Caesar is one of those elder statesmen who visibly enjoys causing discomfort to his underlings; it is partially for this reason that he now abruptly changes his mind upon the entrance of Decius and declares "I will not come" (71). We have not yet heard the dream; Shakespeare leaves it for Caesar himself to recount, as he does now to Decius.

> She dreamt tonight she saw my statue,
> Which, like a fountain with an hundred spouts,
> Did run pure blood, and many lusty Romans
> Came smiling and did bathe their hands in it.
> And these does she apply for warnings and portents
> And evils imminent, and on her knee
> Hath begged that I will stay at home today.
>   (2.2.76–82)

We may notice that here, as in our interpretation of Romeo's last dream, the dead man becomes a statue; this is a recurrent conceit in Shakespearean dreams, and in *The Winter's Tale,* as we will see, the dream action becomes plot as Hermione "dies," becomes a "statue," and is reborn. In Calpurnia's dream the latent dream thoughts are not far removed from the manifest content. She interprets the statue as the body of Caesar and also his funerary monument, and the gushing forth of blood she reads as death. As a prophetic dream this is both an accurate and a curiously lyrical one, graceful in its imagery. It forecasts directly the assassination before the Capitol.

Decius, however, is prepared for the event, and he begins immediately to discredit Calpurnia's prediction. He commences with what is by now a familiar note: "This dream is all amiss interpreted," and offers instead his own "interpretation":

> It was a vision fair and fortunate:
> Your statue spouting blood in many pipes,
> In which so many smiling Romans bathed,
> Signifies that from you great Rome shall suck
> Reviving blood, and that great men shall press
> For tinctures, stains, relics and cognizance.
> This by Calpurnia's dream is signified.
>   (83–90)

It is the dissimulator now who cries, "thou hast misconstrued everything." He takes the manifest content of Calpurnia's dream and attributes to it a clever if wholly fabricated set of latent thoughts, which are the more impressive for their psychological insight. Caesar is flattered, as Decius had predicted, and resolves to go to the Capitol. His last doubts are abruptly erased when Decius suggests that he will be offered a crown and warns that refusal to go will seem like uxoriousness:

>   it were a mock
> Apt to be rendered, for someone to say
> "Break up the Senate till another time,
> When Caesar's wife shall meet with better dreams."
>   (2.2.96–99)

This is a thrust well calculated to strike home. But there is a curious ambiguity about Calpurnia's dream, and the real irony of the situation is that Decius's spurious interpretation of it is as true in its way as Calpurnia's.

The content of her dream, it may be pointed out, does not itself appear in Plutarch. "She dreamed," he writes, "that Caesar was slain, and that she had him in her arms," and he also tells us that "Titus Livius writeth, that it was in this sort. The Senate having set upon the top of Caesar's house, for an ornament and setting forth of the same, a certain pinnacle, Calpurnia dreamed that she saw it broken down."[2] But the dream as we have it, the spouting statue and the smiling Romans, is a Shakespearean interpolation. Like Romeo's last dream, which we have already examined, it is chiefly remarkable for the fact that it permits two opposite interpretations, the one literal and the other metaphorical. For Decius's flattery,

> that from you great Rome shall suck
> Reviving blood, and that great men shall press
> For tinctures, stains, relics, and cognizance

is also a truth. Antony's funeral oration turns on precisely this point, elevating the slain Caesar to the status of a saint or a demigod, exhibiting the bloody wounds to win the hearts of the crowd. And at the play's end Antony shares hegemony—however uneasily—with the *novus homo* Octavius, literal descendant of Caesar's "blood."

The presence of Calpurnia's dream at this crucial point in the plot is thus trebly determined: (1) it has Plutarchan authority and is thus an original element in the story; (2) it acts as a functional device to further the action, showing the deliberate blindness of Caesar to a warning which would have saved his life and demonstrating the cold-blooded manipulation of the conspirators; (3) it symbolically foreshadows events to come, supporting the theme of "all amiss interpreted" which is central to the play's meaning. Interestingly, the accustomed tension between the men who aspire to control dream and those who are controlled by it is diminished in this episode; Decius, who means to assert control, is in a larger sense controlled, since he does not see that his interpretation is true.

For all its richness, however, the scene of Calpurnia's dream is rivaled in significance by a much more tangential scene, which seems at first glance oddly out of place in the plot. The scene of Cinna the poet is in many ways the most symbolically instructive of the whole play: it demonstrates in action the same theme of misinterpretation with which we have been so much concerned. Cinna the poet, a character unrelated to his namesake Cinna the conspirator, appears only in this scene, which may be seen as a kind of emblem for the entire meaning of *Julius Caesar*. We encounter him as he makes his way along a Roman street, and his opening lines describe his dream.

> I dreamt tonight that I did feast with Caesar,
> And things unluckily charge my fantasy.

[2]Ibid., p. 97.

I have no will to wander forth of doors,
Yet something leads me forth.
                              (3.3.1–4)

To "feast with Caesar" here means to share his fate—we may remember Brutus's "Let's carve him as a dish fit for the gods" (2.1.173). Cinna admits that he has had a premonition of danger, but that he has chosen to disregard it; "something"—misconstruction again—leads him forth. He is set on by a group of plebians, their emotions raised to fever pitch by Antony's oration, and they rapidly catechize him on his identity and purpose.

Third Plebian:	Your name sir, truly.
Cinna:	Truly, my name is Cinna.
First Plebian:	Tear him to pieces! He's a conspirator.
Cinna:	I am Cinna the poet! I am Cinna the poet!
Fourth Plebian:	Tear him for his bad verses! Tear him for his bad verses!
Cinna:	I am not Cinna the conspirator.
Fourth Plebian:	It is no matter, his name's Cinna;
	pluck but his name out of his heart,
	and turn him going.

                              (3.3.27–37)

The scene is a perfect illustration of Cicero's verdict: "Men may construe things after their fashion, / Clean from the purpose of the things themselves." The taking of the name for the man—a thematically important element throughout this play, where Caesar is at once a private man and a public title—is symbolic of the overt confusion manifest in much of the action. Cinna's dream is a legitimate cause for anxiety, which he chooses to ignore at peril to himself. Plutarch supplied him with a practical motive: "When he heard that they carried Caesar's body to burial, being ashamed not to accompany his funerals: he went out of his house";[3] in Shakespeare's version the cause is deliberately less exact, more psychological than circumstantial. The warning is given and ignored; the plebians do not care that they attack the wrong man. In one short scene of less than forty lines the whole myth of the play is concisely expressed.

Julius Caesar is a complex and ambiguous play, which does not concern itself principally with political theory, but rather with the strange blindness of the rational mind—in politics and elsewhere—to the great irrational powers which flow through life and control it. The significance attached to the theme of "thou hast misconstrued everything" clearly depends to a large extent upon the reading—or misreading—of the play's many dreams. Here, in the last of his plays to use dreams and omens primarily as devices of plot, Shakespeare again demonstrates the great symbolic power which resides in the dream, together with its remarkable capacity for elucidating aspects of the play which otherwise remain in shadow.

[3]"The Life of Marcus Brutus," in Brooke, *Shakespeare's Plutarch*, II, 139.

Conjuring Caesar: Ceremony, History, and Authority in 1599

Mark Rose

Julius Caesar opens with Marullus and Flavius rebuking the plebeians for transferring their allegiance from Pompey and making a holiday to celebrate Caesar's triumph. It is commonplace to remark that the plebeians in this scene, the cheeky cobbler who makes puns about mending bad soles and the other workmen, are more Elizabethan than Roman. But it is not usually noted that the tribune Marullus sounds strikingly like an indignant Puritan calling sinners to repent:

> O you hard hearts, you cruel men of Rome,
> Knew you not Pompey? Many a time and oft
> Have you climb'd up to walls and battlements,
> To towers and windows, yea, to chimney-tops,
> Your infants in your arms, and there have sat
> The livelong day, with patient expectation,
> To see great Pompey pass the streets of Rome:
> And when you saw his chariot but appear,
> Have you not made an universal shout,
> That Tiber trembled underneath her banks
> To hear the replication of your sounds
> Made in her concave shores?
> And do you now put on your best attire?
> And do you now cull out a holiday?
> And do you now strew flowers in his way,
> That comes in triumph over Pompey's blood?
> Be gone!
> Run to your houses, fall upon your knees,
> Pray to the gods to intermit the plague
> That needs must light on this ingratitude.[1]

Besides the emotionalism and rhetorical urgency which were characteristic of the Puritans and their "spiritual" style of preaching, we can note that the imagery of

"Conjuring Caesar: Ceremony, History, and Authority in 1599" reprinted with permission from *English Literary Renaissance* 19:3 (Autumn 1989): 291–304.

[1] 1.1.36–55. All quotations of *Julius Caesar* are from the Arden edition, ed. T. S. Dorsch (London, 1955).

hard hearts, plagues, chariots, and trembling waters recalls that favorite Old Testament story of the reformers, Exodus. In 1599, when *Julius Caesar* was first performed, similarly styled calls to prayer and repentance might be heard from pulpits all over London.[2]

In the tangled world of Elizabethan England, religion and politics were more often than not indistinguishable, and we need not be surprised to find that Shakespeare, trying to understand the nature of the political contentions of ancient Rome as he found them described in Plutarch's *Lives*, should think of the contemporary struggle in the church. A crucial point of contention between Anglican conservatives and Puritan reformers was whether a clergyman's authority came from above or from below, from the crown or from the congregation. Anglican clergy maintained the importance of episcopal ordination, and thus also the principle of the monarch as the final reservoir of power. The reformers insisted that authority derived from the inward call of the spirit, confirmed by the outward call of the congregation. The prescribed role of the Roman tribunes of the people—the "tongues o' th' common mouth" as Coriolanus contemptuously calls them—was as spokesmen and defenders of plebeian rights. Furthermore, the tribunes were not appointed but elected by the plebeians themselves. Perhaps then the reformers' claim to an authority derived not from the crown but from God and the congregations of the faithful led Shakespeare to conceive an analogy between the ancient tribunes and the Puritan preachers of his day.

That Shakespeare was in fact making this connection is only speculation of course, but the readiness with which this analogy might come to mind is suggested by the fact that a few years later King James made a similar association. Irritated by the independence of the English parliament, he asserted in 1605 that there were in the House of Commons "some Tribunes of the people, whose mouths could not be stopped, either from the matters of the Puritans, or of the purveyance."[3] Moreover, a number of details in the play suggest that some such analogy might be at work in Shakespeare's mind. Casca reports that "Marullus and Flavius, for pulling scarfs off Caesar's images, are put to silence" (1.2.282–83), a phrase that recalls precisely the action which was commonly taken against a Puritan who had become a thorn in the side of authority. In a well-known episode in 1586, for example, Archbishop Whitgift intervened in the running debate at Temple Church between the orthodox Richard Hooker and his Puritan deputy Walter Travers by prohibiting Travers from further

[2]On the "spiritual" style of preaching, which developed in the 1580s and 1590s, see William Haller, *The Rise of Puritanism* (New York, 1938), pp. 19–34, 128–72. David Kaula in " 'Let Us Be Sacrificers': Religious Motifs in *Julius Caesar*," *Shakespeare Studies*, 14 (1981), 197–214, also observes the analogy between the tribunes and the reformers. Kaula develops the point rather differently from the way I do, suggesting that Caesar worship in this play is something akin to Roman Catholic worship and that Caesar himself can be associated with the Pope.

[3]William Cobbett, *Parliamentary History of England* (1806), vol. I, cols. 1071–72. In the ensuing debates over purveyance reform, the principal supporters of reform became associated in the public mind with tribunes. See W. Gordon Zeeveld, "Coriolanus and Jacobean Politics." *Modern Language Review*, 57 (1962), 321–34, who discusses the episode in relation to the tribunes in the later play.

preaching, or in Hooker's phrase, enjoining him to silence.[4] And in 1599 Laurence Barker complained that Londoners would rush to hear any preacher "that will not sticke to reuile them that are in authoritie, that his sectaries may crie he is persecuted, when hee is iustly silenced."[5]

Also suggestive is the exchange at the end of the opening scene when the tribunes go off to "disrobe" the images:

Flavius:	Disrobe the images,
	If you do find them deck'd with ceremonies.
Marullus:	May we do so?
	You know it is the feast of Lupercal.
Flavius:	It is no matter; let no images
	Be hung with Caesar's trophies.

(1.1.164–69)

The language seems to glance at the controversies over garments and the use of images; in the word "ceremonies"—Plutarch speaks of "diadems"—Flavius employs a term of great contemporary resonance, one containing within itself nearly the entire history of fifty years of passionate struggle. Again and again the Puritans condemned what they called "superstitious" and "filthy" ceremonies, the "chains," as one put it, "whereby we were tied to popish religion."[6] With equal determination, the Anglican establishment insisted on the retention of those ceremonies necessary to maintain, in the words of the Book of Common Prayer, "a decente ordre, and godlye discipline" (1599, sig. D1). Over the years the term "ceremony" had been used so often and had acquired so many associations that it had become, as W. Gordon Zeeveld remarks, "a word of extraordinary emotive power with verbal and conceptual values instantly resonant in the theatre."[7]

One form of ceremony that offended the Puritans was the keeping of holidays—the term still carried much of the old sense of holy day—other than those specifically appointed in the Bible. Flavius' dismissive attitude toward the feast of Lupercal may well have sounded Puritanical in the late 1590s when the reformers were making a point of refusing to stop work to celebrate such feasts as saints' days.[8] His comment here recalls the contempt with which he chastises the workmen at the play's start:

Hence! home, you idle creatures, get you home:
Is this a holiday? What, know you not,

[4]*The Works of Mr. Richard Hooker*, ed. J. Keble (Oxford, 1863), III, 570.

[5]*Christs Checke to S. Peter* (1599), sig. M8. On preaching as a crucial area for political control see Christopher Hill, *Society and Puritanism in Pre-Revolutionary England* (London, 1964), pp. 30–78.

[6]Robert Crowley, *An Answere for the tyme* (1566), quoted by W. Gordon Zeeveld, *The Temper of Shakespeare's Thought* (New Haven, Conn., 1974), p. 25.

[7]*The Temper of Shakespeare's Thought*, p. 15.

[8]By the 1590s an anti-holiday attitude had become virtually "official" Puritan doctrine. See Patrick Collinson, *The Elizabethan Puritan Movement* (London, 1982), pp. 436–37, and Hill, *Society and Puritanism*, pp. 145–218, who reports that Puritans were regularly penalized for insisting on working on saints' days.

Being mechanical, you ought not walk
Upon a labouring day without the sign
Of your profession?

(1.1.1–5)

From the first lines of the scene, then, even before Marullus' harangue, a certain aura of Puritanism clings to the tribunes.

The confrontations between the Puritans and the Anglicans often focused on matters of ritual or ceremony, but as the phrase "decent ordre" in the Book of Common Prayer implies, the issues raised were felt to be fundamental and far reaching. The discarding of the symbols of religious authority might lead, as many understood, to the questioning of other images of social authority, and thus to a challenge to the crown itself: no bishop, no king. At stake ultimately was the matter of power in the realm—which is of course also at stake at the opening of *Julius Caesar*.

II

Although the tribunes themselves do not reappear after the first scene, the opposition between puritanical anti-ritualism and a more conservative belief in the efficacy of ceremony is at work throughout the play. Caesar's first appearance shows his concern about ceremonies as he enters speaking about the Lupercalian rite and his desire to have Antony touch Calphurnia. "Set on," he commands, "and leave no ceremony out" (1.1.11). Later Cassius remarks to the conspirators that Caesar "is superstitious grown of late, / Quite from the main opinion he held once / Of fantasy, of dreams, and ceremonies (2.1.195–97). "Ceremonies" here may refer to portents or omens, as it does when Calphurnia comments that although she "never stood on ceremonies" (2.2.13) they now frighten her, but the word's other sense is not lost. We can note, too, Cassius' Puritanical dislike of plays and music, pointed out by Caesar; and in this context Casca's sour dismissal of the ceremony of the offering of the crown as "foolery" may also be suggestive.

In a general way, then, the anti-Caesar parties—both the tribunes and the bitter republicans of the second scene, Cassius and Casca—are associated with anti-ritualism. But Brutus, whom the play carefully distinguishes from the other opponents of Caesar, is no enemy to ceremony as such. Indeed, it is precisely because of his belief in the power of ritual that he comes to the conclusion that Caesar must die. As Frank Kermode observes, anachronistic assumptions about the significance of a coronation ceremony are at work in Brutus' soliloquy in his orchard. For Plutarch, Caesar is already a king *de facto*. But Brutus, thinking more like an Elizabethan subject than a Roman citizen, attaches great importance to the actual crowning: "He would be crown'd: / How that might change his nature, there's the question" (2.1.12–13). Crown Caesar and he will be put beyond reprisal. The ritual itself is what must be prevented.[9]

[9]See Kermode's introduction to *Julius Caesar* in *The Riverside Shakespeare*, ed. G. Blakemore Evans (Boston, 1974), p. 1103.

From the solemn shaking of hands in 2.1 to the bathing in Caesar's blood, the con-spiracy is, under Brutus' direction, carried out in a conspicuously ceremonial manner. As Brents Stirling and others have noted, onstage the ritualistic character of the assas-sination is clear.[10] One by one the conspirators kneel to Caesar, begging him to repeal Publius Cimber's banishment although they know he will not. By arrangement Casca strikes first, rearing his hand over Caesar's head. Each conspirator then stabs in turn, after which they bathe in the blood. But long before the event, Brutus insists that the assassination must be conducted as a sacrifice. His well-known speech evokes both ritual slaughter and the notion of purging or bleeding a sick commonweal in a medic-inal act that he conceives as a kind of exorcism of Caesar's spirit.

> Let's be sacrificers, but not butchers, Caius.
> We all stand up against the spirit of Caesar,
> And in the spirit of men there is no blood.
> O, that we then could come by Caesar's spirit,
> And not dismember Caesar! But, alas,
> Caesar must bleed for it. And, gentle friends,
> Let's kill him boldly, but not wrathfully;
> Let's carve him as a dish fit for the gods,
> Now hew him as a carcass fit for hounds.
> And let our hearts, as subtle masters do,
> Stir up their servants to an act of rage,
> And after seem to chide 'em. This shall make
> Our purpose necessary, and not envious;
> Which so appearing to the common eyes,
> We shall be call'd purgers, not murderers.
>   (2.1.166–80)

Interestingly, some of these motifs recur when Caius Ligarius enters dressed like a sick man and explicitly refers to Brutus as an "exorcist" who gave health: "Brave son, deriv'd from honourable loins! / Thou, like an exorcist, hast conjur'd up / My mortified spirit" (2.1.321–24).

There is, however, an ambiguity in Caius Ligarius' speech, for in Elizabethan usage "exorcise" can mean to raise a spirit as well as to expel one, and this ambigu-ity perhaps foreshadows the ironic turn that events in Rome are to take. Is Brutus an exorcist or a conjurer, Rome's doctor or the means by which the spirit of Caesar is permanently established in the state?

Early in the play, Cassius rather sardonically introduces the notion of conjura-tion when he attempts to move Brutus against Caesar by speaking of the relative power of their names:

---

[10]See Stirling's influential "Or Else This Were a Savage Spectacle," *PMLA*, 66 (1951), 765–74. My reading differs significantly from Stirling's in that I do not see the play as treating ritual with enlight-ened scorn. Naomi Conn Liebler, "'Thou Bleeding Piece of Earth': The Ritual Ground of *Julius Caesar*," *Shakespeare Studies*, 14 (1981), 175–96, is particularly concerned with Shakespeare's use of Roman rituals. Her argument is that in the Caesarean period there was confusion about ritual practices as one social order was coming to an end and another was emerging. Brutus' desire to preserve ritual seriousness, to treat the assassination as a religious sacrifice, suggests, in her reading, his "impossibly idealistic conservatism" (p. 180).

Brutus and Caesar: what should be in that "Caesar"?
Why should that name be sounded more than yours?
Write them together, yours is as fair a name;
Sound them, it doth become the mouth as well;
Weigh them, it is as heavy; conjure with 'em,
"Brutus" will start a spirit as soon as "Caesar".

(1.2.140–45)

Later, in his soliloquy over Caesar's corpse, Antony imagines civil war in Italy with "Caesar's spirit, ranging for revenge" (3.1.270). Antony no doubt is only speaking metaphorically, and yet, together with other allusions to exorcism and conjuration, his picture of the ranging spirit invites us to consider the play's action as an attempt at exorcism that turns into a conjuration, two rituals that are dangerously similar in that each involves the demonstration of power over spirits.[11] In any case, the play makes much of Caesar's spirit, and at the end that spirit does literally range the world, manifesting itself to us as well as to Brutus before the battle of Philippi.

III

But to speak of *Julius Caesar* in terms of spirits and conjuration perhaps seems odd. We may be more accustomed to thinking of this play as a hard-headed political study, one that treats Brutus' attempt to ritualize and purify the assassination with scornful irony. Our approach tends to be in the skeptical vein of Cassius or in that of Antony, who regards the assassination as exactly what Brutus sought to avoid, a butchery. And yet although Antony, the cynical manipulator of the plebeians, may be disenchanted, *Julius Caesar*, with its ghost, its soothsayer, its prophetic dreams and supernatural prodigies, is not. The world of this play is fundamentally mysterious. Minor mysteries such as Cassius' death falling on his birthday are emphasized, and the play implies that Caesar was right to have grown superstitious, to have changed his opinion about dreams: the portents that prefigure the assassination are not merely daggers of the mind. By the play's end even Cassius has lost some of his enlightened skepticism and come to grant some credit to omens.

Of course we do not need to believe that Shakespeare himself had to be superstitious to write *Julius Caesar*. The Elizabethan stage was filled with supernatural beings such as witches, fairies, conjurers, and ghosts. Purged from the church by the new enlightenment of the Reformation, magic reappeared in the

[11]Exorcism, which was associated with the enemies of the Elizabethan establishment, was much in the news in the 1590s in connection with John Darrell, the famous Puritan exorcist whom the authorities put on trial as a fraud. For an account of this affair see D. P. Walker, *Unclean Spirits* (London, 1981), and for a suggestive recent discussion that is particularly concerned with possession and dispossession in relation to *King Lear* see Stephen Greenblatt, "Shakespeare and the Exorcists," in *After Strange Texts*, ed. Gregory S. Jay and David L. Miller (University, Ala., 1985), pp. 101–23.

ostensibly circumscribed and make-believe world of the theater. If sixteenth-century Englishmen could no longer experience the real physical presence of God on the altar in church, they could still experience the pretended physical manifestation of demons and spirits in the theater. We are sometimes inclined to dismiss the Puritan objections to the theater as sour crankiness, but their antagonism can perhaps be sympathetically comprehended as part of their larger campaign against superstition and idolatry.[12] Moreover, there is a real connection between magic, ritual, and drama, and it is sometimes hard to say where the boundary lies between attending a play that is about ritual and participating in a ritual.

Julius Caesar is a case in point. The assassination is so conspicuously ritualized—the conspirators kneeling before Caesar, the repeated stabbing, the ceremonial bathing in Caesar's blood, the clasping of purpled hands when Antony enters—that an audience may well feel that it is not only witnessing but participating in a kind of ceremony. Indeed, in its dramatic self-consciousness, the play calls attention to its special quality as a kind of ritual when, immediately after the death, Cassius speaks of it as an event that will provide high drama in future tongues and states:

Cassius:	Stoop then, and wash. How many ages hence
	Shall this our lofty scene be acted over,
	In states unborn, and accents yet unknown!
Brutus:	How many times shall Caesar bleed in sport,
	That now on Pompey's basis lies along,
	No worthier than the dust!
Cassius:	So oft as that shall be,
	So often shall the knot of us be call'd
	The men that gave their country liberty.
	(3.1.111–18)

This ritual quality is directly related to the special historical status of this play's subject: for the Elizabethans as for ourselves, the assassination of Julius Caesar was probably the single most famous event in ancient history. It would have been quite possible for Shakespeare to have suppressed our knowledge of this history in the interest of illusionism, of making us forget that we are attending a performance, but in fact he does the opposite. For example, the soothsayer who appears in the second scene and again just before the assassination activates our own retrospective foreknowledge. Again and again, Shakespeare in effect reminds us that the story is famous and the outcome known. What does the night of prodigies signify? What is the meaning of the beast in which Caesar's augurers cannot find a heart? What does Calphurnia's dream portend? For the characters these are riddles, and indeed the difficulty of interpreting becomes an important motif in the play. As Cicero says on the night of prodi-

[12]Michael O'Connell explores the seriousness of some of the Puritan objections in "The Idolatrous Eye: Iconoclasm, Anti-theatricalism, and the Image of the Elizabethan Theater," *ELH*, 52 (1985), 279–310.

gies, "men may construe things, after their fashion, / Clean from the purpose of the things themselves" (1.3.34–35). But the audience has no difficulty in construing these signs because we are participating in a reenactment of an event whose most important meanings are already known. Why should the name Caesar be sounded more than any other? Because, as we know, this name will become a title greater even than king. Why should the ghost of Caesar range the world? Because, as we know, the assassination was not the end of Caesarism but effectively the beginning.

A few words about the play's structure as historical drama are necessary. *Julius Caesar* is built upon a tautology: Caesar becomes Caesar, the past becomes the completed past that we know. Much like ourselves, the Elizabethans seem to have imagined ancient Rome in architectural terms, thinking of pillars, arches, and statues; and Shakespeare's Rome is notably a city of statues: Caesar's images, Junius Brutus' statue, the statue of Pompey the Great.[13] Cassius warns Brutus that Caesar has turned himself into a Colossus, and indeed Caesar, who repeatedly suppresses his private fears in order to play out his historical role as "Caesar," does present himself as a kind of monument. As a historical tragedy, then, *Julius Caesar* is built upon the tension between the present tense of dramatic reenactment and the past of history, between the ordinary flesh and blood of life and the immobile statues of antiquity. The play insists throughout upon Caesar's fleshly vulnerability: his falling sickness, his deafness, his near drowning in the Tiber, and his fever in Spain. What Shakespeare shows us is—to employ the grotesque imagery of Calphurnia's dream—marble statues spouting blood; or, conversely, it shows us flesh and blood aspiring to monumentality. Ironically, it is precisely because of his aspiration to a monumentality as fixed as the north star that Caesar is vulnerable to the conspirators' plot. "Hence! Wilt thou lift up Olympus?" (3.1.74) he exclaims the moment before the assassination. This is hubris of course, but in the different sense that the play's historical perspective provides, it is true. "Et tu, Brute?" As Caesar leaves behind the frailty of the flesh and enters history, Shakespeare gives him the one Latin line in the play, underscoring the transformation. The vulnerable man has been revealed as the marmoreal figure of history. Caesar has become Caesar.

What I am suggesting is that the play's mystifications, its magical elements, are associated with this tautological design. Couched in terms of prophecies and omens, our knowledge of events is represented in the drama as a magical necessity embedded in history. The result is that dramatic irony is raised to a metaphysical level and presented as fate. In this manner the play creates a feeling of necessity and persuades its audience that in witnessing Caesar's

---

[13]Collections of engravings of Roman ruins such as Hieronymus Cock's *Praecipua Aliquot Romanae Antiquitatis Ruinarum Monimenta* (Antwerp, 1551) or Antonios Lafreri's *Speculum Romanae* (Rome, 1579) would give a sense of ancient Rome as a city of gigantic columns, arches, and statues. John W. Velz, "The Ancient World in Shakespeare: Authenticity or Anachronism? A Retrospect," *Shakespeare Survey*, 31 (1978), 1–12, observes that "Shakespeare thought of Rome in architectural terms" (p. 11).

death and the collapse of the republican cause it has witnessed something inevitable.

IV

Why should Caesar's assassination and apotheosis as an immortal spirit be ceremonially repeated on the stage of the Globe? Why should Shakespeare conjure up Caesar? Considered not merely as a play about ritual but as itself a version of ritual, Shakespeare's historical drama becomes a ceremony of sacrifice and transcendence that I would like to term a kind of political Mass. As David Kaula has pointed out, there are Eucharistic overtones in Brutus' ceremonial charge to the conspirators to wash their hands in Caesar's blood, an action that echoes the New Testament invocations of Christ having "washed us from our sins in his blood" (Rev. 1.5). So, too, there are allusions to Christian sacrifice in Decius Brutus' interpretation of Calphurnia's dream, in which he claims that the statue spouting blood signifies that Caesar will be the source of renewal for Rome and that Romans will come to him, as to a saint, for "relics" (2.2.83–90). And there are similar overtones when Mark Antony, speaking over Caesar's body, tells the populace that if they heard Caesar's testament they

> would go and kiss dead Caesar's wounds,
> And dip their napkins in his sacred blood,
> Yea, beg a hair of him for memory,
> And, dying, mention it within their wills,
> Bequeathing it as a rich legacy
> Unto their issue.
>
> (3.2.134–39)

"Behind all the oblique allusions to Christian sacrifice," Kaula remarks, "lurks the notion that what the conspirators produce is a disastrous imitation of the true redemptive action.[14] The assassination of Caesar is in other words merely a parody of Christian sacrifice. What I want to suggest by speaking of the play as a kind of political mass, however, is an alternative way of understanding these Eucharistic overtones. Brutus may be misguided in his conception of the assassination, Decius Brutus may be trying to flatter Caesar in order to persuade him to go to the Senate House, and Mark Antony may be a demagogue manipulating a crowd; nevertheless, like the mass, *Julius Caesar* centers upon a sacrificial death that initiates a new era in history, the emergence of imperial Rome. Perhaps the association of Caesar and Christ is not wholly ironic.

Let us recall again the intermingling of religion and politics in the sixteenth century. The struggle within the church, glanced at in the opening scene, rep-

[14]Kaula, "'Let us be Sacrificers': Religious Motifs in *Julius Caesar*," pp. 209–10. The pattern of Eucharistic allusions in the play was also pointed out to me by Frank Burch Brown at the American Academy of Religion in 1985.

resents one aspect of this intermingling. Another is the way the crown penetrated the church. The penetration was literal; in place of the holy rood the royal coat of arms was erected in the chancel arch of English churches. At the same time, religious forms such as the figure of the double nature of the man-god Christ were systematically displaced onto the political sphere. Drained out of the official religion, magic and ceremony reappeared not only on the stage, but in the equally theatrical world of the court, where, for example, something reminiscent of the rejected cult of the Virgin reappeared as the cult of Gloriana with its attendant rites and ceremonies such as the spectacular Accession Day celebrations.

Particularly interesting, given the statues in *Julius Caesar*, the destruction of "popish idols" was paralleled by the rise of the sacred image of Elizabeth, forever young and beautiful. Shakespeare's Caesar turns himself into a monument of greatness; Shakespeare's Queen did something not altogether different, presenting herself as a living idol to be worshiped.[15] Moreover, the Roman imperial theme had immediate significance in sixteenth-century England where Elizabeth, determined to maintain her independence from the threatening powers of Catholic Europe, dressed herself in the symbolism of an empress, the heir ultimately of the Caesars.[16] Even Caesarian triumphs were part of her style. In 1588 she marked the defeat of the Spanish Armada with an entry into London in the ancient Roman manner, and one of the most famous of her late portraits, the procession picture attributed to Robert Peake, is as we now understand a version of the triumph *á l'antique* with affinities to Mantegna's *Triumph of Caesar*.[17] Probably many in Shakespeare's audience would have been prepared to see parallels between the first Emperor, as Caesar was commonly if erroneously regarded, and the great Queen.[18]

I hardly mean to suggest that *Julius Caesar* is to be taken as an allegory, although some in Shakespeare's audience may have interpreted it in this way, as they evidently did *Richard II* a few years later. Nevertheless, the play does have political dimensions, and as a representation of the transformation of the Roman Republic into the Empire, *Julius Caesar* may be understood as yet another of the many originary myths of the Imperial Tudor State, a fable parallel in its way to that of the descent of true British authority from the ancestral

[15]John Phillips comments on the parallel decline of images of Christ and rise of images of Elizabeth; see *The Reformation of Images: Destruction of Art in England, 1535–1660* (Berkeley, Calif., 1973), esp. p. 119. On the displacement of religious themes onto the monarch see Frances A. Yates, *Astraea: The Imperial Theme in the Sixteenth Century* (London, 1975), pp. 29–87, and Roy Strong, *The Cult of Elizabeth: Elizabethan Portraiture and Pageantry* (London, 1977).

[16]See Yates, *Astraea*, esp. pp. 29–87. On the emergence of Tudor imperial claims in the reign of Henry VIII see Richard Koebner, " 'The Imperial Crown of This Realm': Henry VIII, Constantine the Great, and Polydore Vergil," *Bulletin of the Institute of Historical Research*, 26 (1953), 29–53.

[17]See Roy Strong, "Eliza Triumphans," in *The Cult of Elizabeth*, pp. 17–55. The royal entry of 1588 in a symbolic chariot-throne surmounted by a "Crowne Imperiall" is described by John Stowe, *Annales* (1631), p. 751, quoted by Strong, p. 120.

[18]I have noted that Kaula in " 'Let us be Sacrificers': Religious Motifs in *Julius Caesar*" suggests that Caesar can be associated with the Pope. Some in Shakespeare's audience may well have made this connection. Others, however, might have been more interested in the analogy with Elizabeth.

figure of Trojan Brute, or to that of the apocalyptic union of the red rose and the white. Furthermore, by transforming the historical fact of the defeat of Brutus and the republican movement in Rome into a metaphysical confirmation of the inevitability of imperial greatness, Shakespeare's play implicitly confirms the legitimacy of the Tudor state. And yet, even as it does this, *Julius Caesar* is far from univocal. Shakespeare's Caesar may be great, may even be the greatest man who ever lived in the tide of times, but he is also inflexible and pretentious. Nor is Brutus a foul traitor condemned to the deepest circle of Hell like Dante's Brutus, but rather a patriot and an idealist, albeit a misguided one.[19]

In the last years of the sixteenth century it became increasingly difficult for the old Queen to play the role of Gloriana. Elizabeth was still of course a figure of awe and admiration to her people, most of whom, including Shakespeare, had never known any other ruler; nevertheless, many of her loyal subjects were impatiently looking forward to the end of her reign. Office-seekers were anxious for advancement and for the titles of honor that Elizabeth so rarely bestowed, and the Puritans were waiting for a monarch more disposed to continuing the reformation of the church. To make matters worse, the old Queen obstinately refused to name her heir.[20] Perhaps *Julius Caesar* incorporates, in significantly displaced form, something of the ambivalence and frustration with which many regarded the resident deity of England in her final years. In any event, a suggestive doubleness inheres in the play, which allows us at once to do away with Caesar and to submit to him.

Drama, like any form of narrative, has as one of its functions the mediation of contradictions that lie too deep in the culture to be resolved or, sometimes, too deep even to be effectively articulated. Two years after *Julius Caesar* was performed, there was a confused and traumatic revolt in England, the Essex uprising. But this was not a revolution, for no general principles lay behind it, and it was pursued, significantly, in the form of loyalty to the Queen. The last years of Elizabeth's reign are still a long way from the Civil Wars and the public bleeding of King Charles. Nevertheless, the Puritan reformers, however loyal to the person of the Queen they might be as individuals, had made an important step toward the future with their subversive claim to an authority derived not from the crown but from the congregation. No bishop, no king. At stake in the controversy over discarding the ceremonies in the church and the attendant symbols of social legitimation was indeed the matter of power in the realm. In its strategic ambivalence, Shakespeare's play can perhaps be understood as mobilizing some of the contradictory feelings toward the absolute authority of the crown that were beginning to be felt even as early as 1599.

---

[19]Indeed, the play even treats Brutus' republican politics with some sympathy, although the anti-Caesarean voice as it speaks here is perhaps more the antithesis implicit in absolutist monarchy than it is classical republicanism. J. L. Simmons argues suggestively that the republicanism of *Julius Caesar* is colored by the radical ideal of "godly egalitarianism"; see *Shakespeare's Pagan World: The Roman Tragedies* (Charlottesville, Va., 1973), pp. 80–84.

[20]J. E. Neale discusses relevant aspects of the late Elizabethan court in "The Elizabethan Political Scene," in *Essays in Elizabethan History* (London, 1958), pp. 59–84.

"In the spirit of men there is no blood": Blood as Trope of Gender in *Julius Caesar*

Gail Kern Paster

What follows is intended to further two projects of historical reconstruction of the early-modern period: the first involves writing the body into cultural history; the second, deciphering the complex annotation of gender difference in apparently unambiguously gendered characters.[1] In this essay these two projects come together through an interrogation of Shakespeare's use of the bodily signs of blood and bleeding, particularly in *Julius Caesar*. At certain discursive occasions in the play, these signs function as historically specific attributes of gender, as important tropes of patriarchal discourse. The meaning of blood and bleeding becomes part of an insistent rhetoric of bodily conduct in which the bleeding body signifies as a shameful token of uncontrol, as a failure of physical self-mastery particularly associated with woman.

The bleeding body most relevant to my purposes here is that of Julius Caesar himself, in part because Caesar's corpse—that "bleeding piece of earth" (3.1.257)—undergoes a kind of exchange and display that is virtually unique for male protagonists in Shakespearean tragedy.[2] But the gender-specific meanings for blood and bleeding that I am trying to adduce and ground historically lead inevitably beyond Caesar to other Shakespearean Romans whose wounds, like Caesar's, bear the marks of gender difference and hint at the wider cultural meanings of blood and bleeding in early-modern Europe.

I am not claiming that the topos of Caesar's body is at all hidden in the text of the play; the Romans themselves obsessively thematize it. Nor can I claim that discussion of imagery of blood in *Julius Caesar* has any critical novelty, at least not since 1961 when Maurice Charney argued that the "central issue about the meaning of *Julius Caesar* is raised . . . by the imagery

From *Shakespeare Quarterly* 40, no. 3 (Fall 1989), 284–298. Reprinted by permission of *Shakespeare Quarterly*.

[1]Earlier, differently titled versions of this paper were presented at the 1987 MLA Special Session on Gender and Sexuality in Shakespeare and at a seminar on "Theorizing History" at the 1988 Shakespeare Association of America meeting. I am grateful to the chairs of these two sessions, R. L. Widmann and Karen Newman respectively, for their invitations and interest.

[2]Quotations from Shakespeare are from *The Complete Works*, eds. Stanley Wells and Gary Taylor (Oxford: Clarendon Press, 1986), and are cited parenthetically.

of blood."[3] But I would argue that the topos of Caesar's body, which connects obviously with the semantics of blood, takes on new significance in light of Mikhail Bakhtin's now-familiar distinction between two bodily canons and in light of the recent work of Caroline Walker Bynum on the openness of gender symbolism in late-medieval religious discourse and iconography.[4]

Bakhtin describes the grotesque, essentially medieval conception of an unfinished, self-transgressing open body of hyperactive orifices, against which he sees an emerging conception of the "classical" body, a body distinguished by somatic completedness and an opacity of surface that closes it off to undesired physical and social interaction.[5] While Bakhtin himself is silent on gender as logically a major element of bodily canons, Peter Stallybrass has recently demonstrated how some sixteenth-century conceptions of woman render her *"naturally* 'grotesque.'"[6] I would like to tease out the implications of Stallybrass's argument in order to assimilate the classical and grotesque bodily canons to the whole hierarchical structure of gender difference. If woman is naturally grotesque—which is to say open, permeable, effluent—man is naturally whole, closed, opaque, self-contained.

In *Julius Caesar* these bodily canons are evoked diacritically as one way of articulating "the crisis of difference" which engages the Roman state.[7] Shakespeare's construction of the bodily canons differs from Bakhtin's, however, in possessing a metonymic specificity that transvalues what is essentially comic in Bakhtin's formulation into a tragic and also a religious idiom. For Bakhtin the important fluids that the grotesque body takes such pleasure in producing belong to a symbolic category that he calls "gay matter"—dung, urine, sweat, and other bodily effluvia of the "lower stratum."[8] In the high discourse of Shakespeare's Roman tragedy, however, the semiotically vital fluid is blood and the essential bodily process is bleeding. Thus, I would agree with Charney that one way of phrasing the play's central political struggle up to the point at which civil war breaks out is to say that it occurs discursively as a strug-

---

[3]*Shakespeare's Roman Plays: The Function of Imagery in the Drama* (Cambridge, Mass.: Harvard Univ. Press, 1961), p. 48.

[4]See Mikhail Bakhtin, *Rabelais and His World*, trans. Hélène Iswolsky (1968; rpt. Bloomington: Indiana Univ. Press, 1984); and Caroline Walker Bynum, "The Body of Christ in the Later Middle Ages: A Reply to Leo Steinberg," *Renaissance Quarterly*, 39 (1986), 399–439, and *Jesus as Mother: Studies in the Spirituality of the High Middle Ages* (Berkeley and Los Angeles: Univ. of California Press, 1982).

[5]Bakhtin, pp. 19–30.

[6]"Patriarchal Territories: The Body Enclosed" in *Rewriting the Renaissance: The Discourses of Sexual Difference in Early Modern Europe*, eds. Margaret W. Ferguson, Maureen Quilligan, and Nancy Vickers (Chicago: Univ. of Chicago Press, 1986), pp. 123–42, esp. p. 126.

[7]I borrow this term from René Girard in *Violence and the Sacred*, trans. Patrick Gregory (Baltimore and London: Johns Hopkins Univ. Press, 1977), pp. 49–52. For relevant discussions of *Julius Caesar*, see the brief but suggestive comments of C. L. Barber and Richard Wheeler in *The Whole Journey: Shakespeare's Power of Development* (Berkeley and Los Angeles: Univ. of California Press, 1986), pp. 26, 36, and 236, and my *The Idea of the City in the Age of Shakespeare* (Athens: Univ. of Georgia Press, 1985), pp. 69–78.

[8]Bakhtin, pp. 334–35.

gle over kinds and meanings of blood and bleeding. But I would add that the discursive struggle is waged in increasingly gender-inflected terms. Both before and after the assassination, the conspirators use blood as a signifier that differentiates their bodies from Caesar's. They arrogate to themselves references to blood that belong to the symbolic order, and they justify their repudiation of Caesar by marking him discursively with the shameful stigmata of ambiguous gender, especially the sign of womanly blood. The assassination, then, discloses the shameful secret of Caesar's bodiliness: by stabbing and displaying his body, the conspirators cause the fallen patriarch to reveal a womanly inability to stop bleeding. Thus, in the funeral oration, Antony's rhetorical task is not only to deconstruct the term "honourable," which Brutus has appropriated for the conspirators, but to recuperate Caesar's body for his own political uses by redefining Caesar's blood and Caesar's bleeding.

It is important to begin by specifying how blood and bleeding could imply gender inflection in the cultural codes of early-modern England, because influential recent accounts of Renaissance anatomy and physiology can be construed as implying just the reverse. Thomas Laqueur's work, for instance, emphasizes the "flux and corporeal openness" usually associated with human physiology and the fungibility of such bodily fluids as blood, mother's milk, and semen. Both men and women produced semen, the fluid essential for conception; both men and women purged themselves of excess blood which their bodies could not turn into nutriment. Of course, women's purgative bleedings occurred monthly, while men's bleedings were merely occasional responses to a diagnosis of nutritional repletion. But for Laqueur this distinction does not affect the fundamental homology between male and female physiology.[9]

Laqueur's work offers a useful corrective to accounts of Renaissance notions of woman—such as that of Ian Maclean—that reduce gender differences to a rigid and relatively simple set of binary oppositions.[10] The hierarchical model by which woman's cold, moist body was an imperfect version of the hot, dry, well-regulated man's requires analogy rather than polarity as the essential conceptual mode. Further, as I have argued elsewhere, other bodily fluids besides semen and blood—such fluids as tears and urine—were also thought to be fungible.[11] But I would point out that Laqueur's version of the physiology of gender in Renaissance culture fails to account for the possibility of simultaneous and contradictory ways of conceptualizing sexual difference, and that the matter of bleeding in *Julius Caesar* and elsewhere is a relevant case in point. Thus, while menstrual blood might in medical or scientific contexts be regarded as identical in nature to blood produced in other ways, popular culture often followed scriptural prescriptions in demonizing menstrual blood and the men-

---

[9]"Orgasm, Generation, and the Politics of Reproductive Biology," *Representations*, 14 (1986), 1–41, esp. pp. 8–9.

[10]See Maclean's *The Renaissance Notion of Woman: A Study in the Fortunes of Scholasticism and Medical Science in European Intellectual Life* (Cambridge: Cambridge Univ. Press, 1980).

[11]"Leaky Vessels: The Incontinent Women of City Comedy," *Renaissance Drama*, n.s. XVIII (1987), 43–65, esp. pp. 49–50.

struating woman with a variety of taboos. And even medical science could use the menses to prove the natural inferiority of women.[12] Furthermore, because menstrual blood was thought to represent a plethora, menstruation as a process took on an economy of impurity and waste, so that upper-class women who ate rich, moist foods were thought to flow more heavily than their lower-class counterparts.[13]

For my purposes here, however, the most important point about menstrual bleeding is that, unlike the bleedings to which men resorted for purgative purposes, menstruation is an involuntary and thus to some degree a punitive process. Indeed, attitudes towards menstruation in the early-modern period often exhibit a double bind: while the fact of menstrual flow could be used of demonstrate the natural inferiority of women, the cessation or suppression of menses was also blamed for all manner of physical and emotional maladies peculiar to the sex.[14] It seems to me, then, *pace* Laqueur, that physiological homology between menstrual bleeding in women and occasional bloodlettings in men serves not to deny but to establish the difference between the two processes as an issue of self-control. Monthly bleeding signifies as a particularly charged instance of the female body's predisposition to flow out, to leak. Menstruation comes to resemble the varieties of female incontinence—sexual, urinary, linguistic—which served as powerful signs of woman's inability to exercise control over the workings of her own body.[15]

The relevance of this distinction to Caesar may become clear through comparison with other Shakespeare characters in whom shedding blood signifies self-control or its lack. One such instance occurs in Volumnia's vehement praise of male bloodshed:

> . . . It more becomes a man
> Than gilt his trophy. The breasts of Hecuba
> When she did suckle Hector looked not lovelier
> Than Hector's forehead when it spit forth blood
> At Grecian sword, contemning.
> (*Cor.*, 1.3.41–45)

Janet Adelman has seen in this striking image the deep linkage between feeding and phallic aggression in the play, which through the unspoken mediation of the infant's mouth transforms the heroic Hector "from infantile feeding mouth

[12]I do not mean to suggest that the physical inferiority of women was universally accepted; Ian Maclean (pp. 43–46) has demonstrated the extent of disagreement among ancient, patristic, and Renaissance authorities on this question. But I am interested to show how menstruation functions ideologically to support a theory of inferiority.

[13]Patricia Crawford, "Attitudes to Menstruation in Seventeenth-Century England," *Past and Present*, 91 (1981), 47–73, esp. pp. 70–72.

[14]Audrey Eccles, *Obstetrics and Gynaecology in Tudor and Stuart England* (Kent, Ohio: Kent State Univ. Press, 1982), pp. 49–50. An earlier discussion is Hilda Smith, "Gynecology and Ideology in Seventeenth-Century England" in *Liberating Women's History: Theoretical and Critical Essays*, ed. Berenice A. Carroll (Urbana: Univ. of Illinois Press, 1976), pp. 97–114.

[15]Paster, "Leaky Vessels," pp. 49–51.

to bleeding wound."[16] But also at issue, I would argue, is a barely suppressed anxiety that, in bleeding, the male body resembles the body of woman.[17] The physiological fungibility of blood and milk becomes crucial here in two ways, for it provides the symbolic linkage that Volumnia, aroused by Virgilia's feminine squeamishness, must acknowledge in order to deny. Foreheads, like breasts, can yield precious fluids. But in the patriarchal ethos for which Volumnia speaks, male forehead can and apparently must be differentiated from female breast by raising the question of self-control, self-possession, voluntarism. Male bleeding is represented as a "spitting forth," the combative verb serving to deny any causative power to the Grecian swords and to endow the forehead itself with voluntary agency and passion. If struck, the seat of reason will bleed voluntarily from contempt rather than involuntarily from an enemy's external blow. Hecuba gives her milk to Hector, but Hector does not give his blood to Grecian swords. His would seem to be the kind of blood which in its agency and power "more becomes a man," the kind of bleeding that differentiates manliness from motherhood.

It is true, as Caroline Bynum has pointed out, that manliness could be assimilated to motherhood in late-medieval religious discourse, particularly in the conventional iconography of Christ lactating blood.[18] Later, we will see the relevance of this image to the bleeding Caesar. Here it is important only to note that Christ's bleeding was necessarily perceived as a freely willed act and that Christ, unlike Hector, bleeds out of pity, not contempt. To bleed in contempt, then, is to reverse the imputation of woundedness and vulnerability, to deny permeability—or to displace one kind of bodily canon with another. Though an unwanted physical contact has occurred, the more negative implications of male bleeding can be effaced in narrative representation.

A similar inference can be drawn when Martius himself appears, bleeding but seeking to define the physical process as both voluntary and therapeutic: "The blood I drop is rather physical / Than dangerous to me" (1.6.18–19). The evident fact of permeability can be effaced through the assertion of personal control in a therapeutic idiom; he has allowed to flow, he has *dropped* only the excess. Such blood is voluntary in two senses: it is shed as a result of action engaged in freely, and it is shed virtually at will, "the blood *I* drop." When Martius later beseeches Cominius "[b]y th' blood we have shed together" to

---

[16]"'Anger's My Meat': Feeding, Dependency, and Aggression in *Coriolanus*" in *Shakespeare: Pattern of Excelling Nature*, eds. Jay L. Halio and David Bevington (Newark: Univ. of Delaware Press, 1978), pp. 108–24, esp. p. 110.

[17]Another instance of the bloody body as female is the murdered Duncan; see Janet Adelman's recent essay, "'Born of Woman': Fantasies of Maternal Power in *Macbeth*" in *Cannibals, Witches, and Divorce: Estranging the Renaissance*, ed. Marjorie Garber (Baltimore and London: Johns Hopkins Univ. Press, 1987), pp. 90–121, esp. p. 95. That blood is the agent of gender transformation, however, is only implicit in Adelman's remarks, which focus instead on Macduff's reference to Duncan's body as a "new Gorgon." Perhaps more relevant to my purposes is the sleepwalking Lady Macbeth's exclamation: "Yet who would have thought the old man to have had so much blood in him?" (5.1.38–39).

[18]See *Jesus as Mother*, pp. 112–13, and "The Body of Christ in the Later Middle Ages," p. 403.

return him to the fight (1.7.57), his invocation releases all the latent causal ambiguity of a verb that simultaneously signifies blood flowing from others and oneself, and blood being cast off, "shed" like surface exuvia. To have excess blood to shed, therefore, does not create gender difference; what does is the possibility of shedding it at will. The male subject can regard such an action, therapeutically, as purgative and thus define it as enhancing rather than endangering somatic integrity.

The psychic precariousness of this kind of definition is clear in Coriolanus' refusal to show the plebeians his wounds and beg their voices in his election. Janet Adelman is surely right to see this horror as rooted in Coriolanus' fear of dependency, a dependency we have seen imaged in the play through the identification of feeding mouth and bleeding wound.[19] The play's language seems particularly severe in this regard, allowing for no saving categorical distinctions between new and old wounds, between blood and scars. It is only logical then that the imputation of dependency conjoins with the fact of compulsion: the autonomy that Coriolanus has claimed in shedding blood in battle is threatened by his forced, involuntary displaying of his wounds.

The political implication of involuntary display is even clearer on those frequent occasions when Shakespeare associates blood freely flowing with the body of woman or with a bodily passivity linked to the subject position of woman. In *Titus Andronicus,* for instance, Lavinia's bleeding body is likened to "a conduit with three issuing spouts" (2.4.30); in her mouth,

> Alas, a crimson river of warm blood,
> Like to a bubbling fountain stirred with wind,
> Doth rise and fall between thy rosèd lips,
> Coming and going with thy honey breath.
> (2.4.22–25)

The fountain, Albert Tricomi reminds us, "is conventionally associated with the female sexual organs." In scriptural imagery a stopped fountain symbolizes virginity and the flowing or bubbling fountain therefore represents "lost virginity."[20] But the language of Tricomi's interpretation, in service to a moral-allegorical critical practice, sublimates the physicality of what is represented so bloodily onstage: in a precise and wholly conventional metonymic replacement of mouth for vagina, the blood flowing from Lavinia's mutilated mouth stands for the vaginal wound which cannot be staged or represented but which has charged these images of warmth, movement, and breath with a peculiar eroticism.

Furthermore, to the extent that images of fountains and rivers connote ceaseless, natural flow rather than sexual violence, they mask or subordinate the fact of bodily penetration. But blurring the idea of causality for Lavinia's woundedness does not work to reverse the imputation of vulnerability, to

[19] "'Anger's My Meat,'" pp. 114–15.
[20] "The Mutilated Garden in *Titus Andronicus,*" *Shakespeare Studies*, 9 (1976), 89–105, esp. p. 94.

enhance Lavinia's agency, as was the case with Hector's forehead. On the contrary, to liken Lavinia's body to "a conduit with three *issuing* spouts" (emphasis mine) is to make her blood seem to issue from an absent, transcendent source, to make her blood seem hardly her own. As a result, the blood flowing from Lavinia's mouth seems almost to become the sign of an immutable condition—the condition of womanhood—just as the sexual wound of defloration itself is symbolically a wound the female body can never heal. But these meanings are inseparable ultimately from the more conventional meaning of vaginal blood as a sign of male mastery over the body of woman or (as here) of male sexual violence.[21] In a chain of metonymies, Lavinia's inability to prevent her rape is equivalent to her inability to stop bleeding, is equivalent also to her inability to speak her own bodily condition. That the bleeding body of her sexual violation symbolizes—even as it results from—the political incapacity of the male Andronici may partly explain why Titus' own mutilation resembles hers, represents his overmastering by oedipally driven younger males. Even here, though, we ought to note that, unlike Lavinia, Titus mutilates himself, and his wound is at some level, therefore, like Coriolanus' or Hector's, *willed.*

If we can see gender inflection in the symbolism of flowing blood, we can then see the dramatic role of blood in what I would call the bodily canon of the tragic grotesque—a canon represented most obviously by the physical transformation of Julius Caesar. The gender-inflectedness of flowing blood bears significantly upon the assassination of Caesar, for, like Lavinia, Caesar cannot prevent his political victimization, cannot stop bleeding, and—when his body is displayed ceremonially—is dependent on the voices of others to speak the meaning of his wounds. That these conditions combine to position Caesar as a woman in relation to the conspirators—with all the attendant political disabilities—becomes clear both in the play's bodily discourse and in the presentational contrast of Caesar's wounds with the self-wounding of Portia. It is a contrast that precisely reverses the contrasts between Lavinia on the one hand and Coriolanus and Titus on the other, a contrast that underscores the play's marked redistribution of gender attributes.

In the explicitly politicized idiom of *Julius Caesar,* the ideological potentiality of the bodily canons and their use in the attribution of gender become especially apparent. For the conspirators the most disturbing implication of Caesar's desire to be crowned is that it would replace differences with Difference. That is, it would replace a horizontal structure of highly individuated males within a traditionally self-authorizing class with a vertical structure that effaces all forms of patrician differentiation except that of not-being-Caesar. Furthermore, because the conspirators tend to present their own political integrity in somatic

[21]For a cogent discussion of the symbolism of vaginal blood and its relation as well to menstrual blood, see the now-classic essay by Louis Adrian Montrose, " ' Shaping Fantasies': Figurations of Gender and Power in Elizabethan Culture" in *Representing the English Renaissance*, ed. Stephen Greenblatt (Berkeley and Los Angeles: Univ. of California Press, 1988), pp. 31–64, esp. pp. 62–63, n. 44.

terms, their body images and Caesar's necessarily become functionally interrelated. If Caesar grows, the conspirators shrink; if Caesar reveals bodily weakness, the conspirators gain in strength; if Caesar is sick, the conspirators are whole. The process as it works here politically bears an obvious structural resemblance to social and medical constructions of gender—strong man, weak (even sick) woman. Not surprisingly, then, elements of Renaissance sexual binarism come increasingly into play, particularly that gendered equation by which men are associated with spirit and the symbolic order generally, women with matter.[22] To allow Caesar sway over themselves, Cassius implies, is thus symbolically to accede to a shameful feminization:

> . . . Romans now
> Have thews and limbs like to their ancestors.
> But woe the while! Our fathers' minds are dead,
> And we are governed with our mothers' spirits.
> Our yoke and sufferance show us womanish.
> (1.3.79–83)

While the body of the father seems to be reproduced physically in the present, the *gender* of that body—says Cassius—has become shamefully and obviously ambiguous: "Our yoke and sufferance *show us* womanish."

The conspirators can only remake themselves, it would seem, by regendering Caesar; they can throw off the appearance of womanishness by displacing their own sense of gender-indeterminacy onto the body of their adversary and renegotiating the differences between themselves and Caesar in the diacritical terms of the bodily canons. From this point of view, the much-noticed instability of Cassius' representation of Caesar in 1.2 is less a symptom of Cassius' own psychic fragility than it is the necessary discovery of grotesqueness in Caesar, who is notably weak "[a]s a sick girl" (1.2.130) yet prodigiously appetitive and swollen to immense proportions: "Upon what meat doth this our Caesar feed / That he is grown so great?" (1.2.150–51). This contradiction between Caesar's physical inferiority to the other conspirators and his political domination of them bears an obvious resemblance to the chief political paradox of Elizabethan England—the queen herself. Elizabethan political theory, of course, managed the paradox by mystifying the queen's virginity and distinguishing her body iconographically from those of other women.[23] In *Julius Caesar* this contradiction remains necessarily unresolved as Cassius' speech oscillates between literal narratives of Caesar's physical infirmities and explicitly figurative assignments of power, size, godhead:

> When could they say till now, that talked of Rome,
> That her wide walls encompassed but one man?

[22]Maclean, p. 2 and passim.
[23]See Montrose, pp. 49–50; on the cult of Elizabeth, see Roy C. Strong, *Portraits of Queen Elizabeth I* (Oxford: Clarendon Press, 1963) and his *The Cult of Elizabeth* (London: Thames and Hudson, 1977).

> Now is it Rome indeed, and room enough
> When there is in it but one only man.
>   (1.2.155–58)

The speech displays Cassius' need to find Caesar imperiling discursive as well as social boundaries. Caesar transgresses against the social body: by occupying more than his share of Rome, he offends against those norms for interpersonal behavior that Norbert Elias tells us were being promulgated with increasing efficiency throughout Europe in the sixteenth century.[24] The famous first scene has already shown that the right to urban space, to a place within the wide walls of Rome, is a function of vested class interests. The plebeians' enthusiasm for Caesar offends against both time and place, indecorously leading them to wear the wrong clothes, to cull a holiday "out" of time and strew flowers when and where they do not belong.[25] For Cassius such structural disruptions originate in Caesar's own lack of decorum just as his rude refusal to "contain" himself bespeaks a threat to the exclusive community of gender: he would be "but one only man."

This imputation of bodily offence in Caesar—with all its repercussions in the social formation—has two immediate consequences. First, it allows Cassius to place the apparent contradiction between Caesar's political size and strength, on one hand, and his physical weakness, on the other, within the discursive logic of the bodily canons, to thematize his body as monstrously grotesque and structurally disruptive. Even the strange meteorological events on the eve of the assassination arise symbolically from Caesar's grotesque bodily uncontainment:

> . . . Now could I, Casca,
> Name to thee a man most like to this dreadful night,
> That thunders, lightens, opens graves. and roars
> As doth the lion in the Capitol;
> A man no mightier than thyself or me
> In personal action, yet prodigious grown,
> And fearful, as these strange eruptions are.
>   (1.3.71–77)

Second, it allows Cassius and the other conspirators to maintain a sense of somatic integrity, primarily by distinguishing between their own physical self-control and Caesar's lack of it. Caesar is not the only Roman to manifest illness or handicap, but many of the play's references to Caesar's body before the assassination seek to interrogate his bodily condition in terms of self-control. When Caesar chooses to swim the Tiber out of rivalry with Cassius, his body fails him, as it later does by contracting fever on campaign in Spain, and as it will do in the marketplace when the plebeians utter their "deal of stinking

---

[24]*The Civilizing Process*, trans. Edmund Jephcott, 2 vols. (Oxford: Basil Blackwell, 1978), Vol. I (*The History of Manners*), 53–55.
[25]Richard Wilson, "'Is This a Holiday?': Shakespeare's Roman Carnival," *ELH*, 54 (1987), 31–44, esp. p. 32.

breath" (1.2.246). The aged conspirator, Ligarius, by contrast, comes to Brutus' house to "discard [his] sickness" (2.1.320) with the kerchief that was its emblem.

More important, Brutus consistently frames the conspiracy itself in the canonical terms of the classical body—specifically, in terms of what the body contains or "bears": Brutus would be sure that the conspirators individually "bear fire enough / To kindle cowards and to steel with valour / The melting spirits of women . . ." (2.1.119–21). In such bodies vital fluids are represented as having lost the stigma of materiality in order to become symbolic signifieds of patriarchal authority. Similarly, the assertion of somatic integrity in the conspiracy, imaged as a patriarchal body of the whole, requires that oath-taking be superfluous to the common bodily seal of fellowship:

> . . . do not stain
> The even virtue of our enterprise,
> Nor th'insuppressive mettle of our spirits,
> To think that or our cause or our performance
> Did need an oath, when every drop of blood
> That every Roman bears, and nobly bears,
> Is guilty of a several bastardy
> If he do break the smallest particle
> Of any promise that hath passed from him.
>   (2.1.131–39)

To break is to bleed shamefully, to be revealed as bearing other than patriarchal blood. Patriarchal blood in such a formulation is the blood one cannot bleed, the blood that cannot be spilled without changing its nature. "In the spirit of men," says Brutus with more than tautological force,

> there is no blood.
> O, that we then could come by Caesar's spirit,
> And not dismember Caesar! But, alas,
> Caesar must bleed for it.
>   (2.1.168–71)

Later in the same scene, Portia's self-wounding and voluntary self-display corroborate the significance of bodily intactness as an ideological format of gender. Portia stakes her claim to knowledge of the conspiracy by seeking to efface the physical difference that separates her from her husband, difference that Brutus himself seems intent upon marking. Since Shakespeare's text omits any prior references to Portia's illness (which Plutarch explains as a fever brought on by her self-wounding), Brutus' greeting of her is less explicable as a reference to specific illness than as an invocation of difference:

> Portia, what mean you? Wherefore rise you now?
> It is not for your health thus to commit
> Your weak condition to the raw cold morning.
>   (2.1.233–35)

Her response—"Nor for yours neither" (1. 236)—by effectively denying difference in their conditions, undermines both hierarchy and gender as causes for
her exclusion. In fact Portia, appropriating the term "condition," remarks upon
Brutus' own bodily behaviors when contemplating the conspiracy—his sudden
gestures, sighs, stares, head-scratching, foot-stamping. She attributes them to the
involuntary, even potentially transforming effects of "humour" (1. 249). It is an
explanation that opens to question Brutus' own bodily state, even perhaps his own
determinacy of gender. The humor

> . . . will not let you eat, nor talk, nor sleep;
> And could it work so much upon your shape
> As it hath much prevailed on your condition,
> I should not know you Brutus.
> (2.1.251–54)

Portia's desire is to assimilate the bond of marriage with the bond of conspiracy, to have room in Rome rather than dwell in the suburbs of Brutus' good
pleasure. She thus resorts to the only move by which woman's alterity could be
effectively blurred or modified; she replaces the categorical restrictions of definition by gender—which, as Stallybrass says, construct women-as-the-same—
with the privileges of definition by class, or, even more narrowly, of definition
by family:[26]

> I grant I am a woman, but withal
> A woman that Lord Brutus took to wife.
> I grant I am a woman, but withal
> A woman well reputed, Cato's daughter.
> Think you I am no stronger than my sex,
> Being so fathered and so husbanded?
> (2.1.291–96)

Of course, in this claim to exceptional status, Portia affirms politically con-
straining gender norms for the rest of her sex, as Queen Elizabeth did. What
she must distance herself from, above all, is woman's proverbial talkativeness,
a condition linked culturally with the whores who dwelled in the suburbs and
who were conventionally emblematized by the leaking barrel.[27] It was
woman's normative condition to leak; Lavinia's bleeding body, as we have
seen, constitutes the tragic representation of the trope. But Portia, unable by
talking to prove her ability to keep still, turns to self-mutilation. The gesture
seems intended to imitate in little the suicides that Roman patriarchy val-
orized as the supreme expression of personal autonomy. It thus adumbrates
her own and the other suicides at the end of the play. Still, there is an apparent paradoxicality in Portia's act—opening one's body to prove a capacity not
to leak or break—which is worth noting for its relevance to images of Caesar
before and after the assassination. In Plutarch's account the scene of Portia's

---

[26]"Patriarchal Territories," p. 133.
[27]Paster, "Leaky Vessels," p. 52.

self-wounding is graphic, a little grotesque (thanks to the barber), and impressively bloody:

> . . . she took a little razor such as barbers occupy to pare men's nails, and, causing her maids and women to go out of her chamber, gave herself a great gash withal in her thigh, that she was straight all of a gore-blood; and, incontinently after, a vehement fever took her, by reason of the pain of her wound.[28]

In the play, however, though the wound must somehow be physically demonstrable, Shakespeare chooses to present it only after the fact—far less bloodily than does Plutarch and without emphasizing the "incontinent" fever that Portia's pain brought on. Portia does not stand like mute Lavinia with blood flowing uncontrollably, and she does not require a male voice to signify her bodily condition: "I have made strong proof of my constancy, / Giving myself a voluntary wound / Here in the thigh" (2.1.298–300). In this reading Portia calls attention to this bodily site not to remind Brutus of her femaleness, her lack of the phallus, but rather to offer the wound as substitute phallus. Hers is not the involuntary wound of the leaking female body but the honorifically gendered, purgative, *voluntary* wound of the male. She has bled not, like Lavinia, with a wound that cannot heal, but like Coriolanus, like Hector.[29]

In her painful imitation of patriarchal bodily canons, Portia valorizes the conspirators' need to stigmatize Caesar's body discursively with the marks of difference, and, by taking on maleness, she furthers the conspirators' ideological project of regendering Caesar. This project becomes most overt in Decius Brutus' interpretation of Calphurnia's dream, which, as David Kaula has argued, represents Caesar typologically as the redeemer Christ shedding blood for his people. Kaula is right, I think, to see the specific influence here of the medieval cult of the Holy Blood, which publicized miraculous stories of bleeding statues and paintings of Christ.[30] Caesar, as Decius Brutus anticipates, responds positively to this sacerdotal image of himself (perhaps even becoming a victim of witty anachronism on Shakespeare's part in Caesar's ignorance of basic Christian typology about the self-sacrificial nature of the Christ he is made to resemble here).

But even more significant in the exegesis, I would argue, is a detail that Kaula and other interpreters have passed over or evaded: i.e., that Decius Brutus specifically allegorizes Caesar as a lactating figure, a statue or fountain lactating blood:

[28]This passage from *The Life of Marcus Brutus* in Thomas North's *Plutarch's Liues of the Noble Grecians and Romanes* [1579] is reprinted, along with several others, in the Oxford Shakespeare *Julius Caesar*, ed. Arthur Humphries (Oxford: Clarendon Press, 1984), p. 236.

[29]I thus agree with Madelon Sprengnether that in Portia's self-wounding, manliness is equated with injury, "that the sign of masculinity becomes the wound" ("Annihilating Intimacy in *Coriolanus*" in *Women in the Middle Ages and the Renaissance: Literary and Historical Perspectives*, ed. Mary Beth Rose [Syracuse, N.Y.: Syracuse Univ. Press, 1986], p. 96). For an extended riff on possible (if improbable) sexual puns in this speech, see Frankie Rubinstein's entry for "thigh" in *A Dictionary of Shakespeare's Sexual Puns and their Significance* (London: Macmillan, 1984), p. 273.

[30]"'Let Us Be Sacrificers': Religious Motifs in *Julius Caesar*," *ShStud*, 14 (1981), 197–214, esp. p. 204.

Your statue spouting blood in many pipes,
In which so many smiling Romans bathed,
Signifies that from you great Rome shall *suck*
Reviving blood, and that great men shall press
For tinctures, stains, relics, and cognizance.
                                   (2.2.85–89, emphasis mine)

Caroline Bynum has recently demonstrated that images and textual representations of a lactating Christ were familiar in late-medieval Christian worship. The idea took varying forms: the body of the church, itself depicted symbolically as *ecclesia lactans,* was identified with the body of Christ; or Christ's nurturing flesh was identified with nurturing female flesh; or the bodily wound suffered at the Crucifixion was depicted near the breast in order to suggest a bleeding nipple.[31] (All these images are related, furthermore, to the self-sacrificial emblem drawn from natural lore—the mother pelican who, Christlike, pecks her own breast to feed her young.) This iconography depends in the first place on medieval physiology, which, as we have seen, reduced all bodily fluids to blood. Just as medieval typology, for example, could assimilate the blood Christ shed on the cross with the blood shed at his circumcision and even with the monthly bleedings of women, so too could medieval Christianity through the patristic analogy of spirit:flesh::male:female see the humanized Christ as having a female body.[32] What Bynum's brilliant analysis allows us to recognize is the distance between our frame of reference and that of our forebears, who, far more than we, tended to perceive the female body as food and who "assumed considerable mixing of the genders."[33]

But, while late-medieval Christians may not have seen any indecorum in the idea of a male deity giving suck from a flowing breast to spiritually hungry worshippers, such may not be the case with modern students of Shakespeare who have avoided commenting on Decius Brutus' crucial choice of verb here—or even with early-modern Londoners whose cultural attitudes towards the female breast and breast-feeding, as Dorothy McLaren has suggested, were changing.[34] It was still possible, for instance, for King James in *Basilikon Doron* to recommend as one of a king's "fairest styles, to be called a loving nourish-father to the Church."[35] Yet, the idea expressed here by James is left somatically indefinite, a reference to maternal function apart from maternal anatomy. James does not, like the lactating Christ, offer his body, even symbolically, as food, nor was he depicted with a flowing breast. On the contrary, as the breast became increas-

[31]"The Body of Christ in the Later Middle Ages," pp. 414–17 and plate 9, p. 429.
[32]"The Body of Christ in the Later Middle Ages," pp. 421–22. Bynum's latest discussion of this theme appears in *Holy Feast and Holy Fast: The Religious Significance of Food to Medieval Women* (Berkeley and Los Angeles: Univ. of California Press, 1987), pp. 263–65.
[33]"The Body of Christ in the Later Middle Ages," p. 435.
[34]"Marital fertility and lactation 1570–1720" in *Women in English Society 1500–1800*, ed. Mary Prior (London and New York: Methuen, 1985), pp. 22–53, esp. pp. 27–28.
[35]*The Political Works of James I*, ed. Charles Howard McIlwain (Cambridge, Mass.: Harvard Univ. Press, 1918), pp. 3–52, esp. p. 24; quoted also in Stephen Orgel, "Prospero's Wife," *Representations*, 8 (1984), 1–12, esp. p. 9.

ingly eroticized and as suckling of infants or sick adults became the nearly
exclusive province of lower-class women, the image of the flowing breast was
becoming more strictly associated with woman.[36] It is arguable, then, that part
of the complex irony here in the image of a suckling Caesar lies in its semiotic
ambiguity in the matter of gender. Caesar responds to an interpretation of the
image that seems to construe his body, like Christ's, as a magically powerful,
ungendered symbolic source of nurturance; the image seems, in one possible
construction, to offer the childless patrician a suitably powerful patriarchal styl-
ization. But the image also serves to give expression to the conspirators' more
obscure need to re-mark Caesar's body with femaleness and to cause his
body—even if, as here, only discursively—to leak like a woman's. Such bleeding—since it would signify the conspirators' overmastering of Caesar—cannot
truly resemble the freely willed eucharistic offering of Christ nor the patriarchal self-stylization of James. Yet this is exactly how Decius Brutus interprets
blood-flow to Caesar here, flattering him with an ambiguous, equivocal self-
image in which there is a concealed irony: the image of god yields to an image
of woman.

The ironic instability of Caesar's final, haughty affirmation of patriarchal
constancy and phallic power—"Hence! Wilt thou lift up Olympus?" (3.1.74)—is
manifest in the feminizing effect of his bloody death. For there is a precise and
evocative resemblance between the flowing body of Lavinia, with its "three
issuing spouts," and the bleeding corpse of Caesar, its streaming wounds
metaphorized as bodily orifices, "Weeping as fast as they stream forth thy
blood" or "like dumb mouths [which] ope their ruby lips / To beg the voice and
utterance of my tongue" (3.1.202, 263–64). These are no "voluntary wounds,"
nor do they speak for themselves.

Indeed, Antony's recognition that Caesar's body depends on Antony's voice
is at the center of Antony's response to its newly feminized character as a
"bleeding piece of earth" (3.1.257). For Antony cannot deny Caesar's vulnerability, cannot, like Volumnia or Coriolanus, transform the flow of this blood into
a combative spitting forth. On the contrary, both Brutus and Antony respond to
the bloody corpse and to the blood-marked conspirators in the eroticized terms
of male initiation ceremonies—the blooding of maiden hunters, maiden warriors. A familiar canonical analogy is probably Prince Hal, who salutes his
brother after the battle with "full bravely hast thou fleshed / Thy maiden sword"
(*1H4*, 5.4.128–29). Here Brutus urges his conspirators to "bathe our hands in
Caesar's blood / Up to the elbows"—as if entering Caesar's body—"and
besmear our swords" (3.1.107–8). Antony urges the conspirators to "[f]ulfil your
pleasure" (1.160) by killing him too.

Standing over the body of Caesar and speaking the meaning of his death, the
conspirators seem momentarily to have resolved the crisis of difference for themselves in honorifically gendered terms. But the conspirators discover that to femi-

[36]See Marina Warner, *Alone of All Her Sex: The Myth and the Cult of the Virgin Mary* (New York: Knopf, 1976), p. 203, who argues for an increasingly class-specific semiosis of nursing.

nize Caesar by killing him is not to disable him; because, unlike any body's finite material existence, that body's discursivity is subject to seemingly endless renegotiation—and regendering. In a sense, to thematize Caesar's body—as the conspirators have done virtually from the beginning of the play—is already to have conceded the futility of actually killing him and the impossibility of controlling the semiotic uses to which his body and his blood can be put.[37]

While the hostile construction of Caesar as female has helped to sustain the conspiracy, the terms of that construction are neither stable nor exclusionary: Caesar dead is no less obscurely or complexly gendered than Caesar alive, and his femaleness empowers Antony no less than the conspirators themselves. Thus, it may be true, as Richard Wilson has recently argued, that the plebeian riot after seeing Caesar's body and hearing Antony's oration results from "the exposure of Caesar's naked will"; the signifier "will," which Wilson reads as a "phallic pun," is repeated, both as verbal auxiliary and as substantive twenty-seven times in thirty-six lines (3.2.126–61).[38] Yet, even if Antony does seek discursively to reinvest the body with a portion of its original phallic power, he and Shakespeare make even more significant use of what I regard as that body's (connotatively) female affectivity. Even to receive Caesar's body from the conspirators as a token of political exchange and denial of hostile intent suggests Antony's acceptance of its use-value as female and his own new patriarchal responsibilities to it.[39]

Dead, Caesar can be for Antony the perfect, mute Petrarchan object, demonstrably unable (like woman generally) to control the workings of his own body but thereby calling into being whatever powers of articulate closure his body's speaker possesses. Thus, the Petrarchan vocabulary that Antony deploys in signifying Caesar's corpse, first in the Capitol and later in the forum, acknowledges femaleness as a source of Caesar's difference but refigures his body as a discursive site not of contempt or anxiety but rather of desire. Instead of denying Caesar's female vulnerability, he reifies it in the rents and tears of Caesar's mantle: "Look, in this place ran Cassius' dagger through. / See what a rent the envious Casca made" (3.2.172–73). In Antony's sentimental allegorical narrative, Caesar's blood responds to Brutus as to an unkind suitor, with a rather adolescent, even girlish naiveté. As Brutus

> plucked his cursèd steel away,
> Mark how the blood of Caesar followed it,
> As rushing out of doors to be resolved
> If Brutus so unkindly knocked or no—
> For Brutus, as you know, was Caesar's angel.
> (3.2.175–79)

[37]For a related discussion of the semiotic uses of Caesar's toga, see Alessandro Serpieri, "Reading the signs: towards a semiotics of Shakespearean drama" in *Alternative Shakespeares*, ed. John Drakakis (London and New York: Methuen, 1985), pp. 119–43, esp. p. 133.

[38]Wilson (cited in n. 25, above), p. 39.

[39]On woman as object of exchange, see Gayle Rubin, "The Traffic in Women: Notes on the 'Political Economy' of Sex" in *Toward an Anthropology of Women*, ed Rayna R. Reiter (New York: Monthly Review Press, 1975), pp. 157–210.

Particularly telling in this context, then, is Antony's use of the trope of "put[ting] a tongue in every wound of Caesar," a figure that seems to oppose femaleness with a phallicized image of speech. These wounds, however, are "poor poor dumb mouths," as tongueless and silent as Lavinia. Antony "bid[s] them speak for" him, ironically, as if to mark their affective power as constituted by female silence. But the wounds here are also bodily orifices, sites of potential interrogation, places to put tongues in. By fetishizing them to the crowd, Antony can eroticize "sweet" Caesar's female woundedness as the explicit motive of his rhetorical power, the source of his voice. It is he who *puts* the tongue in Caesar's wounds:

> For I have neither wit, nor words, nor worth,
> Action, nor utterance, nor the power of speech,
> To stir men's blood. I only speak right on.
> I tell you that which you yourselves do know,
> Show you sweet Caesar's wounds, poor poor dumb mouths,
> And bid them speak for me. But were I Brutus,
> And Brutus Antony, there were an Antony
> Would ruffle up your spirits. and put a tongue
> In every wound of Caesar that should move
> The stones of Rome to rise and mutiny.
>
>   (3.2.216–25)

The outbreak of civil mutiny in Rome can be seen, then, to result not so much from the disclosure of Caesar's will—his maleness—as from the disclosure of his wounds, his femaleness, and from the affective power these wounds have in flowing to transform Antony from part to whole, from dependent limb to motivated speaker. Antony's oration cannot re-member Caesar nor restore to his bleeding corpse the intact ideal maleness of the classical body. Instead it takes up and redirects the political valences of the conspirators' own rhetoric of blood and bodily conduct, denying the conspirators exclusive rights to the Roman body politic. Womanly blood, however sublimated by Petrarchan discourse, has thus marked Caesar with the bodily sign of the tragic grotesque, but this marking has not achieved the conservative political results the conspirators had aimed for. Like all hegemonic efforts to limit signification and control the procedures of differentiation, the patriarchal attempt to limit and control the semiotics of Caesar's body was open to challenge. When Caesar was alive, his grotesqueness had served as justification for assassination; after he is dead, his grotesqueness diffuses throughout the body politic in the self-transgressions of civil war.

Antony in Behalf of the Play

Kenneth Burke

At times when the standards of criticism are set by a *receptive* class, as in the decadent stages of feudalism, the emphasis of the critic tends to be placed upon *consumption*. Matters of "appreciation" and "enjoyment" are the touchstones. Conversely, in the Art for Art's Sake movement of recent decades, we find the emphasis placed almost wholly upon *production*. Our practical inventors and business promoters of this period tended to emphasize the productive factor, assuming that in the large the matter of consumption would take care of itself—and there was a corresponding trend in aesthetics, with the essence of art being seen in the "self expression" of the artist.

Today, in nonliterary fields, we are stressing neither production nor consumption, but the *integration* of the two. And in the aesthetic field, this emphasis might be paralleled by a tendency to consider literature, not as a creator's device for self-expression, nor as an audience's device for amusement or instruction, but as a communicative relationship between writer and audience, with both parties actively participating. In such an approach, the poet's "self-expression" or the audience's "appreciation" will necessarily figure, but the main emphasis will be elsewhere.

This reader-writer relationship is emphasized in the following article, which is an imaginary speech by Antony. Instead of addressing the mob, as he is pictured in the third act of *Julius Caesar,* he turns to the audience. And instead of being a dramatic character *within* the play, he is here made to speak as a critical commentator *upon* the play, explaining its mechanism and its virtues. Thus we have a tale from Shakespeare, retold, not as a plot but from the standpoint of the rhetorician, who is concerned with a work's processes of appeal.

Act 3, Scene 2. *Antony has entered with the body of Caesar. Brutus has made his defense before the people, has won their sympathies to the cause of the conspirators, and has departed.*

Antony: Friends, Romans, countrymen . . . one—two—three syllables: hence, in this progression, a magic formula. "Romans" to fit the conditions of the play; "countrymen" the better to identify the play-mob with the mob in the

From *The Philosophy of Literary Form*, 3rd edition, revised (Berkeley: University of California Press, 1973), 329–343. Copyright ©1973 The Regents of the University of California. Reprinted by permission. This work first appeared in *The Southern Review* 1 (1935), 308–319.

pit—for we are in the Renaissance, at that point when Europe's vast national integers are taking shape, and all the wisdom that comes of the body is to be obscured by our putting in place of the body the political corpus, while we try to run this bigger hulk with the instincts for the little one—the Hobbesian metaphor—and the gloomy error has exalted us, so that no word handles as much, and as quickly, and as inexpressibly, as this word "countrymen," which must really mean, if pragmatic results are the test, that there is glory solely in being outdone by those within our own borders. Anyway, consider how much better my one-two-three arrangement is than was the opening salutation in Brutus' speech: "Romans, countrymen, lovers." He is an orator—but because you of England have thought the untrustworthy Latins eloquent, and because you don't think you are nearly so clever as you'd like to be, I shall seem closer to you if I apologize for bluntness. Yet how much more competent my opening syllables are: how much *truer*, since true to the processes of a spell, stressing a charm's *threeness*.

My Elizabethan audience, under the guise of facing a Roman mob I confront you at a most complicated moment. As a matter of fact, up to this point in our play you have been treated most outrageously. It can honestly be said that, in no major particular, have you been granted those clear and simple responses to which, as customers, you might feel yourselves entitled. Instead, your author has kept you in as vacillating a condition as this very Roman mob you have been watching with so little respect. I doubt if he distinguishes between the two of you. All that I as Antony do to this play-mob, as a character-recipe I do to you. He would play upon you; he would seem to know your stops; he would sound you from your lowest note to the top of your compass. He thinks you as easy to be played upon as a pipe.

Oh, there have been signs you recognize quickly, that you might feel familiar with the road upon which you have been stumbling. The conspirators have met during storms and in the "vile contagion of the night." They have pulled caps over their eyes. One plucked at another's sleeve. Such labels are easily read by anyone. The streets of Rome have bristled with bad omens. Caesar's wife has cried in sleep that they are murdering Caesar. Outlandish astronomical and biologic marvels have occurred—to point the direction of our plot and give it weight by implicating the very heavens. And finally, Caesar was struck with daggers. Yet these standard things have lured you into a region where you are not competent at all.

Consider the burden you now carry, as I step before the play-mob with the fresh-murdered body of Caesar. We have established a Caesar-principle and a Brutus-principle, though I blush to consider some of the devices whereby the two principles have been set into your minds. Realize for what slight reasons you have been willing to let Caesar die. (The conspirators would not so much as touch him until you also had been brought into their band. And when Casca shouted, "Speak, hands, for me!" stabbing great Caesar, those homicidal hands spoke for you also.) First, we had the portents, beginning with the soothsayer's admonition that Caesar beware the Ides of March. In showing how things were going, these signs prepared you somewhat to go in the same direction.

But in addition, *your sympathies have been poisoned.* Caesar a conqueror, a monarch by reason of his attainments? Yet he was deaf in one ear. He had the falling-sickness, and "swounded" from the intense strain of refusing a crown he coveted. "He had a fever when he was in Spain," cried out "like a sick girl," his feebleness amazing Cassius. Cassius was a better swimmer than Caesar—and when the two of them had leaped into the Tiber on a dare, Cassius had to pull out Caesar, to whom he must "bend his body if Caesar carelessly but nod on him." His wife is barren. For all his determination to be bold, there is a timid and superstitious trait in him. And worst, for an emperor, on a night of storm and portents he appeared on the stage in his nightgown—so let him die. For such reasons as these you are willing to put a knife through the ribs of Caesar.

Still, you are sorry for Caesar. We cannot profitably build a play around the horror of a murder if you do not care whether the murdered man lives or dies. So we had to do something for Caesar—and you would be ashamed if you stopped to consider what we did. I believe we made Caesar appealing by proxy. That is: I, Antony, am a loyal follower of Caesar; you love me for a good fellow, since I am expansive, hearty, much as you would be after not too heavy a meal; and as one given to pleasure, I am not likely to lie awake at night plotting you injury. If such a man loves Caesar, his love lifts up Caesar in your eyes.

I serve a double purpose. Not only do I let Caesar shine a bit warmly by his reflection of my glow, but when the actual *persona* of the Caesar-principle is dispatched by daggers, the principle lives on in me, who continue the function of Caesar in the play. In the next act, the fourth, the *persona* itself will reappear momentarily as a ghost in Brutus' tent—but on the whole, after Caesar's death, I am the plot-substitute for Caesar. No wonder Brutus, in his address to the play-mob but a short time ago, told them that only Caesar's vices had been slain, while his virtues lived on, still active. So they do, in me, whom you like because I am marked by so serviceable a trait as loyalty. And when this play is over, Antony alone of the major characters will live; for you like to have about you such a man as might keep guard at the door while you sleep. Given certain conceptions of danger, I become the sign of safety. A little sunshine-thought, to take home with you after these many slaughterings. Only as much of the Caesar-principle as will let you relax, is left to bid you goodnight—and the Brutus-principle will have died to purchase you this handsome privilege.

I grant that on this last score I am not the perfect recipe. My author has provided purer comfort-recipes for you elsewhere. I show a little too much aptitude at deception, but you should not hold that against me. This trait was merely a by-product of my place in the story: it arose from the fact that upon me fell the burden of keeping things going, and the plottiness of our drama makes naturally for plotting. Besides, recall that I was wholly the reveler as long as Caesar lived. Once he is dead, it is no longer so necessary that I be likable in Caesar's behalf and warm him by my warmth. Henceforth I am no mere

Caesar-adjunct, but the very vessel of the Caesar-principle. So, in expanding to my expanded role, I must break the former mold somewhat. Let *savants* explain the change by saying that carefree Antony was made a soberer man, and a bitter one, by the death of Caesar. But it is an obvious fact that if an important cog in the plot vanishes in the very middle of our drama, something has to take its place. In deputizing for Caesar, I found it impossible to remain completely Antony. Let *savants* explain my altered psychology as they will—*I* know it was a playwright's necessity.

You have been made conspirators in a murder. For this transgression, there must be some expiative beast brought up for sacrifice. Such requirements guided us in the mixing of the Brutus-recipe, for it is Brutus that must die to absolve you of your stabbing an emperor who was deaf in one ear and whose wife was sterile. But let us be fair. There is also the fact that you wrested certain political prerogatives from King John, and have been taught to cherish them. Here also was a source of conviction to be tapped as an ingredient in our formula. We discredited Caesar from the very opening of the play, even before he had appeared (significant timing), by letting you see the tribunes angry with certain commoners who were too cordial in their preparations for the return of Caesar after victory. Caesar, it seems, would try to retract your *Magna Carta* from the Romans. Conversely, it is the Brutus-recipe that would prevent this threatened undoing of English political emancipation. So we make Brutus honorable in your eyes by starting his conduct primarily from this fear, which is always your fear as regards conditions in the contemporary state. He is virtuous because he does for Romans what you want your popular leaders to do for you. He takes on the nobility that comes of being good for private enterprise.

On the other hand, he is a conspirator; hence from the general censure takes corruption. For tough Casca is a Brutus-adjunct; and lean, envious Cassius; and Decius the flatterer. Here are qualities which, if lodged in any but yourselves, are not comforting to contemplate—hence are "vices." Brutus' acts, though done in a good cause, have shadiness. One cannot be stealthy as a thief without partially earning the kind of judgments that are laid against thieves. Nobleness, yes, but dirty business. And if his wife, Portia, speaks for him by her deep affection (as I obediently did for Caesar), note that she is allowed to show this affection only at those moments when he is sinisterly engaged, and answers her evasively. That is: her *love* is conveyed by her *misgivings,* as she worries because her once regular husband roams about at night, in "rheumy and unpurged air" sucking up "the humours of the dank morning," so that even the quality of swamps is drawn upon to discredit Brutus a little, right when Portia is loving him. All told: a fit expiative offering for our offense of murder: worthy, since he was noble and aroused affection, yet yieldable on good legalistic grounds, since he was a conspirator, like a bog. In weeping for his death, you will be sweetly absolved.

At this particular point in the play, however, as I rise to address you, accompanied by Caesar's corpse, Brutus has just confronted the play-mob, stated before them the case of the conspirators, and been exonerated. They have clamored their approval. They are convinced that Caesar would have been a tyrant. And they have shouted to the Brutus-principle, who must die for you, "Live, Brutus! live! live!" It is my task, as I stand before the play-mob, to contrive a *peripety* for my audience, reversing the arrows of your expectations. When my speech is finished, we must have set you to making the preparations for Brutus' death.

Well, a dramatist is a *professional* gambler. He prefers playing with loaded dice. And don't think that we should try to bring about this reversal without first making sure that we had furtively dealt ourselves some trumps. We have stacked the cards a little—not so shamelessly as some of our rival Shake-scenes might have done, but enough. Here, I believe, we have drawn from the well of magic. As follows:

Recall how, in the early rites of communion, whereby one man's interests were made identical with another's, the risks of competitive harms were eliminated by a partnership, a partnership established by three distinct symbolic acts: the sharing of one's wife, the exchanging of blood, the sitting down together at table. Of these, the sharing of the wife is dead, buried beneath notions of virtue that go with later concepts of ownership. Yet we give you something similar, in Caesar's dying words, *"Et tu, Brute?* Then fall, Caesar!"* which suggests that in Caesar's pain there is more than the pain of knives, there is the pain of wrenched intimacy, eliciting a rebuke almost Christlike in its replacing of vengefulness with sorrow, as the victim saw that "Caesar's angel" was among his slayers. At this moment Caesar becomes great—for he must die well, at the expense of Brutus. They had shared affection; hence a promise contracted within the deep-lying terms of magic had been violated.

As for the rites at table: When the conspirators had come, to make sure that Caesar would be on hand at the Senate to be murdered, Caesar welcomed them heartily: "Good friends, go in, and taste some wine with me." And lastly, as for the blood-communion, how grimly it is vivified and mocked (in pious profanation) when the conspirators, at Brutus' word, bathe in the blood of Caesar's wounds. Three magic formulae, outraged—thus Shakespeare speaks to you in accents you had heard while not listening.

I now stand before you, assigned to the definite task of contriving our peripety, turning the arrows of your future while apparently engaged only in turning those of this unruly play-mob. I shall, by what immediately follows, proclaim myself in all thoroughness the Caesar-principle perpetuated. Here I fulfill the pledge I gave when first I came upon the stage after Caesar's murder. I came ostensibly to reassure the conspirators that I was ready to make peace with them, now that the offense was definitely beyond reparation. I shook hands with them, one after the other—but in the very act of doing so, I forgot them, and fell to musing aloud upon the destroyed magnificence of Caesar. In this way I signaled you to the effect that I was not turning against Caesar, even while "shaking the bloody fingers of his foes." (You wanted me to remain with Caesar, since that has been established as my part in this play. I have been given my label—and like children, you insist that a thing's *true* name is the name you first heard it called by. In your insistence that I remain allied with Caesar, repeating my number, you are grateful for the little cue I give you by my absent-minded musings over Caesar's body. In your satisfaction at receiving from me this sign, to restate my identity even as I make peace with the conspirators, you do not stop to ask why the conspirators should not interpret this sign precisely as you do. Your concern with your own aesthetic problem leads you to overlook this straining of verisimilitude, as we thought you would. We judged that, in your eagerness to receive the clue, you would not be overexacting as regard our manner of conveying it.)

Brutus, you will remember, had asked the mob to weigh what he said, and to judge his statements as critics. But, as a matter of fact, he gave them no opportunity to follow his advice. He told them to choose, then stated the issue in such a way that there was no choice. Those that love Rome, he said, must agree that Caesar should have been killed. Those that do not love Rome, should object. If there arc any that do not love Rome, let them step forward in protest. No move— hence, the killing is endorsed.

And now, my countrymen, hear me ask the play-mob to lend me their ears, as I proceed to lay before you a plot in miniature. It will not be a very difficult pattern that I ask you to appreciate: a rudimentary piece of translation, by which I awaken in you the satisfactions of authorship, as you hear me say one thing and know that I mean another. "I come to bury Caesar, not to praise him"—whereat I praise him so roundly that all the vigor of the Caesar-principle is brought to life again.

> . . . if I were dispos'd to stir
> Your heart and minds to mutiny and rage,
> I should do Brutus wrong, and Cassius wrong, . . .

Whereat I stir hearts and minds to mutiny and rage. And as the pattern grows clear, I can subtilize it, making Brutus and his band dishonorable by calling them all, all honorable men. And by the time I mention Caesar's will, saying that I would not read it because it would inflame the people, in accordance with the pattern you wait to hear me read the will. You hear them entreat me, you hear me refuse. Then you observe me stepping down, to be among them, that I may better "realize" Caesar's death for them, and make them tearful coroners while I appraise the wounds:

> If you have tears, prepare to shed them now.
> You all do know this mantle: I remember
> The first time ever Caesar put it on;
> 'Twas on a summer's evening in his tent,
> That day he overcame the Nervii.
> Look! in this place ran Cassius' dagger through:
> See what a rent the envious Casca made:
> Through this the well-beloved Brutus stabb'd;
> And, as he pluck'd his cursed steel away,

> Mark how the blood of Caesar follow'd it,
> As rushing out of doors, to be resolv'd
> If Brutus so unkindly knock'd or no;
> For Brutus, as you know, was Caesar's angel:
> Judge, O you gods! how dearly Caesar lov'd him.
> This was the most unkindest cut of all;
> For when the noble Caesar saw him stab,
> Ingratitude, more strong than traitors' arms,
> Quite vanquish'd him: then burst his mighty heart;
> And, in his mantle muffling up his face,
> Even at the base of Pompey's statua,
> Which all the while ran blood, great Caesar fell.
> O! what a fall was there, my countrymen;
> Then I, and you, and all of us fell down.
> Whilst bloody treason flourish'd over us.
> O! now you weep, and I perceive you feel
> The dint of pity; these are gracious drops.
> Kind souls, what! weep you when you but beheld
> Our Caesar's vesture wounded? Look you here,
> Here is himself, marr'd, as you see, with traitors.

You see my "transference," as I turn from the mantle to the dead man that had worn the mantle. You see the play-mob grow *inflamed* under my talk of *pity* (remember our pattern). There is loud talk of mutiny; the people are about to rush away in anger—but we would "consolidate" our position. And now, rounding out the pattern, I return to the matter of will, which I had refused to read:

> Why, friends, you go to do you know not what.
> Wherein hath Caesar thus deserv'd your loves?
> Alas! you know not: I must tell you then.
> You have forgot the will I told you of.

Whereupon I read them the will of a rich philanthropist—and their vindictiveness against the conspirators is complete. You have been engrossed—faugh! you demons, how you do love plottings, for all your censure of plotters. Or is it machinery that delights you—and are you pleased with joining me to make a smoothly running engine of fatality?

Cassius was right in proposing that they slay me, along with Caesar. But Brutus held it was enough to slay the *persona* of the Caesar-principle, on the ground that the *adjunct* would subside through want of its source:

> Our course will seem too bloody, Caius Cassius,
> To cut the head off and then hack the limbs, . . .
> For Antony is but a limb of Caesar.
>
>   . . . .
>
> And, for Mark Antony, think not of him;
> For he can do no more than Caesar's arm
> When Caesar's head is off.

So the Brutus-principle slays half the Caesar-principle, and spares the other half that will in turn destroy it.

Recall these steps: How first, after the murder, I had sent word by a servant offering to join the cause of the conspirators, if they would guarantee me safety. How I fell to musing over the body of Caesar. How, after *exeunt all but Antony,* I had let loose my full-throated venom:

> O! pardon me, thou bleeding piece of earth,
> That I am meek and gentle with these butchers;
> Thou art the ruins of the noblest man
> That ever lived in the tide of times.
> Woe to the hand that shed this costly blood!
> Over thy wounds now do I prophesy,
> Which like dumb mouths do ope their ruby lips,
> To beg the voice and utterance of my tongue,
> A curse shall light upon the limbs of men;
> Domestic fury and fierce civil strife
> Shall cumber all the parts of Italy;
> Blood and destruction shall be so in use,
> And dreadful objects so familiar,
> That mothers shall but smile when they behold
> Their infants quarter'd with the hands of war;
> All pity chok'd with custom of fell deeds:
> And Caesar's spirit, ranging for revenge,
> With Ate by his side come hot from hell,
> Shall in these confines with a monarch's voice
> Cry "Havoc!" and let slip the dogs of war;
> That this foul deed shall smell above the earth
> With carrion men, groaning for burial.

Then, in my speech before the Romans, I fulfilled my promises, starting those processes by which the Brutus-principle, which killed the Caesar-*persona,* is driven to his death by the Caesar-adjunct.

Thank us for this growing thing by growing with it—and in the following scene we shall allow you to squeeze the last available sum of emotion from the mounting sequence, causing it to drip, not by still hotter pressure, but by a sudden cooling. Prominent among the conspirators, there was a certain Cinna. Now another Cinna comes upon the stage, Cinna the poet, ludicrous, the cartoon of a poet, the aesthete, such as you have long before now been taught to laugh at (our author is treading on safe ground here). He is an earnest but ineffectual wretch, who probably knows a good line when he sees it, and would doubtless have been entranced to write just such verses as Shakespeare wrote; and perhaps he might even have written them had he known, like Shakespeare, how to draw finesses from toughnesses. Yet our dramatist betrays him for the delectation of you, my stinking audience, makes him your laughing stock, ridicules one of his own Guild for your benefit, though you have no desire whatever to write like Shakespeare, would much rather eat beef than hear a play, but cannot go on eating beef forever, and so come here occasionally, demanding firm, beefy diction. The mob stumbles upon this Cinna, overwhelming him. First Citizen, Second Citizen, Third Citizen, and Fourth Citizen each ask him a different question, all at the same time, insisting imperiously that he answer without delay. It is all quite hilarious, as Cinna is in a daze, comically. And when they ask him his name, and he says with assurance, "Cinna," they start pawing at him in earnest—and when he begs them for a little accuracy, insisting that he is not Cinna the conspirator but Cinna the poet, they unanswerably answer that they abominate the name, and so will pummel him for his verses, and the act ends with the brawling group moving from the stage. You somehow know that the poetic Cinna will suffer no fundamental harm. He will merely be slain-not-slain, like a clown hit by cannon balls—yet by this let-down we have reaffirmed in another way the grim intentions of the mob. We have clinched the arrows of your expectancy, incidentally easing our obligations as regard the opening of Act 4.

You will be still more wisely handled by what follows, as our Great Demagogue continues to manipulate your minds. I think particularly of the second scene of the next act, weighted by the steadily organized pressure of events. You will witness a startling quarrel between Brutus and Cassius. After this violence and the sad reconciliation (these men are disintegrating), there will be a contrasted descent to soft tearfulness, as Brutus' drowsy servant plays him a disconsolate little tune in the dead of night (Portia is dead)—and the servant is drowsy, that he may fall asleep as Varro and Claudius have done; then with three men sleeping (and you drooping in sympathy) and Brutus alone awake, there will be, all about, a sleepiness, and a Brutus-loneliness—whereat the Caesar-*persona*, now as a ghost, may return to indicate, by a vague prophecy, that all will be ended for Brutus at Philippi.

Chronology of Important Dates

	Shakespeare's Life	Other Events
1564	Baptized April 26, at Stratford-upon-Avon (born April 23?).	Sixth year of Elizabeth's reign. She is 31 years old.
1576		James Burbage builds The Theater, first permanent playhouse in England, on the outskirts of London.
1582	Marriage to Anne Hathaway.	
1583	Daughter Susanna born.	
1585	Twins (Hamnet and Judith) born.	
1587		Death of Mary Stuart. Rose Playhouse built on the Bankside.
1588		Defeat of Spanish Armada.
1590–92	Active as actor and playwright in London. Known for success of his history plays (*Henry VI* trilogy). Early tragedy: *Titus Andronicus*. First efforts at comedy. Attacked as "upstart crow" (i.e., actor presuming to be a playwright) and defended as "upright" and "civil."	Rival playwrights Kyd (*The Spanish Tragedy*, probably an early *Hamlet*) and Marlowe (*Tamburlaine, Jew of Malta, Dr. Faustus*) active. John Lyly's plays published. Major literary works by Spenser (*The Faery Queene*, I–III) and Sidney (*Arcadia, Astrophel and Stella*) published.
1593–94	Publishes two narrative poems, *Venus and Adonis* and *The Rape of Lucrece*, dedicated to the Earl of Southampton. Becomes a principal member (shareholder, actor, playwright) of leading company of actors, the Lord Chamberlain's Men. Writes *The Taming of the Shrew, Richard III, Two Gentlemen of Verona, Love's Labour's Lost*.	Theaters flourish in London, despite periodic closings (at which time the companies tour) during outbreaks of the plague.
1595–96	*Romeo and Juliet, A Midsummer Night's Dream, Richard II, King John, Merchant of Venice*. Death of Hamnet.	Raleigh's voyages to Guiana. Spenser's *The Faery Queene*, IV–VI.

1597–98	*Henry IV, 1* and *2*. Buys New Place, second largest house in Stratford. Mentioned as leading literary figure, for both his plays and poems. Lord Chamberlain's Men playing at The Curtain, at Holywell, Shoreditch.	Bacon's *Essays*. Chapman's *Homer*.
1599– 1600	*Much Ado about Nothing, Henry V, As You Like It, Julius Caesar, Twelfth Night*. The company builds The Globe Playhouse, on the Bankside.	Essex fighting in Ireland. Death of Spenser.
1601–02	*Hamlet, Troilus and Cressida, All's Well That Ends Well*. Death of Shakespeare's father. The company very nearly gets prosecuted for playing *Richard II* to Essex and his friends just before the attempted coup.	Unsuccessful coup by Essex against Elizabeth. Ben Jonson emerges as playwright (*Every Man in His Humor*).
1603–04	*Measure for Measure, Othello*. The company becomes The King's Men.	Death of Elizabeth. James I succeeds her.
1605–06	*King Lear, Macbeth*.	Jonson's *Volpone*.
1607–08	*Antony and Cleopatra, Coriolanus, Timon of Athens*. Marriage of Susanna, death of Shakespeare's mother.	Midlands riots.
1609–10	*Pericles, Cymbeline*. Unauthorized publication of *Sonnets*. Company adds indoor theater at Blackfriars to its regular playing venues.	Elaborate masques become the fashion at James's court. Jonson's *The Alchemist*.
1611–12	*The Winter's Tale, The Tempest*. Retirement to Stratford.	Publication of the authorized version of the Bible.
1613	*Henry VIII*. Globe Theater burns and is promptly rebuilt.	
1616	Death of Shakespeare, April 23.	Publication of Jonson's *Works*.
1623	Shakespeare's fellow actors, Hemings and Condell, publish the First Folio edition of his plays. Death of Anne Hathaway.	

Notes on Contributors

C. L. BARBER was Professor of Literature at the University of California, Santa Cruz, and the author, among other works, of *Shakespeare's Festive Comedy*, and, together with Richard P. Wheeler, *The Whole Journey: Shakespeare's Power of Development*.

SIGURD BURCKHARDT was Professor of Literature at the University of California, San Diego. He was the author of studies of Goethe and Kleist as well as the posthumously published collection, *Shakespearean Meanings*.

KENNETH BURKE is one of the most influential American critics of the twentieth century. His books include *Philosophy of Literary Form, A Grammar of Motives,* and *Language as Symbolic Action*.

JAMES L. CALDERWOOD is Professor of English and Comparative Literature and Associate Dean of the Humanities at the University of California, Irvine. He has written many books on Shakespeare including *The Properties of Othello* and *Shakespeare and the Denial of Death*. His most recent is *A Midsummer Night's Dream*.

ROSALIE L. COLIE was Professor of English at Brown University. She was the author of a number of books of Renaissance subjects including *Paradoxia epidemica* and *The Resources of Kind* as well as the posthumously published *Shakespeare's Living Art*.

KAREN CUNNINGHAM is Associate Professor of English at Florida State University, Tallahassee. She is the author of articles on Marlowe, Shakespeare, Raleigh, and early modern pedagogy, and is currently writing a book about treason and the drama in sixteenth-century England.

LAWRENCE N. DANSON is Professor of English at Princeton University. He is the author of *Tragic Alphabet: Shakespeare's Drama of Language* and *The Harmonies of the Merchant of Venice* as well as studies of Max Beerbohm and other subjects.

MARJORIE GARBER is Professor of English at Harvard University and Director of the Harvard Center for Literary and Cultural Studies. She is the author of several books on Shakespeare, including *Shakespeare's Ghost Writers: Literature as Uncanny Causality* and most recently of *Vested Interests: Cross Dressing and Cultural Anxiety*.

MICHAEL GOLDMAN is Professor of English at Princeton University. He is the author of a number of books on theater including *The Actor's Freedom* and *Acting and Action in Shakespearean Tragedy* as well as *Shakespeare and the Energies of Drama*.

G. K. HUNTER is Professor of English Emeritus at Yale University. He has edited many Renaissance dramatic texts and is the author, among other books, of *Dramatic Identities and Cultural Tradition: Studies in Shakespeare and His Contemporaries.*

COPPÉLIA KAHN is Professor of English at Brown University. She has edited several important collections including, with Murray M. Schwartz, *Representing Shakespeare: New Psychoanalytic Essays,* and is the author of *Man's Estate: Masculine Identity in Shakespeare.*

MAYNARD MACK is Sterling Professor of English Emeritus at Yale University and the author of many books including *King Lear in Our Time, Alexander Pope: A Life,* and, most recently, *Everybody's Shakespeare.*

GAIL KERN PASTER is Professor of English at The George Washington University. She is the author of *The Idea of the City in the Age of Shakespeare* and, recently, of *The Body Embarrassed: Drama and the Disciplines of Shame in Early Modern England.*

MARK ROSE is Professor of English at the University of California, Santa Barbara, and Director of the University of California Humanities Research Institute. He is the author of books on a range of subjects from Shakespeare to science fiction, including, most recently, *Authors and Owners: The Invention of Copyright.*

EDWARD SNOW is Professor of English at Rice University. He has translated Rilke and has written on Shakespeare and Marlowe as well as on art historical subjects and theories of the gaze. He is the author of *A Study of Vermeer.*

SUSAN SNYDER is Professor of English at Swarthmore College. She is editor of Sylvester's *DuBartas* and of *Othello: Critical Essays,* and the author of *The Comic Matrix of Shakespeare's Tragedies.*

CATHARINE R. STIMPSON is University Professor at Rutgers University. She is the founding editor of *Signs: Journal of Women in Culture and Society* and the author, among other books, of *Where the Meanings Are.*

ALBERT H. TRICOMI is Professor of English at the State University of New York, Binghamton. He is the author of a number of studies on Medieval and Renaissance subjects and of the book *Anticourt Drama in England, 1603–1642.*

EUGENE M. WAITH is Professor of English Emeritus at Yale University. He is the editor of the Oxford Shakespeare editions of *Titus Andronicus* and *The Two Noble Kinsmen* and the author of many books on Renaissance and Restoration drama including *Ideas of Greatness: Heroic Drama in England.*

RICHARD P. WHEELER is Professor of English at the University of Illinois at Urbana-Champaign. He is the author of, among other studies, *Shakespeare's Development and the Problem Comedies* (1981). Before his death in 1980, C. L. Barber requested him to complete the work-in-progress that became *The Whole Journey: Shakespeare's Power of Development.*

Bibliography

Books and Articles on the Early Tragedies

Braunmuller, A. R. "Early Shakespearean Tragedy in its Contemporary Context: Cause and Emotion in *Titus Andronicus, Richard III*, and *The Rape of Lucrece.*" In *Shakespearean Tragedy*, ed. Malcolm Bradbury and David Palmer, 96–128. New York: Holmes and Meier, 1984.

Brooke, Nicholas. *Shakespeare's Early Tragedies*. London: Methuen, 1968.

Hamilton, A. C. *The Early Shakespeare*. San Marino: The Huntington Library, 1967.

Hapgood, Robert. "Shakespeare's Maimed Rites: The Early Tragedies." *Centennial Review* 9 (1965), 494–508.

Hill, R. F. "Shakespeare's Early Tragic Mode." *Shakespeare Quarterly* 9 (1958), 455–469.

Books and Articles on Titus Andronicus

Calderwood James L. "*Titus Andronicus*: Word, Act, Authority." In *Shakespearean Metadrama*, 23–51. Minneapolis: University of Minnesota Press, 1971.

Charney, Maurice. *Titus Andronicus*. New York: Harvester Wheatsheaf, 1990.

Fawcett, Mary Laughlin. "Arms/Words/Tears: Language and the Body in *Titus Andronicus.*" *English Literary History* 50 (1983), 261–277.

Green, Douglas E. "Interpreting 'Her Martyr'd Signs': Gender and Tragedy in *Titus Andronicus.*" *Shakespeare Quarterly* 40 (1989), 317–326.

Hunter, G. K. "Sources and Meanings in *Titus Andronicus.*" In *Mirror up to Shakespeare: Essays in Honour of G. R. Hibbard*, ed. J. C. Gray, 171–188. Toronto: University of Toronto Press, 1984.

Kendall, Gillian Murray. " 'Lend Me Thy Hand': Metaphor and Mayhem in *Titus Andronicus.*" *Shakespeare Quarterly* 40 (1989), 299–316.

Marienstras, Richard. "The Forest, Hunting and Sacrifice in *Titus Andronicus.*" In *New Perspectives on the Shakespearean World*, 40–47. Cambridge: Cambridge University Press, 1985.

Miola, Robert S. "*Titus Andronicus* and the Mythos of Shakespeare's Rome." *Shakespeare Studies* 14 (1981), 85–98.

Palmer, David J. "The Unspeakable in Pursuit of the Uneatable: Language and Action in *Titus Andronicus.*" *Critical Quarterly* 14 (1972), 320–339.

Parker, Douglas H. "Shakespeare's Use of Comic Conventions in *Titus Andronicus*." *University of Toronto Quarterly* 56 (1987), 486–497.

Price, Hereward T. "The Authorship of *Titus Andronicus*." *Journal of English and Germanic Philology* 42 (1943), 55–81.

Spencer, T. J. B. "Shakespeare and the Elizabethan Romans." *Shakespeare Survey* 10 (1957), 39–49.

Wilbern, David. "Rape and Revenge in *Titus Andronicus*." *English Literary Renaissance* 8 (1978), 159–82.

Wynne-Davies, Marion. " 'The Swallowing Womb': Consumed and Consuming Women in *Titus Andronicus*." In *The Matter of Difference: Materialist Feminist Criticism of Shakespeare*, ed. Valerie Wayne, 129–151. Ithaca: Cornell University Press, 1991.

Books and Articles on Romeo and Juliet

Cole, Douglas, ed. *Twentieth Century Interpretations of "Romeo and Juliet."* Englewood Cliffs, N.J.: Prentice-Hall, 1970.

Dickey, Franklin M. *Not Wisely But Too Well: Shakespeare's Love Tragedies*. San Marino: Huntington Library, 1957.

Everett, Barbara. "*Romeo and Juliet*: The Nurse's Story." *Critical Quarterly* 14 (1972), 129–139.

Fly, Richard. "Tempering Extremities: Hazardous Mediation in *Romeo and Juliet*." In *Shakespeare's Mediated World*, 1–26. Amherst: University of Massachusetts Press, 1976.

Garber, Marjorie. "Dream and Language: *Romeo and Juliet*." In *Dream in Shakespeare: From Metaphor to Metamorphosis*, 35–47. New Haven: Yale University Press, 1974.

Kristeva, Julia. "Romeo and Juliet: Love-Hatred in the Couple." In *Tales of Love*, tr. Leon S. Roudiez, 209–233. New York: Columbia University Press, 1987.

Levenson, Jill L. *Romeo and Juliet: Shakespeare in Performance*. Manchester: Manchester University Press, 1987.

Levin, Harry. "Form and Formality in *Romeo and Juliet*." *Shakespeare Quarterly* 11 (1960), 3–11.

Mahood, M. M. "*Romeo and Juliet*." In *Shakespeare's Wordplay*, 56–72. London: Methuen, 1957.

Mason, H. A. *Shakespeare's Tragedies of Love*. London: Chatto & Windus, 1970.

Nevo, Ruth. "Tragic Form in *Romeo and Juliet*." *Studies in English Literature* 9 (1969), 241–58.

Porter, Joseph A. *Shakespeare's Mercutio: His History and Drama*. Chapel Hill: University of North Carolina Press, 1988.

Ryan, Kiernan. "*Romeo and Juliet*: The Language of Tragedy." In *The Taming of the Text: Explorations in Language, Literature and Culture*, ed. Willie Peer, 106–121. London: Routledge, 1988.

Slater, Ann Pasternak. "Petrarchanism Come True in *Romeo and Juliet*." In *Images of Shakespeare*, eds. Werner Habicht, D.J. Palmer, and Roger Pringle, 151–162. Newark: University of Delaware Press, 1988.

Books and Articles *on* Julius Caesar

Charney, Maurice. "The Imagery of *Julius Caesar.*" In *Shakespeare's Roman Plays,* 41–78. Cambridge, Mass.: Harvard University Press, 1961.

Dean, Leonard F., ed. *Twentieth Century Interpretations of Julius Caesar.* Englewood Cliffs, N.J.: Prentice-Hall, 1968.

Girard, René. "Collective Violence and Sacrifice in Shakespeare's *Julius Caesar.*" *Salmagundi* 88–89 (1990–1991), 399–419.

Gless, Darryl J. "*Julius Caesar,* Allan Bloom, and the Value of Pedagogical Pluralism." In *Shakespeare Left and Right,* ed. Ivo Kamps, 185–203. New York: Routledge, 1991.

Goldberg, Jonathan. "The Roman Actor: *Julius Caesar.*" In *James I and the Politics of Literature,* 164–176. Baltimore: Johns Hopkins University Press, 1983.

Greene, Gayle. "The Power of Speech / To Stir Men's Blood': The Language of Tragedy in Shakespeare's *Julius Caesar.*" *Renaissance Drama* n.s. 11 (1980), 67–93.

Hapgood, Robert. "Speak Hands for Me: Gesture as Language in *Julius Caesar.*" *Drama Survey* 5 (1966), 162–70.

Kaula, David. "'Let Us Be Sacrificers': Religious Motifs in *Julius Caesar.*" *Shakespeare Studies* 14 (1981), 197–214.

Miola, Robert S. "*Julius Caesar* and the Tyrannicide Debate." *Renaissance Quarterly* 38 (1985), 271–289.

Rebhorn, Wayne A. "The Crisis of the Aristocracy in *Julius Caesar.*" *Renaissance Quarterly* 43 (1991), 75–111.

Ripley, John. "*Julius Caesar*" *on Stage in England and America, 1599–1973.* Cambridge: Cambridge University Press, 1980.

Siemon, James R. "'Every like is not the same': Figuration and the 'Knot of Us' in *Julius Caesar.*" In *Shakespearean Iconoclasm,* 114–182. Berkeley: University of California Press, 1985.

Stirling, Brents. "'Or Else This Were a Savage Spectacle,'" *PMLA* 66 (1951), 765–774.